Preliminary Injunctions in Patent Litigation

AF184060

Europäische Hochschulschriften Recht

European University Studies in Law

Publications Universitaires Européennes de Droit

Band/Volume **6089**

Arthur von Martels

Preliminary Injunctions in Patent Litigation

Alternative Approaches to Provide Effective Justice under Uncertainty

PETER LANG

Bibliografische Information der Deutschen Nationalbibliothek
Die Deutsche Nationalbibliothek verzeichnet diese Publikation in der Deutschen Nationalbibliografie; detaillierte bibliografische Daten sind im Internet über http://dnb.d-nb.de abrufbar.

Zugl.: München, Univ., Diss., 2018

The author is grateful to have received an IMPRS-CI scholarship from the Max Planck Institute for Innovation and Competition, allowing him to pursue the doctoral research on which this dissertation is based.

D 19
ISSN 0531-7312
ISBN 978-3-631-78698-7 (Print)
E-ISBN 978-3-631-79369-5 (E-PDF)
E-ISBN 978-3-631-79370-1 (EPUB)
E-ISBN 978-3-631-79371-8 (MOBI)
DOI 10.3726/b15798

© Peter Lang GmbH
Internationaler Verlag der Wissenschaften
Berlin 2019
Alle Rechte vorbehalten.
Peter Lang – Berlin · Bern · Bruxelles · New York · Oxford · Warszawa · Wien

Das Werk einschließlich aller seiner Teile ist urheberrechtlich geschützt. Jede Verwertung außerhalb der engen Grenzen des Urheberrechtsgesetzes ist ohne Zustimmung des Verlages unzulässig und strafbar. Das gilt insbesondere für Vervielfältigungen, Übersetzungen, Mikroverfilmungen und die Einspeicherung und Verarbeitung in elektronischen Systemen.

Diese Publikation wurde begutachtet.

www.peterlang.com

Table of Contents

Frequently used Abbrevations

ANDA	Abbreviated New Drug Application
AZ	Aktenzeichen
BGB	Bürgerliches Gesetzbuch; German Civil Code
BGH	Bundesgerichtshof, German Supreme Court
BOA	Boards of Appeal of the European Patent Office
BoC	Balance of Convenience
BIE	Bijblad Industriële Eigendom
BPatG	Bundespatentgericht, Federal German Patent Court
BR	Brussels Regulation
CFI	Court of First Instance of the Unified Patent Court
BW	Burgerlijk Wetboek, Dutch Civil Code
CJEU	Court of Justice of the European Union
CPR	Civil Procedure Rules, UK
DPMA	Deutsches Patent und Markenamt, German Patent and Trademark Office
ECHR	European Convention of Human Rights
ECLI	European Case Law Identifier (number)
ECtHR	European Court of Human Rights
EGMA	European Generic Medicines Association
EMEA	European Agency for the Evaluation of Medicinal Products
EPC	European Patent Convention
EPO	European Patent Office
EU	European Union
FDA	Food and Drugs Administration, US
FSR	Fleet Street Reports
EWCA	England and Wales Court of Appeal
EWHC	England and Wales High Court
GRUR	Zeitschrift für Gewerblicher Rechtsschutz und Urheberrecht
GRUR-INT	Zeitschrift für Gewerblicher Rechtsschutz und Urheberrecht International Edition
GRUR-RR	Zeitschrift für Gewerblicher Rechtsschutz und Urheberrecht Rechtsprechungs-Report
HoL	House of Lords, UK
HR	Hoge Raad, Dutch Supreme Court
IEPT	Case number in the IEPT Database service
IIC	International Review of Intellectual Property and Competition Law
JIPLP	Journal of Intellectual Property Law and Practice
LEXIS	Case number in the Lexis Nexis Database Service
LG	Landgericht (German Regional Court)

NHS	National Health Service (UK)
NJ	Nederlandse Jurisprudentie
NJW	Neue Juristische Wochenschrift
NPE	Non-practicing entity (also known as *patent troll*)
OLG	Oberlandesgericht (German Higher Regional Court)
P&R Approval	Pricing and Reimbursement Approval
PatG	Patentgesetz, German Patent Act
RO	Wet op Rechterlijke Organisatie, Law on Judicial Organsiation (NL)
ROW	Rijkoctrooiwet (Dutch Patent Code)
RV	Wetboek van Burgerlijke Rechtsvordering, Dutch Code of Civil Procedure
SPC	Supplementary Protection Certificate
TRIPS	Agreement on the Trade Related Aspects of Intellectual Property
TRO	Temporary Restraining Order
UPC	Unified Patent Court
U.S.C.	United States Code
USPTO	United States Patent and Trademark Office
Vzr.	Voorzieningenrechter – Kort geding / PI judge (NL)
WTO	World Trade Organisation
ZPO	Zivilprozessordnung, German Act on Civil Procedure

Acknowledgments

In front of the reader lays a work that is the fruit of the research during my time in Munich in 2013–2016. It has been an enriching but challenging experience and it would not be finished without the encouragement, advice and companionship of many.

My first word of thanks of course goes to my *Doktorvater*, Prof. Dr. Ansgar Ohly, who has been most helpful, patient and inspiring in guiding me on this academic journey. I have always very much appreciated our conversations and have got particular good memories of the interesting and enriching Doctoral Seminars and workshops we had in Munich, Schloß Ringberg at the Tegernsee, Tutzing, Bayreuth and Bressanone. I would also like to thank Prof. Dr. Thomas Ackermann for being the Second Reading Professor of this dissertation.

Furthermore, I'm also highly grateful to the *Max Planck Institute for Innovation and Competition* in Munich that not only granted me funding, but also a fantastic place to work. The expertise and resources of the Institute located at the *Marstallplatz* are the best in the world when it comes to Intellectual Property and it has been a joy to be part of that community. I would therefore like to thank Professors Hilty, Drexl and Kur for offering me a place in the IMPRS-CI programme at the Institute, and for all the interesting academic interactions afterwards. A special word of thanks is for Dr. Sylvie Nerisson who worked at the Max Planck Institute, for managing the programme and providing advice.

Gratitude is also due to the many colleagues and friends, from all corners of the world, which I saw on a day-to-day basis in Munich and that made my time in Bavaria unforgettable. The list of names of these people is too long to provide here, but they know who they are. Thanks is equally due to my Dutch friends and family that have visited me in Munich. They too know who they are. Nevertheless, there are a few people I would like to single out at this page: Martin and his wife Lucia for their warm and loyal friendship (both in Germany and in The Netherlands) as well as for their encouragement to me in writing this dissertation. To Henri, for all the dinners and running during our time that we shared a house. A special word of thanks also goes out to Manon and Reinder, your house was always open for me and I truly cherish all the great moments we had. And finally a *grazie mille*, to Sebastian, who encouraged me during the the final evenings of edits to be made.

I would like to dedicate this work to my parents and my fiancé. To my parents, Zweder and Margreet who have always lovingly supported me in every single way and at every single moment of my life. This is something I will always be grateful for and I hope to raise my children in the same way that they have done with me, Julius and Eduard. And to my fiancé, Simona, who I met during my years in Munich: she has not only introduced me to the wonders of Italy but also proved to be the love of my life and the person *con cui voglio percorrere il sentiero della vita.*

Arthur von Martels, Amsterdam, July 2017.

Preface

§1. Introduction

In intellectual property disputes in general – and in patent disputes in particular – injunctions are amongst the most effective and powerful legal measures that can be provided for by a legal system. An injunction is a legal order, given by a court of law, specifically prescribing a particular conduct to be followed or to stop a certain activity. Traditionally, injunctions are granted by a court when monetary remedies do not provide an adequate form of relief. Sometimes, an injunction is combined with a monetary remedy such as damages or restitution of profits. Together, both injunctions and monetary rewards are remedies that can greatly stop, reduce and prevent (the further) infringement of intellectual property rights.[1]

With respect to injunctive relief specifically *in patent disputes*, the focus of literature and research tends to be on injunctive relief with a *permanent* character. These permanent injunctions are granted after the case has been through the normal judicial civil proceedings of a legal system. The case is thus assessed on the merits with ample scope for both the plaintiff (usually the patentee)[2] and the defendant (the alleged infringer) to fully present their arguments in the case at hand. Regardless whether appeal at a higher court is still possible and the initial verdict can still be overturned, these injunctions are, at the very least,[3] characterised by a significantly higher degree of legal scrutiny than the injunctions that will be at the heart of this research; namely that of *preliminary injunctions.*

Known under various names,[4] and required by obligations of International Law and in European Union (EU) jurisdictions by European Union Law,[5] the decision to grant or deny a preliminary injunction is determined early in the course of the legal

---

1 It should be mentioned here that additionally, outside the realm of these civil law remedies, of course other methods exist to stop the infringement, counterfeiting and piracy of intellectual property rights. Criminal sanctions for instance can be an important deterrent and so can technical protection measures, as well as relying on (trade) secrecy.

2 This can not only be initiated by the patent holder itself, but also by its licensee or assignee, that has the legal capacity to act.

3 For more on the hallmarks of a preliminary injunction, as well as on the preliminary injunction proceedings itself, see page 29.

4 Certain specifics regarding the terminology that is used in this work, are discussed at page 25.

5 As will be pointed out on page 133 and further, these are Art. 9 of the European Union Enforcement Directive, 2004/48/EC and Art. 50 (1) of the Agreement on Trade Related aspects of Intellectual Property Rights (TRIPS). To a certain extent, the European Convention of Human Rights (ECHR), the Charter of Fundamental Rights of

dispute. It is also often taken after merely a rudimentary hearing has taken place. This means that the court, when asked to adjudicate, should decide on the request for a preliminary injunction after a relatively limited judicial investigation – as opposed to a decision after normal proceedings on the merits. These proceedings are limited in terms of time, the available evidence that is presented, and the possibility to call in third-party expertise.

This obviously has profound consequences and can result in a certain tension. On the one hand, a preliminary injunction can offer a rights holder speedy, effective and timely relief in preventing or stopping infringement, before a final determination of the legal rights. This relief is (supposedly) temporary of nature, namely, as longs as the proceedings on the merits take. In complex (patent) litigation, this time can range from a few months to even a few years. Nevertheless, on the other hand, a preliminary injunction can have far-reaching consequences. These consequences do not only affect the parties involved but also the wider society, including affecting competitors.

With patents in particular, due to their (often) complex and technical nature, as well as their relationship with other patents and the state of the art, the assessment of a request for a preliminary injunction can be a challenging task for the preliminary injunction court. The abovementioned tension is then often high. Despite this however, preliminary injunctions are generally seen as an often necessary and effective tool in stopping the infringement of patent rights, should the circumstances of a case ask for this.

§2. The main research question

The main research question underpinning this thesis is:

Should the Unified Patent Court provide preliminary injunctions in actual practice, and what can be learned from the different approaches national courts currently have in deciding whether or not to grant this remedy?

It is argued that this research, resulting in the question as formulated above, is of interest for several reasons. Apart from the intellectually appealing tension that underlies the preliminary injunction doctrine – as written above this is the need to provide swift and effective justice versus the challenge to decide on difficult (technical) subject matter in which both granting and denying the request can have profound consequences – there are also at least two more practical reasons. Both these practical reasons are connected to the future establishment of the Unified Patent Court (UPC). The first reason is to find out how preliminary injunctions are currently dealt with in various countries, in order to see whether common principles exist for the UPC to draw upon. The second reason is that the

---

the EU and the Brussels Regulation (BR) also have some effect on the nature, scope and/or role of preliminary injunctions.

start of the UPC is a moment for a new practice regarding the grant of preliminary injunctions. Therefore too, a better understanding of the issues and applicable criteria when granting preliminary injunctions, as well as the consequences of interim relief, may be helpful.

The UPC will likely start to function in 2018, and at the moment of writing the final preparatory efforts are being made in its anticipation.[6] These include the recruitment of judges and staff. As will be seen in the last chapter of this work which is dedicated to the UPC, under the new Court rules, the grant of preliminary injunctions by the UPC is a given statutory possibility. However the judges under this regime are left significant discretion and little guidance on how and when to use this (hence also the phrase 'in actual practice' has been chosen in the wording of the main research question). This means that current national principles and practices will likely be very important sources to draw on, especially in the early years. When these principles and practices are far apart from each other, this may become problematic and lead to a less uniform policy. It may also prove to be quite the contrary: differences between the national courts may exist, but common principles should and could facilitate the transition into a single UPC approach. More research on how courts decide on preliminary injunctions can firstly thus lead to a better understanding of what is likely to happen, and point out some key issues.

Secondly, unburdened by prior decisions and legal tradition, the enactment of the UPC is also an excellent opportunity to *develop* the preliminary injunction practice into a certain direction and shape it into a bespoke mould. This research therefore tries to look at strengths and weaknesses of current approaches. Which direction should the UPC follow and which elements should the Court ideally incorporate in its own substantive legal test when deciding on a request for interim relief in a patent dispute?

These questions will *inter alia* be answered by looking at three key countries in EU patent litigation: Germany, England and The Netherlands. All three countries attract not only a significant proportion of European patent litigation, but they also offer alternative ways of deciding on whether to grant preliminary injunctive relief. To enrichen the analysis, a look will also be taken at the United States as the American practice is characterised by various elements that may be of interest for the UPC to consider. Additionally, more theoretical insights stemming from the literature will be taken along.

6 Note that at the time that this dissertation is being *published*, it has become clear that this date of 2018 has not been met and that for the next step of the project the outcome of a legal challenge pending before the German Constitutional Court is awaited, even though organizational and technical preparations and the ratification process have continued.

§3. Scientific contribution

Whilst works specifically on interim relief of course exist,[7] these works have a different focus and approach to the topic than this work purports to do. Many of these works do not focus on preliminary injunctions as such, but more on provisional measures in a wider sense – sometimes also outside the immediate realm of intellectual property.

A first example is the book written by Schneider in which she has focussed on comparatively analysing most aspects of German-Dutch preliminary relief.[8] This book is rather procedural of nature, focussing much on issues of procedural law and jurisdiction. The authors Berneke and Schüttpelz have written a comprehensive and practically very useful book on the topic, however this only focusses on German law regarding preliminary injunctions, and is not specifically on patents.[9] The same goes for the older work of Leipold, written in 1971, about interim relief in German (general) litigation proceedings.[10] Another German scholar, Heinze, has written an impressive and doctrinally valuable work on interim measures in the context of intellectual property law. However, that work differs from this thesis as it covers more than preliminary injunctions alone and is not on patents specifically. The book also mainly zooms in on how such relief is regulated on a European (Union) level, instead of looking at national practices.[11] A work that *does* go into national legal practices of various countries is the work of Ehrenzeller. Her manuscript however puts a strong emphasis on human rights aspects, and again is not specifically on intellectual property.[12] Very notable too is the Swedish work of Norrgård, who has mainly looked into the Finnish and United States doctrine.[13] Also stemming from Scandinavia is the Danish language work of Petersen.[14] Yet another author, Kramer, has written her book in Dutch. She provides a comparative work going into

7 It seems that particularly German scholars have shown interest in this topic. Many of the more comprehensive works are in the German language. Many of the journal articles on this topic however, are written by English scholars.

8 F. SCHNEIDER, *Die Leistungsverfügung im Niederländischen, Deutschen und europäischen Zivilprozessrecht* (2013 Mohr Siebeck).

9 W. BERNEKE, E. SCHÜTTPELZ, *Die einstweilige Verfügung in Wettbewerbsachen* (2014 NJW Praxis / C.H. Beck Verlag).

10 D. LEIPOLD, *Grundlagen des einstweiligen Rechtsschutzes im zivil-, verfassungs- und verwaltungsgerichtlichenVerfahren* (1971 C.H. Beck Verlag).

11 C. HEINZE, *Einstweiliger Rechtsschutz im europäischen Immaterialgüterrecht* (2007 Mohr Siebeck).

12 S.K. EHRENZELLER, *Der vorläufige Rechtsschutz im internationalen Verhältnis* (2005 Mohr Siebeck).

13 M. NORRGÅRD, *Interimistiskaförbud i immaterialrätten* (2002 Kauppakaari Förlag).

14 C.S. PETERSEN, *Immaterialrettigheder og foreløbige forbud* (2008 Jurist- og Økonomforbundets Forl.).

national practices of interim relief of various European countries.[15] However, the core of her work is on international private law aspects. Somewhat similar to this, is the German book written by Pansch, he looks at various cross-border aspects of preliminary injunctions.[16]

Finally, interim relief is a topic that is of course covered in works on remedies or enforcement that are of a more general nature. These works thus cover more than interim measures alone. Examples are the books by Rademacher[17] and Cotter.[18] Furthermore, apart from being found in dedicated works on the enforcement of patents or intellectual property, the subject of preliminary injunctions is sometimes also covered in individual articles or book chapters. Many of these works are cited in this dissertation.

What sets this thesis apart from the literature that has been cited above? Apart from its dedicated focus on *patents* and *prohibitory preliminary injunctions* – as supposed to interim relief in wider sense – and from being a recent and English-written work on the interesting issues this topic entails, this contribution is novel as it attempts to provide a more *holistic view*. In this thesis, preliminary injunctions are viewed from *five different angles*. Whilst other works may cover some issues that are addressed in this thesis, here an attempt is made to look at several issues at the same time and in relation to each other;

(1) By extensively covering the justifications and risks of granting preliminary injunctions.
(2) By virtue of a legal-comparative analysis of international and national law: a selection of national European jurisdictions, at EU and European law, at TRIPS and at the US approach.
(3) In giving a short overview of how legal theory has approached the decisionmaking process taken by the preliminary injunction court.
(4) By looking beyond formal, statutory and procedural aspects, and trying to map which issues are important in decisionmaking *in practice*. Since the reasoning of the courts is very important to look at here, there will be various cases to illustrate the relevant issues. Although legal cases (and preliminary injunction proceedings are of course no exception to this) to a large extent hinge on the specific facts and circumstances which are central to the proceeding, it is submitted that the issues raised in cases in this thesis are rather exemplary. The selected cases thus give a good overview of how the courts deal with issues that they encounter.

---

15 X.E. KRAMER, *Het kort geding in internationaal perspectief* (2001 Kluwer Uitgeverij).

16 R. PANSCH, *Die einstweilige Verfügung zum Schutze des geistigen Eigentums im grenzüberschreitenden Verkehr* (2003 Carl Heymanns Verlag).

17 C. RADEMACHER, *Die gerichtliche Durchsetzung von Patent-und Markenrechten in Deutschland, Japan und den USA* (2010 Nomos Verlagsgesellschaft).

18 T.F. COTTER, *Comparative Patent Remedies: A Legal and Economic Analysis* (2013 Oxford University Press).

(5) The last angle is on preliminary injunctive relief in the nearby future. This work attempts to forecast the issues that will play a role when the UPC comes into force, its likely approach and it will finally make a proposal for UPC judges to be followed, based on all what is learned in preceding chapters.

§4. A concise overview of the chapters

At this point, in order to offer a better understanding of the issues this dissertation covers, a brief overview of the upcoming chapters in this thesis will follow.

Part I – The theoretical underpinning

In the *first chapter* of this work the scene will be set by describing various fundamental issues that surround preliminary injunctions in patent litigation. What are the main arguments for the enforcement of patent rights in the first place? Why is interim litigation uncertain? And what is the property and liability rules framework and the place of preliminary injunctions therein?

The second and third chapter look at the 'pros and cons' of preliminary injunctions in patent litigation. *Chapter two* starts by taking a critical look at the independent economic and doctrinal justifications for prohibitory preliminary injunctions. Why, apart from being legally prescribed, should society have and grant the remedy? The *third chapter* looks at the potential risks the remedy entails.

After these two chapters, in *chapter four*, a case-study follows, looking at a key example of preliminary injunctions in practice. This is on preliminary injunctions with respect to generic competition in the pharmaceutical industry. This is largely based on the data and findings from the European Commission. This chapter offers an excellent example of the role the remedy can have, and the issues that can occur. It also demonstrates that preliminary injunctions can be beneficial for society, but are not without risk.

In *chapter five*, a review is made of various approaches stemming from the field of Law & Economics: what insights can be learned from this discipline about the court's decisionmaking process on whether or not to grant preliminary injunctions and what exactly from these models can be extracted and used in practice?

Part II – International and national law

In chapter six and seven, we will look at the current legal framework. Firstly, in the *sixth chapter*, this will happen regarding the international (TRIPS) and European level. The latter will of course specifically address the EU Enforcement Directive, but it will also shortly cover cross-border enforcement and the influence of the ECHR. *Chapter seven* looks at the national legal frameworks and practices of the four selected national jurisdictions. It will be seen that across the board there are many similarities, but that there are also a number of interesting differences, when it comes to how courts deal with preliminary injunctions in patent litigation.

Part III – A look into the future

Chapter eight looks at upcoming changes that will transform the patent litigation landscape in Europe when the UPC starts with its work. It will be examined which changes and challenges the UPC will likely bring end encounter when it comes to preliminary injunctions. Subsequently, an attempt will be made to – within the framework of the UPC Agreement and Rules of Procedure – to provide suggestions for the newly to be formed Court. This will happen in the form of a *recommended practices.*

§5. Limitations

This work is mainly based on research during my time in Munich in 2013–2016. As is apparent from above, quite some ground will be covered in this thesis: both in terms of the number of issues as regarding the multitude of jurisdictions that are dealt with. At the same time, the length of this dissertation is of course limited. It is thus important to stress therefore, that by no means this work attempts to give an exhaustive analysis of the remedy in all its aspects. Nor does it attempt to provide a review of cases as handed down by national courts. Rather it attempts to illustrate the main and most interesting issues and developments. It also attempts to highlight the different ways and approaches courts have to decide on a request for this type of interim relief.

Other limitations that should be stressed from the outset, are the following:

This work will specifically be focussing on what in Common Law jurisdictions is known as a *prohibitory injunction.* These injunctions are negatively formulated and thus prohibit certain actions. This is something opposed to what in Common Law is known as a mandatory injunction. These positively prescribe a specific form of conduct that should be followed by one of the involved parties. Furthermore, this thesis will also *not* focus on other forms of interim relief. This includes interim relief such as to secure evidence,[19] or interim relief to provisionally seize assets, such as movable or immovable property, or the blocking of bank accounts[20] such as *freezing injunctions* for instance do.[21]

Neither will the thesis look into interim awards that are given outside the traditional judicial setting where the bulk of patent litigation in most countries takes place: namely national courts. Therefore, interim awards that are granted in arbitration panels under rules of the World Intellectual Property Organisation (WIPO)

---

19 Art. 7 of the EU Enforcement Directive 2004/48/EC.

20 Art. 9 (2) of the EU Enforcement Directive 2004/48/EC.

21 Freezing injunctions (also known under the former name of *Mareva* injunctions) are Common Law injunctions which, once granted, temporarily freeze the defendant's assets in order to comply with a legal ruling.

are not considered.[22] Furthermore, it will not cover practices of the United States International Trade Commission (ITC). Whilst it is admitted that the latter forum is gaining importance, it has been decided to not review this forum in more detail. This is due to the comparative nature that the thesis strives to have: therefore, it has been decided to focus on the same type of judicial bodies, namely national courts.

Largely left out too, are issues of a more *procedural nature* and that of *jurisdiction*.[23] This is due to limitations in the size of this work and a different focal point of interest herein.[24] Instead, the emphasis is more on the function and use of preliminary injunctions, and on the aspect of judicial decisionmaking.

Finally, it is important to underline that the main attention of this work will be directed to *inter partes* proceedings, sometimes also known as 'contradictory' proceedings. Here the defendant is summoned to appear in court and the proceedings take place between parties *before* an interim injunction is given. This work is thus not so much on *ex parte* type of preliminary injunctions: these are given for usually a very short effective time span, without a summary trial and without the other party being heard. There also should be extreme urgency. Ex parte injunctions are not covered as such, as these remain quite rare in most countries with respect to patent infringement. Whilst much that is written in this work is just as applicable to ex parte injunctions as it is to inter partes preliminary injunctions, the focus remains on *inter partes* prohibitory preliminary injunctions because these are most common in patent litigation.[25] Nevertheless, in the case an ex parte injunction is granted, usually a 'normal' preliminary injunction trial is held within a short time,

---

22 See Art. 48–49 of the *WIPO Arbitration Rules, as well as the Rules on Expedited Arbitration* (valid from June 1st 2014). These WIPO provisions set out the possibilities to obtain interim awards or emergency relief at WIPO arbitration tribunals. At this point it is important to make one important comment with respect to arbitration: note that according to Art. 48 (d) of WIPO's 2014 Arbitration Rules, the request for a preliminary injunction to a court, shall *not be deemed incompatible with an Arbitration Agreement*, or deemed to be a waiver of such an agreement. After obtaining a preliminary injunction therefore, it is still possible for the parties to take the route of alternative dispute resolution via the arbitration process offered by WIPO.

23 This said, certain aspects of international jurisdiction (cross-border enforcement) under the umbrella of the Brussels Regulation and under the Unified Patent Court, namely between national courts and the UPC are briefly taken along.

24 But see the work of others, notably HEINZE, KRAMER, EHRENZELLER and BERNEKE/SCHÜTTPELZ, who have dealt with these issues in considerable detail. See W. BERNEKE, E. SCHÜTTPELZ, *Die einstweilige Verfügung in Wettbewerbsachen* (2014 NJW Praxis / C.H. Beck); C. HEINZE, *Einstweiliger Rechtsschutz im europäischen Immaterialgüterrecht* (2007 Mohr Siebeck); X.E. KRAMER, *Het kort geding in internationaal perspectief* (2001 Kluwer Uitgeverij); S.K. EHRENZELLER, *Der vorläufige Rechtsschutz im internationalen Verhältnis* (2005 Mohr Siebeck).

25 For an interesting work on the possibility of whether *ex parte injunctions* in patent litigation are possible under Dutch Law, and if so under which conditions, see the master thesis of W.F. DAMMERS, *Examining ex parte in rei patenti* (2009); available

in order to decide on the keeping or lifting of the granted relief. Such a proceeding *will* be covered in the thesis, as it effectively allows a preliminary injunction to stay in place until the trial on the merits. It is also granted according to the same criteria as otherwise.

§6. Terminology

A few remarks on terminology should still be made: in the English language legal literature, preliminary injunctions are also known as 'interlocutory injunctions', and also called sometimes 'interim injunctions' or 'provisional injunctions'. In practice and in the bulk of the literature, these terms are used interchangeably. Differences predominantly seem to be stemming from either arbitrary choice or a different legal tradition or time of writing. In England traditionally there seemed to be a preference for the term 'interlocutory injunction', even though legislative changes now officially denote it as an 'interim injunction'.[26] In the United States however, there has traditionally seemed to be a preference for the term 'preliminary injunction'. This said, from henceforth on, for reasons of consistency and the ease of reading, the term 'preliminary injunction' will be used for the type of remedy that is central to this work. This is also the case in the non-English language jurisdictions that will be dealt with in this work, namely Germany and The Netherlands. In these countries, a prohibitory preliminary injunction is called respectively '*die einstweilige Unterlassungsverfügung*' or '*het voorlopig inbreukverbod (na kort geding)*'.

Furthermore, unless otherwise mentioned, the term 'plaintiff' in this dissertation coincides with the patentee and the applicant for a preliminary injunction. Equally, the term 'defendant' coincides with the (alleged) infringer.

Lastly, unless otherwise mentioned, the neutral terms of 'preliminary injunction court' or 'the court' are used to refer to the judicial body which decides on the grant of a preliminary injunction. This is also so in those cases when a single judge does so.

---

via the website of the University of Tilburg, The Netherlands: http://arno.uvt.nl/show.cgi?fid=99971 (last accessed on 17 April 2017).
Dammers concluded affirmatively to his hypothesis on the possibility of Dutch courts to grant ex parte injunctions in patent cases, but only if strict conditions are met. These conditions require extraordinary urgency and imminent harm, full and frank disclosure by the plaintiff and a situation where it is necessary and proportionate not to hear the other party and summary proceedings cannot be awaited.

26 This is nowadays the terminology that is used in the Civil Procedural Rules (CPR) in England.

Part I: The Theoretical Underpinning

Chapter 1: Setting the Scene: Preliminary Injunctions, Patents and Uncertainty

§1.1. Introduction

As stated before, an injunction is a legal order given by a court of law, prescribing or prohibiting a certain behaviour that the addressee of the injunction should adhere to.[27] A natural starting point of this dissertation is to raise the key question of what are to be considered as the *hallmarks* of preliminary injunctions and preliminary injunction proceedings? It is submitted that there are three specific characteristics that make the preliminary injunction itself distinct from permanent (also known as

27 Breaching a (preliminary) injunction leaves the party to which the injunction was directed at the risk of being held of 'in contempt of the court'. The breaching party hereby disrespects the court's authority to decide upon the grant of a preliminary injunction and thereby, indirectly, disrespects the authority of the State. This act can lead to severe punishments, when the contemnor – the addressee of the (preliminary) injunction – is proven guilty in a separate contempt proceeding. The exact punishment differs per country, but can range from imprisonment or severe financial penalties. As Golden explains, in the United States for instance, contempt is criminalised and can lead to prison sentences but more likely in the case of patent infringement are high fines or treble damages. See: J.M. GOLDEN, 'Injunctions as more (or less) than "Off Switches": patent infringement injunctions' scope' *Texas Law Review* 90 (2012), pp. 1399–1472. See: pp. 1409–1415.
However, despite this, Golden argues at pp. 1112–1413 that in the United States, the differences between injunctions and monetary remedies are less large than one would think on first sight. One reason is that in practice, the punishment for contempt boils down to merely heightened, but still limited monetary sanctions since criminal sanctions and the stigma associated to those, are usually off the table. Moreover, the contempt also should be *proved.* Under such circumstances Golden argues, an injunction, rather than acting as a clear 'off-switch' for infringement, serves instead primarily as a gateway to a potential set of enhanced monetary remedies.
It is submitted that Golden's observation touches upon a certain Law and Economics theory called 'efficient breach'. This is when a voluntary breach is better for the party than to abide by the contract, or in this case the court's order. However, it is assumed in this disseration that the breaching of a preliminary injunction order is not something that a rational party in general would do and that injunctions and the contempt proceedings form deterrents that are robust enough to stop further infringement from occurring. Therefore, although it is submitted that Golden offers a very interesting insight, the true 'strength' of injunctions is not questioned further in this dissertation.

final) injunctions and, at the same time, also make preliminary injunction proceedings different from that of a trial on the merits.

These three characteristics are the following:

(1) A preliminary injunction is a decision that is taken under circumstances of *heightened uncertainty.* This is due to the brevity in time that a court should make its decision in, and (thus) the more limited nature of the investigation by the court in comparison with a final injunction and a trial on the merits. As an example, observe that with a permanent injunction in a patent dispute, *at least* the liability of the other party in infringing the right has been established.[28]

---

28 This is a difference with the situation of *temporarily enforceable decisions of permanent* (non-preliminary) *nature* as is the case in Germany for instance with *vorläufige Vollstreckbare Urteile.* Although these types of decisions are to certain extent like a preliminary injunction – namely both are temporarily enforceable measures and bridge an interval period until all the merits of the case have been scrutinised – the reader should be reminded that the substance of a case in a temporarily enforceable decision of permanent nature has already undergone a more thorough examination than in most cases where a preliminary injunction is given. Consider a situation that is particularly apparent in Germany, due to the bifurcated patent system in that country (although the situation is not only limited to there). In Germany, the situation can occur that the infringement court (Landgericht) decides on the infringement issue, but the validity issue is still to be decided upon by the patent validity court (Bundespatentgericht). If the infringement court is convinced that the Bundespatentgericht will ultimately rule in the plaintiff's favour, and if the latter is willing to post a bond – in case the infringement court is mistaken with its assessment on the patent's validity – the court can give an injunction that has a status of being temporarily enforceable (*vorläufige Vollstreckbarkeit*). That this 'injunction gap' is a real issue, is for instance shown by Florian Müller, in his analysis of the smartphone patent assertions in Germany. He writes that in his research, there was not one case in which a final or preliminary injunction was granted in which an infringement proceeding was stayed and a patent later upheld. However, there were multiple cases with later invalidated patents which were enforced for a considerable amount of time. See: F. MÜLLER, 'Analysis of 222 smartphone patent assertions: more than 90% go nowhere, rest lacks impact' *FOSS Patents weblog* (published October 1st 2014). Available at: http://www.fosspatents.com/2014/10/analysis-of-222-smartphone-patent.html (last accessed 16 April 2017).
Harhoff *et al.* confirm a similar picture: "Our empirical analysis confirms the anecdotal evidence – bifurcation creates 'invalid but infringed' situations in which a court finds infringement of a patent that is subsequently invalidated. (..) we find that 12% of infringement cases with parallel invalidity proceedings produce such divergent decisions. In a total of 142 cases, patents were held infringed that were (partially) invalidated. Our analysis also shows that the length of the potential injunction gap is substantial." D. HARHOFF, K. CREMERS, F. GAESSLER, C. HELMERS, 'Invalid but infringed? An analysis of Germany's bifurcated patent litigation system' *Zentrum für Europäische Wirtschaftsforschung, Discussion Paper* No. 14–072 (2014). See: p. 3.

This is not yet the case with a preliminary injunction where the *likelihood* that the defendant will be held liable of infringement at a later stage of the litigation should be assessed. In addition, the question whether the patent is *likely* to be held invalid is often taken along during the proceedings and should be anticipated by the court. As will be seen in the chapter on Law and Economic theories,[29] but also in practice, this increased level of uncertainty is widely recognised by both academics as the judiciary.

(2) Another difference with permanent injunctions is that a granted preliminary injunction is intended to be *temporary of nature* and not a replacement of final adjudication. A preliminary injunction is intended to be in place for as long as the trial on the merits takes. This is a difference with other legal mechanisms that are being developed to provide faster relief to parties, such as accelerated patent proceedings on the merits.[30] This can also be seen as a difference with various emergency measures – such as Temporary Restraining Orders – which are meant *to only last during* the preliminary injunction proceedings itself, but not in the *interval* between preliminary (injunction) proceedings and the trial on the merits.

(3) The preliminary injunction itself is not a wholly free-standing remedy, nor is the proceedings in which it is decided upon a completely free-standing proceeding. In other words, neither the interim remedy and interim proceedings operate in a vacuum. Both are interrelated with a final injunction and a trial on the merits. The influence between preliminary and final decisions is mutual of nature and works in several ways. It is submitted the mutual influence can be subdivided into that of *congruential* and *temporal* dimensions. Firstly, the more *congruent* the criteria to decide upon preliminary and final proceedings are, the stronger the relationship between preliminary and final relief will be, as the judge in preliminary proceedings tries to anticipate the result at trial. This of course may have a bearing on a party's decision to proceed with litigation after a preliminary injunction has taken place. In light of this, a party may take another look at its chances. The latter is particularly so, because it is not uncommon that in many jurisdictions the same judge which ruled on the preliminary injunction also looks (again) at the matter during the trial on the merits. Secondly, as mentioned, there are also important *temporal* links between preliminary and final decisions to be made. The longer it takes for a final decision to take place after a preliminary injunction has been given, *the stronger the influence of that decision becomes.* This has its impact, as will be seen below, on a party's decision whether to litigate or to settle after a preliminary injunction has been handed down.

---

29 See page 111 a.f. of this dissertation.

30 This is for instance the case in The Netherlands, with the *Versneld Regime Octrooizaken*, see page 159 of this dissertation. Experiments with accelerated proceedings on the merits have also taken place in other countries.

That said, however, with respect to time there are also of course important differences between both preliminary and final proceedings and remedies. After all, the *relative consequences of harm* (stakes) are often different at the time of a request of a preliminary injunction and at the time of the final hearing on the merits.[31] This also means that at different times another remedy may be more preferential. Whilst enjoining a party may be the most optimal solution for a litigant at the preliminary injunction stage, it may be a solution that is worth nothing anymore two years later down the road, where only damages can (attempt to) make whole.

Figure 1. Two examples of relief by a preliminary injunction (own image).

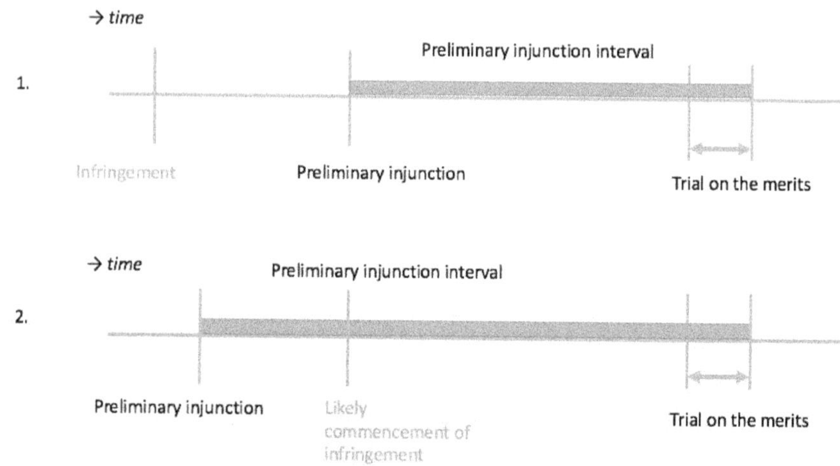

§1.2. Justifications for patent protection

There is an abundance of (philosophical and economic literature on the) theoretical justifications for patent protection and an overview of this would be incomplete and superficial by default.[32] However, since preliminary injunctions

31 As Davis notes, this is an important factor and has impact on whether or not to grant a preliminary injunction, even if the judge's view of that probability remains stable all the time. For this, see: J.P. DAVIS, 'Taking uncertainty seriously: revising injunction doctrine' *Rutgers Law Journal* 34, No. 2 (2003), pp. 362–462. See: p. 398.

32 See for more on this, inter alia, the works of: F. MACHLUP, *An Economic Review of the Patent System – Study of the Subcommittee on patents, trademarks and copyrights of the Committee on the Judiciary of the United States Senate* (1958 US Government Printing Office). See: pp. 21–22, W.M. LANDES, R.A. POSNER, *The Economic Structure*

specifically with respect to patents are at the heart of this work, it is perhaps good to give a very brief overview of several main theoretical justifications for patent protection.[33]

The *natural law theory* is based on the idea that man has a natural property right in his own ideas. The use of these ideas by others then amounts to stealing and there is a *moral duty* of society to protect those with ideas. In the patent context, it is the innovator that is to be protected from this theft.[34] Therefore a right of exclusivity provided by the state is justified as forming a deterrent to prevent the stealing of intellectual ideas from happening.

The *incentive theory* is based on the view that ideas and knowledge are public goods and that without patent protection and actual enforcement of these patent rights, the inventions that are based on these ideas could be easily reproduced or copied by those free-riding on the work of others. Others, that have taken the time, the risk and made the investments to innovate.[35] From this point of view, patent infringement can reduce and stifle incentives to create and to innovate. Hence the premise here is that without patents, less or no innovation occurs and that therefore strong patent protection and strong enforcement is key. This view is often seen as

---

of Intellectual Property Law (2003 Harvard University Press). See: pp. 295–311, M. LEMLEY, 'Ex ante versus ex post justifications for intellectual property' *The University of Chicago Law Review* 71, No. 1 (2004), pp. 129–149. P. DRAHOS, *A Philosophy of Intellectual Property* (1996 Dartmouth Publishing) and the work of E.C. HETTINGER, 'Justifying Intellectual Property' *Philosophy and public affairs* 18, No. 1 (1989), pp. 31–52.

33 It should be noted that the theories mentioned below have lesser or higher degrees of plausibility and have their own strengths and weaknesses. This is not the place to go into these aspects here, but see the concise and informative work of Nelson and Mazzoleni that reviews the strengths and weaknesses of four broad theories of patent protection. R.D. NELSON, and R. MAZZOLENI, 'Economic theories about the costs and benefits of patents' *Intellectual Property Rights and Research Tools in Molecular Biology* (1997 National Academy Press). See: pp. 17–27. Available via: http://www.ncbi.nlm.nih.gov/books/NBK233537/pdf/Bookshelf_NBK233537.pdf (last accessed on 17 April 2017). Apart from these theoretical works, also see the article of B.H. HALL, D. HARHOFF, 'Recent research on the economics of patents' *National Bureau of Economic Research Working Paper Series* (2012). Available at: http://www.nber.org/papers/w17773.pdf (last accessed on 17 April 2017), in which the authors give an overview of empirical research undertaken to assess the strengths of the most popular patent theories. See esp. at pp. 12–22.

34 F. MACHLUP, *An Economic Review of the Patent System – Study of the Subcommittee on patents, trademarks and copyrights of the Committee on the Judiciary of the United States Senate* (1958 US Government Printing Office). See: p. 21.

35 M. LEMLEY, 'Ex ante versus ex post justifications for intellectual property' *The University of Chicago Law Review* 71, No. 1 (2004), pp. 129–149. See: p. 129.

the most 'standard' justification for patent protection. It is ex-ante of nature, as it attempts to impact human behaviour before the right comes into being.[36]

The *disclosure/dissemination* function is stooled upon the insight that there is a *social contract* between the inventor and society or, in the words of Machlup, there is exclusivity in exchange for secrets.[37] In turn for (full) disclosure of the technical working of the invention, the patentee will gain a monopoly status, namely a certain period of exclusivity. Society on the other hand will benefit from the knowledge of how the invention functions. This way, also, the wasteful duplication of investments is prevented as far as possible and society benefits by becoming able to build further on the teachings of others.[38]

The fourth theory is the so-called *commercialisation function* of patents.[39] This function recognises that patenting often takes place early and that much work is then yet to be done in order to develop an idea or innovation into a viable commercial invention. This theory illustrates that patents can be a vehicle to attract investments to further the goal of the actual marketing of the inventions into a commercial product. Without patent exclusivity, investors might be reluctant to invest into a new technology which can be replicated easily, without a deterrent. Additionally, patent rights themselves are easily tradeable rights, which highly facilitates the bargaining, the acquisition and selling of these rights.[40]

The last justification is based on the *prospecting function* of patents. This function is stemming from the work of Edmund Kitch.[41] Although maybe more controversial than the other theories above,[42] the prospect theory still has become rather established. This theory states that patent systems are often tailored to granting

---

36 Idem, at p. 130.

37 F. MACHLUP, *An Economic Review of the Patent System – Study of the Subcommittee on patents, trademarks and copyrights of the Committee on the Judiciary of the United States Senate* (1958 US Government Printing Office). See: p. 21.

38 Ibidem.

39 R.D. NELSON, and R. MAZZOLENI, 'Economic theories about the costs and benefits of patents' *Intellectual Property Rights and Research Tools in Molecular Biology* (1997 National Academy Press) See: pp. 17–27, esp. p. 22. Available via: http://www.ncbi.nlm.nih.gov/books/NBK233537/pdf/Bookshelf_NBK233537.pdf (last accessed on 17 April 2017).

40 Ibidem.

41 E. KITCH, 'The Nature and the Function of the Patent System' *Journal of Law and Economics* 20, No. 2 (1977), pp. 265–290. Kitch comes to this insight by making an analogy between patent rights and that of mineral claims on public land during the second half of the 19th century in America. See: pp. 271–275 of his article.

42 For interesting view on this theory, J.F. DUFFY, 'Rethinking the Prospect Theory of patents' *University of Chicago Law Review* 71, No. 2 (2004), pp. 439–510. See: pp. 441–447.

patents that are relatively broad[43] in scope,[44] that should be applied for at an early technological stage. Furthermore, the patent systems only require disclosure of an invention that works, but there is no requirement for it yet to be fully developed or to be commercially valuable.[45] The theory argues that such broad patents put the innovator into the driver's seat, to allow him to seize the possibility to explore the opportunities for the creation of derivative and subsequent inventions. As Nelson and Mazzoleni also write, further development and inventions might become possible and stimulated via the input of this initial invention.[46]

At this point it is crucial to underline one important assumption that underpins all these theories: all these justifications have in common that they require an adequate level of enforcement for them to effectively work in the way they suggest. A sufficient level of enforcement is thus a prerequisite to offer incentives, to provide disclosure and to offer prospects. It is to the role of enforcement of patent rights, specifically via preliminary injunctions, that we now turn.

§1.3. Uncertainty in litigation

Uncertainty is an omnipresent feature of law. It is for instance clear that uncertainty can affect people's compliance with legal standards,[47] and a party's view on the scope of legal rights, such as intellectual property rights.[48] Uncertainty is

43 That is, at least broader than the incentive function would require. See E. KITCH, 'The Nature and the Function of the Patent System' *Journal of Law and Economics* 20, No. 2 (1977), pp. 265–290. See: p. 267.

44 This happens by allowing the drafting of very general or abstract claims in patent applications.

45 E. KITCH, 'The Nature and the Function of the Patent System' *Journal of Law and Economics* 20, No. 2 (1977), pp. 265–290. See: p. 270.

46 R.D. NELSON, and R. MAZZOLENI, 'Economic theories about the costs and benefits of patents' *Intellectual Property Rights and Research Tools in Molecular Biology* (1997 National Academy Press). See: pp. 17–27, esp. p. 23. Available via: http://www.ncbi.nlm.nih.gov/books/NBK233537/pdf/Bookshelf_NBK233537.pdf (last accessed on 17 April 2017).

47 J.E. CALFEE, R. CRASWELL, 'Some effects of uncertainty on compliance with legal standards' *Virginia Law Review* 70, No. 5 (1984), pp. 965–1003.

48 S.E. STERK, 'Property rights, liability rules and uncertainty about property rights' *Cardozo School of Law Working Paper* No. 205 (2007). Available at: http://papers.ssrn.com/sol3/papers.cfm?abstract_id=1016168 (last accessed on 17 april 2017). Sterk points out for instance that the uncertainty about the scope of legal rights is more pervasive for users in the patent realm than it is in the copyright realm. Factors contributing to this uncertainty with patents are that 'independent creation' is not a defence to an infringement claim, that patent searches are difficult to undertake for individuals due to the large number of incomprehensive databases, the difficulty in claims evaluation for users and that there is the possibility for the patentee to file continuation applications. See: pp. 49–50.

also something that is present during *litigation*. This is very clear in the process of decisionmaking by the court, as is the case when it decides on the grant of a preliminary injunction. As Leubsdorf writes, uncertainty is a central feature of remedial law,[49] when courts decide on the need for the *grant* and the *type* of remedy. Not only are courts in their decisionmaking confronted with uncertainties about what will happen (i.e. which future harms may occur)[50] or uncertainties what might have been (i.e. what if infringement has *not* occurred),[51] but courts also face uncertainties about the effect – the impingement – that a selected remedy will have.[52]

A court has several methods to its disposal to try to deal with this uncertainty. For instance, the choice of remedy can take away some uncertainties. In fact, the (preliminary) injunction itself is seen as a solution for the court in tackling some of the uncertainty, as this relieves the court of the difficult task to establish the exact scope of calculating damages for harms.[53] However, a choice of remedy does not take away all the uncertainty, and a certain estimation often remains impossible to avoid when making a decision.[54] Therefore, courts have developed a number of strategies to deal with uncertainty, as an alternative for 'ordinary' fact finding when there is more legal certainty. The use of probabilities[55] and

49 J. LEUBSDORF, 'Remedies for uncertainty' *Boston University Law Review* 61 (1981), pp. 132–172.

50 Idem, at p. 137.

51 Idem, at p. 134. Furthermore, Leubsdorf writes on p. 137 that both these uncertainties are speculative of nature.

52 Idem, at p. 138. Here Leubsdorf points out that both injunctions and damages can have unpredictable effects.

53 D. LICHTMAN, 'Uncertainty and the standard for preliminary relief' *John M. Olin Law & Economics Working Paper* No. 166 (2002). See: p. 5. Available at: http://papers.ssrn.com/sol3/papers.cfm?abstract_id=344640 (last accessed on 17 April 2017). Arguing "Another response is that injunctions offer an easy way for courts to hide their uncertainty, a result not attainable via traditional money damages. In a case where a preliminary injunction issues and the plaintiff goes on to win on the merits, the court's uncertainty never appears on the public record." Furthermore; J. LEUBSDORF, 'Remedies for uncertainty' *Boston University Law Review* 61 (1981), pp. 132–172. See: p. 142.

54 J. LEUBSDORF, 'Remedies for uncertainty' *Boston University Law Review* 61 (1981), pp. 132–172. See: p. 142. Leubsdorf states that in other cases, the difficulty of framing an injunction is a ground for awarding damages. Nevertheless, as he writes: "Often, however, neither damages nor injunctions permit the court to avoid impossible estimation."

55 Idem, at p. 148. He writes on tht page: "The more courts seek to find the unfindable, the more they are likely to rely on probabilities disguised as findings of particular facts. What purports to be a finding that a plaintiff will be disabled for ten years, is actually an assertion that most similarly injured people are disabled about that long. The same can be said of findings that a plaintiff would have reaped specified

expectations[56] are two of these strategies, as will later be seen. Whilst these strategies can be helpful in dealing with uncertainty, they too cannot completely remedy uncertainty and factor it out of the equation.

Why is this a problem? Uncertainty in judicial decisionmaking when it comes to deciding on the grant of preliminary injunctions can be troublesome, since it can result into three connected, but distinct issues: 1) it can impact optimal decision rules,[57] 2) lead to erroneous decisions being taken[58] and 3) result in a haphazard application of the remedy.[59]

---

profits had the defendant made timely delivery of goods, or that a plaintiff could have preserved some of those profits had he made appropriate efforts to mitigate his damages. Reliance on probabilities may be inherent in all fact-finding. Judges and juries seldom pass on violations that have actually occurred in the court-room. Rather, they appraise evidence, and draw inferences leading more or less persuasively from the evidence to what has occurred or will occur."

56 Idem, at pp. 150–151. Leubsdorf writes: "Although expectations arrived at by a judge or jury are likely to be crude estimates, this approach may be less arbitrary than a system that awards full damages when the trier of fact "finds" when it "finds" that a given harm was caused by a violation, and no damages the contrary."

57 D. LICHTMAN, 'Uncertainty and the standard for preliminary relief' *John M. Olin Law & Economics Working Paper* No. 166 (2002). Available at: http://papers.ssrn.com/sol3/papers.cfm?abstract_id=344640 (last accessed on 17 April 2017). See pp. 7–11, pointing out that uncertainty about values of probabilities and harms can have large ramifications, from a Law and Economics point of view: "Decision rules that are optimal when all values are known precisely are not necessarily optimal in the face of uncertainty." Lichtman points out that this uncertainty is pervasive, capable of for instance affecting cost-benefit analysis, but also a similar analysis in tort law: "Judge Learned Hand famously proposed that an injurer should escape liability only where the marginal cost of any remaining precaution is greater than the expected reduction in the probability of harm multiplied by the expected loss. That certainly works if all of those quantities are known with certainty. But, again, what happens when we acknowledge that different courts likely read the same evidence differently?"

58 It is submitted that this is one of the strongest arguments in favour of a cautious attitude towards granting preliminary injunctions, see page 89 of this dissertation.

59 On this, also see D. LICHTMAN, 'Uncertainty and the standard for preliminary relief' *John M. Olin Law & Economics Working Paper* No. 166 (2002).
Available at: http://papers.ssrn.com/sol3/papers.cfm?abstract_id=344640 (last accessed on 17 April 2017). At p. 7 it is held by Lichtman: "There is another interpretation of uncertainty, however, and where it applies uncertainty cannot be ignored. Under this interpretation, an uncertain value is a value that different courts *would estimate differently even given the same evidence*, or, equivalently, a value that a single court *would estimate differently given the same evidence on different occasions*. This is exactly what happens when, for example, a group of people try to guess the number of pennies in a jar. Each looks at the same evidence and yet each offers up

Before these issues are further explored in the upcoming chapters, it is important to first review what the *sources* of this uncertainty are, in the context of preliminary relief in patent disputes. It is submitted that these sources of uncertainty can be subdivided into technical complexity, legal and economic uncertainties.

§1.3.1 (Technical) complexity in patent litigation

A specific patent-related argument arguing for caution and restraint with respect to the granting of preliminary injunctions is that patent issues can be too (technically) complex to be dealt with in preliminary relief proceedings, due to the technically complicated subject-matter of the technology which is central to the litigation. The reasoning behind this view is that the institution of preliminary injunctive relief proceedings is 1) a *general, all-purpose instrument* of law, and 2) that the typical issues central to patent litigation are not suitable to be dealt with in a preliminary injunction request, due to the speed and brevity of the proceedings. These 'typical issues' refer to the infringement analysis but also the examination of the validity of the patent. Both require a good understanding of (technically) complex subject-matter and the issues involved. The challenge for the court to reach this level of good understanding is further aggravated by the difficulty to collect and to be presented evidence and arguments on technical issues within such a short timeframe. Finally, as is shown in cases on the merits, the understanding, interpretation and evaluation of the technical merits of many inventions in patent litigation requires specific expertise: this can be provided for by court appointed experts, or can be provided for in briefs that are offered by experts that have been selected by the parties. In preliminary injunction proceedings, there is often little or no possibility for this.

However, that being said, it is difficult to attach a particular value to this source of uncertainty from a general point of view. It is submitted that the argument of 'technical complexity' has its main value on a case-by-case basis, rather than as a general argument against the use and (un)desirability of preliminary injunctions in patent litigation. Therefore, it is not uncommon to see in practice, as will be demonstrated in later chapters, that a defendant sometimes attempts to brand a dispute as 'too complex', in order to frustrate the adjudication in the context of preliminary relief. This is especially the case in The Netherlands[60] where, unlike other jurisdictions, 'suitability' of the case is a specific prong, and this factor

---

a different estimate. If the guesses are unbiased, they might converge toward the right answer; but any specific guess can be too high or too low." Emphasis added. He also writes, at p. 8, "(..)on this interpretation of uncertainty, courts might on average converge to the same estimate as before, but any court in isolation can overstate or understate the harm."

60 See for instance, Vzr. Rechtbank Den Haag, *Rhodia Chimie v PPG Industries Chemicals B.V.*, April 25th, 2012, KG ZA 12–244 and Vzr. Rechtbank Den Haag, *Unilever N.V. v. Procter & Gamble Nederland B.V. et al*, December 19th 2013, KG ZA 13–1038.

includes the concept of complexity. Overall however, as is demonstrated later, the argument seems to be rarely accepted in practice because Dutch courts seem reluctant to give up their chance to look at the dispute, and doing so would have the same effect as denying the preliminary junction to the plaintiff on substantive grounds.

A few remarks of general nature can still be made here however. Firstly, it not always the case that patent litigation requires great technical expertise; sometimes the technical issue covered by a patent is clear. Secondly, many judges in the field of patent litigation have a good understanding of technical issues themselves. Whilst judges are maybe not experts in all technical fields, this can – to a certain degree – be resolved by allocation of judges. Another development is the establishment of specialised patent chambers. Perhaps the furthest in this is The Netherlands, where all Dutch preliminary injunction proceedings related to (alleged) patent infringement take place at the *Voorzieningenrechter* in The Hague. The abovementioned factors may not go so far as taking away the point that patent litigation can be (technically) complex, but they do attempt to mitigate it.

Nevertheless, as written, it often will be a struggle to hear a patent case in preliminary injunction proceedings, due to the (technical) complexity of the subject-matter, the scramble to get sufficient expertise and evidence on (technical) issues and finally to have sufficient (preparation) time. It is submitted that this can be more of a problem for financially restricted or smaller parties involved in litigation, than it is for larger parties. It also affects the preliminary injunction court itself, as this body will have a limited amount of resources (in time, staffing and budget) that can be allocated to individual cases. Courts seem to be mindful of this; when complexity for instance was invoked in the litigation between Apple and Samsung in The Netherlands, the court pointed out that under Dutch law the court should be reluctant to view a case as unsuitable for *kort geding* but thereby it also considered *the nature of the parties* involved:

> "Although without any doubt complex, the case is not too complicated for a *kort geding*. *The Voorzieningenrechter* stresses firstly **that it should be reluctant in deciding that a preliminary injunction should not be granted merely on the basis that a case is too complicated.** The patents in this procedure, do furthermore not involve too complicated technology (..) Also, **these type of companies <of a large size and with large interests> should furthermore be regarded as being capable of organising a team of lawyers and patent attorneys**, in order to make possible a legal procedure on short term. Arguments of this nature run against the claim of Samsung that it has not been able to prepare adequately in this case, especially with respect to the patents Apple invokes, or that from that point of view there is an abuse of (procedural) law."[61]

61 Vzgr. Rechtbank Den Haag, *Apple Inc v Samsung Electronics,* August 24th· 2011, KG ZA 11–730. See: par. 4.5. Emphasis added.

This case fits well with what will be seen: generally speaking, courts are reluctant to give up a case, due to alleged unsuitability for a preliminary proceeding. The argument of unsuitability due to (technical) complexity is not accepted *prima facie*. Finally, one should bear in mind that, as will become clear, the bar of evidence is lower in preliminary injunction cases than it is in permanent injunction cases. Rock solid proof of infringement and patent validity is not required. What matters for the parties is to sufficiently convince the court that it is likely that either the plaintiff or defendant will succeed in the main proceedings, and what matters for the court is that it is confident that a made decision will be likely be upheld at a trial on the merits.

§1.3.2. Legal and economic uncertainties

In taking a decision whether or not to grant a preliminary injunction against an alleged patent infringer, a court should make a decision with respect to a range of factors. Theory assumes however that a court cannot make this decision with full confidence and that these factors are often surrounded by clouds of uncertainty. It is submitted that this uncertainty can be grouped under several different headings. These are provided in this paragraph.

Two caveats should be made before this. Firstly, it should be noted that whilst all jurisdictions take the elements of uncertainty given below into account, the actual degree that they do so differs strongly per jurisdiction. In England for instance, the analysis of the likelihood that the plaintiff will win is much more limited than in other countries in the sense that the case must only 'not be frivolous'. Equally, the (economic) assessment of harms plays a pivotal role in the United States but is of much less significance in The Netherlands. Therefore, the 'birds-eye' overview of this paragraph is somewhat artificial. Nevertheless, it is submitted that it has value as it highlights the dynamics which play a role in all preliminary injunction requests, regardless of the fact whether they are explicitly addressed in the different jurisdictions. Secondly, it should be stressed that also courts *within* a specific jurisdiction do of course not face the same uncertainties every time that they are asked to decide upon the grant of a preliminary injunction. This of course depends much on the specifics and facts of the individual case: what is uncertain in one case, may be much more clear in another. This results in various degrees of likelihood that the preliminary court makes a 'correct decision' in relation to a later judgment on the merits. In the same light, there are cases where a patent's validity may explicitly be undisputed by both parties, whilst in other cases it forms a key battleground.

Figure 2. Legal and economic uncertainties (own image).

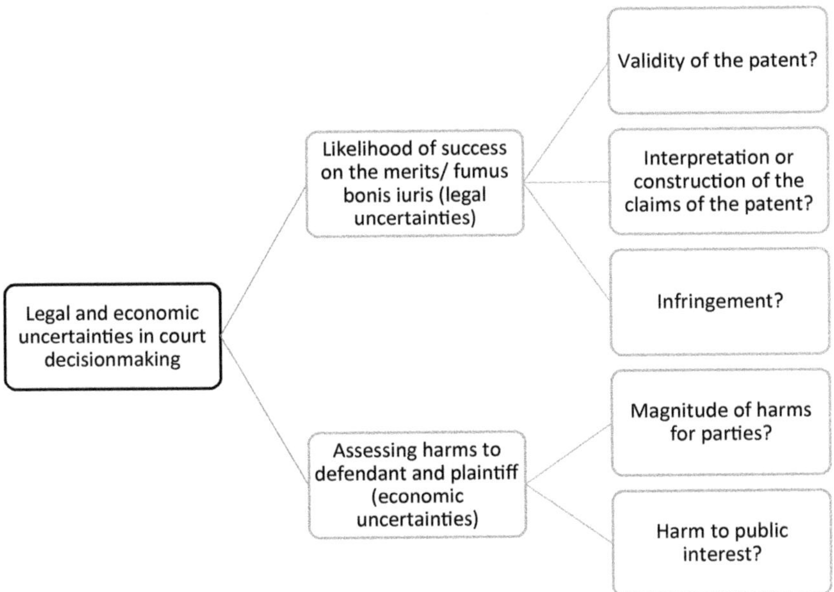

§1.3.2.1. Legal uncertainties

Firstly, the preliminary injunction decision is based on the differing probabilities of whether the plaintiff will prevail on trial at a later stage. This is often also referred to as 'the likelihood of success' and is also known under the Latin phrase *fumus boni iuris.*

There are three main reasons of uncertainty that are related to the 'likelihood of success' that the plaintiff will win at trial.[62] These uncertainties stem from legal issues – as opposed to economic ones – which the court has to consider.[63] Hampered by a limited possibility to be presented arguments and evidence, a limited amount of time and having to deal with often sharply opposing views of the involved parties, the preliminary injunction court has to anticipate how the trial-court later will decide on the following issues:

62 Y.T. WU, 'How will Ebay v Mercexchange affect preliminary injunction?' *NTUT Journal of Intellectual Property Law and Management* 3, No. 1 (2014), pp. 34–55. See: pp. 40–41.

63 R. SHEHADEH, M. STEWART, 'An economic approach to the "Balance of hardships" and "Public interest" tests for Preliminary Injunction Motions in Patent Infringement Cases' *Journal of the Patent and Trademark Office Society JPTOS* (2001) No. 5, pp. 341–358. See: p. 341.

1. The validity of the patent;
2. The claim interpretation / claim construction of the patent claims;
3. Whether patent infringement has occurred or not;

The first source of uncertainty refers to the notion[64] that a granted patent is not necessarily a valid patent. The reality is that patent offices all over the world grant inventors patents that upon further and later examination prove to be invalid.

The second source of uncertainty refers to the issue that even if a patent as such is valid, the infringement question is in the end about how the patent's *claims* are to be interpreted.[65] The extent of these claims is often most central in litigation, and their scope is very often strongly disputed. A court must anticipate how these claims will be interpreted at the trial on the merits and how this will impact the alleged assertion of infringement by the plaintiff. This is by no means a straightforward task. It seems especially challenging for 'lower instance' courts, bearing the often complex technology in mind.[66]

Thirdly, preliminary injunction courts should consider whether *infringement* has genuinely taken place. This is mostly not as clear-cut as the plaintiff-patentee presents it to be. The defendant's conduct may turn out not to amount to infringing behaviour at all. It may neither be literal infringement nor infringement that qualifies as such under the Doctrine of Equivalence. Furthermore, the conduct may also fall under certain exceptions such as an experimental use/research exception for generic companies.[67] In the latter case, pharmaceutical generic companies are

64 See below at page 67 of this dissertation, where this issue is considered in more detail.

65 Y.T. WU, 'How will Ebay v Mercexchange affect preliminary injunction?' *NTUT Journal of Intellectual Property Law and Management* 3, No. 1 (2014), pp. 34–55. See: p. 40.

66 Moore concludes on p. 38 of her article, although this is not specifically on the grant of preliminary injunctions, that: "This empirical study of the Federal Circuit's de novo review of district court claim constructions leaves little doubt that the present system of adjudication is flawed. The 33% reversal rate of district court claim constructions *suggests that judges are not, at present, capable of resolving these issues with sufficient accuracy.* This infuses the patent system with a high degree of uncertainty until the Federal Circuit rules on claim construction." Emphasis added. K.A. MOORE, 'Are district judges equipped to resolve patent cases? *Harvard Journal of Law and Technology* 15, No. 1 (2001), pp. 1–39. This said, much of course depends on the way a court system is set up, i.e. regarding the bundling of judicial expertise in chambers as well as the experience of judges.

67 On this, see for instance, A. TRIDICO, J. JACOBSTEIN, L. WALL, 'Facilitating generic drug manufacturing worldwide: Bolar exemptions worldwide' *WIPO Magazine*, No. 3 (2014). Available at: http://www.wipo.int/wipo_magazine/en/2014/03/article_0004.html (last accessed on 14 April 2017) and P. GARLAND, K. LARUSSON, 'Data exclusivity, Bolar exemption and generic drugs in the EU' *European Intellectual Property Law Review* (2007), pp. 128–133.

allowed to conduct research activities – for instance on a drug's bioequivalence – during the period of time that the patentee's exclusive right is still effective. In the United States this is stipulated in 35 USC Par. 271(e)(1)[68] and in the EU it is currently permitted by virtue of Directive 2004/27/EC.[69] The exception is also provided for under the UPC Agreement.[70]

It is important to stress again at this point that the preliminary injunction court dealing with the request for a grant of a preliminary injunction court does *not* have to find definitive answers to these questions. However, it should have the confidence that its decision, guided by these questions, will anticipate the judgment that follows an actual trial on the merits.

§1.3.2.2. *Economic uncertainties: assessing the economic harms that may occur to the plaintiff and to the defendant*

The preliminary injunction court does not only have to make a decision on how the plaintiff's case will be ruled at a later stage from a legal point of view. Often, there are considerations of a more *economic* nature involved too.

Primarily, this means that the court should attempt to develop a better understanding of the economic harms which may follow from granting or denying the preliminary injunction. The court should do so for both parties. It can also be necessary to involve into the analysis the question whether it is warranted to give an injunction with respect to the public interest.[71] Furthermore, as Lichtman correctly states, an approximation of the magnitude of the involved harms can be necessary

---

Another example of an exception of a patentee's exclusive right would be if a company does this via a compulsory licensing scheme on the government's instructions. Art. 31 TRIPS provides for this in the case of an emergency situation.

68 This provision stipulates that: "*It shall not be an act of infringement* to make, use, offer to sell, or sell within the United States or import into the United States a patented invention (..) *solely for uses reasonably related to the development and submission of information under a Federal law* which regulates the manufacture, use, or sale of drugs or veterinary biological products." Emphasis added.

69 See Art. 10 of the Directive 2004/27/EC and then especially Art. 10 (6): "Conducting the necessary studies and trials with a view to the application of paragraphs 1, 2, 3 and 4 and the consequential practical requirements shall not be regarded as contrary to patent rights or to supplementary protection certificates for medicinal products." The abovementioned paragraphs describe the scope of the provision.

70 According to Art. 27 (b) of the Unified Patent Court Agreement, this exemption is also part of the Unified Patent Court system: "The rights conferred by the patent shall not extend to any of the following: (..) acts done for experimental purposes relating to the subject matter of the patented invention."

71 R. SHEHADEH, M. STEWART, 'An economic approach to the "Balance of hardships" and "Public interest" tests for Preliminary Injunction Motions in Patent Infringement Cases' *Journal of the Patent and Trademark Office Society JPTOS* (2001) No. 5, pp. 341–358. See: pp. 355–357.

in order to establish the level of the bond. This bond, for a wrongfully issued injunction, is set for the defendant's benefit when the court proves to be wrong.[72]

Lichtman argues that it is difficult for the court to make a well-balanced decision on determining the magnitude of economic harms as the court is *unlikely to have good information about the relative harms* facing the parties.[73] And indeed, as will be seen in subsequent chapters, establishing the magnitude of harms is, at the very least, a rather complex issue and often requires economic analysis by the parties and the court involved.[74] A patentee for instance will attempt to quantify how the infringer's action will damage its business position.[75] The competition by the infringer can lead to diverted sales, price erosion (due to the undercutting of the price by the infringer) and can result in the more limited ability for the patent holder to price-discriminate. The latter is because of the restricted possibility of the targeting of different groups of consumers, by adjusting the price of the product according to a consumer's maximum 'willingness to pay', this way maximising profits.[76]

How strong these effects are, to a large extent depends on how much market power the contested patent confers. In other words, do suitable alternatives exist and (where applicable) what role does the patent play in the overall product? Furthermore, what can also be taken into consideration is how the infringement affects the patentee's offering of non-patented complementary products or complementary (maintenance) services.[77] Relevant too may be whether the patentee and defendant are in direct competition with each other. Are they producing for the

72 D. LICHTMAN, 'Uncertainty and the standard for preliminary relief' *John M. Olin Law & Economics Working Paper No. 166* (2002). See: pp. 12–13. Available at: http://papers.ssrn.com/sol3/papers.cfm?abstract_id=344640 (last accessed on 17 April 2017). Licthman also provides an additional noteworthy reason: a defendant may be deterred to cause further harms even in the absence of an injunction as a high estimation of harms may lead the defendant to believe that it may incur these harms in damages to be paid when it comes to a trial on the merits.

73 D. LICHTMAN, 'Uncertainty and the standard for preliminary relief' *John M. Olin Law & Economics Working Paper No. 166* (2002). See: p. 2. Available at: http://papers.ssrn.com/sol3/papers.cfm?abstract_id=344640 (last accessed on 17 April 2017). He therefore argues, on p. 11, that the difficulty in doing so has affected the preliminary injunction standard which is traditionally used in the United States. There, the assessment of economic harms is a key part of the test.

74 R. SHEHADEH, M. STEWART, 'An economic approach to the "Balance of hardships" and "Public interest" tests for Preliminary Injunction Motions in Patent Infringement Cases' *Journal of the Patent and Trademark Office Society JPTOS* (2001) No. 5, pp. 341–358. See: p. 344.

75 Idem, at pp. 345–354.

76 Ibidem.

77 Idem, at pp. 351–352.

same market?[78] These effects should of course not only be claimed by the patentee, but they should be *proven and quantified* as far as possible as well, thereby bearing in mind the nature of preliminary injunction proceedings. A loss of sales due to diversion and a drop in prices once the infringer has entered the market, can for instance be shown in figures. It is then up to the preliminary injunction court to accept or reject a causal link between the infringer's activities on the one hand and the fall in sales and prices on the other hand. The court should subsequently decide on whether to prevent recurring infringement.

Simultaneously, *the defendant* will attempt to convince the court of the negative effects that will occur to its own business activities if a preliminary injunction is granted against him. Furthermore, the defendant may also argue in the *public interest*: an elimination of competition by a preliminary injunction enjoining the defendant can also result in a loss of consumer welfare. As Shehadeh and Stewart explain well, there is a tension between the entry of competitors and patent protection in the light of the public interest and they warn that a preliminary injunction, from this perspective, should perhaps not be granted too early:

> "From an economic perspective, the elimination of a desired product or service from the marketplace necessarily reduces some consumers' welfare. Generally, one would expect the public interest to be well served by such an exclusion only if a substantial compensating benefit would be gained as a result of restricting consumer choice. The public-policy justification for government enforcement of a patent holder's "right to exclude" rests on the belief that (1) intellectual property protection will stimulate invention and innovation and (2) in the long run the gains from innovation will more than compensate for the loss in consumer welfare brought about by the exclusion of goods or services accused of patent infringement. Because there is an economic cost associated with the exclusion of a good or service that consumers desire, however, it seems clear that accused goods or services should not be precipitously excluded from the marketplace."[79]

Whilst the abovementioned harms are already challenging enough to establish for either the defendant or the plaintiff, there are other harms that are more *indirect* and even more difficult to quantify and link to the infringement. Think for instance of the loss of goodwill which may occur to the patentee when the preliminary

---

78 C. LAWSON, 'The interlocutory injunction dilemma in patent infringement and invalidity disputes' *Australian Intellectual Property Journal* 21, No. 2 (2010). See: pp. 73–99. Version accessed via: https://research-repository.griffith.edu.au/bitstream/handle/10072/35487/66020_1.pdf;jsessionid=E8F91C09631731896AA6D48887041040?sequence=1 (last accessed on 17 April 2017). See the conclusion of the article.

79 R. SHEHADEH, M. STEWART, 'An economic approach to the "Balance of hardships" and "Public interest" tests for Preliminary Injunction Motions in Patent Infringement Cases' *Journal of the Patent and Trademark Office Society JPTOS* (2001) No. 5, pp. 341–358. See: pp. 355–356. Emphasis added.

injunction is not granted.[80] This may also negatively affect future business with other companies or obstruct further financing by investors. Lastly, what about extra costs for instance that the patentee has to make, in order to face the competition? One can think of advertising expenses; these are costs that would not have existed if the patentee had retained its monopoly position.

§1.4. The property and liability rules framework and preliminary injunctions

§1.4.1. The framework itself

No work on patents and injunctive relief would be complete without making a reference to a key topic in Law and Economics theory; that of property and liability rules. It is especially of interest to see what the specific role is of preliminary injunctions within (the application of) this framework. For this, a short introduction to a few main concepts related to this framework should take place first.

Our starting point is the 'Coase Theorem'.[81]This states that in a world with zero transaction costs (the costs that are *related* to any economic exchange and which in turn also *impact* this exchange)[82] the initial allocation of rights or entitlements does not matter, as these rights will be transferred to their highest value use due to

---

80 See for instance C. LAWSON, 'The interlocutory injunction dilemma in patent infringement and invalidity disputes' *Australian Intellectual Property Journal* 21, No. 2 (2010), pp. 73–99. Version accessed via: https://research-repository.griffith.edu.au/bitstream/handle/10072/35487/66020_1.pdf;jsessionid=E8F91C09631731896AA6D48887041040?sequence=1 (last accessed on 17 April 2017). See p. 3 of the PDF.

81 The theorem is based on the work of R. COASE, 'The problem of social cost' *Journal of Law and Economics* 3 (1960), pp. 1–44, although he did not formulate the theorem himself in that article. For a good introduction, see: the work of Schwab. S. SCHWAB, 'Coase defends Coase: why lawyers listen and economists do not' *Michigan Law Review* 87, No. 6 (1989), pp. 1171–198. See: pp. 1173–1174.

82 Examples of transaction costs are for instance search costs, enforcement costs and bargaining costs. Note that the term 'transaction costs' itself is highly debated. Economists differ between a 'neoclassical' definition, highlighting the costs of trading across a market, and a 'property rights' definition concerning the costs of establishing and enforcing property rights. For more on the history and use of this term, see, D. W. ALLEN, 'Transaction costs' (2000) in C. MÉNARD (editor), *Transaction costs and Property rights* (2004 Edward Elgar Publishing), pp. 304–337. For an interesting article on the works of Coase and the different reception some of his thoughts have had from lawyers and economists, see the book review of Schwab. S. SCHWAB, 'Coase defends Coase: why lawyers listen and economists do not' *Michigan Law Review* 87, No. 6 (1989), pp. 1171–1198.

private bargaining.[83] This bargaining becomes problematic when transaction costs are high, instead of zero, as the Theorem assumes. In that case, the allocation of rights *does* become important.[84] It is then that we turn to the writing of Calabresi and Melamed, which has become influential in the field as those authors linked the issues of allocation of rights, remedies and transaction costs together.[85]

Calabresi's and Melamed's main finding was that transaction costs matter whether a property rule or a liability rule is preferred, and the choice of remedy can impact the allocation of rights.[86] The property rule gives the holder of an entitlement the possibility to rely on exclusivity. It thus allows to enjoin the infringer. The liability rule does not give the option to enjoin but only a right to receive an amount of damages for the injury done by the defendant. In other words, as Hylton writes, property rules seek to secure and settle expectations with respect to an entitlement whilst liability rules in contrast aim merely to reallocate the burden of a loss, after it has occurred.[87]

Building on this insight, Calabresi and Melamed argue that when transaction costs are low, property rules are preferable to liability rules.[88] This is because in that

---

83 R.P. MERGES, 'Of property rules, Coase and Intellectual Property' *Columbia Law Review* 94, No. 8 (1994), pp. 2656–2673.

84 Idem, at p. 2656. As Merges writes: "But where transaction costs are positive, this result cannot be assumed. Thus, ultimately Coase admonishes us to pay attention to transaction costs in allocating property rights and setting rules for their exchange."

85 G. CALABRESI, D. MELAMED, 'Property rules, liability rules and inalienability: one view of the cathedral' *Harvard Law Review* 85 (1972), pp. 1089–1128. Also see: R.P. MERGES, 'Of property rules, Coase and Intellectual Property' *Columbia Law Review* 94, No. 8 (1994), pp. 2656–2673. See: p. 2664 a.f.

86 G. CALABRESI, D. MELAMED, 'Property rules, liability rules and inalienability: one view of the cathedral' *Harvard Law Review* 85 (1972), pp. 1089–1128. See: pp. 1106–1110.

87 K. HYLTON, 'Property rules and liability rules once again' *Boston University School of Law Working Paper, Law and Economics* No. 05–17 (2005). Available at https://papers.ssrn.com/sol3/papers.cfm?abstract_id=818944 (last accessed on 17 April 2017). See esp. p. 2 of the Working Paper, thereby partly quoting Jeremy Bentham.

88 G. CALABRESI, D. MELAMED, 'Property rules, liability rules and inalienability: one view of the cathedral' *Harvard Law Review* 85 (1972), pp. 1089–1128. See: pp. 1106–1110. The value of the finding has been questioned for instance in the work of L. KAPLOW, S. SHAVELL, 'Property rules and liability rules: an economic analysis' *Harvard Law Review* 109, No. 4 (1996), pp. 713–790. At p. 718, they write: "we will cast doubt on the belief that property rules are best when transaction costs are low – assertedly because the use of property rules will induce parties to bargain and reach desirable out- comes – whereas liability rules are best when transaction costs are high – supposedly because the use of liability rules will induce injurers to act desirably, mimicking the outcomes that would otherwise have been reached through bargaining. We find that this belief is often contradicted (...)." However, Hylton disagrees with this and maintains that the fundamental proposition of Calabresi and Melamed – namely that the property rules are to be preferred above liability

situation, the individual who wants to acquire a property from another individual, will find a mutually agreeable price to purchase it due to bargaining activities. When transaction costs are high on the other hand – i.e. due to a large multitude of actors or large information asymmetries between parties – liability rules seem to be more effective, and thus from an economic perspective preferable.[89] In this situation, bargaining between the prospective purchaser and holder of an entitlement is no longer required. The entitlement can be used against a fixed cost, compensating the holder for its use by others.

§1.4.2. *The role of preliminary injunctions in (the application of) the framework*

Having given an extremely concise overview of the main findings of Coase, Calabresi and Melamed, the question is whether preliminary injunctions play a specific role in the debate. It is submitted they do.

The first observation is that it is clear that the request to decide on a preliminary injunction implies *that the legal protection of entitlements cannot be postponed* until the conclusion of the litigation about the assignment of the contested entitlement, after trial. This is, as Brooks and Schwartz recognised, "at odds with the usual law and economics understanding in the sense that the assignment and protection of entitlements can be separated and handled sequentially so long as damages at the conclusion of the case are adequate."[90] According to them, many scholars that build on the framework of Calabresi and Melamed often look at entitlement protection

rules in situations of low transaction costs – remains valid. Hylton does so by basing himself on research that takes into account the *subjective valuations* of entitlement holders, based on the specific rule used. See the work of K. HYLTON, 'Property rules and liability rules once again' *Boston University School of Law Working Paper, Law and Economics* No. 05-17 (2005). Available at https://papers.ssrn.com/sol3/papers.cfm?abstract_id=818944 (last accessed on 17 April 2017). Furthermore, see the interesting work of R.A. EPSTEIN, 'A clear view of the cathedral: the dominance of property rules' *Yale Law Journal* 106 (1997), pp. 2091–2120. Epstein also argues in favour of property rules above liability rules. This in order to preserve the stability of possession and social expectations that are necessary for the growth of any complex social order, although he acknowledges that in certain situations liability rules can be used but only with extensive procedural protections.

89 G. CALABRESI, D. MELAMED, 'Property rules, liability rules and inalienability: one view of the cathedral' *Harvard Law Review* 85 (1972), pp. 1089–1128. See: pp. 1106–1110.

90 R.R.W. BROOKS, W.F. SCHWARTZ, 'Legal uncertainty, economic efficiency, and the preliminary injunction doctrine' *Stanford Law Review* 58 (2005), pp. 380–409. See: p. 384, including footnote 9. With 'the usual Law and Economics understanding' the authors refer the work of Calabresi and Melamed in G. CALABRESI, D. MELAMED, 'Property rules, liability rules and inalienability: one view of the cathedral' *Harvard Law Review* 85 (1972), pp. 1089–1128.

in isolation of the assignment of rights.[91] But due to the lack of certainty that exists at the time prior to the preliminary injunction decision is taken, it is not possible for the parties to make efficient trade-offs in the way Calabresi and Melamed have predicted.[92] Thus: *prior to the preliminary injunctions, and until the issue is resolved, truly efficient trade-offs cannot be made.*[93] If the remedy of preliminary proceedings did not exist, this indeterminacy could last long, namely until a trial on the merits, thereby hampering the possibility of any efficient trade-offs.

Therefore, secondly, the following can be submitted with respect to the relationship between transaction costs and preliminary injunction (proceedings): preliminary injunctions, when granted, *have an effect on reducing transaction costs.* Due to the decision to issue a preliminary injunction (1) some degree of uncertainty, even if merely to a certain extent, is taken away. The grant also (2) identifies the defendant as a (likely) infringing party. It is submitted that both effects correspond with the abovementioned findings of Coase, Calabresi and Melamed in the sense that both can contribute to a more efficient bargaining between parties, i.e. in the attempt to reach a settlement.[94]

Thirdly, as Lawson, Brooks and Schwartz observe, whilst doctrinally a preliminary injunction itself can be seen as an example of a property rule in action, *it also has some characteristics of a liability rule* for at least two parties that take place in the proceedings. These are the preliminary injunction judge and the plaintiff. For the *preliminary injunction judge,* this observation is related to the *decisionmaking process,* the proceeding, itself. As Lawson indicates, this is because the preliminary injunction judge is "essentially addressing the patent dispute in the context of a liability rule."[95] In considering a preliminary injunction, it should ask itself the question

---

91 R.R.W. BROOKS, W.F. SCHWARTZ, 'Legal uncertainty, economic efficiency, and the preliminary injunction doctrine' *Stanford Law Review* 58 (2005), pp. 380–409, esp. footnote 9 on p. 384.

92 Ibidem.

93 Brooks and Schwartz, also argue that the availability of an adequate final remedy is not a justification to deny a preliminary injunction from an efficiency point of view. As they write on p. 385, "adequate compensation at the conclusion of the case does not provide parties with sufficient incentive to engage in efficient conduct before and during the case."

94 In the same light, see the work of Lichtman, arguing that injunctions facilitate bargaining by establishing clear property rights, thereby not restricting bargaining due to different views of how much damages a court would award. See D. LICHTMAN, 'Uncertainty and the standard for preliminary relief' *John M. Olin Law & Economics Working Paper* No. 166 (2002). Available at: http://papers.ssrn.com/sol3/papers.cfm?abstract_id=344640 (last accessed on 17 April 2017).

95 C. LAWSON, 'The interlocutory injunction dilemma in patent infringement and invalidity disputes' *Australian Intellectual Property Journal* 21, No. 2 (2010), pp. 73–99. Version accessed via: https://research-repository.griffith.edu.au/bitstream/handle/10072/35487/66020_1.pdf;jsessionid=E8F91C09631731896AA6D48887041040?sequence=1 (last accessed on 17 April 2017). See: p. 18 of the PDF.

that if infringement is to be found, whether the court assessed damages (at trial) are sufficient to properly value the patent?[96] If the answer to this question negative, this can be a reason to grant a preliminary injunction at the time it is requested.

For the *plaintiff*, this is because the plaintiff can *use the asymmetric information* which exists between parties at preliminary injunction hearings.[97] The authors Brooks and Schwartz thereby base themselves on the work of Kaplow and Shavell[98] and again stress that although in the form of a property rule, the preliminary injunction does have characteristics of a liability rule:

> "(..) the granted preliminary injunction in essence converts a property rule into a temporary liability rule: the party seeking the injunction has a limited call option, wherein she will have to pay court determined damages if it turns out that the entitlement belongs to the other party. Knowing her private value and the distribution of harms to the other party from complying with the injunction, the liability-rule-like preliminary injunction harnesses the party's private information."[99]

Concluding, it is therefore clear that preliminary injunctions occupy a special place in the property and liability rules landscape. They have some hallmarks of both and their availability is of significance with respect to transaction costs and the notion that the assignment and protection of entitlements cannot be separated and handled sequentially.

§1.5. Chapter conclusion

This opening chapter has firstly reviewed what are seen as three hallmarks of preliminary injunctions and preliminary injunction proceedings. These are: 1) a decision taken under heightened uncertainty; 2) which is supposedly temporary of nature; and 3) which has a congruential and temporal relationship with final injunctions and the trial on the merits, instead of being a completely freestanding remedy. Subsequently, a few common justifications for patent protection have been briefly provided. As has been stated, these justifications can only fulfil their intended goals – to offer incentives, disclosure and prospects – when patents are sufficiently enforced. A preliminary injunction, being an enforcement tool, can then help achieve to provide an adequate level of protection since, as will be seen in the

---

96 Ibidem.

97 R.R.W. BROOKS, W.F. SCHWARTZ, 'Legal uncertainty, economic efficiency, and the preliminary injunction doctrine' *Stanford Law Review* 58 (2005), pp. 380–409. See: p. 387.

98 L. KAPLOW, S. SHAVELL, 'Property rules and liability rules: an economic analysis' *Harvard Law Review* 109, No. 4 (1996), pp. 713–790. See: p. 725.

99 R.R.W. BROOKS, W.F. SCHWARTZ, 'Legal uncertainty, economic efficiency, and the preliminary injunction doctrine' *Stanford Law Review* 58 (2005), pp. 380–409. See: p. 387, footnote 20.

following chapter, it can be an effective remedy in certain situations. This can allow the justifications for patent protection to prosper.

In this chapter, we have also looked at the difficult aspect of uncertainty. Although uncertainty may be an ubiquitous factor of Law and within litigation, its presence is not to be taken lightly here and the various sources that generate this uncertainty in the context of the preliminary injunction doctrine have been reviewed. Whilst actual practice is perhaps not so stark as theory – after all not every source of uncertainty mentioned in this paragraph is explicitly addressed in every jurisdiction in an equal manner – it has become clear that the preliminary injunction court faces a difficult task and that they have quite a few legal and economic uncertainties to reckon with and to anticipate on. These include the likelihood of infringement and patent validity, claim construction and the magnitude of harms to parties and public.

Lastly, we have shortly reviewed the property and liability rules debate, and then specifically the place of preliminary injunctions therein. As has been written, no academic work on injunctions would be complete without a reference to the works of Coase, Calabresi and Melamed that helped in shaping the discourse. It is concluded that herein, preliminary injunctions have a somewhat special position given their rather hybrid nature. Furthermore, it is apparent they can reduce transaction costs and they impact the notion that the protection and the assignment of entitlements can be handled separately.

Chapter 2: Independent Economic and Doctrinal Reasons in Favour of the Availability of the Remedy of Preliminary Injunctions

§2.1. Introduction

Apart from international and national legal obligations to provide the remedy of preliminary injunctions, there are more independent doctrinal justifications as well. Authors of legal and economic writing on preliminary injunctions have used varying formulations to describe the main justifications for *why* the institution of the preliminary injunction is useful or necessary. Below, the main justifications that are regularly cited are set out. These will be analysed on their value.

Please note four points beforehand.

Firstly, the question that is raised here is *not* when or whether a preliminary injunction should be given in a specific, concrete case. Instead, it is about justifications *for the availability of the legal remedy itself.*

Secondly, it should be stressed that the viewpoint from this chapter is that of a more theoretical and overarching one. Even when a justification is not explicitly addressed or mentioned by the court in a specific case, this does not mean that this is not a justification for the remedy itself nor that it does not have this function in practice. As will be seen, when looking comparatively at the actual standards used by courts in different jurisdictions, national courts interpret justifications differently and attribute different values to them. Sometimes for instance 'irreparable harm' is an explicit condition to be fulfilled and is prescribed in the legal test by the court. However, this is not the case everywhere and it may be a factor that is more on the background in other jurisdictions.

Thirdly, there is of course a certain overlap between justifications for preliminary injunctions and for permanent injunctions. For instance, a justification for both types is that they are issued because damages would be difficult to estimate. That said, below an attempt will be made to highlight the specific interim nature of the preliminary injunction.

Lastly, mentioned below are the general and doctrinal justifications, which can be further elaborated upon when looking at practice. When one for instance looks at the pharmaceutical industry, certain justifications for a preliminary injunction are regularly invoked which are not mentioned in this chapter. These can however be grouped under one of the doctrinal justifications below. For instance, the loss of a privileged position within a medical reimbursement scheme may qualify as irreparable harm for doctrinal purposes.

§2.2. To preserve the status quo between the parties: more than an effect?

The preservation of the status quo, or in other words to *preserve the existing state of affairs between the parties*, is a frequently cited, although controversial justification for the remedy of the preliminary injunction to be available for litigants. In some jurisdictions, it has been of such prominence, that it *de facto* has been incorporated into the legal test governing preliminary injunctive relief.[100] Courts, especially in Common Law countries, have often seen it as one of the more traditional goals – if not *the main* goal – of the remedy of preliminary injunctive relief.[101] However, also the German legislator has included this notion in its Code on Civil Procedure.[102]

Lord Justice Cotton has formulated the goal of a preliminary injunction as follows:

---

100 The preservation of the status quo can have two faces, as POWERS explains. Both as a purpose/justification of a preliminary injunction and as part of the legal test governing the grant of a (preliminary) injunction. With respect to the US, he comments at pp. 1027–1028 of his article: "Many courts note that the *purpose of a preliminary injunction is to preserve the status quo* existing between the parties. Such statements of purpose, while notable, need not go beyond functioning as mere platitudes, throwaway lines in a judicial opinion that do not figure in the substantive test applied by the court a greater showing by movants seeking preliminary relief that alters the status quo. More interestingly, some Federal Circuit courts sometimes *incorporate the status quo issue into their substantive preliminary injunction doctrine* and require a greater showing by movants seeking preliminary relief that alters the status quo." Emphasis added. J. POWERS, 'A status quo bias: behavioural economics and the Federal Preliminary Standard' *Texas Law Review* 92 (2014), pp. 1027–1051. The latter is mostly the case with respect to *mandatory* preliminary injunctions in the United States. Also see on this, R. LEE, 'Preliminary injunctions and the status quo' *Washington Law Review* 58 (2001), pp. 109–166. See: pp. 115–121. Note that also the *American Cyanamid* test in England, as will be seen, makes a reference to the status quo in the test too, namely at the balancing of convenience prong when comparing the harms of the parties with each other.

101 L.B. VAUGHN, 'A need for clarity: toward a new standard for preliminary injunctions' *Oregon Law Review* 68 (1989), pp. 839–884. See: p. 849. Similarly, see M. DENLOW, 'The Motion for a Preliminary Injunction: Time for a Uniform Federal Standard' *The Review of Litigation* 22, No. 3 (2003), pp. 495–539. See: p. 516.

102 See Paragraph 935 of the German Code of Civil Procedure (ZPO), which states: "Einstweilige Verfügungen in Bezug auf den Streitgegenstand sind zulässig, wenn zu besorgen ist, *dass durch eine Veränderung des bestehenden Zustandes* die Verwirklichung des Rechts einer Partei vereitelt oder wesentlich erschwert werden könnte." Emphasis added.

> "the object of [an interlocutory injunction] which is to keep things *in statu quo*, so that that if at the hearing the plaintiffs obtain a judgment in their favour, the defendants will have been prevented from dealing in the meantime with the property in such a way as to make the judgment ineffectual."[103]

This 'freezing' of the case most commonly arises, Spry continues, where property may be damaged, destroyed or removed or when the value of other rights of the plaintiff may be diminished.[104] In these cases, the basis to grant the preliminary injunction, despite the possible hardships for to who it is addressed, is to act to preserve the subject matter which is in dispute or otherwise to protect the plaintiff's position.[105]

On first sight, a prohibitory preliminary injunction can indeed serve the purpose of preservation of a physical object or the preservation of an actual (physical) situation. For instance, one can think of the preservation of a tree. In the patent context, one can think of a situation in which a generic entrant has not yet entered the market. A *goal*, but also *effect* of a preliminary injunction can then indeed be to maintain the status quo. After all, a prohibition of felling a tree or the blocking of market entrance will keep the situation more or less as it is. The tree will remain standing and the patentee will maintain its exclusive status on the market. However, as Zuckerman points out, doctrinally, this may be an incorrect interpretation of the law[106] as the law is not so much concerned with keeping in status quo the object of a right, but with *preservation of the legal right* itself from injury.[107] The problem with 'maintaining the status quo' from this perspective however, he argues, is that before the court has adjudicated, the court cannot know which of the contenders is right. Therefore, whether the court grants or denies preliminary relief, it risks harming rights and upsetting the status quo.[108]

Apart from being doctrinally difficult and somewhat hypothetical, it is furthermore submitted that maintaining the status quo is everything but a practical justification. When *infringement is already occurring*, it is difficult, if not impossible to maintain the status quo in practice. As Lawson states, in his article on Australian preliminary injunctions in patent litigation:

---

103 L.J. Cotton cited in I.C.F. SPRY, *Equitable Remedies* (1990 Sweet & Maxwell). See: pp. 446–447.

104 I.C.F. SPRY, *Equitable Remedies* (1990 Sweet & Maxwell). See: p. 445.

105 Ibidem.

106 A.A.S. ZUCKERMAN, 'Interlocutory remedies in quest of procedural fairness' *The Modern Law Review* 56 (1993), pp. 325–341. See: p. 327.

107 Ibidem. Note that Zuckerman gives the example of a preliminary injunction against felling a tree. Zuckerman argues that the status quo does not refer to the physical object, which would dictate a prohibition of felling the tree. Instead he writes: "the only right with a claim to preservation is the right of the lawful owner to resist interference with his freedom to deal with the tree, whether it be felling or preserving it."

108 Ibidem.

> "whether the court awards or denies an interlocutory injunction, **one of the parties will suffer damage,** while the aspiration of the relevant principles **might be to maintain the status quo** between the parties until their rights can be finally adjudicated and determined, **this is in practice an impossible task where parties are already in the market**."[109]

The *timing factor* that the concept entails, is another reason that 'maintaining the status quo' can maybe be more seen as a theoretical justification than as a practical concept. As Mei for instance writes, the status quo is featured in the English *American Cyanamid* guidelines, but much around its use is unclear:

> "However, for this term to be a helpful legal criterion, it is necessary to answer the question: Existing when? At what point of time? Should it be the date immediately before the defendant did the first act that is alleged to have been wrongful; the date when the plaintiff first learned of that act; the date when the plaintiff first complained to the defendant; or the date when the plaintiff issued his writ?"[110]

Vaughn concludes – and this is, it is submitted, particularly relevant regarding the short and swift nature of preliminary injunction proceedings – that it is a concept which relies heavily upon both parties' views and the evaluation of facts and this at a time when there is very little time and opportunity to assess these facts.[111, 112]

---

109 See the following article: C. LAWSON, 'The interlocutory injunction dilemma in patent infringement and invalidity disputes' *Australian Intellectual Property Journal* 21, No. 2 (2010), pp. 73–99. Version accessed via: https://research-repository.griffith.edu.au/bitstream/handle/10072/35487/66020_1.pdf;jsessionid=E8F91C09631731896AA6D48887041040?sequence=1 (last accessed on 17 April 2017). See: page 21 of the PDF.

110 G. MEI, 'Interlocutory injunctions in IP Infringement actions in England and Wales and in Ireland – *American Cyanamid* revisited' *International Review of Intellectual Property and Competition Law* 46, No. 2 (2015), pp. 175–202. See: p. 192. Also see Vaughn: "At some point in the relationship or transactions between the parties *the court must identify it.* Classically, that time was the last peaceable status between the parties. But when courts attempted to inquire into that peaceable situation, *they have tripped over another component of a status-quo oriented purpose: the parties' subjective description of that time.* One person's last non-contested status was often another's declaration of war." L.B. VAUGHN, 'A need for clarity: toward a new standard for preliminary injunctions' *Oregon Law Review* 68 (1989), pp. 839–884. See: p. 850. Emphasis added.

111 Idem, at p. 850.

112 Similar criticism is also directed to the application of the status quo with respect to *mandatory* preliminary injunctions in the United States, which has resulted into 'a rift' between the courts with some courts requiring a heightened standard when a mandatory preliminary injunction is requested. T. R. Lee, has researched the attitude of the American courts on this. He states that there is a difference amongst courts in dealing with them: some courts hold the preservation of the status quo as utterly irrelevant, whilst others see this as a critical factor in

Therefore, due to its doctrinal unclarity and uncertainty about its application, it has been commented that the 'preservation of the status quo' is something which can be "manipulated to reach a certain conclusion"[113] and furthermore is "not capable of being an independent criterion."[114]

It is submitted that perhaps the best answer to the pervasiveness of the concept is offered by Lee. In his historical work on (mandatory) preliminary injunctions, he looked at the historical role of the status quo. He writes that instead of according much doctrinal significance to the concept of preservation of the status quo, his research shows that the concept was seen by courts and commentators *as a common effect* of preliminary injunctions.[115] It is submitted that Lee's observation may also be relevant for a neutral description of the role of the status quo with respect to modern day prohibitory preliminary injunctions. Rather than to see this is an undisputed independent doctrinal purpose of the remedy, it instead denotes an effect that *can* happen once a preliminary injunction is granted. Over time, this effect has – wrongly, it is submitted – sometimes been seen as the goal of a preliminary injunction. Instead, it is argued that there should not be too much weight attributed to seeing the concept as something of more value, let alone as an independent criterion for the remedy.[116]

---

their determination to issue interim relief. He also argues that the ambiguity of the concept and its exact status has influenced the standard used by American courts. See T. R. LEE, 'Preliminary injunctions and the status quo' *Washington Law Review* 58 (2001), pp. 109–166. See: p. 124. Lastly, as Powers writes: "numerous academics and judges have rejected its application as unnecessary at best, and pernicious at worst." The author tries to explain, with the help of Behavioural Law and Economics, *why* it nevertheless is the case that US Courts still continue to use it. J. POWERS, 'A status quo bias: behavioural economics and the Federal Preliminary Standard' *Texas Law Review* 92 (2014), pp. 1027–1051.

113 G. MEI, 'Interlocutory injunctions in IP Infringement actions in England and Wales and in Ireland – *American Cyanamid* revisited' *International Review of Intellectual Property and Competition Law* 46, No. 2 (2015), pp. 175–202, esp. p. 193. Also calling it a manipulative and subjective concept, but then in the *American* preliminary injunction context is Vaughn. See: L.B. VAUGHN, 'A need for clarity: toward a new standard for preliminary injunctions' *Oregon Law Review* 68 (1989), pp. 839–884. See: p. 850.

114 G. MEI, 'Interlocutory injunctions in IP Infringement actions in England and Wales and in Ireland – *American Cyanamid* revisited' *International Review of Intellectual Property and Competition Law* 46, No. 2 (2015), pp. 175–202. See: p. 197.

115 T. R. LEE, 'Preliminary injunctions and the status quo' *Washington Law Review* 58 (2001), pp. 109–166. See: pp. 129–130.

116 Zuckerman, arguing from the English perspective, writes that the idea that the purpose of the interlocutory injunction is to maintain the status quo, has largely survived due to its ambiguity and the limited practical significance that was given to it. A.A.S. ZUCKERMAN, 'Interlocutory remedies in quest of procedural fairness' *The Modern Law Review* 56 (1993), pp. 325–341. See: p. 327.

§2.3. To prevent irreparable harm: the inadequacy of damages to make whole

Figure 3. The most important sources of irreparable harm, leading to the inadequacy of damages (own image).

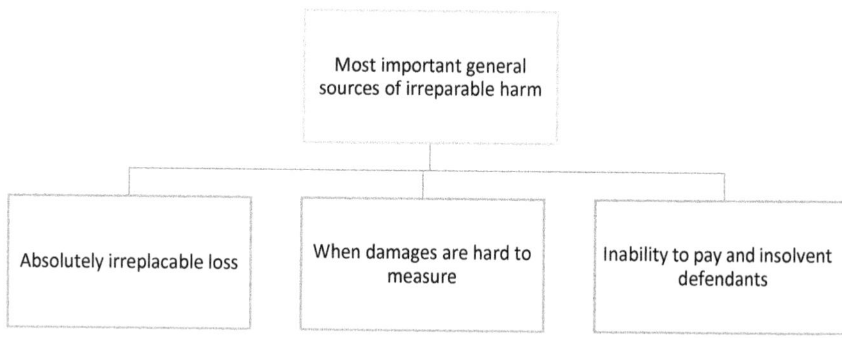

Arguably, the most cited, and in this author's view also the strongest justification for the remedy of preliminary injunctions is that of *to prevent irreparable harm*. This justification, as will be pointed out, is firstly an explicit part of the legal test in some countries. However, it is also culturally, historically and as Laycock argues, *rhetorically* centrally positioned in a number of jurisdictions. Laycock argues that some courts have the tendency to almost reflexively explain their decisions in terms of irreparable injury.[117]

But what exactly constitutes irreparable harm? Can damages not always make whole, implying that an injunction is not necessary? McGowan raises this very straightforward question in the light of Law and Economics theory:

> "**Why should any sort of harm be treated as beyond the power of money to cure?** After all, law and economics has succeeded to the point where much law is a sort of economics, and it is a tenet of at least one influential strand of the neoclassical economic approach that all human behavior **can be generalized into preferences which, employing the assumption of rationality, can be counted as costs and benefits and thus analyzed using price theory**. We have economic theories of marriage, sex, childbirth, adoption, and so on, for goodness' sake. Why not simply recognize that everything has a price and then set it?"[118]

117 D. LAYCOCK 'The death of the irreparable injury rule' *Harvard Law Review* 103, No. 3 (1990), pp. 687–771. See: p. 770.

118 D. MCGOWAN, 'Irreparable harm' *Lewis and Clark Law Review* 14, No. 2 (2010), pp. 577–596. See: p. 585. Emphasis added.

But whilst Law and Economics theory has become very influential over the years and has clearly been capable of revealing new insights, this does not mean that 'setting a price to it' comes without costs. Also, injunctions in some situations quite simply have lower costs vis-à-vis damages. It is submitted that these costs can either be *real costs* (in terms of investigation and research or trying to establish the magnitude of harm) or alternatively they can be costs in terms of *accuracy* (i.e. resulting in less or more legal errors due to decisions taken). From this perspective, McGowan submits, the Law & Economics techniques work best when prices exist and can be discovered rather than being made up.[119] This is something that in practice is not the case with many harms.

This does not mean that accepting and embracing the concept of irreparable harm makes life much easier though. Irreparable harm is a highly illusive and difficult to define concept, and its meaning has been interpreted in many different ways. Variations on what type of injury constitutes irreparable harm span from "a very grievous injury",[120] to "harms for which there is no substitute at all", or for "harms that are very difficult to quantify or estimate".[121]

And indeed, Laycock shows that the concept of irreparable harm is in practice a concept of enormous elasticity and a concept which accommodates much.[122] This also explains why it has been so pervasively used over the years.[123] What all the variations have in common however, is that *any other remedy, most importantly damages*, would be inappropriate, inadequate or simply insufficient.

§2.3.1. Is 'to prevent irreparable harm' a distinct justification?

Although the argument of 'preventing irreparable harm' has strong overlaps with other justifications for the remedy of preliminary injunctions,[124] it can and should be seen as a *distinct justification* for the following three reasons.

Firstly, the irreparable harm justification is *wider* than harm due to delay of justice alone. In practice the concept functions as an *umbrella term* for a multitude of different sources leading to the harm.

---

119 Idem. Noting that "Things are more dicey where notional prices have to be made up." See McGowan's interesting critique on this issue at pp. 585–586.

120 Lord Cranworth, as cited in I.C.F. SPRY, *Equitable Remedies* (1990 Sweet & Maxwell). See: p. 448.

121 D. LICHTMAN, 'Uncertainty and the standard for preliminary relief' *John M. Olin Law & Economics Working Paper No. 166* (2002). See: p. 3. Available at: http://papers.ssrn.com/sol3/papers.cfm?abstract_id=344640 (last accessed on 17 April 2017).

122 D. LAYCOCK 'The death of the irreparable injury rule' *Harvard Law Review* 103, No. 3 (1990), pp. 687–771. See: p. 694.

123 Ibidem.

124 Several of these are mentioned in this chapter, especially the justifications to 'preserve the status quo' and 'to prevent a delay of rights'.

Secondly, what constitutes irreparable harm should be always assessed in relationship with *other remedies*, such as damages. Spry makes a similar argument: he too presents 'irreparable injury' not as an absolute but instead he stresses the close connection between irreparable harm on the one hand and to damages on the other hand:

> "Because often any decision whether a prospective injury will be irreparable involves questions of degree, it is commonly preferable that here also the court should simply take these considerations into account, together with other relevant matters, in the exercise of its discretion, **on the basis that the smaller is the expected injury [hence the less the irreparability] or the more fully the plaintiff will be protected by damages, the less likely it is that interlocutory relief is appropriate**, especially if hardship would thereby be caused to the defendant."[125]

A third, final reason why this should be regarded as a separate justification, is due to its absolutely *central position* in some legal systems.[126] As will be seen in the chapter setting out the national legal frameworks and practices, both the legal tests in English and American courts explicitly address the question of irreparability. In England, by asking whether damages are adequate and in the United States by asking whether the plaintiff will suffer irreparable harm in the absence of a preliminary injunction.

§2.3.2. The main sources of irreparable harm

A) An irreplaceable loss

An irreplaceable – or irreparable – loss occurs when damage cannot be adequately compensated for by money. Outside the area of patent litigation, a good example of an irreplaceable loss would be losing something of great value such as the

---

125 I.C.F. SPRY, *Equitable Remedies* (1990 Sweet & Maxwell), pp. 448–449. Emphasis added.
Furthermore, see a similar comment made by Dean. On p. 23 he states that 'adequacy of damages' and 'irreparable harm' are relative phrases and that whether harm is irreparable depends on whether it is *inappropriate* to wait to make the party whole again. See R.J.C. DEAN, 'Varying the plaintiff's burden: an efficient approach to interlocutory injunctions to preserve future monetary judgments' *The University of Toronto Law Journal* 49, No. 1 (1999), pp. 1–52.

126 Douglas Laycock writes on this in his work about irreparable harm in the context of the evolution of the so-called 'irreparable injury rule'. He explains that the irreparable injury rule has been part of Anglo-American law for hundreds of years. This 'irreparable injury rule' states that equity will not act if a legal remedy would be adequate. In other words, the rule states that if damages are adequate, a preliminary injunction is not (likely) to be granted by the court. See D. LAYCOCK 'The death of the irreparable injury rule' *Harvard Law Review* 103, No. 3 (1990), pp. 687–771. See: p. 688.

demolition of an old, but historically valuable building, the loss of a species of animals or the destruction of an environmentally significant area due to the construction of a motorway. It is in these cases that "damages are obviously inadequate, awarded only as a second-best case when it is too late for an injunction to do any good, or where there is some other reason to deny specific relief, such as disproportionate cost."[127]

A similar, patent-related example of irreplaceable loss is more difficult to think of *prima facie*, if one considers patents mainly as economic assets, i.e. considering mainly the monetary value a patent can generate. Much of this value for the patentee can be (attempted to be) calculated. However, it is submitted that such a narrow perspective should be avoided. Instead, if one takes a *wider perspective* and looks at the larger and more intangible role patents play in society (such as spurring investment and providing incentives to innovation) this irreparability argument makes more sense. Without a preliminary injunction, a company may lose a valuable business opportunity leading to less future investment. The consequence is that *society* is thereby benefitting less from the innovative fruits of that investment, and this can be regarded as amounting to irreparable harm. And indeed; as will be seen, courts frequently accept a similar argument as a reason to grant a preliminary injunction, especially in the area of pharmaceutical products.

Equally, if one takes a similar wider perspective, what is also to be seen as irreplaceable loss is when damages *are not able to offer sufficient compensation* for harm that has taken place. We will see below that often harm is difficult to calculate, but also it should be pointed out that not all harms are covered by compensation anyhow. This is often the case with *consequential damages*.[128, 129] These are not damages that stem directly from the infringement itself, such as lost profits, but as is the case in originator-generic competition in the pharmaceutical industry for instance, are that of an erosion of a market share, the loss of a special regulatory position or loss of a specific reimbursement price level.[130] These damages are often not only irreversible as such for the patentee, but also a generic company is not obliged to

---

127 D. LAYCOCK 'The death of the irreparable injury rule' *Harvard Law Review* 103, No. 3 (1990), pp. 687–771. See: p. 709.

128 R. SUBIOTTO, *Generic pharmaceuticals – expert paper* (June 17th 2014); available from the website of the Organisation for Economic Cooperation and Development (OECD): http://www.oecd.org/officialdocuments/publicdisplaydocumentpdf/?cote=DAF/COMP/WD(2014)75&docLanguage=En (last accessed on 19 April 2017).

129 The literature does not always clearly make a distinction between this argument and the difficulty to calculate damages adequately (on which more in the subsequent paragraph). Indeed, these arguments to a certain extent overlap and are not mutually exclusive. It is submitted that consequential damages are more difficult to calculate and are therefore considered as being more irreparable.

130 For which, in the determination of this specific reimbursement level, it is of no matter whether the patent is infringed or not.

compensate this kind of harm for the patentee in any way as these damages are consequential.[131]

Lastly, in the same light are *litigation costs*. Whilst these are often well calculable, litigation costs are mostly not sufficiently compensated. These costs can, in patent litigation, be very significant,[132] but in Europe these are not always ordered to be reimbursed. In general, compensation of full litigation costs is not awarded and the losing party is not held liable for these costs.[133] Extended legal proceedings aimed towards obtaining ex post remedies such as damages are thus relatively expensive and a quicker and cheaper preliminary injunction proceeding from that point of view is more attractive.

B) The difficulty to calculate damages

This source of harm refers to those situations when damages are difficult to calculate or are hard to measure in an accurate manner. Then they are considered to be inadequate. This argument is often raised and frequently accepted by courts in preliminary injunction cases that deal with civil rights – notably freedom of speech[134] and the right to strike – and that of personal injury or emotional distress.[135] But also with commercial transactions this argument can be persuasive, especially with respect to intellectual property infringement.[136] Attributing a correct value to intellectual property assets – whether these assets are protected by trademark protection, copyright protection, design protection or patent protection – can indeed

131 R. SUBIOTTO, *Generic pharmaceuticals – expert paper* (June 17th 2014). See: p. 4. Available from the website of the Organisation for Economic Cooperation and Development (OECD): http://www.oecd.org/officialdocuments/publicdisplaydocumentpdf/?cote=DAF/COMP/WD(2014)75&docLanguage=En (last accessed on 19 April 2017).

132 Idem. Subiotto mentions litigation costs exceeding €1 million in the United Kingdom and well over €400.000 in other European jurisdictions for this type of litigation.

133 Ibidem.

134 For the relationship between preliminary injunctions and freedom of speech, mainly in the context of copyright, see the interesting article written by M. LEMLEY, E. VOLOKH, 'Freedom of speech and injunctions in Intellectual Property Cases' *Duke Law Journal* 48 (1998), pp. 147–242.

135 D. LAYCOCK 'The death of the irreparable injury rule' *Harvard Law Review* 103, No. 3 (1990), pp. 687–771. See: p. 712.

136 Note that this source of harm is also seen as a ground to grant a *permanent injunction*, as Chan rightly submits: "Judge Posner noted two disadvantages to damages: They may be expensive for courts to assess and they may substantially overvalue or undervalue the right. Both cut in favour of injunctive relief." See: N.P. CHAN, 'Balancing judicial misvaluation and patent hold-up: some principles for considering injunctive relief after eBay' *UCLA* 59 (2011–2012), pp. 746–787. See: p. 759 and pp. 759–768.

sometimes be notoriously difficult, and is a task for which courts are often not well-equipped.[137] Although various methods exist and are used by the courts to *approximate* harm, damages and lost profits, this does not always offer a satisfactory solution. Establishing the right level of harm and damages is even more difficult with respect to estimating future damages that *may* occur, instead of those harms that already have happened. A factor which can influence the calculation of harm and damages significantly with respect to patents is for instance whether a *functioning market* for the drug or the technology at hand already exists. Furthermore, alternative and competing technologies that are being developed should also be taken into consideration.

Another factor that significantly complicates the calculation of damages for the court is that parties themselves often have very different views of their harms. This results in different views on how much the enforcement or lack of enforcement of a patent is worth. These estimations of harms and appropriate monetary damages by the parties are influenced by *biases* regarding the value of their harm (i.e. by overstating the harm when enjoined or when infringement occurs) and due to *tailoring* (the latter is when many different terms influence each other, making it difficult to price one aspect without influencing others).[138] Both can further contribute and result into the difficulty of properly estimating or valuing the level of damages by the court.[139, 140]

The plain acknowledgement that harm and damages are hard to compensate is one thing, but as Chan writes, the misvaluation of harms and the calculation and fixation of the corresponding damages rate is especially problematic when courts (begin to) systematically undercompensate or overcompensate patentees and both these entail their own negative consequences. Undercompensation takes away

---

137 N.P. CHAN, 'Balancing judicial misvaluation and patent hold-up: some principles for considering injunctive relief after eBay' *UCLA* 59 (2011–2012), pp. 746–787. See: p. 761.

138 D. MCGOWAN, 'Irreparable harm' *Lewis and Clark Law Review* 14, No. 2 (2010), pp. 577–596. See: p. 587.

139 McGowan states that parties never have perfect information and they are always subject to biases. The immeasurability of harm, he argues, is therefore a relative notion with respect to the work of the court: "Immeasurability thus is a strictly comparative concept: Harm should be deemed irreparable when parties' bargaining could more closely approximate an efficient price (net of transaction costs) than could courts, or when parties able to bargain at reasonable cost could not reach one." D. MCGOWAN, 'Irreparable harm' *Lewis and Clark Law Review* 14, No. 2 (2010), pp. 577–596. See: p. 588.

140 For an interesting article on the problems of damages calculation, specifically regarding lost profits and reasonable royalties, see the insightful article of Blair and Cotter. In line with this paragraph, they state, on p. 2, that rules for estimating patent damages have been complex, contradictory and difficult to apply. R.D. BLAIR, T.F. COTTER, 'Rethinking patent damages' *Texas Intellectual Property Law Journal* 10 (2001). See: pp. 1–94.

the incentives to invest and innovate which the carefully calibrated patent system strives to offer.[141] It may also encourage infringement in lieu of ex ante licensing negotiations.[142] Overcompensation is also troubling, since it then provides incentives for the patentee to litigate rather than negotiate. This instead of, upon noticing (likely) infringement, an attempt is made to negotiate a licensing agreement with the infringer, the patentee may then rather opt for overvalued damages it can get awarded by the court.[143] Chan argues that this can result in another issue, namely in the patentee not properly disclosing its patent as the patentee may prefer laying low hoping on inadvertent infringement due to the possibility to then obtain overvalued damages.[144] Lastly, overcompensation of the damages of the patentee also has effects on other parties' incentives to create, invest and innovate. One example of this is for instance the depressing of the market for substitute products: as the costs of possible infringement go up, firms are discouraged to develop substitute products, this resulting into a broader level of exclusivity than was granted solely by the patent.[145] In the same light, the overcompensation of damages for the patentee can also limit other firms from trying to design *around* a patent, when there is a chance that they may be found to infringe the patent and then pay excessive damages to the patent holder.[146]

Because of the risk to miscalculate harms and damages, with the significant problems that can arise from this, a preliminary injunction is a valuable remedy to the court's toolbox and can be a welcome alternative instead of solely offering litigants the possibility to obtain (inadequate) damages at a later stage.[147]

---

141 N.P. CHAN, 'Balancing judicial misvaluation and patent hold-up: some principles for considering injunctive relief after eBay' *UCLA* 59 (2011–2012), pp. 746–787. See: p. 763–764.

142 Idem. However, at p. 764 footnote 102, Chan also writes that this can be tempered if the court issues punitive damages in cases of wilful infringement. For example, one can think of treble damages. However, not all jurisdictions do offer such a remedy.

143 N.P. CHAN, 'Balancing judicial misvaluation and patent hold-up: some principles for considering injunctive relief after eBay' *UCLA* 59 (2011–2012), pp. 746–787. See: p. 764 and further.

144 Idem, at p. 766. Chan also rightly notes in footnote 112, p. 766, that even though formally, disclosure occurs by the publication of the patent, patent publications itself are not an effective way in conveying technical information and that many scholars believe that disclosure primarily happens when patentees educate other firms about their patented technology. This is something that may not happen, or happen less, in the case of systematic overcompensation by the court.

145 Idem, at p. 767.

146 Ibidem.

147 In the same light, see C. HEINZE, *Einstweiliger Rechtsschutz im europäischen Immaterialgüterrecht* (2007 Mohr Siebeck). See: pp. 138–139.

C) The inability to pay and insolvent defendants

Even in the case when damages would be regarded as appropriate *and* would be able to be adequately calculated, this remedy is worth little if damages *are not, or cannot be, paid* by the defendant. This may for instance be due to his inability to pay or in the case of his insolvency.[148] A preliminary injunction in these cases is then more useful to the plaintiff, since preventing (further) damage from occurring in the first place is better than instead of relying on damages which may be awarded eventually, but never paid.

After all, when insolvency occurs, an outstanding claim for damages against an insolvent defendant would put the plaintiff in the position of a general creditor. In most bankruptcy cases, the number of general creditors is usually rather considerable and normally all pre-bankruptcy claims, regardless of the value and origin are treated equally. This means that a plaintiff with a claim for monetary damages – based on intellectual property infringement – would likely be unable to monetise this damages claim or obtain only a portion of its value. An exception to this general rule is when it is deemed by the bankruptcy court to be in the interest of the estate to for instance fulfil the contract of a creditor, with the goal of benefitting all creditors.

As unjust this may be for the patentee, Laycock submits rightly that a bankruptcy court is not created to award adequate damages but its purpose, at least in practice, is to give all general creditors *equally inadequate damages.*[149] In any case, the above forms another justification for a preliminary injunction to be awarded instead of relying on damages later, in order to minimise harm for the patentee in the first place.

§2.4. To prevent delay rendering rights meaningless *(periculum in mora)*

This source is *temporal* of nature. The time that the litigation takes can lead to rendering rights effectively meaningless.[150] This results into one of the main arguments for a preliminary injunction in the context of patent protection. The ticking of the

---

148 Subiotto also mentions the possibility of a debtor purposefully avoiding compensation by entering into administration or by liquidating itself, to later reappear as a different corporate entity. R. SUBIOTTO, *Generic pharmaceuticals – expert paper* (June 17th 2014). See: p. 5. The document is available from the website of the Organisation for Economic Cooperation and Development (OECD): http://www.oecd.org/officialdocuments/publicdisplaydocumentpdf/?cote=DAF/COMP/WD(2014)75&docLanguage=En (last accessed on 19 April 2017)

149 D. LAYCOCK 'The death of the irreparable injury rule' *Harvard Law Review* 103, No. 3 (1990), pp. 687–771. See: p. 717.

150 Zuckerman refers to this as the undermining of the practical utility of the actual judgment. He also refers to another reason to prevent delay, though in this context this is deemed to be a less pressing reason. This is the deterioration or disappearance of evidence. See A.A.S. ZUCKERMAN, 'Quality and Economy in Civil Procedure – The case for commuting correct judgments for timely judgments'

clock can lead to a risk of what Heinze described in German as 'überholende *Innovation*', literally translated as 'overtaking innovation'. His argument is that because time is a decisive factor for the effectiveness of legal proceedings and because of the fast pace that innovation occurs with, the patentee can only reap the benefits for a limited period of the duration of its exclusive right.[151] Heinze adds, however, that the value of this argument can be completely dependent on the specific industry. Industries that have a fast pace of innovation – and thus have a corresponding technology lifecycle – are characterised by patented technologies which lose their value rapidly due to the emergence of new technologies. Then, at the end of the patent's lifetime, the underlying technology may be technologically and commercially outdated.[152] In other words, it is submitted that the value of these patents lies in the *early years* of its possible exploitation.

A similar, yet distinct, situation is something that will be considered more when looking at generic entry of pharmaceutical products. This is the situation of delay of adequate enforcement possibilities *at the end* of the period of which patent protection is granted.[153, 154] The issue of 'overtaking innovation' is not the problem here: what is however, is *the ineffectiveness of the patent owner to strike back against infringement.* From that point of view it is submitted that when the remedy of preliminary injunctions would not exist, the effective life of a patent would be the regular patent life minus the period it normally takes for a patent to be litigated. This way, the patentee would suffer significantly less protection than it is entitled to and delayed justice would then effectively result into denied justice.[155] This problem is exacerbated for some classes of patents, especially medical and pharmaceutical

---

Oxford Journal of Legal Studies 14, No. 3 (1994), pp. 353–387. See: pp. 360–362 and further.

151 C. HEINZE, *Einstweiliger Rechtsschutz im europäischen Immaterialgüterrecht* (2007 Mohr Siebeck). See: pp. 144–146.

152 Ibidem.

153 Ibidem.

154 This period of regular patent protection is a maximum of 20 years. An exception to this 20-year period can be found in the EU, in which the period of protection of certain patented inventions can be extended by Supplementary Protection Certificates (SPCs). These *de facto* prolong the patentee's exclusivity for a maximum of 5 to 5,5 years. Protection on the basis of the SPC will commence after the patent, by which the invention is initially protected, expires. SPC protection is available for human or veterinary medicines, insecticides or herbicides. The legal basis for this sui-generis form of intellectual property protection is: Regulation (EC) No 469/2009 of the European Parliament and of the Council of 6 May 2009 concerning the Supplementary Protection Certificate for medicinal products.

155 Zuckerman also uses the beautiful Latin saying '*venter non patitur dilationem*' for this; the stomach does not brook delay. See: A.A.S. Zuckerman, 'Quality and Economy in Civil Procedure – The case for commuting correct judgments for timely judgments' *Oxford Journal of Legal Studies* 14, No. 3 (1994), pp. 353–387. See: p. 361.

related ones: these patents are often only profitable in the *final years* of their lifecycle, as after a long period of extensive clinical testing and after obtaining regulatory approval, the patent owner can only reap the benefits relatively late in the patent's statutory lifetime.

Another practical problem, related to delay in the enforcement of rights, is a time-related issue of a more general nature: without an injunction, the plaintiff should commence with a separate proceeding in order to obtain damages. It can only do so after its infringement claim has been held as valid after a trial on the merits. Obviously, this process is time-consuming, whilst instead a preliminary injunction can give immediate relief. Such an extra proceeding is also inaccessible to some, as it involves further litigation costs and administrative hassle in proving damages. Both the extra time, costs and work involved in taking the case further, may lead to the situation that the plaintiff refrains from taking further steps altogether, this again rendering rights meaningless.

§2.5. To protect rights given: the need for enforcement

As has been argued at the beginning of this dissertation,[156] there are strong theoretical justifications for the protection of inventions by patents. However, as has also been stated at that instance, *the grant* of property rights is of course only part of the story. The strength of any legal system (and the patent system is no exception to this) is also based on the way granted rights are respected.[157] And indeed, one of the key justifications for injunctive relief – both at a trial on the merits and at the preliminary stage – is the clear connection between substantive law and enforcement law. Rights can only be only relevant when there is sufficient enforcement and the main goals of patent law can only be obtained when this is adequate.

The role of injunctions in the enforcement of patent rights – in relationship with other remedies such as damages – is not undebated and its role depends largely on the view that one sees for these type of property rules.[158] One can take the view that,

156 See above, at page 32 of this dissertation.

157 But note the argument of Hilty, who submits that – in his article on the enforcement of intellectual property rights from a more general point of view, not limited to the issue of interim relief and patents – that much enforcement no longer takes place with a view to the right holder's original rights but that enforcement is increasingly used for other purposes. Examples of these practices that he gives are: to defend outdated business models, to squeeze undesirable competitors out of the market or other activities that do not fit with the initial function of intellectual property rights. See: R.M. HILTY, 'The role of enforcement in delineating the scope of IP Rights' *Max Planck Institute for Innovation and Competition Research Paper* No. 15–03 (2015).
Examples of abovementioned practices by virtue of preliminary injunctions will also become apparent in the subsequent chapters of this dissertation.

158 The property and liability rules debate is a good example of the differing views that exist on this, see page 46 and further of this dissertation.

in principle, patents should be protected by a property rule and that they should therefore be enforced by (preliminary) injunctions. This also because interim relief is a unique remedy in protecting patentees prior to the moment that infringement occurs, or until a trial on the merits can take place. In those situations, one can see it then as the most desirable form of enforcement that a property rule can provide for.

A further argument for a court not to hesitate too much with offering strong protection and by enjoining another party relatively swiftly, is mentioned by Heinze. He points out that patents are rights that have been *already under scrutiny* at an earlier stage.[159] After all, unlike some other intellectual property rights, these are property rights that (can) have already been examined at an earlier stage. They have been examined for novelty[160] and for inventive step[161] by the European Patent Office (EPO), or sometimes domestically by national European patent granting bodies.[162] The argument for the grant of preliminary injunction for patents is then that – until proven otherwise – patents should be presumed to be valid. Therefore, in order to preserve the various functions of patents as referred to in the justifications (be it by offering incentives, disclosure or prospects) these should by enforced by the courts. The grant of an injunction may be the most effective way in doing so. It can therefore be argued that the courts should not be too cautious in offering injunctive relief in general and (considering the preventive nature of interim relief) with preliminary injunctions in particular.

The value of this argument specifically for patents can be questioned however: the present author does not find this argument to be as convincing in practical terms as it is as convincing from a theoretical point of view. The main reason for this is because it is evident that patent quality is an issue.[163] Although the exact number is disputed, a considerable numbers of patents that are granted turn out to be held as invalid when challenged. This may be because upon further research, after the grant of the patent, it becomes clear that the patent should not have been granted in the first place due to for instance the existence of prior art. According to the *European Generic Medicines Association*, one-third of the patents subject to litigation in *pharmaceutical* patent proceedings for instance is revoked during litigation

159 C. HEINZE, *Einstweiliger Rechtsschutz im europäischen Immaterialgüterrecht* (2007 Mohr Siebeck). See: pp. 147–148.

160 Art. 54 EPC.

161 Art. 56 EPC.

162 The substantive patentability requirements that national patent offices set are similar and in line with those found in Art 54 and 56 EPC, however the actual (level of) examination that national patent offices undertake before granting a patent differs per jurisdiction.

163 On the issue of 'patent quality', see the paper of Hilty in which he looks at this phenomenon and possible remedies to deal with problems related to this. R.M. HILTY, 'The role of patent quality in Europe' *Max Planck Institute for Intellectual Property and Competition Law Research Paper* No. 11 (2011).

and another one-third is amended during the course of proceedings.[164] This number of two-thirds of fully or partially invalidated patents in litigation across the EU is not too far off from a number that has been given by researchers of the *Technische Universität München*. Their research shows that at least 75% (the researchers even speak of 'a conservative estimate') of all patents in Germany *would be a partially or fully revoked if ever challenged in court.*[165] The authors point to similar numbers of invalidated patents in other jurisdictions.[166]

Of course, the exact percentage is not the point here. More relevant is the notion that if a random patent is litigated, the chance is relatively high that in the end the patent will be ruled as being invalid. A preliminary injunction based on a possible invalid patent is an undesirable situation and this itself is something that should be taken along. This is especially so, bearing in mind the special nature of preliminary proceedings in which there is relatively little time to examine infringement and validity in the same depth as normally at a trial in the merits. The above

164 See the viewpoint of the EUROPEAN GENERIC MEDICINES ASSOCIATION, *Submission to the European Commission's consultation on civil enforcement of intellectual property rights: public consultation on the efficiency of proceedings and accessibility of measures* (2013). Available at: http://ec.europa.eu/internal_market/consultations/2012/intellectual-property-rights/contributions/registered-organisations/european-generic-medicines-association_en.pdf (last accessed on 19 April 2017).

165 J. HENKEL, H. ZISCHKA, 'Why most patents are invalid – extent, reasons and potential remedies of patent invalidity' (June 2015, working paper). Available at: https://www.tim.wi.tum.de/fileadmin/w00bcy/www/Research/Publications/Henkel/Henkel_Zischka_Patent_Validity.pdf (last accessed on April 25 2017). Note that Henkel's and Zischka's research focusses on a *random selection of patents* – thus this is not restricted to invalidity of patents involved in litigation, which is deemed to be a non-random selection in itself.

166 Idem; see page 8 of the paper, in which Henkel and Zischka give an elaborate overview of research that has been carried out on rates of patent invalidity rights in other jurisdictions. They write: "High rates of invalidation are not specific to Germany. Early studies on U.S. patent litigation unveil an invalidation rate of 60% to 70% for the period 1948 to 1954 (Federico, 1956) and roughly 65% from 1953 to 1978 (Koenig, 1980). Allison and Lemley (1998) report an overall invalidation rate of 46% for the period of 1989 to 1996. More recently, Mann and Underweiser (2012) find for the years 2003 through 2009 that the Federal Circuit held 60% of the patents in the cases it adjudicated not valid. In other countries, invalidation rates are in similar ranges. For Australia, Weatherall and Jensen (2005) report a rate of full or partial invalidation of 53% (first and second instance) for the period of 1997 to 2003. Oyama (2012) finds an invalidation rate of 73% at the Japanese district courts, and a UK study examining the years 2000 to 2008 indicates an overall rate of about 50% partially or fully invalid in the first instance (Helmers and McDonagh, 2013). France seems to be special case, with according to Véron (2010) only 27% of the cases before the court of first instance in Paris between 2000 und 2009 resulting in a revocation decision."

however, should by no means be interpreted as an argument *against the* remedy of preliminary injunctions *as such*. Instead, it is believed that this calls for some caution on behalf of the courts in granting a preliminary injunction too easily. Finally, it is argued that there are stronger arguments in favour of preliminary injunctions than this particular one.

§2.6. To preserve the ability for the court to do judgment later

Above, under the heading of 'preservation of the status quo', we have already looked at the preservation of the existing state of affairs *between the parties*. However, there is another justification for preliminary injunctions that is somewhat connected to this: the preservation of the existing state of affairs results in the possibility for the court to deliver its judgment later.[167] More time would, so it is assumed here, result into more clarity and this in turn would lead to a more accurate judgment on the merits in the end.[168] It is submitted that this can not only be seen as a distinct justification from 'preserving the status quo between the parties', but also it is somewhat less controversial as it is not directly linked to parts of the legal test as is the case with maintaining the status quo between parties.[169] Although this justification stresses the interim function of a preliminary injunction, for reasons that have already been provided in §2.2 such a function seems to be rather theoretical of nature, since preliminary injunctions in practice always change the existing state of affairs regardlessly.

§2.7. Possible positive effects on innovation

Apart from the more general justifications such as 'the link between substantive law and enforcement law' and 'to prevent delay', which can have an effect on the decision to opt for a preliminary injunction, there is also some literature pointing directly to the link between innovation incentives and the remedy of interim relief.

Brooks and Schwartz argue that preliminary injunctions promote better investment incentives, basing themselves on the findings in their model-based work.[170]

---

167 M. DENLOW, 'The Motion for a Preliminary Injunction: Time for a Uniform Federal Standard' *The Review of Litigation* 22, No. 3 (2003), pp. 495–539. See: p. 506, where he names this as one of the purposes of a preliminary injunction.

168 A.A.S. ZUCKERMAN, 'Quality and Economy in Civil Procedure – The case for commuting correct judgments for timely judgments' *Oxford Journal of Legal Studies* 14, No. 3 (1994), pp. 353–387. See: pp. 353–354 a.f.

169 As is sometimes the case in the United States and to a certain extent as well under the English doctrine.

170 R.W. BROOKS, W.F. SCHWARTZ, 'Uncertain breach of contract and efficient preliminary remedies', *American Law and Economics Association Annual Meeting Working Paper* (2008). Available at http://law.bepress.com/cgi/viewcontent.cgi?article=2440&context=alea (last accessed on April 20th 2017).

They argue that a preliminary injunction can reduce both overinvestment and underinvestment.[171]

Whilst the reduction of underinvestment due to the lack of legal clarity is intuitively clear, that of prevention of overinvestment ('the offsetting effect') is a little more difficult in the patentee-infringer context.[172] It is submitted by the present author that this refers to ongoing legal uncertainty that still exists, even if a preliminary injunction has been taken, since a preliminary injunction is not always confirmed at trial. There is a probability that this decision was taken erroneously. This is something that in patent litigation, considering the complexity and uncertainty attached to this, is not unlikely. This of course also entails a risk of paying compensation to the defendant. Most importantly however is that the notion of Brooks and Schwartz seems to confirm that underinvestment due to lack of uncertainty is much reduced.

Llobet has researched how patent protection via litigation, including that via preliminary injunctive relief, affects *cumulative innovation*.[173] This is when subsequent innovative developments occur on the basis of already existing (patented) inventions. Obviously, there is a certain tension here: whilst offering stronger patent protection benefits the patentee, this can however also discourage entry and thus the incentives for future, further research to be taken.[174] Llobet shows that increasing the level of protection, apart from restricting entry and thus incentives for future innovators, does not necessarily increase the patentee's profits. This is because often an important part of the revenue for a patentee stems from licensing fees from future innovators, who are deterred when the level of patent protection increases.[175] This is even more the case for 'valuable' or 'better' patents, since an infringer, after a trial on the merits, may be held liable for lost profits and the more valuable the patent is, the costlier this becomes. Therefore, Llobet argues that valuable inventions

171 Idem, at p. 4. They write: "the possibility of securing a preliminary injunction can reduce both overinvestment and underinvestment. The preliminary injunction places a floor on the tendency to underinvest resulting from legal uncertainty. This may in some circumstances lead to efficient investment, and in all cases provide better investment incentives than that observed in the traditional model without legal uncertainty. So there is a final irony to be noted. Given the tendency to overinvest when there is legal certainty, the offsetting effect of the availability of preliminary injunctions promotes better investment incentives in the presence of legal uncertainty than in its absence."

172 Idem, at pp. 18–20. It is noted that the model of Brooks and Schwartz, in the work mentioned in the previous footnotes, is not one in the patent-infringement context, but in a buyer-selling setting and features a mandatory preliminary injunction. Nevertheless, it is submitted here that the insights and dynamics remain the same.

173 G. LLOBET, 'Patent litigation when innovation is cumulative' *International Journal of Industrial Organisation* 21 (2003), pp. 1135–1157.

174 Idem, at p. 1136.

175 Idem, at p. 1137.

should obtain weaker protection instead, allowing the patentee to facilitate the licensing of future entrants.[176]

With respect to preliminary injunctions, Llobet comes to a different conclusion; he seems to have a positive view towards the remedy of preliminary injunctions and especially to protect patents of higher value. He argues that it seems *socially optimal* that "pre-emptive injunctive relief should be granted to innovations that have a higher market value, together with more protection to the corresponding patentees."[177] He also writes that "the use of a preliminary injunctive relief seems to benefit relatively more better inventors by increasing their licensing revenue."[178] This is because he concludes that entry and litigation with respect to *preliminary injunctive relief* is independent of the quality of the patent.[179] A main reason for this is that because infringers do not run the risk to be ordered to compensate for the plaintiff-patentee's foregone profits, if they lose the preliminary injunction proceedings.[180, 181]

§2.8. Providing temporary clarity

Finally, as we have already seen in the context of the property and liability rule framework,[182] the grant of preliminary injunctive relief can provide temporary clarity about a legal situation or dispute. It is clarity which in turn is a requirement for *efficient transactions*; this way, transaction costs are also reduced.[183] A granted

176 Idem, at p. 1137.
177 Idem, at p. 1153.
178 Idem, at p. 1153.
179 Idem, at p. 1151. Llobet writes: "When a PIR is requested, entry and litigation do not depend on v <the quality of the patent>. This is an important difference with respect to our benchmark case, because here better inventions do not deter more entry." At p. 1152 he continues: "This result means that the capacity that the patentee has to capture profits from future innovation is independent of the quality of the original invention as opposed to the case where PIR is not available." Note that the clarification between <brackets> is added by the author of this dissertation.
180 G. LLOBET, 'Patent litigation when innovation is cumulative' *International Journal of Industrial Organisation* 21 (2003), pp. 1135–1157. See: p. 1138.
181 The economic effects that preliminary injunctions have on innovation is most definitely a topic worthy of further research. However, as Brooks and Schwartz note, it is surprising that Law & Economics scholars have not focussed more on preliminary injunctions, since it is a feature of the law that is 'cast with economic content'. See: R.W. BROOKS, W.F. SCHWARTZ, 'Uncertain breach of contract and efficient preliminary remedies', *American Law and Economics Association Annual Meeting Working Paper* (2008). See: p. 4. Available at http://law.bepress.com/cgi/viewcontent.cgi?article=2440&context=alea (last accessed on April 20th 2017).
182 See page 46 a.f. of this dissertation.
183 Ibidem.

preliminary injunction is thus the starting point, the base line, of further negotiations between patentee and infringer and can facilitate the conclusion of a settlement.

§2.9. Chapter conclusion

Having looked at several justifications for the remedy of preliminary injunctions in patent litigation, it is good to draw a conclusion at this point.

It has become clear that, apart from the national and international legal obligations that exist for countries to provide preliminary injunctions and to which we will turn later, there are ample other reasons to do so, as strong independent reasons exist for (the grant of) the remedy. That being said, it is equally clear that not all the justifications of preliminary injunctions are of the same value. It is submitted that the most persuading justifications for preliminary injunctions – both from the perspective of patent litigation as from a more general point of view – is that they can *prevent various sources of irreparable harm from occurring*, thereby highlighting the inadequacy of damages. Furthermore, they can *prevent delay which renders rights meaningless*. The latter is highly necessary in patent litigation where it can take a considerable time until the trial on the merits takes place, and also to protect patentees at the end of their patent's lifetime.

Whilst *maintaining the status quo between parties* is traditionally seen as an important justification for preliminary injunctions, it is submitted that in practice it is a more difficult concept to apply and it therefore should not be seen as one of the main justifications for the remedy. To a lesser extent, the same applies to the justification *of providing a link between substantive law and enforcement law*. Whilst this argument is sound in theory, this is less so in practice, as many patent rights are less strong than they seem on first sight. This problem is aggravated together with the drastic nature a preliminary injunction can have. The last justifications for the remedy that were mentioned – namely *preserving the ability for the court to do judgment later, providing temporary clarity* and that of preliminary injunctions having *possible positive effects on innovation* – definitely have more merit to them. These also contribute to the overall picture that preliminary injunctions are entitled to, and deserve, their own place in the remedy landscape.

Chapter 3: Potential Risks with the Grant of Preliminary Injunctions in Patent Litigation

§3.1. Introduction

Above, we have seen that despite the heightened uncertainty that forms one of the hallmarks of preliminary injunctions and proceedings – due to the (technical) complexity of the cases together with the economic and legal uncertainties – a preliminary injunction can nevertheless fulfil a useful role. However, this does not mean that they should therefore be granted too easily and freely by courts: as will be seen, they can also have significant drawbacks for the defendant as well as entail costs of a more social nature. These will be subject of this chapter.

Just as in the preceding chapter, the viewpoint taken here is that of a more doctrinal one. This means that the problems which are described in this chapter may not be as severe in practice as they appear to be from a theoretical point of view. The extent to which they do, of course depends on the constellation of facts of a particular case, and the exact way the legal system of a country is set up and functions.

§3.2. Possible lock-in effect leading to biased decisionmaking

From a doctrinal perspective, with a two-stage litigation process as a preliminary injunction proceeding, there is always a risk of a *lock-in effect.* As Lynch writes, sometimes judges first rule on the grant of a preliminary injunction and then later also on the same issue at the trial on the merits.[184] Basing himself on psychological and economic insights, Lynch argues that judges who rule in a preliminary injunction proceeding first as well as later on the trial on the merits, "are *less likely* to change their mind and that this difference systematically biases outcomes (..)."[185, 186] This result can happen consciously, but often also subconsciously. It is in fact a process driven by confirmation bias and cognitive dissonance, in order to justify

184 K.J. LYNCH, 'The lock-in effect of preliminary injunctions' *Florida Law Review* 66 (2014), pp. 779–821.

185 Idem, at p. 813.

186 Also see: R.R.W. BROOKS, W.F. SCHWARTZ, 'Legal uncertainty, economic efficiency, and the preliminary injunction doctrine' *Stanford Law Review* 58 (2005), pp. 380–409. At p. 386 footnote 16, the authors comment: "Parties often pursue preliminary actions, knowing that they are likely to get the same judge at the final stage (especially in state courts) and that judge is unlikely to switch her views of the merits subsequently."

past decisions that are made.[187] Foster mentions the same psychological effect.[188] Lynch also writes that despite an obvious solution to this, namely the inclusion of a second decision-maker in the procedure (i.e. a second, different judge), the proceedings at trial can nevertheless still suffer from the lock-in effect. He argues also that judges are often bound together as a subgroup.[189] They share many psychological connections, expect collegiality, can understand a taken decision from the perspective of a colleague and often they share a similar background.[190] It is thus here submitted that the lock-in effect may thus be more pervasive than one first thinks.

§3.3. The subsequent trial on the merits is a legal fiction

This argument boils down to the observation that in practice, the trial on the merits which *is supposed* to follow after preliminary injunction proceedings (and to which the preliminary injunction court tries to anticipate on) is nothing more than legal fiction.[191] The reality is that often parties consider the case as 'done' after a grant of a preliminary injunction, because they deem the trial on the merits to be no longer relevant from a practical point of view. This may be due to the fact that a settlement is reached[192] or with an eye on the time that it will take until a decision on the merits

---

187 K.J. LYNCH, 'The lock-in effect of preliminary injunctions' *Florida Law Review* 66 (2014), pp. 779–821. See: p. 785.

188 J.J. FOSTER, 'The preliminary injunction – a 'new' and potent weapon in patent litigation' *Journal of the Patent and Trademark Office Society* (1986) pp. 281–291. See: p. 288 where he writes: "Even if the litigation continues, such a major victory so early in the case will continue to have a substantial psychological effect on the defendant and, perhaps, the court. An early decision that patentee is "right" and defendant is "wrong" may, absent some dramatic turn-around, continue throughout the litigation."

189 Idem, at p. 790 and at p. 814.

190 Ibidem.

191 This argument is pointed out for example in the following works: G. MEI, 'Interlocutory injunctions in IP Infringement actions in England and Wales and in Ireland – *American Cyanamid* revisited' *International Review of Intellectual Property and Competition Law* 46, No. 2 (2015), pp. 175–202. See: p. 195. Also see the report of the EUROPEAN GENERIC MEDICINES ASSOCIATION, *Patent-related Barriers to Market Entry for Generic Medicines in the European Union* (May 2008). Report drafted by K. ROOX, J. PIKE, A. BROWN, S. BECKE. See: p. 20.

192 J.J. FOSTER, 'The preliminary injunction – a 'new' and potent weapon in patent litigation' *Journal of the Patent and Trademark Office Society* (1986) pp. 281–291. See: p. 288 where he writes: "A preliminary injunction may effectively end the case, as a practical matter. The effect of such an injunction on the defendant, particularly its officers and other businessmen, would usually be substantial, increasing the pressure to abandon the market or to negotiate a license. Psychologically, the patentee is put in an excellent position in negotiations to settle the dispute."

is concluded. It can also be that parties believe that an outcome on the merits may not be different. Finally, due to the enjoining by the court, it can also be that the defendant may have gone bankrupt meanwhile.

As Deutsch rightly argues, this is worrying. Although certain procedural rights of due process are curtailed during preliminary proceedings, this is deemed as being an acceptable trade-off, *because* there is likely to be a trial on the merits in which these can be invoked.[193] If this often tends not to be the case in practice, the theoretical possibility of later invoking these rights of due process is in practice not worth much. Zuckerman stresses the link between the assumption of provisionality and the assumption of corrective compensation which is central to the preliminary injunction doctrine: he argues that these two terms are intimately connected.[194] He observes that a vicious circle is possible: "In the absence of final judgment, which will reveal whether the interlocutory injunction did or did not interfere with legitimate rights, there can be no occasion for corrective compensation."[195] He also writes that "The poor prospect of corrective compensation may itself contribute to the ending of the litigation at the interlocutory stage, and thus render final judgment less likely to be reached."[196] In the same light, but more from a legal-theory perspective, is the contribution of Petersen. He raises the question what it means when preliminary injunction proceedings become a substitute to ordinary civil litigation, given that due to the high rate of settlements after a granted preliminary injunction the course of litigation ends there.[197]

It is submitted that this 'legal fiction' changes the (intended) role and effect of a preliminary injunction considerably and that this should in turn also change the perception society and courts have of it. Instead of merely seeing a preliminary injunction as a temporary 'order measure', the remedy in practice tends to morph

---

193 A. DEUTSCH, 'Preliminary injunction proceedings in German intellectual property disputes' *Journal of Intellectual Property Law & Practice* 8, No. 2 (2013), pp. 136–145. See: p. 139. He writes: "This abrogation of the basic right of due process of law ('rechtliches Gehör') is justified by the preliminary character of an injunction *and the later possibility of opposing it.*" He thereby cites the German Bundesgerichtshof in NJW 1995, 2477 and NJW 2004, 2443.

194 A.A.S. ZUCKERMAN, 'Quality and Economy in Civil Procedure – The case for commuting correct judgments for timely judgments' *Oxford Journal of Legal Studies* 14, No. 3 (1994), pp. 353–387. See: pp. 369–374. In his article, he proposes a non-interlocutory accelerated procedure as an alternative to be considered, in order to achieve a better balance between quality judgments and timely judgments. It is submitted that a somewhat similar procedure is now available in some jurisdictions, indeed specifically for patent litigation. See for instance the *vro proceedings* in The Netherlands, written about on page 159 of this dissertation.

195 Idem, at p. 373.

196 Ibidem.

197 C.S. PETERSEN, *Immaterialrettigheder og foreløbige forbud* (2008 Jurist- og Økonomforbundets Forl.). See: chapter 2.

into what is *de facto* a final ruling. It is submitted that this should have ramifications on how the individual case is assessed, and how the remedy from a general perspective is viewed.

§3.4. Negative effects on competition and innovation

Why do patentees file a motion for a preliminary injunction? The motivation for this coincides with the general motivation why patentees undertake patent litigation,[198] and this can be grouped into two categories. Firstly, this is to extract money, directly or indirectly. This can be either opting for damages or by obtaining an injunction that can be used to stop infringement which in turn can facilitate the negotiation of a licensing agreement (on better terms for the patentee) which covers the issue of (past) financial compensation. Secondly, litigation can be used as a tool to protect a position in a business market, by hurting a competitor's revenue or to exclude the competitor entry from the market place altogether.[199] Preliminary injunctions are no different in their capability in achieving these goals and can serve as a tool to meet these ends. In fact, the unique power of a preliminary injunction is to immediately put pressure on the other party,[200] as for that other party there is less time to seek and prepare for alternatives.

Regardless of the plaintiff's motivation, obtaining a preliminary injunction has effects on competition. Whilst the primary goals of preliminary injunctions are not rooted in terms of innovation and competition – it is of course a *multi-purpose remedy of general civil law* – it is clear that with respect to intellectual property in general and patents in particular, they can have effects on competition and innovation. These effects are both positive of nature as well as negative.[201] A few of these negative, or at the very least 'questionable' effects of preliminary injunctions are mentioned subsequently.

§3.4.1. 'Working around' the contested patent and the preliminary injunction: a waste of resources?

The longer the preliminary injunction is in place, the higher the incentives are for the defendant to (re)design around the contested patent that is central to the litigation.[202] A preliminary injunction, or the threat thereof, may thus lead to the

198 On this, see Y.T. WU, 'How will Ebay v Mercexchange affect preliminary injunction?' *NTUT Journal of Intellectual Property Law and Management* 3, No. 1 (2014), pp. 34–55. See: p. 47.

199 Ibidem.

200 Ibidem.

201 With respect to the positive effects on competition and innovation, see the previous chapter of this dissertation.

202 The assumption is made, in this paragraph, that redesign is possible. This may not always necessarily be the case, either for technical reasons or because it is

situation that an already designed, made or working product or process of the defendant which has (allegedly) infringed a patented invention might require 'working around' (redesigning) by the defendant. This in order to circumvent the patent and the scope of the preliminary injunction. Such an activity may not only entail substantial (sunk) costs – in terms of missed market opportunities, labour and efforts – but also may require the extra costs of purchasing a different set of patents.[203] Depending on the patent, these costs can be significant and in some instances even prohibitive.[204] Furthermore, during the process of redesigning, the production is often ceased, leading to a temporary loss in production.

Forced redesign may thus be deemed to be an inefficient undertaking for an individual firm. The *individual* costs for a firm of being the addressee of a preliminary injunction can be, and in practice often are, significant. How much depends on the actual patent or industry involved as well as the number of alternatives that are possible: sometimes certain patented (software-related) inventions for instance are fairly easy to redesign around.[205]

From a *social costs* perspective, Golden has rightly pointed out that the literature is divided on the desirability of designing around and that the there are opposing views on the costs and benefits that society incurs due to this.[206] Some commentators see the pressure to design around as something positive, rather than negative, because the designing around can often lead to a technologically better product.[207]

---

prohibitively expensive to do so. In such cases, the infringer may also choose to settle, under non-optimal terms, see below, at page 82 and further.

203 S.E. STERK, 'Property rights, liability rules and uncertainty about property rights' *Cardozo School of Law Working Paper No. 205*, (2007); available at: http://papers.ssrn.com/sol3/papers.cfm?abstract_id=1016168 (last accessed on 17 april 2017). See: p. 50.

204 Ibidem, at footnote 189, in which Sterk cites the work of M.A. LEMLEY, P.J. WEISER 'Should property or liability rules govern information?' *Texas Law Review* 85, No. 4 (2007), pp. 783–841. See: pp. 797–798. Sterk argues that the abovementioned authors state that the cost of redesign, in some sectors, can be tens of millions of dollars and in fact so large that it is *not feasible* any more to do so from a commercial perspective.

205 See for instance a Dutch Apple-Samsung case, where the court took this into account in its decision to grant a preliminary injunction to Apple as it was straightforward for Samsung to design around the infringing use. See: Vzr. Rechtbank Den Haag, *Apple v Samsung*, August 24th 2011, KG-ZA 11–730. See: par. 4.2–4.4.

206 J.M. GOLDEN, 'Injunctions as more (or less) than Off Switches: patent infringement injunctions' scope' *Texas Law Review* 90 (2012), pp. 1399–1472. On pages 1406–1409, Golden goes into the issue of redesign in patent law.

207 See for instance J.M. GOLDEN, 'Injunctions as more (or less) than Off Switches: patent infringement injunctions' scope' *Texas Law Review* 90 (2012), pp. 1399–1472, citing at p. 1408 in footnotes 30 and 32 the work of F. Scott Kief who argued that "[w]hile at first blush [designing around] may seem wasteful, as redundant, it becomes immediately apparent that such secondary inventive activity is usually

However, other authors, including Machlup and Kitch (whose works already have been mentioned before)[208] see this differently. They argue that "the production of the knowledge of how to do in a somewhat different way what we have already learned to do in a satisfactory way would hardly be given highest priority in a rational allocation of resources."[209] They also point out that patents are a good way to prevent duplicative investments in follow-on innovation.[210] Golden himself makes an interesting analogy between roadwork and patent law. He writes that roadwork might produce temporary blockages or slowdowns to the public, but that this can encourage drivers to experiment with finding new ways to travel – this is something which Golden deems as positive – in order to reach their destination. He continues that "the likelihood of causing such experimentation is unlikely to be considered a positive justification to undertake the roadwork in the first instance, but such design around-activity can reduce the social costs of the work, therefore helping to make these costs tolerable."[211]

Although some positive social spin-offs may well be the case, it is nevertheless submitted that the decision to grant a preliminary injunction is taken amidst the

---

a very good thing." This is because "[o]ften, a second-generation product is better than the first." F. SCOTT KIEF, *Principles of Patent Law* (Fourth edition, 2008). See: p. 71.

208 See page 32 and further of this dissertation.

209 Ibidem, J.M. GOLDEN, 'Injunctions as more (or less) than Off Switches: patent infringement injunctions' scope' *Texas Law Review* 90 (2012), pp. 1399–1472, citing Machlup at p. 1408, footnote 34 of his work. See F. MACHLUP, *An Economic Review of the Patent System – Study of the Subcommittee on patents, trademarks and copyrights of the Committee on the Judiciary of the United States Senate* (1958 US Government Printing Office). See: p. 51.

210 J.M. GOLDEN, 'Injunctions as more (or less) than Off Switches: patent infringement injunctions' scope' *Texas Law Review* 90 (2012), pp. 1399–1472, thererby citing Kitch, at p. 1409, footnote 35; <A patent> "puts the patent owner in a position to coordinate the search for technological and market enhancement of the patent's value so that duplicative investments are not made and so that information is exchanged among the searchers." See: E. KITCH, 'The Nature and the Function of the Patent System' *Journal of Law and Economics* 20, No. 2 (1977), pp. 265–290. See: p. 276.
Another interesting insight from Kitch on this issue, although not mentioned by Golden, is the following: "After a patent is issued, other firms have an incentive to invent substitute technologies even if the substitute technology is less efficient than the patented technology but can be produced more cheaply than the existing royalty rate. *Even more efficient inventions should not, from a social point of view, be produced unless the cost of producing them is less than or equal to their saving over the existing technology, absent any royalty on that technology.*" See his work on pp. 278–279. Emphasis added.

211 J.M. GOLDEN, 'Injunctions as more (or less) than Off Switches: patent infringement injunctions' scope' *Texas Law Review* 90 (2012), pp. 1399–1472. See: p. 1409.

fog of uncertainty with a higher than normal risk of an erroneous decision. At the same time, if the firm is enjoined, it faces high individual costs that can potentially put it out of business. Therefore, one can question about what the true value of the social cost justifications are.

§3.4.2. *Hold-up problems*

An argument in favour of damages, or at the very least for caution with the grant of *permanent* injunctions, is that of the risk of hold-up problems. This is no different with respect to *preliminary* injunctions. 'Hold-up' occurs when the patentee can extract more from the infringer than the value of the patent actually provides for.

As will be seen, for instance in the chapter on preliminary injunctions and generic entry of pharmaceuticals, it is clear that preliminary injunctions are regularly granted in situations when the patent is of critical importance to the marketing of the product and that imminent infringement may hinder this exploitation. This can be when the patented innovation is the sole part really representing the *value* of the product. For example, in the pharmaceutical industry, the marginal costs of producing the pills itself are relatively low, whilst the patent represents the undertaken and costly research and development phase prior to the development of the pharmaceutical. Or it can also be in the case when the patent central to the dispute is a *critical and necessary* component of a multi-component product. In such a case a preliminary injunction is often seen as justified.

However, sometimes requests for a preliminary injunction occur with respect to (weak) *patents on a minor part of the product* and this is a situation when hold-up can occur. By obtaining a preliminary injunction for a (weak or questionable) patent that protects a minor part of the product, the plaintiff can prevent entry of other parties to the market, or demand excessive royalties. This would be consistent with the theoretical findings of Shapiro. He showed that both (potential) holdup problems and also hold-up power is the greatest for (weak) patents covering a minor feature of a high-margin product.[212]

A way for courts to deal with this situation is by denying an injunction altogether and later offering damages instead, or by raising the bar for obtaining (preliminary) injunctive relief. It is submitted that these solutions are not too drastic as 'hold-up' is considered to lead to problematic issues. Chan argues[213] that hold-up problems can lead to the same inefficient incentives as with overvaluation of harms and damages by the court.[214] These include the supressing of the development of legitimate substitutes, the undermining of the patent system's disclosure benefits and the shifting

---

212 C. SHAPIRO, 'Injunctions, hold-up and patent royalties' *American Law and Economics Review* 12, No. 2 (2010), pp. 280–318. See: p. 285.

213 N.P. CHAN, 'Balancing judicial misvaluation and patent hold-up: some principles for considering injunctive relief after eBay' *UCLA* 59 (2011–2012), pp. 746–787. See: pp. 772–774.

214 As discussed at the main text at footnote 143 of this dissertation.

of resources to litigation rather than towards negotiations.[215] Chan also adds that hold-up leads to unique problems of its own: one of them is that overcompensation from hold-up can encourage inventors at the margin to focus on producing products that are likely to cause hold-up in the future and which can then be monetised. These inventions are often of little innovative character and usually concern obvious steps forward and are thus suitable of being replicated by another firm. Subsequently, this other firm is then accused of patent infringement.[216] Whilst this alone is worrying enough, one should also bear in mind that every Euro or dollar spent by a firm in producing these type of little innovative inventions is less capital spent on more innovative research activities.[217]

Whilst the problem of hold-up is of course not restricted to *preliminary* injunctions alone, it is submitted that certain characteristics of preliminary injunction proceedings – including the shorter and more shallow investigation into key issues of validity and infringement than at the trial on the merits – can result in a heightened chance of false-positive decisions. This, as Cotter puts it, can subsequently lead to a risk of exacerbating hold-up problems.[218]

§3.4.3. Settlements and (the threat of) preliminary injunctions

Litigation, and the *threat of litigation*, does of course not take place in a vacuum and the proceedings and the result obviously affect the chances and terms of a settlement;

> "A wide range of commercial arrangements involving intellectual property can be regarded as settlements of intellectual property disputes, either **literally** (in the sense that litigation has been initiated and is dropped once an agreement is reached) or **effectively** (because negotiation takes place **in the shadow** of possible litigation). Virtually every patent license can be viewed as a settlement of a patent dispute: the royalty rate presumably **reflects the two parties' strengths or weaknesses in patent litigation** in conjunction with the licensee's ability to invent around the patent."[219]

Of course the above is no different in the case when litigation takes place in the context of (the threat of) preliminary injunction proceedings.

It is submitted that whilst settlements can be useful after a final ruling, it is submitted that settlements based on a temporary verdict – a decision whether or not

215 N.P. CHAN, 'Balancing judicial misvaluation and patent hold-up: some principles for considering injunctive relief after eBay' *UCLA* 59 (2011–2012), pp. 746–787. See: pp. 772–773.

216 Idem, at p. 773.

217 Ibidem.

218 T.F. COTTER, *Comparative Patent Remedies: A Legal and Economic Analysis* (2013 Oxford University Press). See: p. 179.

219 C. SHAPIRO, 'Antitrust limits to patent settlements' *RAND Journal of Economics* 34, No. 2 (2003), pp. 391–411. See: p. 392. Emphasis added.

to grant a preliminary injunction – insufficiently reflects the definitive legal status of rights and these can force parties into early negotiations and settle on terms that they would not have done under normal circumstances. Both the *likelihood* and the *value* of settlements are influenced by both the remedy as the proceedings, as will be seen.

The outcome of the preliminary injunction proceedings in combination with external circumstances

After the decision on a request for a preliminary injunction has taken place and the remedy has either been granted or denied, a settlement can be the next step towards ending the dispute and so offer a final outcome, instead of further litigation on the merits. A settlement can then be induced, also thanks to *external circumstances.* One of these is *time.* As Bernieri asserts, a good example of this in practice can be found in Italy (although this country is of course not the only one where litigation on the merits can take longer than the parties deem to be acceptable). She writes: "the practical importance of preliminary measures in Italy follows from the long duration of trials which makes preliminary injunctions (as well as other interim measures) usually the most important decisions and *often the final turning point for a settlement.*"[220]

It may also be the case that other external circumstances play a role. This can be, for instance, that the *level of demand* of the (disputed) technology which the patent covers has changed or that meanwhile *increased competition has emerged* on the market. Therefore, a settlement, which was first maybe an unattractive alternative for one party or for both parties, may then become an increasingly interesting option to consider.

The influence of the actual preliminary injunction and of the proceedings itself

Whilst above we have looked at the preliminary injunction *in combination* with external circumstances, the literature points out that (the threat) of a preliminary injunction and of the preliminary injunction proceedings *itself* can have a number of effects in raising the chances of a settlement, by breaking down barriers that stand between the parties. The most important of these barriers is those of *information problems* and to a lesser extent in the context of preliminary injunctions those of *bargaining problems, principal-agency problems* and *psychological* issues.[221] It is

220 From: R.J.F.M.C. BERNIERI, *Ex-post liability rules in modern patent law* (2010 Intersentia Publishing). See: p. 161. Emphasis added.

221 G.P. MILLER, 'Preliminary judgments' *New York University Law and Economics Working Papers* No. 138 (2008). See respectively pages 8, 15, 18, 20. This article is not about preliminary injunction proceedings as such, but on *preliminary judgments.* Miller proposes a more merits-based mini trial, with the judge being less limited than it is in summary proceedings and in which the taken decision converts into a final judgment after a certain period of time. By contrast, current

deemed useful to elaborate a little more on information problems, as overcoming this is key to reaching a settlement.

The *information* that is gained from the preliminary injunction proceedings itself may contribute to nudging parties into *reaching a settlement.* That these proceedings and the court's decision on whether to grant an injunction, can have effect on a litigant's behaviour is demonstrated by the findings of Jeitschko and Kim.[222] Their in economics grounded research is on the 'informational effects' of preliminary injunctions. Their model focusses on two types of effects that are now described below.[223]

Firstly, this is that preliminary injunction *proceedings* are capable of revealing (private) information,[224, 225] and secondly, that the preliminary *injunctions* themselves (the actual court order) have an effect on settlement negotiations due to the informational transmission that takes place. The former can for instance be the plaintiff revealing information about his level of damages, the latter for example be the hearing on the motion and the court's decision revealing information about the (strength of the) merits of the case. One of the conclusions of Jeitschko and Kim is:

---

preliminary injunction proceedings are more limited in scope. Miller argues that although rulings on preliminary injunctions can serve *some* of the functions of preliminary judgments, they are not an adequate substitute for the preliminary judgment as he envisions. See p. 41 a.f.

222 T.D. JEITSCHKO, B.C. KIM, 'Signalling, learning and screening prior to trial: informational implications of preliminary injunctions' *EAG Discussion Paper* (2011). Available at the website of the US Department of Justice: https://www.justice.gov/sites/default/files/atr/legacy/2011/02/23/267542.pdf (last accessed on 21 April 2017). Their paper is an interesting contribution, focussing specifically on preliminary injunctions, to the volume of literature on how the transmission of information affects the behaviour and strategies of parties before and after litigation. In the same line, also see: S. SCOTCHMER, *Innovation and incentives* (2004 MIT Press). See: p. 202.

223 T.D. JEITSCHKO, B.C. KIM, 'Signalling, learning and screening prior to trial: informational implications of preliminary injunctions' *EAG Discussion Paper* (2011). See: p. 2. Available at the website of the US Department of Justice: http://www.justice.gov/atr/public/eag/267542.pdf (last accessed on 21 April 2017).

224 But, as Lichtman argued, this is not specifically limited to preliminary hearings in the context of injunctions, but rather an argument for having informative hearings early in litigation in general. D. LICHTMAN, 'Uncertainty and the standard for preliminary relief' *John M. Olin Law & Economics Working Paper* No. 166 (2002). See: p. 5, footnote 4. Available at: http://papers.ssrn.com/sol3/papers.cfm?abstract_id=344640 (last accessed on 17 April 2017).

225 Also see G. LLOBET, 'Patent litigation when innovation is cumulative' *International Journal of Industrial Organisation* 21 (2003), pp. 1135–1157. See: p. 1137. He refers to this in his model, as parties having *private information* about the qualities of their invention.

> "In the wake of the **hearing** on the motion and the **court's ruling**, litigants are able to glean information about the case strength and, thus, **reassess their chances of ultimately prevailing at trial.** In particular, when the court declines to enjoin the defendant and denies the request for an interlocutory injunction, litigants' beliefs that the plaintiff will ultimately prevail at trial are diminished. **As a consequence, lower settlement offers are made by the defendant, yet these are accepted with greater frequency,** precisely because the alternative of continued litigation is less attractive to the plaintiff."[226]

The inverse is of course also true: in case of the grant of a preliminary injunction, a settlement will become less likely, since the plaintiff will be confident about its chances later on in the continuation of the litigation.[227]

An example of the information transmission in preliminary injunction proceedings having an impact on *the value of a settlement,* is given by the lawyers Baumann and Belvis in a patent litigation specific case. They point out, basing themselves on their experiences, that clients opting for a preliminary injunction should be warned that requesting a preliminary injunction is not without risk for plaintiff and that the playing field after such a proceeding and ruling can be slanted much more in favour of the defendants due to the particular *claims construction* that is made on the plaintiff's motion. This cannot only influence the decision with respect to the motion for a preliminary injunction, but it can also affect *the value* of a potential settlement:

> "an adverse claim construction from a preliminary injunction ruling **will significantly reduce the settlement value of the cases**. One would have to turn a completely blind eye toward human nature to believe that a defendant would put the same amount of money on the table after it has a favourable claims construction than when the issue was unresolved. **The cloud of uncertainty over claims construction can be a very powerful motivation for settlement. That motivation is lost or at least significantly reduced, if an adverse claims construction flows from a preliminary injunction ruling.**"[228]

---

226 T.D. JEITSCHKO, B.C. KIM, 'Signalling, learning and screening prior to trial: informational implications of preliminary injunctions' *EAG Discussion Paper* (2011). See: p. 26. Emphasis added. Available at the website of the US Department of Justice: http://www.justice.gov/atr/public/eag/267542.pdf (last accessed on 21 April 2017).

227 Ibidem.

228 J.J. BAUMANN, G.P. BELVIS, 'Better things come to a patent owner who waits – the need to fully assess the strategic risks of seeking preliminary injunctive relief in patent cases' *Intellectual Property Litigation* 16, No. 4. (2005), p. 2. Emphasis added. In the same light, see: G.P. MILLER, 'Preliminary judgments' *New York University Law and Economics Working Papers* (2008) Paper No. 138, who argues against the 'world of settlements' that he sees we're living in: "Settlements, moreover, do not always achieve satisfactory outcomes. Defendants claim they are forced to settle frivolous lawsuits for exorbitant sums in order to avoid burdensome

The impact of preliminary injunctions on (litigation) costs of rival firms

The writing of Lanjouw and Lerner[229] is one the few *empirically* driven economics papers on the specific topic of preliminary injunctions in patent litigation.[230] In their research, the authors consider the links between (the threat of) preliminary injunctions, the financial resources of parties and their (potential) payoffs from litigation.[231]

The authors find that litigation proceedings with the goal of obtaining a preliminary injunction are used extensively and strategically as 'weapons' by plaintiffs in order to drive up the costs of rivals. Firstly, the proceedings itself increase litigation costs for a defendant to continue with a case until a trial on the merits. Secondly, because of the costs of being under the injunction for the defendant: as long as the preliminary injunction is in place, a sharp reduction in cash flow will occur.[232]

Therefore, instead of merely preventing 'irreparable harm' to the plaintiff's own business position,[233] one of Lanjouw and Lerner's conclusions is that "compared to other means of increasing an opponent's costs, the option to seek preliminary injunctive relief may give plaintiffs a particularly effective threat to use against capital-constrained defendants because of the extra financial burden that they experience if actually enjoined."[234] Merely the *threat* (as well as the actual use) of starting preliminary proceedings can be sufficient for a defendant to surrender and choose for a settlement, even before the decision of the court in the preliminary injunction proceeding has taken place.[235] Striking too, is that the authors also conclude that the financial status of firms does indeed play a determining role in this. They write that: "the availability of this threat tilts payoffs against weaker firms in favour of their less constrained rivals."[236, 237] Another of their conclusions

litigation expenditures or to limit their exposure to class actions. Plaintiffs claim that scorched earth defense tactics force them to settle too cheaply." See pp. 2–3.

229 J.O. LANJOUW, J. LERNER, 'Tilting the table? The use of preliminary injunctions' *Journal of Law and Economics* 44, No. 2 (2001), pp. 573–603.

230 The authors use a sample of 252 patent suits that were filed in six different US Federal Districts between 1990 and mid 1991. For more specifics on the data which is used in the model by Lanjouw and Lerner, see pp. 589–595 of their article.

231 J.O. LANJOUW, J. LERNER, 'Tilting the table? The use of preliminary injunctions' *Journal of Law and Economics* 44, No. 2 (2001), pp. 573–603. See: p. 575.

232 Idem, at pp. 573–574.

233 Idem, at p. 575.

234 Idem, at p. 601.

235 Idem, at p. 583.

236 Idem, at p. 600.

237 One alternative explanation to the relationship between financial status and court actions is a certain *reputation of litigiousness* that a firm can build up, Lanjouw and Lerner argue on p. 599. However, they argue that this does not explain the whole effect: "The importance of creating and maintaining a reputation for litigiousness

in this light is then rather intuitive perhaps: low-cost firms hold out longer in settlement negotiations after their activities have been enjoined by the grant of a preliminary injunction.[238]

The above, it is submitted, is worrisome enough in any industry, but is extra worrisome for a reason which is *directly linked to innovation.* One perspective on innovation is that significant innovative capacity is rooted in smaller companies. An example of these are start-ups, which are often venture-backed.[239] The point is that these frequently will have (relatively) smaller financial buffers, resulting in less funds to either freely allocate towards litigation purposes or to survive in times with a reduced cash flow in the interval between a granted preliminary injunction and the trial on the merits.[240] This is an interval that may be months or years. The situation may be even worse if one accepts the intuition that many start-ups or smaller companies are less diversified in their activities than larger firms are, so that a preliminary injunction has an extra strong effect on daily business.[241]

---

may increase when a firm expects to be engaged in future disputes. Larger firms may expect to be involved in litigation more frequently because they have more patents. If requesting injunctions contributes to a reputation for being aggressive, then reputational concerns might induce a positive relationship between firm size and the likelihood of an injunction request. While this may explain part of the significance of our plaintiff measures, it is unlikely to represent the entire explanation for this effect."

238 See J.O. LANJOUW, J. LERNER, 'Tilting the table? The use of preliminary injunctions' *Journal of Law and Economics* 44, No. 2 (2001), pp. 573–603. See: p. 600.

239 Idem: Lanjouw and Lerner at p. 575 point to this as well: "(..) where innovative industries may be driven by smaller, more vulnerable, venture-capital-based firms reliant on the profits -or potential profits- derived from intellectual property assets."

240 Ibidem.

241 The crux of this point, also seems to be confirmed in the work of Harhoff *et al.* with respect to temporary enforceable final patent injunctions that create an 'injunction gap' as well. In Germany, these are known as *vorläufige vollstreckbare Urteile* and as stated before these share some characteristics with preliminary injunctions (see footnote 28 of this dissertation). Harhoff *et al.* point out: "We also show that bifurcation reduces the likelihood that an alleged infringer challenges a patent's validity. *Because challenging the validity of a patent requires a separate action at a different court, the alleged infringer may refrain from doing so despite the potential invalidity of a patent.* We find evidence that *in particular smaller firms are less likely* to file an invalidity action at the BPatG when they are sued for infringement. The effect is robust to controlling for various time varying and invariant patent-, litigant-, and case- level characteristics. *This suggests that more resource-constrained firms are less likely to challenge a patent's validity.*" See p. 3, emphasis added. D. HARHOFF, K. CREMERS, F. GAESSLER, C. HELMERS, 'Invalid but infringed? An analysis of Germany's bifurcated patent litigation system' *Zentrum für Europäische Wirtschaftsforschung, Discussion Paper* No. 14–072 (2014).

In the same light, the scholars Ayres and Klemperer warn of the effects that preliminary injunctions may have on innovation too. They point out that both uncertainty and delay in patent litigation may have unforeseen virtues.[242] In their view, denying immediate interim relief when infringement occurs can have a purpose. The starting point of their analysis is the notion that different types of uncertainty exist.[243] These are the type of uncertainty whether or not a valid patent will be *un*enforced (so-called *Type I uncertainty*, a false-positive decision) and secondly, the type of uncertainty whether or not an invalid patent will be enforced (so-called *Type II uncertainty*, a false-negative decision).[244] The costs associated with Type I uncertainty are deemed to be less high than the costs associated with Type II uncertainty.[245] The authors argue that practices and remedies aimed at reducing Type I uncertainty – such as strong preliminary injunctive relief – are likely to lead to an increase of Type II uncertainty.[246] Questioning whether this is good for innovation, Ayres and Klemperer argue that the number of preliminary injunctions with respect to patents should be low.[247]

The main gist of their article which is most relevant here,[248] is that both authors argue that a preliminary injunction standard leading to a practice of the non-enforcing of valid patents, instead of a preliminary injunction practice of actually enforcing invalid patents, may be more desirable in terms of economic efficiency:

> "enforcing invalid patents creates ex post pricing distortions without enhancing innovation while <our model showed that> failing to enforce otherwise-valid patents could reduce the ex post distortions without reducing, or without substantially reducing, innovation incentives."[249]

---

242 I. AYRES, P. KLEMPERER, 'Limiting patentees' market power without reducing innovation incentives: the perverse benefits of uncertainty and non-injunctive remedies' *Michigan Law Review* 97, No. 4 (1999), pp. 985–1033. See: p. 986.

243 Idem, at p. 987.

244 Idem, at pp. 987–988.

245 Idem, at p. 988. The authors state that: "recent efforts of the Federal Circuit to expand the use of preliminary injunctions may not be cost-justified as they are likely to expand Type II uncertainty and reduce Type I uncertainty. The costs of Type I uncertainty and delay are not as great as previously thought, and we may not want to expend substantial resources to eliminate this feature of the current system. Appreciating the benefits of uncertainty argues against giving patentees a presumptive right to preliminary injunctions against infringement, and militates instead in favor of relatively stingy ex post measures of make-whole damages."

246 Ibidem. Also see: pp. 1022–1024.

247 Idem, at p. 1020 and further.

248 Idem, at pp. 1019–1022.

249 Idem, at p. 1019. Brackets added.

Therefore, a policy of reducing the number of granted preliminary injunctions may perhaps be sensible, *by increasing the patent holder's burden to justify its request for a preliminary injunction.*[250] The ratio behind this, is that allowing a limited level of interim infringement – that is until a trial on the merits has taken place and the court can establish with more certainty the questions of infringement and patent validity – has the benefit of restricting the patentee's market power, by allowing entry of other parties and some reduction in price.[251] At the same time, allowing a limited amount of infringement would not substantially reduce the profitability of the patent.[252] The amount of entry would be limited anyhow because potential infringers will compete down the market price reducing the probability of further infringement and having to pay potentially higher damages if the patent is enforced after the trial on the merits.[253] They conclude therefore that the advantages preliminary injunctions are seen to have should be reconsidered[254] and they argue that courts should become more reluctant and cautious in granting them:

> "The essentialist notion of "patents" as "property" that by nature entails the right to exclude has led courts to discourage interim infringement even when the consumer costs of monopoly dramatically outweigh the benefits to the patentee (and any plausible impact on innovation incentives). If courts can free themselves of this notion, however, they can shift away from issuing injunctions, as the issuance is not mandated by statute but is within the courts' equitable discretion."[255]

§3.5. An erroneous decision and the question of compensation

Uncertainty can be seen as a problem as it is linked to judicial errors. Or in other words to the court failing to reach the 'right' or 'correct' result. The thesis here is that the higher the uncertainty, the higher is the chance of an erroneous decision. With an erroneous decision is meant that a decision after the trial on the merits differs from the decision taken in the preliminary injunction procedure.[256] Because of the heightened uncertainty surrounding the decision to grant preliminary injunctions, erroneously granted preliminary injunctions are not uncommon. Such

---

250 Idem, at p. 1022.
251 Idem, at p. 1021.The underlying economic principles are due to what Ayres and Klemperer call the 'Stationarity intuition' for patents with a fixed lifetime and for patents with an increased length after an extension, the 'Ramsey intuition' See pp. 989–993 of their work.
252 Idem, at p. 1021.
253 Ibidem.
254 Idem, at p. 1033.
255 Idem, at pp. 1029–1030.
256 Or later, with the benefit of hindsight, would likely be taken at such a trial.

a 'wrong' decision has economic effects, as will be seen below, for both the parties involved in the litigation as for society as a whole. Also, it is submitted that this issue has effects on the concepts of legitimacy and fair justice; high judicial error rates can, on the long term, erode the confidence that stakeholders – such as patentees, other market parties and the general public – have in the working and functioning of the patent system.[257]

With respect to economic effects, Grosskopf and Medina have rightly noted that harms which may be created by an erroneously issued preliminary injunction can be of two types; potentially reparable harms and completely irreparable harms.[258] The first refers to the undeserved and errant transfer of wealth from a party who is legally entitled to it to a non-entitled party.[259] Potentially, these private losses can be repaired.[260] The latter refers to losses that are absolutely irreparable by nature – i.e. a deadweight loss, a direct net-loss of social welfare – or those which are practically irreparable by an ex-post remedy – i.e. the harms to consumers and third parties – as these can also not be repaired.[261]

§3.5.1. Potentially reparable harms – harms due to an undeserved wealth transfer

An undeserved wealth transfer is when an errant transfer of wealth takes place from an entitled party to a non-entitled one. Jurisdictions can provide a legal mechanism to offer some degree of compensation to the defendant that has been wrongfully enjoined by a wrongfully issued preliminary injunction and thus when an undeserved wealth transfer has taken place. Although in general, parties are not held responsible for wrong judicial decisions and therefore are not liable to compensate for harms occurring by this, this is somewhat different in the case of (enforcing) preliminary injunctions.[262] This is due to the special nature of the remedy which has an "explicit awareness of the possibility that it will be proved wrong."[263] Indeed, this is also enshrined in the law.[264]

257 For general arguments on the link between substantive and enforcement law, also see page 67 of this dissertation.

258 O. GROSSKOPF, B. MEDINA, 'Remedies for Wrongfully-Issued Preliminary Injunctions: The Case for the Disgorgement of Profits' *Seattle University Law Review* 32 (2009), pp. 903–941. See: pp. 919–920.

259 Ibidem.

260 Idem, at p. 920 and p. 923, where the authors state that "the remedy determines which part of the harm is socially reparable."

261 Idem, at p. 920 and p. 924. Note that although reallocation of the damage, i.e. via compensation, would be possible the damage cannot be eliminated.

262 Idem, at p. 903.

263 Idem, at p. 904.

264 See Art. 50 (3) and (7) TRIPS and Art. 9 (3) and (7) of the EU Enforcement Directive.

As written above, the consequences of the losses that occur to an undeserved wealth transfer between litigating parties can *potentially* be remedied and there are various types of mechanisms that can provide a wrongfully enjoined defendant monetary compensation. Some form of reinsurance for defendants could for instance be offered in the form of a bond, and other mechanisms are for instance that of the remedy of restitution or that of damages. However, these mechanisms do often *only on paper* really make whole and their usefulness in providing full compensation in practice is not to be overstated. An erroneously taken preliminary injunction in general thus remains costly to the party which is wrongfully enjoined. A wrong decision should therefore be avoided in the first place altogether. Some examples of these mechanisms and their shortfalls may demonstrate this.

- In some jurisdictions *a bond* is foreseen in, when a preliminary injunction is granted and this bond is to be posted to the court directly or in the form of a bank guarantee. Whilst this is relatively easily accessible form of financial compensation for the defendant, there are problems with it. Often, a bond actually covers only a fraction of the harm that occurs due to the erroneous decision. Firstly, this is because the way the bond amount is set does not reflect the actual damages, but it is mainly a tool to provide first and accessible security.[265] Secondly, this is because the level of the bond is set at an early stage, when the damages are very unclear and possible damages may be underestimated.[266] Furthermore, often the amount is set to unrelated issues to the damages, such as the financial means of the plaintiff or the public interest of the case.[267] Finally, in certain countries, such as the United States, the bond is the *upper limit* of a party's liability and caps this, since further damages for a wrongfully issued preliminary injunction (beyond the amount of the bond) are not possible.[268] Unsurprisingly, authors have therefore expressed concerns with respect to relying on bonds too much.[269] Also, some jurisdictions in practice do not request bonds from parties, such as The Netherlands.

---

265 O. GROSSKOPF, B. MEDINA, 'Remedies for Wrongfully-Issued Preliminary Injunctions: The Case for the Disgorgement of Profits' *Seattle University Law Review* 32 (2009), pp. 903–941. See: p. 908.

266 Ibidem.

267 Ibidem.

268 Idem, at p. 921. Also see the older but still interesting article of Marotta who is critical of this: "Since an entire company can potentially be destroyed by an injunction, a rule which limits the recovery for a wrongfully enjoined party to the amount of a bond, is archaic." (p. 47). P. MAROTTA, 'The injunction bond in high technology litigation: the need for reform' *Santa Clara High Technology Law Journal* 4, No. 1 (1988), pp. 19–47.

269 For instance, Leubsdorf is also very sceptical of relying on bonds too much. He argues that estimating their magnitude is often tricky, that not all damages can be made whole by money and he warns that if high bonds become a requirement

- Equally, *restitution* (which is gains-based recovery) has problems too, in the case of prohibitively formulated preliminary injunctions, as no money has been paid nor has property been transferred.[270] Also, courts have shown reluctance to provide restitution for an unjustified monopoly status, if the upheld patent turns out to be invalid.[271] Doctrinally, this approach is deemed to be acceptable because the plaintiff benefitting from this upheld monopoly status did nothing wrong in the context of unjust enrichment and nothing was taken from the defendant due to the injunctive relief.[272] However, that this is not satisfactory and should be reconsidered is argued by Grosskopf and Medina, who point out many justifications in favour of a restitution-based remedy.[273] They forcefully argue that the disgorgement of profits is more appropriate than relying on damages in the case of an erroneously taken decision as liability can lead to overdeterrence.[274] They also add that the latter offers the wrong incentives to apply for a preliminary injunction.[275]

---

for obtaining a preliminary injunction, this may deter parties of asking for one in the first place. See: J. LEUBSDORF 'Preliminary injunctions, in defense of the merits' *Fordham Law Review* 76 (2007), pp. 33–47. See: pp. 40–43 and p. 47.

270 O. GROSSKOPF, B. MEDINA, 'Remedies for Wrongfully-Issued Preliminary Injunctions: The Case for the Disgorgement of Profits' *Seattle University Law Review* 32 (2009), pp. 903–941. See: pp. 911–912.

271 Idem, at pp. 910–912. The authors argue that this is the case in Common Law jurisdictions, thereby also citing the case of EWCA *SmithKline Beecham PLC v. Apotex Europe Ltd.* (2007) Ch. 71, 89. Here the English Court of Appeal rejected a claim for such restitution, thereby also pointing to the courts of the United States and Australia which have decided that restitution is not to be provided to a harmed party in the case of an erroneous court decision.

272 O. GROSSKOPF, B. MEDINA, 'Remedies for Wrongfully-Issued Preliminary Injunctions: The Case for the Disgorgement of Profits' *Seattle University Law Review* 32 (2009), pp. 903–941. See: p. 912.

273 Idem, at p. 928.

274 Idem, at p. 933.

275 Without developing a fully-fledged preliminary injunction standard, it is submitted that GROSSKOPF AND MEDINA, in their article 'Remedies for Wrongfully-Issued Preliminary Injunctions' make an interesting contribution to the debate. They persuasively argue that a restitutionary remedy can be extremely useful in removing the improper motives to apply for a preliminary injunction (p. 941). They also argue that the right amount of plaintiff-liability should deter frivolous applications and that it does not deter a plaintiff when it has a legitimate reason to opt for a preliminary injunction (p. 935) and that the disgorgement of profits is the best way to deal with this (p. 939). They further write that taking away the benefits that the plaintiff receives from an erroneously given preliminary injunction, instead of relying on the compensation of the harms caused by this injunction, can better advance the aim of minimising social harm (p. 940).

- This brings us to *damages*. Damages have the problem that their magnitude is often difficult to assess, both in their size and with respect to the causal relationship between the harm and wrongfully issued preliminary injunction.[276] Also, a separate damage proceeding is (often) necessary for them to be awarded to the injured party, or these should be agreed on in negotiations by the parties in the form of a settlement. Both may not always be easy undertakings. In fact, one of the reasons to opt for a preliminary injunction (as well as for the court to grant a preliminary injunction) – namely the difficulty in calculating and obtaining damages – is then actually *caused* by the *erroneously* granted preliminary injunction.

Lastly, it should be mentioned that apart from the private losses that occur with an undeserved wealth transfer, there are also *social harms* that occur from this. An undeserved wealth transfer can adversely affect the purpose of the assignment of a legal entitlement, thereby for instance affecting the incentives to invest and innovate.[277] [278]

§3.5.2. Deadweight losses and practically irreparable harm

Whilst the harms of an underserved wealth transfer are thus potentially able to be remedied, this is most definitely different with deadweight losses. This is also different with respect to the losses of consumers and third parties in the case an erroneously preliminary injunction has been issued. These can be practically irreparable, for instance due to lack of standing.

A deadweight loss is harm that can never be undone, not even with compensation. It may for instance be generated due to the lack of the production and consumption of a product or due to an elimination of competition that occurs because

276 C. HEINZE, *Einstweiliger Rechtsschutz im europäischen Immaterialgüterrecht* (2007 Mohr Siebeck). See: pp. 160–16. Heinze argues that establishing the magnitude of damages of the defendant, in the context of damages due to an erroneous decision, is even more difficult than establishing the magnitude of harms of the plaintiff in considering the grant of a preliminary injunction.

277 O. GROSSKOPF, B. MEDINA, 'Remedies for Wrongfully-Issued Preliminary Injunctions: The Case for the Disgorgement of Profits' *Seattle University Law Review* 32 (2009), pp. 903–941. See: pp. 919–920.

278 It is not entirely clear from their article whether the social harms of an undeserved wealth transfer are potentially reparable, but from the contrast Grosskopf and Medina make on p. 920 and p. 293 – making a distinction between social costs of a deadweight loss and social costs of an undeserved wealth transfer which can be eliminated – it is understood that this can happen, at least if an adequate compensation is provided for.

of an erroneously granted preliminary injunction.[279, 280] *The consumer* in such cases has then ended up paying a monopoly price for the patented product in the period between the grant of a preliminary injunction and the trial, as the plaintiff-patentee was able to charge its monopoly price in absence of competition by the alleged-infringer. *Other competitors* may also have been shut out of the market, together leading to less demand, supply, business and research.

Additionally, as Boyce and Hollis point out,[281] this not only leads to the result that consumers shoulder the burden of a monopoly price, but also to the situation that this way preliminary injunctions create *extra profits* to be shared between the litigating firms:

> "the patent holder gets monopoly profits less a (possible) payment to the imitator; and the imitator bears no risk of having to pay even larger damages to the incumbent. This is, in effect, an anti-competitive settlement between firms enforced by the court."[282]

A deadweight loss is thus harm that cannot be undone and this is *a distinct issue* from that of whether any compensation would be practically possible in the first place. It should be stressed that even if such harm could potentially be undone, *a consumer* for instance is often *not* provided by law to a claim for damages for this type of harms. Equally, *third parties* to the defendant/infringer (such as suppliers) are normally not entitled to a claim for damages either,[283] nor can they benefit from the bond as they were not directly enjoined by the injunction.[284] Restitution is rarely an option for them either.[285] Such harms can thus also, *practically speaking*, be irreparable for these parties.

In other words, the wrongfully issued preliminary injunction, resulting in less competition, can lead to a *deadweight loss* which is shouldered by the consumers and

279 O. GROSSKOPF, B. MEDINA, 'Remedies for Wrongfully-Issued Preliminary Injunctions: The Case for the Disgorgement of Profits' *Seattle University Law Review* 32 (2009), pp. 903–941. See: p. 919.

280 Heinze argues persuasively that indeed false-positive granted preliminary injunctions in intellectual property litigation are very worrying, since this leads to the inefficient use and the shrinking of the *public domain.* This, he points out, may especially force smaller and middle-sized companies to maintain a larger distance from another's intellectual property rights than the property right as such foresees in. See C. HEINZE, *Einstweiliger Rechtsschutz im europäischen Immaterialgüterrecht* (2007 Mohr Siebeck). See: pp. 156–157.

281 J.R. BOYCE, A. HOLLIS, 'Innovation, imitation and preliminary injunctions in patents' (2002), pp. 1–35. See: p. 30. Available at: http://citeseerx.ist.psu.edu/viewdoc/summary?doi=10.1.1.214.6747 (last accessed on 21 April 2017).

282 Idem, at p. 30.

283 Ibidem.

284 O. GROSSKOPF, B. MEDINA, 'Remedies for Wrongfully-Issued Preliminary Injunctions: The Case for the Disgorgement of Profits' *Seattle University Law Review* 32 (2009), pp. 903–941. See: p. 909.

285 Ibidem.

other parties that are not part of the litigation proceedings and have no possibility of a claim against the plaintiff.

§3.5.3. *An insufficient remedy to compensate and further effects*

An insufficient remedy in the case of a (likely) wrong decision can also discourage the defendant from litigating the case further after the preliminary injunction proceedings (also when he eventually might win the case) if during the period between the grant of the preliminary injunction and trial on the merits, the defendant is enjoined. This is because this preliminary injunction interval may cover most of the time that the patent is economically valuable.[286] In such a case, the defendant may then not have sufficient incentives to continue litigating, as he would not recover the damages that are sustained during the preliminary injunction interval anyway. This is problematic, as preliminary injunctions are issued with the implicit assumption that the dispute should eventually be resolved during a trial on the merits.[287] When this is not the case, this has ramifications for the quality of the patent system and the trust stakeholders have in this. Furthermore, from a more ex ante perspective, a sufficient remedy enabling the defendant to gain compensation in the case an erroneous preliminary injunction is granted, can help prevent "rash and flimsy" applications for a preliminary injunction by plaintiffs in the first place, thereby resulting in less burden on the judicial system.[288]

§3.6. Chapter conclusion

Whilst we have already seen in chapter 2 that there are strong independent justifications in favour of the availability and the grant of preliminary injunctions, this chapter has also pointed out that there are significant (social and private) risks, effects and costs that can be linked to them. In other words, whilst a preliminary injunction *can* do justice and provide effective relief, the process of granting the injunction and the grant itself can at the same time be seen as entailing risks and undesirable consequences. Especially concerning here, it is argued, is that the preliminary injunction proceeding is often the final station of the litigation. An important check built into the judicial system – namely the trial on the merits – is then not utilised. Equally, the use of a preliminary injunction (or threatening to do so) in forcing the defendant to accept a settlement as well as, lastly, the court's risk of

---

286 O. GROSSKOPF, B. MEDINA, 'Remedies for Wrongfully-Issued Preliminary Injunctions: The Case for the Disgorgement of Profits' *Seattle University Law Review* 32 (2009), pp. 903–94. See: p. 922.

287 Ibidem. In the same light, see page 76 and further of this dissertation.

288 O. GROSSKOPF, B. MEDINA, 'Remedies for Wrongfully-Issued Preliminary Injunctions: The Case for the Disgorgement of Profits' *Seattle University Law Review* 32 (2009), pp. 903–94. See: p. 929.

making an erroneous decision with significant consequences for society, are serious issues that should be noted.

However, these potential downsides do not mean that simply not granting preliminary injunctions at all is a (better) solution, in avoidance of the abovementioned risks. Apart from the legal obligation to make the remedy of the preliminary injunction available, such an approach would also put an intolerable high burden on the shoulders of the plaintiff. In other words, as Zuckerman stated: "for, clearly, a system which does not offer some such relief pending judgment would confer an enormous, in many cases decisive, advantage on defendants."[289]

289 A.A.S. ZUCKERMAN, 'Quality and Economy in Civil Procedure – The case for commuting correct judgments for timely judgments' *Oxford Journal of Legal Studies* 14, No. 3 (1994), pp. 353–387. See: p. 374.

Chapter 4: A Case Study of the Role of Preliminary Injunctions in Practice: Generic Entry in the Pharmaceutical Market

§4.1. Introduction

It has been demonstrated above that preliminary injunctions have both justifications and risks arguing in favour or against them. It is submitted that this is shown very well in a sector in which preliminary injunctions are routinely used and which also is a sector that happens to be well-documented: this is the pharmaceutical sector,[290] where preliminary injunctions are frequently requested in originator-generic competition.

§4.2. Preliminary injunctions and the (generic) pharmaceutical market

Apart from the vast economic value of the industry itself,[291] the pharmaceutical sector is also an essential sector having a direct impact on the health of citizens as well as on the affordability of the health system.[292] Pharmaceuticals are often seen as a key factor in driving health expenditures.[293] Patents play a role in safeguarding both the economic value of the findings as well as fostering a climate of innovation, stimulating further Research and Development. Preliminary injunctions play an important role too in this market and can be considered as a regularly used tool of enforcement in a rather specific context. According to the European Commission, interim injunctions in the EU are hardly ever sought *between originator*

---

290 It is noted that for the purpose of this dissertation, 'pharmaceuticals' are widely defined. It can also include for instance small medical devices (like catheters) or methods for patients to actually apply pharmaceutical products, such as insulin pumps or application patches.

291 The economic value of the pharmaceutical sector in the EU is large. According to the European Commission's Sector Enquiry, the total market value approximated €214 billion euros at retail prices. This averages on €430 per capita and will likely increase since the EU population is ageing. See: EUROPEAN COMMISSION, *Pharmaceutical Sector Inquiry Final Report* (2009). See: p. 1. Available at: http://ec.europa.eu/competition/sectors/pharmaceuticals/inquiry/staff_working_paper_part1.pdf (last accessed on 20 April 2017).

292 Idem, at p. 19.

293 Ibidem.

pharmaceutical companies,[294] but this is markedly different from the situation between originator companies and generic companies.

> "According to the data submitted by respondent companies, hardly any interim injunctions were issued in litigation between originator companies. This is in contrast to the findings on litigation between originator and generic companies, where interim injunctions are more regularly sought. (..)"[295]

It should be stressed here that seeking a preliminary injunction is only *one way* for a patentee to manage generic competition.[296] Other of these so-called 'extension strategies' – since the life of the patent is de facto being extended – which are widely used by pharmaceutical patentees are for instance applying for an SPC, seeking additional patent protection by modifying certain aspects of an already patented product (so-called *evergreening* or *life-cycle management*), by virtue of second pharmaceutical/medical use claims or by means of test data protection and the use of trademarks. All these tactics can have varying degrees of success against the competition by generic companies.[297]

Unsurprisingly, generic companies have shown themselves to be concerned about the use of patents and patent litigation in hindering generic entry and these concerns include the use of preliminary injunctions.[298] The *European*

294 One of the reasons for this is given in the *Sector Inquiry*. A respondent argues that this is because in this type of litigation often secondary medical use or process claims are central to the dispute and infringement is less obvious. That makes these type of cases less suitable for preliminary injunction proceedings. See: EUROPEAN COMMISSION, *Pharmaceutical Sector Inquiry Final Report* (2009). See: par 3.2.3.4. Available at: http://ec.europa.eu/competition/sectors/pharmaceuticals/inquiry/staff_working_paper_part1.pdf (last accessed on 20 April 2017).

295 EUROPEAN COMMISSION, *Pharmaceutical Sector Inquiry Final Report* (2009). See: par 3.2.3.4. at 1196 and 1197. Available at: http://ec.europa.eu/competition/sectors/pharmaceuticals/inquiry/staff_working_paper_part1.pdf (last accessed on 20 April 2017).

296 For a concise review of these strategies, see the article of B. WHITEHEAD, S. JACKSON, R. KEMPNER 'Managing generic competition and patent strategies in the pharmaceutical industry' *Journal of Intellectual Property Law & Practice* 3, No. 4 (2008), pp. 226–235. Also see: EUROPEAN COMMISSION, *Pharmaceutical Sector Inquiry Final Report* (2009). See: pp. 60–61. Available at: http://ec.europa.eu/competition/sectors/pharmaceuticals/inquiry/staff_working_paper_part1.pdf (last accessed on 20 April 2017).

297 B. WHITEHEAD, S. JACKSON, R. KEMPNER, 'Managing generic competition and patent strategies in the pharmaceutical industry' *Journal of Intellectual Property Law & Practice* 3, No. 4 (2008), pp. 226–235.

298 EUROPEAN GENERIC MEDICINES ASSOCIATION, *Patent-related Barriers to Market Entry for Generic Medicines in the European Union* (May 2008). Report drafted by K. ROOX, J. PIKE, A. BROWN, S. BECKER.

Generic Medicines Association (EGMA) points out five concerns which are related to this. The EGMA argues that preliminary injunctions in this industry are often granted inappropriately and instead should only be used as exceptional remedies, when delay in granting relief would lead to irreparable harm for the originator.[299] The EGMA also argues that varying preliminary injunction standards have resulted into divergent practices within the EU.[300] It writes in its report,[301] that in practice:

- interim injunctions in certain countries are handed out very easily as national courts feel uncomfortable in changing the status quo (of the market) based on a *prima facie* assessment;
- in various countries, European patents are presumed to be *prima facie* valid, this even when opposition proceedings at the European Patent Office (EPO) are pending or prior invalidity decisions have taken place in other Member States in parallel proceedings. Also, courts often lack the technical expertise to properly decide upon infringement and validity questions on the face of the issue. During interim proceedings, they do not have the benefit of appointing a technical expert;
- the time until a decision on the merits has been reached can be very long. This may be due to a backlog of cases, lack of judicial experience and the impossibility to appoint technical experts. This can result in a long delay until the moment the generic producer can enter, if it is enjoined earlier due to a preliminary injunction;
- the 'balance of convenience' should lie in *not* granting a preliminary injunction in the case of follow-on patents after the expiry of the basic patent, since the patentee should have already recouped its costs during the lifetime of the basic patent. This is not the case everywhere;
- the harm that occurs due to generic entry does not seem to be irreparable for an originator, as this can be calculated and compensated for with damages. It are often commercial issues (i.e. is the harm of the patentee outweighing that of the defendant?) which drive litigation strategy, instead of the merits of the patent infringement issue. Because often a preliminary injunction proceeding is the final station of litigation (as the trial of the merits stage is in practice often not reached) the issue of actual infringement is then ultimately of little significance;

299 Idem, at p. 19.

300 Ibidem.

301 Idem, at pp. 19–21. The listed concerns hereafter are partly paraphrased, but an attempt has been made to stay as close to the wording of the EGMA report as possible.

All in all, the EGMA argued for caution and reluctance in the granting of preliminary injunctions in the originator-generic context.[302]

We will return to some of these concerns of the EGMA later in this and subsequent chapters of this dissertation. To begin with, we will do so with the findings of the European Commission in the *Pharmaceutical Sector Inquiry*, in paragraph §4.6. and further.

§4.3. Characteristics of the pharmaceutical market regarding supply and demand

Several specific characteristics of the pharmaceutical sector shape supply and demand of this market. Because we will refer regularly to pharmaceuticals later on in the thesis as well, a short explanation of these characteristics is warranted here.

The *supply* of the market is served by both originator and generic companies.[303] The research and development of new pharmaceutical products (often for unmet medical needs) as well as the subsequent testing, is done by *originator* companies.[304] Originator companies are sometimes also known as branded companies, since they heavily rely on trademark protection, as well as on patents. The supply from the originator side is heavily influenced by the process of regulatory approval, as pharmaceuticals are meticulously regulated from a health and safety point of view. Both in the US as in Europe, a new pharmaceutical drug must go through various phases of (pre)-clinical trials,[305] which can easily take up to a decade, before

---

302 The EGMA concluded in its report that: "*In conclusion, the standard for obtaining an interim injunction should be returned to its roots as an equitable remedy.* This means that a litigant should be required to establish irreparable harm that cannot be compensated by monetary damages before a court takes the far-reaching step of enjoining a product. *Applying this standard would serve the dual goal of encouraging patent owners to commercially develop or license their innovations, and of ensuring that injunctions are not used simply as a tactic in litigation, which is essentially the reality today.*" See: p. 21. Emphasis added.

303 EUROPEAN COMMISSION, *Pharmaceutical Sector Inquiry Final Report* (2009). See: p. 22. Available at: http://ec.europa.eu/competition/sectors/pharmaceuticals/inquiry/staff_working_paper_part1.pdf (last accessed on 20 April 2017).

304 Idem, at pp. 23–27.

305 C. DESOGUS, *Competition and Innovation in the EU Regulation of Pharmaceuticals* (2011 Intersentia Publishing). See: pp. 15–18. She writes that these tests not only concern the safety of the drug, but also take place to establish the minimal effective dose, the optimal regime of administration and whether there are side effects or advantages over other drugs. For the legislative basis in the EU, see Directive 27/2004/EC of the European Parliament and the Council of 31 March 2004, amending Directive 2001/83/EC on the Community code relating to medicinal products for human use. (OJ L 136/35).

the pharmaceutical is approved.[306] Degosus submits, correctly, that this leads to two effects.[307] Firstly, the long path from the first synthesis of the substance to a marketable pharmaceutical means that the costs a company incurs are sunk and should be recouped in the relatively short time of protection that a patent or the SPC offers. Secondly, only a very small amount of substances make it through all the clinical tests successfully and an even lesser number becomes highly profitable.[308] This shows the immense importance of efficient patent enforcement for originator pharmaceutical products, especially for those pharmaceuticals which are successful in the marketplace and experience high demand.

The other main source of supply of pharmaceutical products comes from *generic* companies. Generic companies provide pharmaceuticals that have lost their exclusivity status and have the same active ingredients as the originator product. They are to be seen as just as effective.[309] Their key selling point is that of costs: their produced pharmaceuticals are offered substantially cheaper than originator products and without generic supply, public health expenditure would be much higher. They are therefore vital in keeping the public expenditures of the health system affordable.[310] Therefore, delays in market entry of generic products can be costly for society. Arguably, generic companies also have a positive effect in stimulating originator companies into research, to come up with new medicines.[311] Note that the market introduction of generic pharmaceuticals is regulated. Whilst depending somewhat on the type of pharmaceutical, overall this can be a much quicker and less costly process than the launch of a novel pharmaceutical product. This because the long series of clinical trials an originator product should go through can often be

306 Idem, at p. 17.

307 C. DESOGUS, *Competition and Innovation in the EU Regulation of Pharmaceuticals* (2011 Intersentia Publishing). See: p. 19.

308 As Desogus mentions, at page 19 of her work, only 1 in 10 000 substances that is synthesised, passes all stages of clinical testing with success. Also, about 1 in 60 000 compounds is deemed to become a highly successful one, resulting in global sales over $100 million per annum.
It is submitted that this is also known as the 'lemons problem'. From the outset it is difficult to impossible to predict which investment will be successful and this notion is a strong argument to justify strong patent enforcement, in order to compensate the inventor for all the other investments that did *not* pay off.

309 EUROPEAN COMMISSION, *Pharmaceutical Sector Inquiry Final Report* (2009). See: p. 22. Available at: http://ec.europa.eu/competition/sectors/pharmaceuticals/inquiry/staff_working_paper_part1.pdf (last accessed on 20 April 2017).

310 Idem.

311 BRITISH GENERIC MANUFACTURERS ASSOCIATION, *Response by the British Generic Manufacturers Association (BGMA) to the DG Competition Pharmaceutical Sector Inquiry Preliminary Report* (2004). See: p. 2.

(largely) skipped when it is proven that the generic product has the same properties as the originator's pharmaceutical, the so-called reference product.[312]

The *demand side* of the market is characterised by the fact that in general, the end users, namely the patients, are not sovereign and independent in the way that they select pharmaceuticals.[313] In fact the pharmaceutical market is four-sided.[314] Along with the patient, there are other actors that are considered to be influential in driving demand for a drug: these are the doctor (in selecting the pharmaceutical for a certain medical condition), the pharmacist (in administering the drugs and maybe to prescribe a cheaper substitute) and the government (mostly paying for the drugs).[315]

§4.4. Generic entry and regulatory approval

A generic company that plans to launch a generic product will do so after it has achieved the required regulatory approval from the relevant authorities. After obtaining at least market approval,[316] but mostly also after obtaining Pricing and Reimbursement (P&R) approval,[317] the generic company can decide to launch the

---

312 EUROPEAN COMMISSION, *Pharmaceutical Sector Inquiry Final Report* (2009). See: p. 39. Available at: http://ec.europa.eu/competition/sectors/pharmaceuticals/inquiry/staff_working_paper_part1.pdf (last accessed on 20 April 2017).

313 C. DESOGUS, *Competition and Innovation in the EU Regulation of Pharmaceuticals* (2011 Intersentia Publishing). See: p. 20.

314 Idem, at p. 27.

315 Idem, at pp. 20–27.

316 In the process of marketing approval, the relevant health authorities control for aspects of quality and safety, as well as bioequivalence of the generic drug to the patented drug. This is done purely on the basis of scientific criteria. Other aspects such as the level of reimbursement and – importantly here – *the patent status* of a product are *not* taken along in this risk-benefit assessment. An applicant can obtain this approval through different routes: a national procedure (which offers authorisation only to that country) or a centralised, decentralised or mutual procedure route. The latter procedures can directly or indirectly lead to an EU-wide marketing approval. See: P. DYLST, A. VULTO, S. SIMOENS, 'Overcoming challenges in market access of generic medicines in the European Union' *Journal of Generic Medicines* 9, No. 1 (2012), pp. 21–28. Also see the EUROPEAN COMMISSION, *Pharmaceutical Sector Inquiry Final Report* (2009). See: p. 115. Available at: http://ec.europa.eu/competition/sectors/pharmaceuticals/inquiry/staff_working_paper_part1.pdf (last accessed on 20 April 2017).

317 P&R Approval foresees in a link between the generic entrant and the (national) health insurance system of an EU Member State. As Pignatti et al. explain, most EU Member States try to influence public health expenditure by pricing and reimbursement decisions and by demand-side policies. These demand-side policies are aimed at the three 'consumers' of pharmaceuticals. These are medical prescribers (influenced via i.e. therapeutic guidelines, budgeting), pharmacies (influenced via i.e. the right of substitution) and patients (influenced via i.e. co-payments). These

generic product *even prior* to the expiration of the patent or SPC. This is called 'launching at risk' because the generic company runs the risk of being sued for patent infringement by the originator.

In the United States there is even specific legislation for this: the *Hatch Waxman Act* regulates generic pharmaceutical competition.[318] Under Paragraph IV of the Act, it is possible for a generic company to obtain prior *Food and Drug Administration* (FDA) Market Approval, before the patent of the originator has expired. It does so by the filing of an Abbreviated New Drug Application (ANDA), in which the generic company is allowed to rely on the clinical trials undertaken by the originator.[319] This way, early generic entry is facilitated.[320] Along with the ANDA, the generic company should, inter alia, notify the relevant patentee(s) and point out why it believes the patent is invalid or infringed.[321] This way, patentees with questionable patents are

---

policies vary widely per Member State and even within Member States, but these decisions must adhere to certain transparency criteria which are laid down in Directive 89/105/EEC. In order to be part of the system of the abovementioned health insurance policies – and thus essentially to become commercially successful – a pharmaceutical needs P&R Approval. This de facto determines the commercial degree of access to the market in a particular country. This can amount to direct price control or a reimbursement level decision. Whilst some countries grant automatic P&R Approval under the same conditions as the originator reference product – notably for this dissertation this is the case in the UK and Germany – this is different in other countries. See for more on this: F. PIGNATTI, H. BOONE, I. MOULON, 'Overview of the European Regulatory Approval System' *Journal of Ambulatory Care Management* 27, No. April-June (2004), pp. 89–97. See: p. 93. Also see C. DESOGUS, *Competition and Innovation in the EU Regulation of Pharmaceuticals* (2011 Intersentia Publishing). See: pp. 21–27 for a good overview of these cost-containment measures. Lastly, see: EUROPEAN COMMISSION, *Pharmaceutical Sector Inquiry Final Report* (2009). See: p. 54 and p. 132 a.f. Available at: http://ec.europa.eu/competition/sectors/pharmaceuticals/inquiry/staff_working_paper_part1.pdf (last accessed on 20 April 2017), and P. DYLST, A. VULTO, S. SIMOENS, 'Overcoming challenges in market access of generic medicines in the European Union' *Journal of Generic Medicines* 9, No. 1 (2012), pp. 21–28. See: p. 24.

318 The *Hatch Waxman Act* is the colloquial acronym for the legislation that is officially entitled as the 'United States Drug Price Competition and Patent Term Restoration Act' (Public Law 98–417). It was enacted in 1984.

319 FEDERAL TRADE COMMISSION, *Authorized Generic Drugs: Short Term Effects and Long Term Impact* (2011). See: pp. 2–4. Available at: http://www.ftc.gov/sites/default/files/documents/reports/authorized-generic-drugs-short-term-effects-and-long-term-impact-report-federal-trade-commission/authorized-generic-drugs-short-term-effects-and-long-term-impact-report-federal-trade-commission.pdf (last accessed on 21 April 2017).

320 Idem, at p. 3. Also see the relevant legislation at 21 USC §355 (j). Market approval is required for any new drug under 21 USC §355 (A).

321 It can also be that in the ANDA, the generic company states that it will wait with entry until the patent(s) expire(s).

challenged by competitive forces. The patentee, upon receiving notice, has 45 days to react. If the patentee subsequently starts infringement proceedings against a *Hatch Waxman* Paragraph IV ANDA, the necessary market approval for the entrant is withheld by the FDA.[322] This results into effectively barring generic entry until either the alleged infringement issue is resolved or when a period of maximum 30 months has expired.[323] After that period, or at an earlier moment if infringement is not found, the FDA may give its approval and the generic company can proceed with the launch of its generic product.

The main attraction for generic companies of the Hatch Waxman Act, Paragraph IV, is that the *first approved ANDA applicant* obtains protection vis-a-vis other Paragraph IV ANDA applicants, leading to a *First Mover Advantage.* It is to this concept that we now turn.

§4.5. Preventing generic entry versus First Mover Advantage

Generic entry negatively affects the prices and volumes of originator companies.[324] Combined, this can heavily influence the revenue that originator companies enjoyed prior to the loss of exclusivity due to generic entry. As soon as the generic product hits the market, the sales and prices of the branded product, formerly under patent exclusivity, will steadily go downwards. This is because the demand side of the market (i.e. patients, governments, pharmacists) will have a cost incentive to switch to the generic equivalent of a certain drug. They can save on public health expenses and still obtain a fully equivalent product. The originator's options in reacting to this development are limited and boil down to reducing the price of its own product and instead relying on its trademark and reputation. It can also offer a generic product to the market itself. Nevertheless, it is clear that the originator's revenues and profits will drop, in comparison to the numbers during the period that the originator enjoyed exclusivity. The figure below, from the Commission's *Pharmaceutical Sector Inquiry,* neatly visualises this. It shows the 'possible effects of delayed generic entry in terms of welfare distribution, for given levels of consumption of the product – patent litigation'.

---

322 21 USC §355 (j) (D) (BB).

323 Ibidem.

324 EUROPEAN COMMISSION, *Pharmaceutical Sector Inquiry Final Report* (2009). See: p. 77 a.f. Available at: http://ec.europa.eu/competition/sectors/pharmaceuticals/inquiry/staff_working_paper_part1.pdf (last accessed on 20 April 2017). This report shows that in the EU, prices drop around 20% on average one year after generic entry. In some Member States however, this could be as much as 90% (p. 78). After two years, the originator's average price drop for the product is 50%, in comparison with the situation prior to the loss of exclusivity (p. 85). With respect to volumes, the *Pharmaceutical Sector Inquiry* shows that within two years, a generic penetration rate of 50% market share is not uncommon (p. 89).

Figure 4. The effects of an interim injunction and generic entry. Source of this image is p. 377 of the European Commission's Pharmaceutical Sector Inquiry.

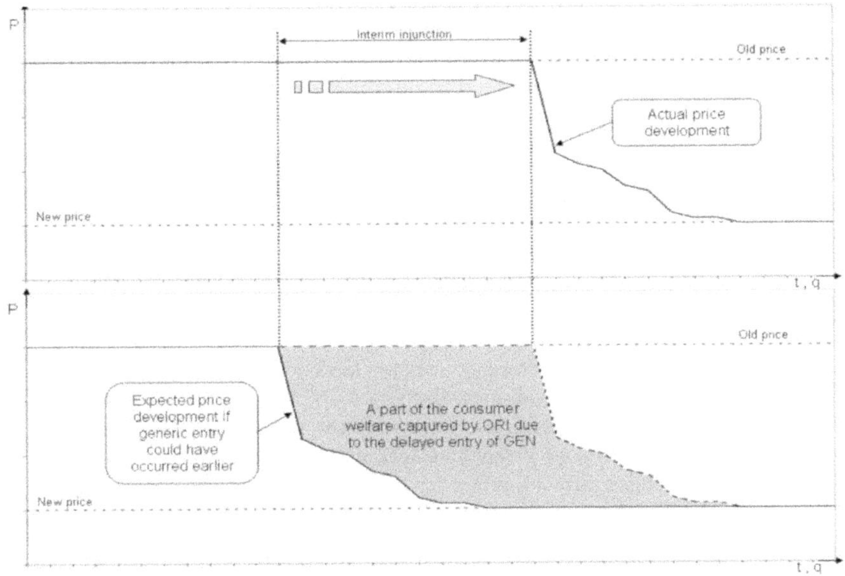

First Mover Advantage: This is now the right moment to point out why generic companies undertake the practice of 'launching at risk' and to determine why generic entry is so attractive for certain companies. The most important reason is the *First Mover Advantage*. Becoming the first generic company on the market after the patentee's monopoly, can attract much sales and lead to a rapidly developed and significant market share. This position can be established both *de facto* or *de iure*, and the latter is for instance created by the regulatory framework of the Hatch Waxman Act as provided for in the United States.

In the US, the first generic company to file a Paragraph IV ANDA application is legally protected with a privileged position for 180 days. During this period, other (later) generic companies have to wait to enter the market,[325, 326] as the FDA will

325 FEDERAL TRADE COMMISSION, *Authorized Generic Drugs: Short Term Effects and Long Term Impact* (2011). See: p. 3. Available at: http://www.ftc.gov/sites/default/files/documents/reports/authorized-generic-drugs-short-term-effects-and-long-term-impact-report-federal-trade-commission/authorized-generic-drugs-short-term-effects-and-long-term-impact-report-federal-trade-commission.pdf (last accessed on 21 April 2017),

326 Note that this exclusivity period of 180 days is not absolute *erga omnes*: generic products offered by originator companies can still compete, since they can rely

withhold their marketing approval. The first generic applicant thus has valuable time to build up its market share. This is a core part of the US government's policy that is in place to offer incentives to generic companies. This way, there is an incentive for companies to make generic medicines available from the first day after the relevant patent or SPC protection expires. By doing so, the health system can save more money due to the increased competition and the corresponding average price drop of the patentee's product. The EU lacks a similar statutory mechanism as provided for by the Hatch Waxman Act.

A citation from a Marketing Director of a generic company shows the economics of First Mover Advantage in the pharmaceutical sector. He describes why this First Move Advantage is valuable vis-a-vis other generic competitors entering the market at a later stage. He also illustrates how short the effective time span of this First Mover Advantage actually is, taking into account the market dynamics of the pharmaceutical industry;[327]

> "Being first to market with a generic product is a key strategy for generic companies including Mylan. Being first with a product enables us **to establish supply** to key customers. **When further generics come onto the market, as the incumbent supplier we will usually be given first option to keep the supply (albeit at a lower price).** This is a huge advantage for us particularly because it **allows us to maintain our market share, but it also allows us to manage our stock and so reduce the possibility of write-off costs.** The generic pharmaceutical market is

---

on their branded drug that was already admitted to the market by the FDA. These so-called authorised generics are chemically identical to the originator's branded drug and then sold by the brand-name company without the name or trademark, against a lower price. This practice has gained much controversy, since some state that this undermines the true purpose of Paragraph IV of the *Hatch Waxman Act*, namely in offering incentives to the first ANDA applicant in the form of a privileged market position. This practice is however not relevant for this dissertation, as patents or preliminary injunctions play no direct role in this. FEDERAL TRADE COMMISSION, *Authorized Generic Drugs: Short Term Effects and Long Term Impact* (2011). See: p. 1 and 4. Available at: http://www.ftc.gov/sites/default/files/documents/reports/authorized-generic-drugs-short-term-effects-and-long-term-impact-report-federal-trade-commission/authorized-generic-drugs-short-term-effects-and-long-term-impact-report-federal-trade-commission.pdf (last accessed on 21 April 2017).

327 It should be noted here that the concept of First Mover Advantage is not only of relevance in this context nor is it only restricted to the pharmaceutical industry. In fact, it is a very rewarding effect for companies, as is argued by Levine and Boldrin. They argue, agreeing with other academics, that competition and first-mover incentives are to be seen as the strong drivers of innovation and instead they question the notion that the monopoly of patents should be seen as doing so. See: M. BOLDRIN, D.K. LEVINE, 'The case against patents' *The Journal of Economic Perspectives* 27, No. 1 (2013), pp. 3–22.

highly competitive and it is within the first **few weeks or months of launch that the bulk of profits on a product can be made**, particularly where a company is the only generic on the market for a period. If a number of generics then enter the market and compete on price, the profit margins reduce. Successful generic companies rely on the strategy of first market entry as it is a **key factor** for profitability."[328]

§4.6. Main findings and data from the EU Pharmaceutical Sector Inquiry with respect to preliminary injunctions

Whilst the *EU Pharmaceutical Sector Inquiry* looks into a multitude of issues,[329] most relevant for us are the findings and data that the report provides regarding the practice of interim injunctions. Although it should be acknowledged that the Inquiry relied on the provision of voluntarily provided data within a specific times-pan, it is submitted that the research provides a good snapshot of the industry. The numbers and findings it presents are likely to be a fairly good indicator of what is actually occurring regarding the interactions and competition between originator and generic companies.[330] With respect to preliminary injunctions, the following observations are made.

Firstly, it provides data on the *share of granted requests for a preliminary injunction.* The Inquiry indicates that in 44% of the aggregated EU cases in which an originator company requested a preliminary injunction, this relief was granted.[331] However this level varies widely between the various EU Member States: around 75% of the requests for a preliminary injunction was granted in Germany, Belgium and Sweden and in 67% of the cases in Italy. This is in stark contrast with the UK (in the range of 30–35%) and The Netherlands (where only in 14% of the cases the request was honoured).[332]

Secondly, it provides data on *the average duration of a granted preliminary injunction.* The Inquiry points out that over 50% of the issued interim injunctions in

---

328 Citation from the Marketing Director of Mylan in the United Kingdom, in the case of *Cephalon v Orchid* before the English High Court: EWHC, *Cephalon & Ors v Orchid & Anor, trading as Mylan*, November 19th 2010, EWHC 2945 (pat.).

329 The *EU Pharmaceutical Sector Inquiry* looks at length at practices regarding settlements, data exclusivity, advertising, litigation, marketing authorisation and regulatory approval, as well as patent strategies with respect to granting authorities. The Inquiry does so both with originator-generic competition as with originator-originator competition.

330 To improve readability, all data below is given in percentages only. It is also submitted that with respect to absolute numbers of some findings, the data sample that the European Commission uses, seems to be somewhat on the low side.

331 EUROPEAN COMMISSION, *Pharmaceutical Sector Inquiry Final Report* (2009). See: p. 230. Available at: http://ec.europa.eu/competition/sectors/pharmaceuticals/inquiry/staff_working_paper_part1.pdf (last accessed on 20 April 2017).

332 Idem, at p. 230.

the specific context of originator-generic competition in pharmaceutical patent disputes was in place less than a year,[333] with an average EU duration of 18 months.[334] Germany was well below this average (less than 6 months) as was the UK (circa 9 months). The Netherlands was substantially above this, with more than 42 months.[335] In Italy, an interim injunction in the pharmaceutical sector has an average duration of almost 60 months.[336]

Thirdly, the data sheds *some light on the closure of the case*. Regarding the cases in which a preliminary injunction was granted, over half of the cases was eventually formally closed[337] because either a final judgment was taken (in 27% of the formally closed cases) or a settlement had been agreed on between the parties (in 73% of the formally closed cases).[338]

- When a final judgment was made by a court, this resulted into a positive judgment for the originator company in circa 2/3 of the cases.[339]
- In the majority of cases, a settlement was agreed on after the grant of a preliminary injunction.[340] In 40% of these settlements, the result was deemed to be favourable for the generic company. For example, it allowed generic entry at a certain stage or that a value transfer from the originator to the generic company took place.[341] In 10% of the cases a value transfer took place vice versa, so from the generic company to the originator firm or generic entry was delayed until the end of the patent protection period. In 25% of the settlements made, it was not possible to unequivocally establish in whose favour the settlement was.[342]
- The European Commission in the *Pharmaceutical Sector Inquiry* commented that the results above – on final closure – show that despite the high level of granted interim injunctions, the picture may be more nuanced than one would expect. This certainly is the case when it is taken into account that normally success on the merits and urgency should be proven if a preliminary injunction is to be granted.[343] The Commission adds that the combination of actual generic success in litigation and that of a settlement rate that seems to be favourable to generic

333 Idem, at p. 232.
334 Idem, at p. 232.
335 Idem, at p. 232 (figure).
336 Idem, at p. 232 (figure).
337 In the other half of the cases in which a preliminary injunction was granted, no formal closure had been made at the time of the Inquiry, thus the case was still pending.
338 Idem, at p. 234.
339 Idem, at p. 234.
340 Not given is data on when a settlement has been agreed after a preliminary injunction has been *denied*. It is submitted that this is a likely scenario in which parties may do so too.
341 Idem, at p. 234.
342 Idem, at p. 234.
343 Idem, at p. 234.

companies, leads to the conclusion that "it would seem that in almost a half of the closed cases the grant of interim injunctions might not have been justified, whilst in another 25% of the cases that were settled the situation is unclear."[344]

- Last, but certainly not least, the results show that in 11% of the cases, national courts reached *contradicting decisions* with respect to the same underlying issues in patent disputes.[345] This is because the court in one Member State held the patent to be valid, whilst in another it was held that the patent was invalid. Whilst 11% at first glance may not seem to be a high number, the Commission concludes: "This is a significant finding since the existence of conflicting final judgments inevitably harms the legal certainty for the companies that are active in a given product on other EU markets."[346]

§4.7. Analysis of the findings of the Pharmaceutical Sector Inquiry

It is submitted that the findings which the European Commission presents in the Sector Inquiry are rather worrying and are in line with some of the observations that the EGMA made earlier in this chapter.

- It is clear that – as is apparent from the differences between Member States in the numbers of granted preliminary injunctions, the injunctions' duration as well as the contradicting decisions between national courts – that there is not a single EU practice yet for this form of interim relief.
- Furthermore, it is evident that once granted, preliminary injunctions are in force for a considerable amount of time on average. It is submitted that even a relatively short preliminary injunction of less than six months can already have considerable effects, both for the enjoined party, competitors and for consumers.
- The number of erroneously granted preliminary injunctions seems to be significant, as the Commission's data and conclusion on this show. Also, this is something that patentees are apparently quite aware of as the high rate of settlements which are favourable for the generic company shows.

It is submitted that a more harmonised and perhaps cautious decisionmaking process when deciding on granting a preliminary injunction can be important steps in mitigating these problems in the future. The start of the UPC from this point of view may prove to be a welcome development and a break with the current European practices.

344 Idem, at pp. 234–235.
345 Idem, at pp. 236–237.
346 Idem, at p. 237.

Chapter 5: How Courts Can Deal with Preliminary Injunctions from the Perspective of Law & Economics Theory

§5.1. Introduction

When faced with a request for a preliminary injunction, how should a preliminary injunction court decide on this and what should be taken into account? This issue will be now addressed, in the light of Law & Economics theory. Law & Economics scholars have come up with different standards on how judges should handle preliminary relief. It is submitted that it is possible to classify the different approaches into two schools of regulation.[347] On the one the one hand there are proponents of tight judicial control, believing that the preliminary injunction court is in the best position to decide about the need for interim relief. On the other end of the spectrum there are also scholars opting for a more flexible approach or even liability approach, with markedly a less strong position for the court in deciding on the request to grant a preliminary injunction and on assessing the evidence. Proponents of this school of thought believe that it are the parties that are in the best position to decide on the need for a preliminary injunction.[348]

We will now look briefly at these different theoretical approaches. At the end of this chapter there is a table in which the main results are also given in a concise overview.[349]

§5.2. Tight judicial control in decisionmaking under uncertainty

§5.2.1. The Leubsdorf-Posner approach

This approach is characterised by a very instrumentalist vision, clearly resembling a cost-benefit perspective, in the sense that a preliminary injunction is only desirable if the expected harm of the plaintiff from not granting the preliminary injunction, outweighs the expected harm that the defendant shall suffer by grant

347 F.R. ROMEU, 'An economic theory of the regulation of preliminary measures' *European Journal of Law and Economics* 30 (2010), pp. 267–300. See: p. 275. Romeu also mentions other forms of regulation to control a plaintiff's behaviour, namely criminal or administrative sanctions and a pigouvian tax.

348 Ibidem.

349 For this table see page 128 below.

of the preliminary injunction.[350] It is submitted that this is also the best known, and most cited, approach Law & Economics has offered in the past as an answer to *when* an preliminary injunction should be granted. In his influential article,[351] Leubsdorf attempted to propose a model, that would form the basis of preliminary relief, "incorporating much, but not all, of that was learned so far on interlocutory injunctions."[352] His standard is based on the following key contribution;

> "the dilemma, of course, exists only because the court's interlocutory assessment of the parties' underlying rights **is fallible in the sense that it may be different from the decision that ultimately will be reached.** The danger of incorrect preliminary assessment is the key to the analysis of interlocutory relief. **It requires investigating the harm an erroneous interim decision may cause and trying to minimise that harm.** And it decisively distinguishes the preliminary from the final injunction."[353]

Leubsdorf's contribution thus evolves around two elements: the concept of *uncertainty*, and the *costs of an erroneous decision*: these elements are, it is submitted to a certain degree always present in judicial decisionmaking, but they are particularly present with preliminary injunctions due to the limited amount of scrutiny that takes place. The preliminary injunction *standard* therefore aims *to minimise expected errors* that are likely to occur.[354] Therefore this is indeed a strategy that attempts to lower risk under uncertainty. An added benefit is that, minimising legal errors also has a wider effect than just with the case at hand. Legal errors not only cause direct harm in the present case but they can also have a negative effect on the (future) incentives to obey the law and to bring a lawsuit in general,[355] for instance with respect to infringement claims.

Directly building further upon the idea of Leubsdorf was Posner. This American judge (and esteemed Law and Economics scholar) developed Leubsdorf's view further. Posner subsequently used it later in his scholarly writing as well as in a number

---

350 F.R. ROMEU, 'An economic theory of the regulation of preliminary measures' *European Journal of Law and Economics* 30 (2010), pp. 267–300. See: p. 272, where Romeu also calls the Leubsdorf-Posner approach the "conventional wisdom of Law and Economics scholars." Furthermore, see: J. LEUBSDORF, 'Preliminary injunctions, in defense of the merits' *Fordham Law Review* 76 (2007), pp. 33–47. See: p. 34. R.R.W. BROOKS, W.F. SCHWARTZ, 'Legal uncertainty, economic efficiency, and the preliminary injunction doctrine' *Stanford Law Review* 58 (2005), pp. 380–409. See: p. 392.

351 J. LEUBSDORF, 'The standard for preliminary injunctions' *Harvard Law Review* 91, No. 3 (1978), pp. 525–566.

352 Idem, at p. 541.

353 Ibidem.

354 Ibidem. With an error being that of when the outcome of the preliminary injunction proceeding does not match the subsequent outcome of the trial on the merits.

355 A.M. POLINSKY, S. SHAVELL, 'Legal error, litigation, and the incentive to obey the law' *Journal of Law and Economics and Organisation* (1989), pp. 99–108.

of judgments that he presided.[356] In doing so Posner came up with an economic formula to represent Leubsdorf's initial contribution in a more algebraic manner. A preliminary injunction should then be *granted* to the plaintiff if the following conditions in the formula are satisfied:

$$p\,(H_p) > (1\text{-}p)\,H_d$$

Or, in Posner's words: "Where P is the *probability* that the plaintiff will prevail in the full trial on the merits (and therefore 1-P the probability that the defendant will prevail), H_p is the irreparable harm that the plaintiff will suffer if a preliminary injunction is not granted to maintain the status quo pending the trial and H_d is the irreparable harm the defendant will suffer if the preliminary injunction is granted."[357] The court should thus establish the values of *probabilities* and *harms*. As Romeu notes, the public interest can also be taken along this way: this is done by tweaking the respective magnitudes of the formula elements H_p and $H_{d,}$[358] The likelihood of prevailing on the merits at trial is established, and forms an important part of the approach.[359] Equally, the theory entails that demonstrating irreparable harm is a necessity for obtaining a preliminary injunction, except for 'statutory exceptions' of social policy, where reparable harm can also be a ground to issue a preliminary injunction for social policy reasons.[360]

It is obvious that the Leubsdorf-Posner approach fits well with one of the two main goals Posner has set out for civil litigation, namely minimising expected error costs and minimising litigation costs.[361]

---

356 Most notably R. POSNER in the judgment Federal Circuit of the United States Court of Appeals, 7th Circuit, *American Hospital Supply Corporation v Hospital Products Limited* (1986). For a good background and analysis of this often cited case and how it fits within the American preliminary injunction doctrine, see: A. HEINY, 'Formulating a theory for preliminary injunctions: American Hospital Supply Corp. v Hospital Products Ltd.' *Iowa Law Review* 72 (1987), pp. 1157–1170.

357 R.A. POSNER, *Economic Analysis of Law* (1973 Little, Brown and Co). See: p. 565. Also see: J.P. DAVIS, 'Taking uncertainty seriously: revising injunction doctrine' *Rutgers Law Journal* 34, No. 2 (2003), pp. 362–462. See: esp. p. 380. And also: F.R. ROMEU, 'An economic theory of the regulation of preliminary measures' *European Journal of Law and Economics* 30 (2010), pp. 267–300. See: p. 272.

358 F.R. ROMEU, 'An economic theory of the regulation of preliminary measures' *European Journal of Law and Economics* 30 (2010), pp. 267–300. See: p. 272.

359 J.P. DAVIS, 'Taking uncertainty seriously: revising injunction doctrine' *Rutgers Law Journal* 34, No. 2 (2003), pp. 362–462. See: p. 378. J. LEUBSDORF, 'Preliminary injunctions, in defense of the merits' *Fordham Law Review* 76 (2007), pp. 33–47. See: p. 34.

360 R.R.W. BROOKS, W.F. SCHWARTZ, 'Legal uncertainty, economic efficiency, and the preliminary injunction doctrine' *Stanford Law Review* 58 (2005), pp. 380–409. See: esp. p. 389, at footnote 30 of their article.

361 J.P. DAVIS, 'Taking uncertainty seriously: revising injunction doctrine' *Rutgers Law Journal* 34, No. 2 (2003), pp. 362–462. See: p. 364, for this comment of Posner.

The Leubsdorf-Posner approach has, despite the already described general acclaim, also faced its fair share of criticism: amongst this is for instance that the theory is silent on the role of liability for the harms that a preliminary measure may cause,[362] on the use of mathematics by the judge in establishing values of the parameters[363] (such as harm and probability of success),[364] and for the implicit assumption that judges make no errors.[365]

§5.2.2. A refinement of Leubsdorf's formula: Davis' Modified Framework

The so-called 'Modified Framework', presented by Davis,[366] is an interesting refinement to the Traditional Framework.[367] It attempts to address a main perceived key weaknesses of the Leubsdorf-Posner standard. The framework of Davis is, just as the

---

362 Idem, p. 273. Also see: F.R. ROMEU, 'An economic theory of the regulation of preliminary measures' *European Journal of Law and Economics* 30 (2010), pp. 267–300. See: p. 273.

363 See J.P. DAVIS, 'Taking uncertainty seriously: revising injunction doctrine' *Rutgers Law Journal* 34, No. 2 (2003), pp. 362–462. See: esp. pp. 413–414. F.R. ROMEU, 'An economic theory of the regulation of preliminary measures' *European Journal of Law and Economics* 30 (2010), pp. 267–300. See: p. 274. Also, on this subject, see: R.R.W. BROOKS, W.F. SCHWARTZ, 'Legal uncertainty, economic efficiency, and the preliminary injunction doctrine' *Stanford Law Review* 58 (2005), pp. 380–409. See: p. 407.

364 See for instance the article of Lichtman in which he, it is submitted, persuasively argues that courts are often just as uncertain about estimates of harm as about their prediction of the outcome of a case on the merits. D. LICHTMAN, 'Uncertainty and the standard for preliminary relief' *John M. Olin Law & Economics Working Paper No. 166* (2002). Available at: http://papers.ssrn.com/sol3/papers.cfm?abstract_id=344640 (last accessed on 17 April 2017).

365 This is at the heart of the work by Davis, on which more below. J.P. DAVIS, 'Taking uncertainty seriously: revising injunction doctrine' *Rutgers Law Journal* 34, No. 2 (2003), pp. 362–462. Also see D. LICHTMAN, 'Uncertainty and the standard for preliminary relief' *John M. Olin Law & Economics Working Paper No. 166* (2002). Available at: http://papers.ssrn.com/sol3/papers.cfm?abstract_id=344640 (last accessed on 17 April 2017). See: pp. 2–3.

366 J.P. DAVIS, 'Taking uncertainty seriously: revising injunction doctrine' *Rutgers Law Journal* 34, No. 2 (2003), pp. 362–462.

367 Please note that Davis, in his article speaks about 'The Traditional Framework', under which he means the Leubsdorf-Posner approach, as well as the four-factor test that is used by the US Federal Courts. Although it is submitted that these are to be seen as distinct, in some legal writing however, including Davis' article, these are combined into a single category. One of the reasons for this is because, in practice, US courts sometimes rely on a Leubsdorf-Posner style approach to assist them during actual litigation. See for instance Davis' article at pp. 378–381, esp. at footnotes 59–62. To prevent confusion, the present author has decided to only refer directly to the Leubsdorf-Posner formula in this dissertation.

Leubsdorf-Posner standard, concerned with the minimisation of error costs under the fog of uncertainty.[368] Davis' goal is to minimise these errors costs even further: he argues that *the uncertainty about the merits of a case* should be further taken into account when deciding on the remedy such as a preliminary or final injunction.[369] Instead of seeing (1) the assessment of the merits and (2) the selection of the remedy as two distinct stages, he argues for a more holistic approach.[370]

Key to the Leubsdorf-Posner model, Davis points out, is the *likely result* at the trial, but it may be that this likely result is wrong, something he argues that is generally not considered nor taken along in the Leubsdorf-Posner model.[371] That does "not minimise expected error costs if the actual result at trial *is not necessarily the same* as the right result."[372] Therefore, Davis argues that there is a distinction between the actual result at trial and the right result and this is *because the probability of winning is not the same as probability of being right.* A numerical example that Davis provides in his article may illustrate the idea behind his framework in the best possible way.[373]

---

368 J.P. DAVIS, 'Taking uncertainty seriously: revising injunction doctrine' *Rutgers Law Journal* 34, No. 2 (2003), pp. 362–462. See: esp. p. 368 and p. 378.

369 Idem, at p. 368.

370 Idem, at p. 364 and subsequently pp. 383–387.

371 Idem, at p. 378, at p. 381 and at p. 383.

372 Idem, at p. 383. Emphasis added.

373 Idem, at pp. 384–387. A numerical example, here paraphrased from an example given by Davis in these pages of his article, may point this out best: in this example, a judge finds that Party P (which is the plaintiff) in the preliminary injunction proceeding has submitted evidence that leads the judge to believe that Party P is 60% *is right* about the issue that is contested in litigation (i.e. that the patent is valid or infringed, or that a road is indeed a private road instead of a public road) and that evidence is not conclusive, since decisionmaking happens under the fog of uncertainty. *Based on the evidence* (with emphasis added here) that is presented however, the judge may be confident that the chance of Party P *winning at the actual trial* approximates 95%. The irreparable harm of P is valued on €10.000, if the preliminary injunction is wrongly denied, and of €100.000 of irreparable harm to Party D (which is the defendant) if the preliminary injunction is wrongly granted. The Leubsdorf-Posner formula would lead the judge to grant the preliminary injunction, since the harm that it seeks to minimise is that the plaintiff gets the request denied, but will win at trial. If the court has erroneously denied Party P a preliminary injunction, it will cost Party P $10.000 in harm, with the *expected average harm* from an error to be 0.95 x €10.000. This totals €9.500. Since D has 5% chance of prevailing on trial, and if a preliminary injunction would have been erroneously given, the expected harm on average would be €5.000 (0.05 x €100.000). Since 5.000 is smaller than 9.500, the preliminary injunction is subsequently to be granted by the court. Note that the example of Davis has a more elaborate and different context than is provided by the present author above, but features the same numbers and elements.

Davis' contribution with the Modified Framework is the following: the standard that should be used in the preliminary injunction analysis should measure error more accurately,[374] and *should reflect a judge's degree of confidence* which party *should win* rather than the judges prediction which party *will win* at the trial; thus, the judge should take into account the possibility of an adjudicative error.[375] [376]

In algebraic form, the Modified Framework proposes that a preliminary injunction should be granted to the plaintiff if:

$$Rp \times Hp > (1-Rp) \times Hd.$$[377]

Here, *Rp* is the likelihood that the plaintiff is right, *instead of will prevail at trial as is stipulated in the Leubsdorf-Posner standard, Hp* is the expected irreparable harm to the plaintiff from wrongly denying the injunction, and *Hd* is the expected irreparable harm, to the defendant from incorrectly granting the injunction.[378] *(1-Rp)* is the probability that the defendant *is right* (instead of that he will prevail at trial).

---

374 Idem, at p. 385.

375 A continuation of the (numerical) example from above (footnote 373) again illustrates this well. Again this is paraphrased from the example of Davis in pp. 384–387. Given before was the observation that the court was 60% confident that P *is right* about the issue at hand, i.e. the validity or infringement of a patent or the legal status of a road. Davis' suggestion is then that the PI should be denied to Party P, instead of granted, as would be so under a Leubsdorf-Posner approach. This for the following reason: the judge should follow up on its view that of 60% that the plaintiff is right, rather than think of the likelihood, based on this evidence as presented, that D will win at trial which would be 95%. This leads to an expected average harm for Party P of 0.60 x €10.000 = €6.000. Using the same insight for Party D, this means that the average expected harm from an error about the D's legal rights is 0.40 x €100.000 = €40.000. Since €40.000 is larger than €6.000 the preliminary injunction should be denied This way, the average expected error costs are minimised (in any case relatively to the result as calculated by the Leubsdorf-Posner formula).
The table below summarises the numbers above, where LP is the Leubsdorf-Posner formula and MF Davis' Modified Framework.

Exp Average Harm P under LP	0.95 x €10.000 = €9.500
Exp Average Harm D under LP	0.05 x €100.000 = €5.000
Exp Average Harm P under MF	0.60 x €10.000 = €6.000
Exp Average Harm D under MF	0.40 x €100.000 = €40.000

376 As Davis argues, his approach does not require that the judge casts away the rules that govern civil litigation, but instead for the judge to, within these rules, to take into account the possibility of an error. J.P. DAVIS, 'Taking uncertainty seriously: revising injunction doctrine' *Rutgers Law Journal* 34, No. 2 (2003), pp. 362–462. See: esp. p. 370.

377 Idem, at p. 386.

378 Idem, at p. 386. Note that the example that Davis gives on this page, with the case featuring Penelope and Dwayne, is correct: the given formula on p. 386 seems to the present author, it is submitted, to be incorrectly described.

In doing so, it allows the court for a *much larger degree of discretion* into what it believes is correct. The merits of the case will influence the selection and nature of remedy.[379] This approach allows and prescribes the judge to take into account doubts about the merits she expects to have after trial.[380] The court is then less restricted than under the Leubsdorf-Posner approach to deal with the uncertainty *about the evidence*, in its assessment whether on the basis of this the plaintiff will prevail at trial: after all, the relying on the evidence may create a substantial possibility of error.[381] This way, it is submitted, a higher degree of judicial discretion is used to offer a more balanced approach: just as in the Leubsdorf-Posner formula, a balancing test takes place, but here, a court is allowed to have doubts on the merits presented and it can consider the likelihood of making an error by granting or denying preliminary injunctive relief based on this. In the end, apart from allegedly reducing error costs more than the Leubsdorf-Posner approach does, Davis' Modified Framework is therefore perhaps more comfortable from the perspective of a corrective theory of justice as well.[382, 383]

Davis expects much criticism to his approach, but defends it with vigour.[384] Some criticism that he anticipates is of a similar nature to the Leubsdorf-Posner formula, that has been pointed out above.[385] The lack of space disallows us to review these arguments here. Most notable however, is that Davis argues against the notion that the difficulty in estimating the relative harms and relative likelihood of being right is likely to create *more* errors costs instead of less.[386] He also points out that

379 Idem, at p. 398.

380 Idem, at p. 378.

381 Idem, at p. 374.

382 Note that also Romeu notes that the Leubsdorf-Posner formula is unsatisfactory from a corrective theory of justice point of view. See: F.R. ROMEU, 'An economic theory of the regulation of preliminary measures' *European Journal of Law and Economics* 30 (2010), pp. 267–300. See: p. 274.

383 For further arguments given by Davis on why the Modified Framework should be seen as a better alternative, and on its proposed working in detail, see J.P. DAVIS, 'Taking uncertainty seriously: revising injunction doctrine' *Rutgers Law Journal* 34, No. 2 (2003), pp. 362–462. See: pp. 397–428.

384 Idem, at pp. 398–415.

385 See the accompanying main text at footnote 363 of this dissertation.

386 J.P. DAVIS, 'Taking uncertainty seriously: revising injunction doctrine' *Rutgers Law Journal* 34, No. 2 (2003), pp. 362–462. Davis acknowledges at pp. 401–404 that arguments questioning the uncertainty about the relative harms and the establishing of the likelihood of which party is right (instead of relying on the ordinary burden of persuasion) have some force. These issues, such criticism points out, would increase error costs, instead of reducing them. However, Davis disagrees with this view, and argues that the Modified Framework should reduce errors costs overall: with respect to the establishing of relative harms for instance, Davis points out, with an economics-reasoned response, that as long as the judge correctly gauges which party values a favourable decision more highly, and when he does

a judge does not have to undertake a formal mathematical analysis and that rough estimations are already sufficient.[387]

§5.3. Alternatives to tight judicial control in decisionmaking under uncertainty

Because courts and judges are not infallible and the uncertainty surrounding the legal situation during preliminary proceedings can be high, not all commentators have agreed with the view that judicial control should be this central in the preliminary injunction court's analysis. Various contributions have therefore emerged that can be seen as alternatives to tight judicial control. Illustrative of these are the models proposed by Brooks and Schwartz and to a lesser extent that of Romeu. These models have in common that they give the involved (contesting) parties a much larger role than parties have under the approaches of Leubsdorf-Posner and Davis. This is, as will be seen, based on the assumption that the involved parties can better than the court assess the need for a preliminary injunction on the one hand and the risks associated with an erroneous preliminary injunction on the other hand. These models also propose that preliminary injunctions have a different function within society than merely minimising errors alone.

§5.3.1. The PI liability rule

Whilst the previous two standards can be regarded as strong examples of tight judicial control, the standard proposed by Brooks and Schwartz in their writing can be seen as having a more liability-rule approach.[388] This rule is then also called the 'PI liability rule'.[389] Brooks and Schwartz argue that the main purpose for preliminary

---

not overestimate the ratio of the stakes to the parties (something that the judge can hedge towards the ordinary burden of persuasion) the Modified Framework produces *lower* expected error costs than is the case under the current approach, as used in the American courts (and also by the Leubsdorf-Posner formula).

387 J.P. DAVIS, 'Taking uncertainty seriously: revising injunction doctrine' *Rutgers Law Journal* 34, No. 2 (2003), pp. 362–462. See: p. 413.

388 R.R.W. BROOKS, W.F. SCHWARTZ, 'Legal uncertainty, economic efficiency, and the preliminary injunction doctrine' *Stanford Law Review* 58 (2005), pp. 380–409.

389 Please note that Brooks and Schwartz also come with another, fairly similar rule, named 'The interim efficiency rule'. Both the 'PI liability rule' and 'The interim efficiency rule' approach feature a quasi-automatic grant of preliminary injunctive relief, as long as the court deems the request to be 'not frivolous'. Both also, ignore the merits of the case at hand: the probability of the plaintiff winning later at trial is not important nor is meeting the criterion of 'irreparable harm' any longer required. This 'interim efficiency rule' will not be examined here, since it does not add much to the further analysis. Furthermore, as Leubsdorf submits – also focussing mainly on the PI liability rule in his article – the 'interim efficiency rule' is not entirely clear in all aspects, for instance whether a bond is required or

injunctions should be to offer efficient incentives before and during litigation. According to the authors, the "preliminary injunction proceeding is a dynamic process that compels consideration of ex ante motivations and strategic behaviours".[390] Or in the words of Leubsdorf, who responded directly to the proposal of Brooks and Schwartz in an essay, their approach "seeks rather to promote efficient conduct during the litigation by removing the incentives of parties to act inefficiently in the hope that the court will not hold them liable."[391] The approach thus entails that a preliminary injunction should be granted in order to induce socially benefical behaviour during the pendency of litigation.[392]

The PI liability rule that Brooks and Schwartz propose stipulates that a preliminary injunction would be almost always quasi-automatically awarded by the court when requested by the plaintiff, and when there is (1) uncertainty over the correct result of the case and this uncertainty is established;[393] (2) in the plaintiff's request a genuine (i.e. a "non frivolous") issue over an entitlement is shown;[394] and (3) the plaintiff is prepared to assume full liability, for when it turns out that at the conclusion of the trial on the merits, the preliminary injunction was granted incorrectly.[395] In doing so, the plaintiff will obtain the preliminary injunction if it posts a (high) bond and guarantees to be fully liable for the defendants' costs should the latter eventually win.[396] This way according to Brooks and Schwartz, inefficiency is avoided whilst offering compensation too: the plaintiff will only request a preliminary injunction *if its gain from obtaining one is higher than the costs it imposes on the other party*.[397] An added benefit of the PI liability rule is that the court no longer

not. See also p. 41 at footnote 40 of J. LEUBSDORF, 'Preliminary injunctions, in defense of the merits' *Fordham Law Review* 76 (2007), pp. 33–47.

390 R.R.W. BROOKS, W.F. SCHWARTZ, 'Legal uncertainty, economic efficiency, and the preliminary injunction doctrine' *Stanford Law Review* 58 (2005), pp. 380–409. See: p. 386.

391 J. LEUBSDORF, 'Preliminary injunctions, in defense of the merits' *Fordham Law Review* 76 (2007), pp. 33–47.

392 R.R.W. BROOKS, W.F. SCHWARTZ, 'Legal uncertainty, economic efficiency, and the preliminary injunction doctrine' *Stanford Law Review* 58 (2005), pp. 380–409, esp. p. 390; J. LEUBSDORF, 'Preliminary injunctions, in defense of the merits' *Fordham Law Review* 76 (2007), pp. 33–47. See: p. 34.

393 Idem, at p. 33.

394 Idem, at p. 35.

395 R.R.W. BROOKS, W.F. SCHWARTZ, 'Legal uncertainty, economic efficiency, and the preliminary injunction doctrine' *Stanford Law Review* 58 (2005), pp. 380–409. See: pp. 405–406.

396 J. LEUBSDORF, 'Preliminary injunctions, in defense of the merits' *Fordham Law Review* 76 (2007), pp. 33–47. See: p. 33. Also see: R.R.W. BROOKS, W.F. SCHWARTZ, 'Legal uncertainty, economic efficiency, and the preliminary injunction doctrine' *Stanford Law Review* 58 (2005), pp. 380–409. See: p. 405.

397 J. LEUBSDORF, 'Preliminary injunctions, in defense of the merits' *Fordham Law Review* 76 (2007), pp. 33–47. See: p. 35. Again, also see R.R.W. BROOKS,

has to conduct a comparative analysis of the irreparable harms, but only look at the defendant's compliance costs.[398] As can be seen too, establishing the probability of winning (the likelihood of success) is taken out of the court's hands almost completely. Brooks and Schwartz point out that the PI liability rule is especially compelling in the case of asymmetric information amongst the litigating parties and the court. This is something that they deem, correctly it is submitted, often to be the case in preliminary injunction proceedings.[399]

The PI liability rule thus entails four key differences with the approaches of Leubsdorf-Posner and Davis as described above: Firstly, the requirement of 'irreparable harm' is completely removed from the picture: this is because both *reparable* as *irreparable injury* should be prevented by a preliminary injunction, if this is the most efficient result.[400] Therefore, the court does not need to engage in an analysis of irreparable harms.[401] Also, a second difference is that according to the PI liability rule, any ex post compensation cannot eliminate the social loss that stems from earlier inefficient conduct.[402] Thirdly, the merits of the case (e.g. did infringement occur, and is the patent valid?) are considered to be mostly irrelevant. Lastly, it is clear that the role of the court has been largely marginalised and limited to checking the non-frivolous nature of the plaintiff's request.

The PI liability rule has been criticised by Leubsdorf himself. He argues that the PI liability rule undermines the rights conferred by the law: a plaintiff can then easily enjoin the defendant without much regard of the latter's substantive rights but almost solely on the basis that he believes his activities are more efficient or

---

W.F. SCHWARTZ, 'Legal uncertainty, economic efficiency, and the preliminary injunction doctrine' *Stanford Law Review* 58 (2005), pp. 380–409. See: p. 405. It is submitted, that the wording and examples given by Leubsdorf, in his response to Brooks and Schwartz, are more clear than the examples given by Brooks and Schwartz. In their given example, the plaintiff uses an injunction to compel the defendant to fulfil a contract; this instead of the enjoining function of an injunction that is at the heart of the dissertation. It is submitted here that the underlying idea of Brooks and Schwartz is not changed.

398 R.R.W. BROOKS, W.F. SCHWARTZ, 'Legal uncertainty, economic efficiency, and the preliminary injunction doctrine' *Stanford Law Review* 58 (2005), pp. 380–409. See: p. 405.

399 Idem, at p. 405.

400 Idem, p. 405. Also see: J. LEUBSDORF, 'Preliminary injunctions, in defense of the merits' *Fordham Law Review* 76 (2007), pp. 33–47. See: p. 33.

401 R.R.W. BROOKS, W.F. SCHWARTZ, 'Legal uncertainty, economic efficiency, and the preliminary injunction doctrine' *Stanford Law Review* 58 (2005), pp. 380–409. See: p. 405 and also J. LEUBSDORF, 'Preliminary injunctions, in defense of the merits' *Fordham Law Review* 76 (2007), pp. 33–47. See: esp. p. 33 and pp. 37–39.

402 R.R.W. BROOKS, W.F. SCHWARTZ, 'Legal uncertainty, economic efficiency, and the preliminary injunction doctrine' *Stanford Law Review* 58 (2005), pp. 380–409. See: p. 393.

profitable and when he is willing to take on full liability.[403] Also, with respect to relying on such compensation, it has already been pointed out that monetary damages do not always make whole.[404] A bond too has its limits.[405] Furthermore, whilst uncertainty may often be problematic for the court, this is not an absolute and there are different degrees of uncertainty.[406] Grosskopf and Medina additionally point out that relying on damages-based liability may lead to over-deterrence and that this offers the wrong incentives to the plaintiff to opt for a preliminary injunction.[407] Lastly, it is submitted by the present author that since the occurrence of irreparable harm and the merits is no longer evaluated, this can amount to denial of due process.

It is indeed submitted that the PI liability rule goes rather far and it is agreed upon with what Grosskopf and Medina conclude: the approach of Brooks and Schwartz seems an interesting but unpractical approach. Interesting since it shows the effects of preliminary injunctions on a plaintiff's ex ante incentives,[408] but at the same time it seems unpractical as it will be very difficult to make a plaintiff fully internalise the consequences of a wrongly-issued preliminary injunction.[409] Thus, it is here agreed with the abovementioned criticism of Leubsdorf and Grosskopf and Medina that it is better that the judges have a higher degree of judicial discretion and should be allowed to consider the merits of the case.[410]

---

403 J. LEUBSDORF, 'Preliminary injunctions, in defense of the merits' *Fordham Law Review* 76 (2007) pp. 33–47. See: pp. 36–37.

404 Idem, p. 41. A similar observation to this aspect of the model of Brooks and Schwartz has been made by O. GROSSKOPF, B. MEDINA, 'Remedies for Wrongfully-Issued Preliminary Injunctions: The Case for the Disgorgement of Profits' *Seattle University Law Review* 32 (2009), pp. 903–94. See: p. 932.

405 J. LEUBSDORF, 'Preliminary injunctions, in defense of the merits' *Fordham Law Review* 76 (2007), pp. 33–47. See: pp. 40–43, where the author points out that the magnitude of injunction bonds is difficult to assess, that bonds can offer inadequate compensation and that the need to post a bond may make the remedy unavailable for certain plaintiffs.

406 Idem, at p. 36.

407 O. GROSSKOPF, B. MEDINA, 'Remedies for Wrongfully-Issued Preliminary Injunctions: The Case for the Disgorgement of Profits' *Seattle University Law Review* 32 (2009), pp. 903–94. See: p. 933.

408 Idem, at p. 934.

409 Idem, at p. 933.

410 Leubsdorf concludes: "There is little foundation for courts to disregard the strength of a plaintiff's claim or the irreparable threatening to parties, or to rely on the plaintiff's fear of liability under the injunction bond as the unique safeguard against improvident relief." See: J. LEUBSDORF, 'Preliminary injunctions, in defense of the merits' *Fordham Law Review* 76 (2007), pp. 33–47. See: p. 47. Also see: O. GROSSKOPF, B. MEDINA, 'Remedies for Wrongfully-Issued Preliminary Injunctions: The Case for the Disgorgement of Profits' *Seattle University Law Review* 32 (2009), pp. 903–941. See: p. 934.

§5.3.2. *Romeu's dual standard*

Neatly wedged between the two extremes of tight judicial control and a liability approach, there is yet another theoretical alternative to be explored. Romeu in his article at first scrutinises the characteristics, the advantages and the disadvantages of both liability-based and judicial control.[411] Based on his findings, Romeu proposes a *dual standard* as a general civil law theory – thus beyond the scope of patent infringement alone – on how to deal with requests for a preliminary injunction.[412] He argues in favour of a (strict) liability regime that should deal with the request first, in a summary manner, however, as a second stage, he prescribes a more elaborate standard of review by the court in the form of tighter judicial control if this determined to be necessary.[413] The latter would be the case when the liability system fails,[414] i.e. in failing to filter for absolutely undesirable measures, when monetary damages cannot make whole adequately and when third parties cannot bring a claim, meaning that their interests are not taken along in any way.[415] This way expected harms are minimised.[416]

As Romeu explains, the legal test is therefore worded as follows:

> "The Court shall grant the request for an interlocutory injunction if, cumulatively, (1) the claim is not unviable (2) risks derived from the delay are not inexistent and (3) the plaintiff is notoriously solvent (if not a bond is requested). However, in cases in which the preliminary measure can cause irreparable harm that it would be difficult to repair in monetary terms, the judge shall issue the measure only if the harm that it shall cause is not greater than the harm that it can avoid, taking into account

411 F.R. ROMEU, 'An economic theory of the regulation of preliminary measures' *European Journal of Law and Economics* 30 (2010), pp. 267–300. See: pp. 277–282, Romeu concludes that in his view, a liability regime for harms is a more optimal way of regulation than judicial control. He mentions that liability control is speedier than judicial control, generates less administrative costs and is less prone to create judicial errors since establishing liability happens at a later stage with more information and under less time pressure.

412 F.R. ROMEU, 'An economic theory of the regulation of preliminary measures' *European Journal of Law and Economics* 30 (2010), pp. 267–300. See: pp. 297–298.

413 Idem, at p. 298.

414 Idem, at p. 281 ("the judicial control of preliminary measures should be used only when the liability system may fail").

415 Idem, at pp. 279–282.

416 F.R. ROMEU, 'An economic theory of the regulation of preliminary measures' *European Journal of Law and Economics* 30 (2010), pp. 267–300. See: esp. pp. 275 and p. 273. Whilst not explicitly mentioned, Romeu states that he in this paper takes the goal of the Leubsdorf-Posner standard for granted, in providing a good answer *when a measure is desirable* (namely, the minimisation of expected harms). Also, see his writing on p. 279, which is on judicial errors and the virtues of the liability system.

> the probability that the plaintiff's claim will be accepted and the types of harms that both parties can suffer."[417, 418]

Romeu's contribution is not specifically written with patent litigation in mind[419] and it is clear that his approach hinges on the idea that most cases can be dealt with at the first stage, with the judge exercising summary control, whilst a smaller number of lesser suitable cases for such an approach are dealt with in the second stage under a more intense and elaborate level of review by the court.[420] Romeu has not written explicitly what occurs regarding liability in the case of an erroneous decision. However, in this, the first (liability) stage presupposes that the plaintiff is liable for an erroneous decision. Romeu has expressed his favour for a strict liability regime elsewhere.[421] Furthemore, it is clear that merits play a scarce role at the first stage, namely only to establish whether the claim is not unviable in the first place. The merits have more influence in the second category of cases. Equally, it is evident what the role of 'irreprable harm' is in this test; irreparable harm invokes a test with a higher standard of review for those cases at the second stage.[422]

Whilst Romeu's approach is an interesting contribution to the (debate on the) development of a new standard for preliminary injunctions in general civil litigation, the actual viability of such a standard with respect to specifically patent litigation is questionable because, it is here submitted, injunctions in this area can lead to numerous examples in which the liability system fails. We have seen that this is the case when the interests of other parties, such as consumers, would not be taken along and because of the notion that monetary damages do not always make the damage by an erroneously granted preliminary injunction undone, as is exemplified by deadweight losses. However, Romeu's approach does provide an interesting view on how the judicial standard in granting preliminary injunctions can differ, depending on the *suitability* of a case. It should be noted that Romeu too, just as Brooks and Schwartz puts emphasis on the view that the optimal filtering of preliminary measures is at first by virtue of a liability regime[423] and there should be less emphasis on judicial control. Unlike Brooks and Schwartz seem to do however,

---

417 Idem, at p. 297.

418 It is submitted that, as one can see, this 'second step' of Romeu's contribution is based on the Leubsdorf-Posner approach.

419 In fact, F.R. ROMEU, 'An economic theory of the regulation of preliminary measures' *European Journal of Law and Economics* 30 (2010), pp. 267–300. See: p. 269 states that the focus of his work is on preliminary measures that are adopted in civil litigation cases involving patrimonial issues.

420 Idem, at p. 298.

421 Idem, at pp. 285–286.

422 F.R. ROMEU, 'An economic theory of the regulation of preliminary measures' *European Journal of Law and Economics* 30 (2010), pp. 267–300. See: pp. 297–298.

423 See footnote 411, above.

Romeu recognises the shortcomings of a liability regime and explicitly provides exceptions to this, leading to the second stage of his standard.[424]

§5.3.3. The relative consequences model of Norrgård

Yet another alternative approach is provided for by the author Marcus Norrgård,[425] who argues for a model that makes the *threshold to obtain a preliminary injunction* completely dependent on the interests of the parties.[426] This is an, as he calls it, *inverse sequential approach*, where the *economic harm of the parties influences the standard of proof* that the plaintiff should fulfil – that is, to prove the likelihood of success on infringement and validity – in order to gain a preliminary injunction.[427] It therefore differs from the Leubsdorf-Posner approach, which is a model that *concurrently* determines both aspects, something which is more difficult to apply and can result into higher (magnified) errors being made. The approach of Norrgård would mean that:

> "the graver the consequences of the plaintiff compared with the defendant's consequences, the lower the threshold for a preliminary injunction, and the other way around: the greater the harm to the defendant (compared to the plaintiff's) the higher the threshold. (...)"[428]

Assessing the economic consequences of a preliminary injunction is thus vital and should be the starting point of the court's analysis in making a decision on this, as this influences the burden of proof. Key to this view, is the notion that economic consequences are *relative* of nature:

> "If the defendant's harm from being enjoined is very small compared to the applicant's harm from not being granted a preliminary injunction, it could suffice that the applicant proves that there is "a serious question" to be tried. In patent cases, such situations might be quite rare, but still it is possible that the defendant has engaged in infringing activities with a small investment and without a loss of revenue if the injunction is granted, whereas the loss to the plaintiff might be substantial in case of an infringement."[429]

---

424 F.R. ROMEU, 'An economic theory of the regulation of preliminary measures' *European Journal of Law and Economics* 30 (2010), pp. 267–300. See: p. 298.

425 M. NORRGÅRD, *Interimistiskaförbud i immaterialrätten* (2002 Kauppakaari Förlag).

426 M.L. NORRGÅRD, A. NYLUND, 'The requirements for preliminary injunctions in the unified patent court' in R.M. BALLARDINI, M.L. NORRGÅRD, G.N. BRUUN, *Transitions in European Patent Law: Influences of the European Patent Package* (2015 Kluwer International Law Publishing), pp. 189–206. See: p. 204.

427 Ibidem.

428 Idem, at p. 204.

429 Idem, at p. 204 (sic).

Also, as another consequence of this *relative nature*, is the notion that €1 million in harm is considered to be less harm for an economically strong party than the same amount is for an economically weak party.[430] This model then also implies that if infringement *is obviously clear* (and is likely to be confirmed at trial later), the nature of the harm does not matter and then an assessment of the harms of the defendant should not take place,[431] as the latter would influence the former in that case.

However, in most cases, *where infringement is not immediately obvious*, the situation is as follows: when the economic harms of the plaintiff outweigh those of the defendant, this should entitle the plaintiff to a preliminary injunction when the likelihood that infringement has occurred (and will be confirmed at trial later), is larger than it has not.[432] Finally, it should be stressed that with this approach, unlike in the Leubsdorf-Posner theory, the proof of 'irreparable harm' is not required per se for the grant of a preliminary injunction. It is about relative economic harm for the parties, where the economic strength of a party in dealing with a certain magnitude of harm also plays a role.[433]

§5.4. Chapter conclusion

As can be seen from above, there seem to be two main schools of thought on how a preliminary injunction request should be handled. Arguing for tight judicial control are the approaches of Leubsdorf-Posner and Davis and to a certain extent Norrgård, whilst the liability rule is endorsed by Brooks and Schwartz and to a certain extent by Romeu. All these approaches attempt to offer a better solution, from a Law and Economics theoretical perspective, in reducing the chance that a non-optimal preliminary injunction is taken.

Of course, the above-mentioned contributions are both simplified and highly stylised models of reality, and they cannot (easily) be used and applied one-on-one

430 M. NORRGÅRD, *Interimistiskaförbud i immaterialrätten* (2002 Kauppakaari Förlag). See: p. 342.

431 M.L. NORRGÅRD, A. NYLUND, 'The requirements for preliminary injunctions in the unified patent court' in R.M. BALLARDINI, M.L. NORRGÅRD, G.N. BRUUN, *Transitions in European Patent Law: Influences of the European Patent Package* (2015 Kluwer International Law Publishing), pp. 189–206 and also C.S. PETERSEN, *Immaterialrettigheder og foreløbige forbud* (2008 Jurist- og Økonomforbundets Forl.). See: p. 204.

432 M.L. NORRGÅRD, A. NYLUND, 'The requirements for preliminary injunctions in the unified patent court' in R.M. BALLARDINI, M.L. NORRGÅRD, G.N. BRUUN, *Transitions in European Patent Law: Influences of the European Patent Package* (2015 Kluwer International Law Publishing), pp. 189–206. See: p. 204.

433 C.S. PETERSEN, *Immaterialrettigheder og foreløbige forbud* (2008 Jurist- og Økonomforbundets Forl.). See: pp. 296–297.

in patent litigation cases in practice.[434, 435] Therefore it is submitted that the *main value* of these theoretical models is to be seen in the fact that they point out alternatives, certain strengths and weaknesses of different approaches and issues that the court may encounter when deciding on a request for a preliminary injunction in practice. They also show the relevance of certain decisions and certain variables in the overall process of decisionmaking.

Some more specific takeaways can be noted down as well:

- Most theories put the court (or judge) central to the decisionmaking in deciding on the grant of a preliminary injunction, and highlight that the court should have discretion in doing so.[436]
- In almost all cases, the purported role of the legal standard is to reduce the chance of the court making an erroneous decision.[437]
- The majority of tests take require the court to somehow take into account the parties' interests and hardships (i.e. the economic consequences of granting or denying a preliminary injunction to the parties).[438]
- The strength of the case (the merits, i.e. the likelihood of success at trial) plays a role in the majority of tests as well at some stage.[439] The exact role of the merits however differs between the approaches, and ranges from mainly determining the likelihood of winning at trial to actually influencing the threshold.
- All tests require the court to at the very least filter for abusive practices of applying for a preliminary injunction.
- The various approaches differ whether solely irreparable harm can warrant the grant of a preliminary injunction, or whether a preliminary injunction can also be issued in cases of *reparable* harm. Also, it is clear that the nature of the harm can sometimes influence the outcome of the test.
- Urgency does not play an explicit role in any of the tests and – given that all approaches are non patent specific, but more general of nature – neither does patent validity. Both are, as will be seen, critical factors in actual practice. It is noted however, that these factors can be taken along in a 'likelihood of winning' factor that is sometimes prescribed in the theoretical approaches.

---

434 The exception to this is the Leubsdorf-Posner model, that has been used in some real-life cases, for instance by judge Posner himself.

435 One complication is that the models are tailored towards litigation in general and not purely towards patent litigation. Only that of Norrgård is more specifically in the context of intellectual property.

436 In favour: Leubsdorf-Posner, Davis and Norrgård. Against: Brooks/Schwartz and in some cases Romeu. Davis puts the role of the judge most central.

437 In favour: Leubsdorf-Posner, Davis, Norrgård and Romeu, exception: Brooks/Schwartz.

438 The exception to this is only the theory of Brooks/Schwartz and in extreme cases Norrgård when there is clear and obvious patent infringement.

439 With again as the exception to this, is the model of Brooks/Schwartz.

- There seem to be differing views between the approaches on the amount of liability a plaintiff should incur in the case an erroneous decision to grant a preliminary injunction is taken.[440]

It is therefore difficult to select one optimal theoretical model from the given alternatives, as a benchmark for regulating preliminary injunctions. All have characteristics speaking out in favour or against them. Instead, and this is also more relevant for legal practice, it is deducted from the majority of the teachings of these theoretical approaches, that it is vital that the legal system ensures – at an *absolute minimum* – that:

- The court is central to decisionmaking and has discretion to grant or deny a preliminary injunction.
- The court is key, in order to balance interests of litigating parties and third parties, and filter for abusive practices.
- The merits of a case should play a role in this decisionmaking process.

Lastly, Romeu adds that in any case, whatever standard a jurisdiction may decide on, it is crucial that this should be formulated clearly. This is not so in current practice, Romeu submits, and he argues that courts in both Civil Law and Common Law countries have disregarded the language of statutes regarding the degree of judicial control, liability and bond requirements, resulting into what he calls ineffectiveness, legal uncertainty and deep confusion.[441] Furthermore, he also writes that "the optimal standard of review may differ from legal sector to legal sector, and from types of cases to types of cases."[442] And this, it is submitted here, is indeed an idea that is worth taking further. In that light, it can therefore be argued that a detachment from the general system of civil litigation, with the formation of more specialised and dedicated courts like the UPC – thereby for instance having the possibility of setting an own standard of review and creating a specific legal test – may then be seen as a step taken in the right direction.

---

440 The theories of Leubsdorf-Posner, Davis and Norrgård are silent on this. Although not commented on by the authors, it is here assumed that judges may then fall back on the given liability practice that already exists in a country. Note that Brooks/Schwartz and Romeu are, or seem to be, in favour of (strict) liability, because then the plaintiff internalises the risk of opting for a preliminary injunction, something that is central to their view. Also placing plaintiff-liability central, but then with a different outcome, is the work of Grosskopf and Medina. Although their work is not mentioned in the comparative overview of this chapter, it is interesting to add that they have opted for a benefits-based liability, taking away the profits of the plaintiff. See footnote 275 of this dissertation.

441 F.R. ROMEU, 'An economic theory of the regulation of preliminary measures' *European Journal of Law and Economics* 30 (2010), pp. 267–300. See: p. 297.

442 Ibidem.

§5.5. A schematic overview of different Law & Economics theories

	The Leubsdorf-Posner rule (1978)	Modified framework (Davis 2003)	The PI – Liability rule (Brooks / Schwartz 2005)	Dual Standard (Romeu 2010)	Relative consequences model (Norrgård 2002)
What is the aim of the PI standard?	To minimise expected error costs that occur due to uncertainty. A PI is only desirable if the expected harm of the plaintiff from not granting the PI, outweighs the expected harm that the defendant shall suffer by grant of the PI	To minimise expected error costs, by taking into account the possibility of adjudicative error, thereby acknowledging uncertainty	A PI should be granted to induce socially beneficial behaviour during the pendency of litigation	To offer a double standard of liability and judicial control, thereby having many of the advantages of the liability model whilst offering judicial control as well for when the liability system fails. This way, expected harms are minimised	To offer a (flexible) threshold to obtain a preliminary injunction which is completely dependent on the interests of the parties
Role of the judge?	Strong judicial control	Very strong judicial control	Limited judicial control	Limited judicial control, but more intense when required	Mostly strong judicial control

	The Leubsdorf-Posner rule (1978)	Modified framework (Davis 2003)	The PI – Liability rule (Brooks / Schwartz 2005)	Dual Standard (Romeu 2010)	Relative consequences model (Norrgård 2002)
Main test?	Focus on probability of winning as well as harm to the parties of the PI decision. Looks at the probability of plaintiff winning on trial, multiplied with the irreparable harm for the plaintiff without a PI granted, compared with the probability of the defendant of winning, multiplied by the irreparable harm for the defendant with a PI The former probability should be larger than the latter, if a PI is to be granted. The probability is established based on the evidence as presented	Reflects a judge's degree of confidence which party *is right* rather than the judge's prediction which party *will win after trial based on the evidence as presented* Thus taking into account the possibility of adjudicative error. The likelihood that the plaintiff is right, multiplied with the irreparable harm for the plaintiff with incorrectly denying a PI, compared with the probability of the plaintiff being wrong, multiplied by the irreparable harm for the defendant from incorrectly granting a PI	Quasi-automatic injunction of interim injunctive relief: The PI would be awarded when a non-frivolous issue over entitlement is shown and the plaintiff is prepared to assume liability (via a bond)	Two level test: The court shall grant the request for a preliminary injunction if, cumulatively, (1) the claim is not unviable (2) risks derived from the delay are not inexistent and (3) the plaintiff is seen as solvent (if not, a bond is requested). However, in case of (a) irreparable harm that is difficult to repair in monetary terms, the judge shall issue the measure only if the harm that the PI can cause is not greater than the harm that it can avoid, thereby taking into account the (b) probability that the plaintiff's claim will be accepted and the (c) types of harms that both parties can suffer	A sequential consideration of harms and likelihood, instead of a concurrent assessment of these elements as under the Leubsdorf-Posner model The graver the consequences of the plaintiff compared with the defendant's consequences, the lower the threshold for a preliminary injunction, and the other way around: the greater the harm to the defendant (compared to the plaintiff's) the higher the threshold

	The Leubsdorf-Posner rule (1978)	Modified framework (Davis 2003)	The PI – Liability rule (Brooks / Schwartz 2005)	Dual Standard (Romeu 2010)	Relative consequences model (Norrgård 2002)
Liability for wrong decision?	Theory silent on this	Theory silent on this	Full liability for plaintiff, this is established through a (high) bond	Theory is not explicit in this, but the first (liability) stage presupposes that the plaintiff is liable for an erroneous decision. Romeu has expressed his favour for a strict liability regime elsewhere in his article	Theory silent on this
Anticipation of the strength of the case (merits)?	The likelihood of prevailing on the merits at trial is established, and forms an important part of the approach	Merits influence selection and nature of remedy. Approach allows and prescribes the judge to take into account doubts about the merits he expects to have after trial	Merits of the case are scarcely considered, only to establish uncertainty and whether abuse does not take place	Merits play a scarce role at the first stage, only to establish whether the claim is not unviable. They have more influence in the second category of cases	Merits influence the threshold that is used to grant a preliminary injunction
The role of irreparable injury?	Demonstrating irreparable harm is a necessity for a preliminary injunction, except for 'statutory exceptions' of social policy, where reparable harm can also be a ground to issue a preliminary injunction for social policy reasons		Both reparable as irreparable injury should be prevented by a PI; it is the most efficient result that matters. Therefore, the court does not need to engage in an analysis of irreparable harms	Irreparable harm invokes a test for with a higher standard of review (stage two cases)	Unlike Leubsdorf-Posner, irreparable harm is not required. It is about relative economic harm for the parties, where the economic strength of a party in dealing with harm also plays a role

Source: the respective works of the mentioned authors, as cited in this chapter.

Part II: International and National Law

Chapter 6: International and European Obligations and Preliminary Injunctions

§6.1. Introduction

As will be seen, preliminary injunctions have their roots in three different levels of legislation: on the international level, for European countries on the European (and EU) level and, last but not least, they also have a basis in the national legal frameworks of individual states. This chapter focusses on the obligations stemming from International Law and European (Union) law. Subject to review here are the following sources of law: the TRIPS Agreement, the EU Enforcement Directive, the European Convention of Human Rights and the Brussels Regulation. The former two sources were specifically drafted for intellectual property law enforcement. Whilst the latter two are not, they without a doubt also have effect on litigation in this area. All the sources of law mentioned in this chapter remain of relevance with the start of the UPC Agreement.

§6.2. The international level: the TRIPS Agreement

The United States and the predecessor of the EU, the European Community, have pushed for a common minimum of protection of intellectual property at the International Law level. They did so already at the time of early GATT-TRIPS[443] negotiations at the end of the 1980s and in the early 1990s.[444] The signatories of TRIPS, namely Members of the World Trade Organisation (WTO) – now encompassing most nations in the world – have thereby agreed on common principles and minimum standards for the protection of intellectual property rights.

The TRIPS Agreement, effective since January 1st 1995, not only stipulates key principles which form the cornerstone of trade and intellectual property exploitation – for example the Most Favoured Nation principle[445] and the principle of

---

443 The General Agreement on Tariffs and Trade (GATT) is, together with The Agreement on Trade Related aspects of Intellectual Property Rights (TRIPS), one of the main pillars of World Trade Organisation (WTO) membership.

444 J. STRAUS, 'Reversal of the Burden of Proof, the Principle of 'Fair and Equitable Procedures' and Preliminary Injunctions under TRIPS Agreement' *Journal of World Intellectual Property* 3, No. 6 (2000), pp. 807–823. See: p. 812.

445 Art. 4 TRIPS provides that, subject to certain exceptions, advantages in the context of intellectual property rights given to the nationals of one Member to the Agreement, should also be provided to the nationals of all other Member States to the Agreement.

National Treatment[446] – but it also prescribes minimum standards on a whole range of other topics concerning the protection of intellectual property rights, including those concerning (interim) enforcement measures.

With respect to the enforcement of intellectual property rights in general, Art. 41 (2) TRIPS obliges Member countries that enforcement should be *effective* and *fair*. Signatory countries should provide expeditious remedies to prevent infringements and remedies which constitute a deterrent to further infringements.[447] The actual minimum standards relating specifically to *provisional* enforcement measures are stated in Section 3, Part 3 of TRIPS. This section consists of merely one article, namely Art. 50. The key paragraphs of this article are to be given here in full and the most important elements for preliminary injunctions are highlighted in bold:

> 1. The judicial authorities shall have the authority to order **prompt and effective** provisional measures:
> (a) **to prevent an infringement of any intellectual property right from occurring**, and in particular to prevent the entry into the channels of commerce in their jurisdiction of goods, including imported goods immediately after customs clearance;
> (b) to preserve relevant evidence in regard to the alleged infringement.
>
> 2. The judicial authorities shall have the authority to adopt provisional measures inaudita altera parte where appropriate, in particular where any delay is likely to cause irreparable harm to the right holder, or where there is a demonstrable risk of evidence being destroyed.
> 3. The judicial authorities shall have the authority to require the applicant to provide any reasonably available evidence in order to satisfy themselves with a sufficient degree of certainty that the applicant is the right holder and that the applicant's right is being infringed or that such infringement is imminent, and to order the applicant to provide a security or equivalent assurance sufficient to protect the defendant and to prevent abuse.
> 4. Where provisional measures have been adopted inaudita altera parte, the parties affected shall be given notice, without delay after the execution of the measures at the latest. A review, including a right to be heard, shall take place upon request of the defendant with a view to deciding, within a reasonable period after the notification of the measures, whether these measures shall be modified, revoked or confirmed.
> 5. (..) Omitted here.
> 6. (..) Omitted here.

---

446 Art. 3.1. TRIPS stipulates that Members to the Agreement shall not treat nationals of other states worse than their own nationals regarding the protection of intellectual property rights. Note that this concept was introduced already in the Bern and Paris Conventions before.

447 Art. 41 (1) TRIPS.

7. Where the provisional measures are revoked or where they lapse due to any act or omission by the applicant, or where it is subsequently found that there has been no infringement or threat of infringement of an intellectual property right, the judicial authorities shall have the authority to order the applicant, upon request of the defendant, **to provide the defendant appropriate compensation for any injury caused by these measures**.
8. To the extent that any provisional measure can be ordered as a result of administrative procedures, such procedures shall conform to principles equivalent in substance to those set forth in this Section.

As can be seen and as can be expected with these types of general agreements that are signed by a vast number of different countries (each with different political, economic and legal characteristics and diverse growth trajectories) only a very loosely defined baseline is set, resulting in true minimum standards.[448] Note that common concepts in some preliminary injunction tests such as a requirement of 'urgency' and 'balancing of interests' are not mentioned for instance. Also, as with other provisions in Part 3 of TRIPS, the wording of the provision merely defines the results to be achieved, rather than stipulating how to do so. Art. 50 TRIPS also lacks the elements necessary to make it directly operative in the courts of most countries.[449]

Despite this, Art. 50 TRIPS sets some important conditions which should be take into account by the signatories of the Agreement. First and foremost, the signatories to TRIPS have agreed, in the first and third paragraphs of Art. 50, on the need that provisional measures *should* exist, that they should be *effective* and that these measures are *principally* to be decided upon by a court.[450] Furthermore, a key notion is stated in Art. 50 (3) TRIPS, in recognising that courts are not infallible certainly at this stage of the proceedings. The Article sets the level of required evidence with some nuance, thereby taking into account the

---

448 This does by no means imply that the present author is of the opinion that the drafters of TRIPS have been too little ambitious in their work nor that TRIPS is not an important international agreement. It is actually of great significance, especially in the political context and in establishing more equal (trade) conditions between a large and diverse set of countries, most notably between developed and lesser developed countries. Art. 50 is even more relevant for countries which did not provide a similar level of protection before. However, despite this, one should still recognise the facts that TRIPS only establishes a general legal framework on many issues, including interim relief, and also that many Western countries already had a system in place for preliminary injunctions in patent disputes prior to TRIPS. These were largely aligned with the obligations that were later prescribed by the TRIPS Agreement.

449 C.M. CORREA, *TRIPS, A Commentary on the TRIPS Agreement* (2007 Oxford University Press). See: p. 434.

450 Nevertheless, note that Art. 50 (8) TRIPS, under certain conditions also gives the possibility for administrative authorities to take certain provisional decisions.

uncertainty and swift nature that forms a hallmark of preliminary injunction proceedings. This results into the wording of 'reasonably available' and 'has to lead to a '*sufficient* degree of certainty'. Equally, it is stated in Art. 50 (3) that the judicial authorities of states can require some form of security for compensatory purposes, should the decision to grant interim relief prove to be wrong, as well as to prevent abusive practices.

In doing the above, it is submitted that the drafters of Art. 50 of TRIPS have done two things: firstly, they have made *some* form of injunctive interim relief for the enforcement of intellectual property rights mandatory for all signatories. Secondly, they have set a few minimum requirements that function as checks and balances and which are also aimed at preventing abuse of the mechanism to obtain a preliminary injunction. These are that the grant of preliminary injunctions is subject to some degree of judicial control and there is some form of security or compensation available in the case of an erroneous decision.[451] Furthermore, the grant of the request is subject to the plaintiff providing sufficient evidence.[452] Lastly, a reasonable period in which a proceeding on the merits should be initiated is demanded.[453] These elements are all laudable.

At the same time, Art. 50 TRIPS does *not do much more* than lay down an absolute minimum, leaving a more precise implementation completely up to the Member States. Although this is wholly understandable considering the economic and political differences between the signatories of the TRIPS Agreement, this also opens the door to potential legal divergences and differences in the way jurisdictions deal with a request for a preliminary injunction. Nevertheless, it is clear that Art. 50 TRIPS is in line with other provisions of the TRIPS Agreement, in the sense that the drafters were, as with other provisions, reluctant in stipulating further detailed procedures that should be taken into account by the signatories. Additionally, this lack of specifics may not be negative per se and such criticism can be turned on its head: the wording of TRIPS allows the signatories plenty of flexibility and manoeuvring room for their own legal tradition and own policy accents.

Having given a brief overview of the substance and spirit of Art. 50 TRIPS, three interesting points remain to be made with respect to this provision: (1) its interpretation; (2) whether TRIPS allows a preliminary injunction to be given prior to infringement; and (3) on the meaning of provisional measures *inaudita altera parte* in conjunction with the phrase 'irreparable harm'.

Firstly, regarding the issue of *the interpretation* of Art. 50 TRIPS, Straus makes an important comment by stressing that a procedure for preliminary injunctions

---

451 Art. 50 (7) TRIPS.

452 Art. 50 (3) TRIPS.

453 According to Art. 50 (6) TRIPS, this period – unless the court stipulates a different period thereby basing itself on judicial discretion to do so as provided for by national legislation – amounts to 20 working days or 31 days, whichever is shorter.

should be *fair and equitable* by underlining the connection to other provisions in the Agreement. He writes: "As is clearly revealed by the structure of TRIPS Part III, the maxims of fair and equitable procedures set out in Art. 41 (2) and 42,[454] [of TRIPS] also control Article 50."[455, 456] This is particularly relevant with respect to the position of the defendant in interim relief proceedings. As Straus writes, "(..) any interpretation of Article 50 which would not also carefully take into account the interests *of the defendant* would violate the fair and equitable procedures rule (..)."[457]

Secondly, as Gervais writes in his Commentary on the Agreement,[458] TRIPS allows, even though whilst not expressly mandated in Art. 50 (1), to allow preliminary injunctions to be granted *before* the actual infringement takes place: the wording of Art 50 (3) seems to point to this. This is especially clear when comparing the current wording of Article 50 (1) TRIPS with an earlier draft of Art. 50 (1) TRIPS, from which the removal of the square brackets around the words 'from occurring' seems to point in this direction.[459] This, Gervais submits "reflected a concern about

---

454 Articles 41 (2) and 42 TRIPS on fair and equitable procedures read as follows: Article 41 (2) TRIPS:
"Procedures concerning the enforcement of intellectual property rights shall be fair and equitable. They shall not be unnecessarily complicated or costly, or entail unreasonable time-limits or unwarranted delays." Article 42 TRIPS:
"Members shall make available to right holders civil judicial procedures concerning the enforcement of any intellectual property right covered by this Agreement. Defendants shall have the right to written notice which is timely and contains sufficient detail, including the basis of the claims. Parties shall be allowed to be represented by independent legal counsel, and procedures shall not impose overly burdensome requirements concerning mandatory personal appearances. All parties to such procedures shall be duly entitled to substantiate their claims and to present all relevant evidence. The procedure shall provide a means to identify and protect confidential information, unless this would be contrary to existing constitutional requirements."

455 J. STRAUS, 'Reversal of the Burden of Proof, the Principle of 'Fair and Equitable Procedures' and Preliminary Injunctions under TRIPS Agreement' *Journal of World Intellectual Property* 3, No. 6 (2000), pp. 807–823. See: pp. 813–814.

456 Of course, one can argue that many of the provisions expressly stipulated in Art. 50 TRIPS – namely the possibility to ask for security for the defendant, the requirement of convincing evidence to be given by the plaintiff and similar aspects – tend to already foresee to a certain extent in offering a fair procedure.

457 J. STRAUS, 'Reversal of the Burden of Proof, the Principle of 'Fair and Equitable Procedures' and Preliminary Injunctions under TRIPS Agreement' *Journal of World Intellectual Property* 3, No. 6 (2000), pp. 807–823. See: p. 814. Emphasis added.

458 D. GERVAIS, *The TRIPS Agreement: drafting history and analysis* (2003 Sweet and Maxwell). See: p. 306.

459 This earlier draft of the TRIPS Agreement (the so-called *Brussels draft*, from December 1990, see, Gervais pp. 21 and 73) stated of what is now Art. 50 (1) TRIPS the

injunctions to forestall an infringement from being initiated."[460] Other commentators seem to agree with this view of Gervais.[461]

Lastly, the drafters of the TRIPS Treaty have *only explicitly chosen* for the addition of the phrase 'irreparable harm' in the context of 'provisional measures *inaudita altera parte*'.[462] This Latin term means 'when the other party is not heard' and this would refer, amongst others, to *ex parte preliminary injunctions.* These are opposed to the type of preliminary injunction proceeding that we are mainly dealing with in this thesis, which are given after proceedings between parties. As will be seen below, a similar observation – namely that the concept of 'irreparable harm' is seemingly only connected to *ex parte* preliminary injunctions – can be made in the context of the EU Enforcement directive.[463] What does this observation entail?

With respect to this provision in the TRIPS Agreement, it is submitted that to be read along with the phrase 'irreparable harm' are two key words in Art. 50 (2), namely '*in particular*'. Correa states, in the same light, that it is clear that the provision of Art. 50 (2) is then applicable in the vaguely defined situation of 'where appropriate' *as well* in two more specifically detailed cases. The first is when irreparable harm can occur due to delay and the second when there is a demonstrable risk of

---

following: "The judicial authorities shall have the authority to order prompt and effective provisional measures: (a) to prevent an infringement of any intellectual property right <*from occurring*>(..)". Emphasis added. The bracketed text was, as Gervais states, later removed and does no longer appear in the current wording of this TRIPS provision. D. GERVAIS, *The TRIPS Agreement: drafting history and analysis* (2003 Sweet and Maxwell). See: p. 308.

460 Idem, at pp. 306–308.

461 See, for instance, SASCHA VANDER on Art. 50 TRIPS in a German language Commentary on TRIPS: J. BUSCHE, P.T. STOLL, *TRIPS* (2007 Carl Heymanns Verlag). See: p. 653. He writes: "Die Möglichkeit dieses vorbeugenden Rechtsschutzes ergibt sich war nicht unmittelbar aus Art. 50 Abs 1, jedoch aus dem Zusammenhang mit Art. 50 Abs. 3, der ausdrücklich von einer Verletzung und einer drohenden Verletzung spricht." The view that preliminary injunctions prior to infringement can be given has also been confirmed by the *Declaration on Patent Protection; Regulatory Sovereignty under TRIPS* (2014). This declaration has been signed by a large group of academics. The project lead was by R.M. HILTY and M. LAMPING. See esp. par. 10.1 of the document, stating "Articles 44 and 50 of the TRIPS Agreement do not require the authority finding an infringement to grant injunctive relief." The Declaration is available at: https://www.mpg.de/8132986/Patent-Declaration.pdf (last accessed on 25 April 2017).

462 Art. 50 (2) TRIPS.

463 This then refers to Art. 9 (4) of the EU Enforcement Directive, see the comments of Ohly on this provision of the Enforcement Directive: A. OHLY, 'Three principles of European IP enforcement law: Effectiveness, proportionality, dissuasiveness' in J. DREXL (ed). *Technology and Competition – Contributions in honour of Hanns Ullrich* (2009 Larcier), pp. 257–274. See for more on this, page 145 a.f. of this dissertation.

evidence being destroyed.[464] It is mainly the former (delay) that is the subject of our attention here. Furthermore, as Vander points out, the wording of Art. 50 (2) seems to point out that a *special reason* is required when a preliminary injunction *inaudita altera parte* can be granted.[465] The bar for this special reason may be relatively high.[466] All-in all, it is submitted that this would seem to point to a sliding scale. A preliminary injunction can indeed be granted if (reparable) harm occurs, but if the defendant's basic right to be heard prior to the grant of a preliminary injunction in the sense of Art 50 (2) is not respected, the level of harm that is required for the grant of a preliminary injunction will shift upwards and *harm should then be of a more irreparable and more concrete nature.*[467]

Additionally, it is also noted that in the case an *inaudita altera parte* injunction is granted, a further safeguard in TRIPS in the form of Art. 50 (4) is also provided for. This means that an ex post notice should be given after grant and the right to be heard by the defendant is also prescribed to occur in a subsequent review.

§6.3. The (supranational) European level

§6.3.1. Introduction

Despite the increasing influence of both International Law and European harmonisation on substantive and procedural patent law, this has mainly impacted the scope and grant of patent rights as such.[468] The actual *enforcement* of patent rights in Europe is still very much a national issue. Indeed, it are the domestic courts that decide on the enforcement of a patent right in their jurisdiction, thereby taking into account (mainly) *national law.*[469] This is in stark contrast with for instance

---

464 C.M. CORREA, *TRIPS, A Commentary on the TRIPS Agreement* (2007 Oxford University Press). See: p. 436.

465 S. VANDER in J. BUSCHE, P.T. STOLL, *TRIPS* (2007 Carl Heymanns Verlag). See: p. 655. "Allgemein ist ein besonderer Grund anzunehmen, soweit wegen einer Anhörung des Antragsgegners die Gefahr besteht, dass die Rechtsverfolgung des Rechtsinhabers nachhaltig behindert oder ausgeschlossen wird."
He writes as well: "Die schlichte Möglichkeit eines bevorstehenden Schadens auf Seiten des Rechtsinhabers ist nicht ausreichend, um das Prozessrecht des vermeintlichen Verletzers auf rechtliches Gehör vor Erlass einer Maßnahme auszuschließen."

466 Ibidem.

467 C.M. CORREA, *TRIPS, A Commentary on the TRIPS Agreement* (2007 Oxford University Press). See*:* p. 436.

468 The European Patent Office can grant European patents ex Art. 4 (3) EPC.

469 This is also stipulated in Art. 64 (3) of the European Patent Convention (EPC): "Any infringement of a European patent shall be dealt with by national law."
Of course, however, although decided upon by a *national* court, a preliminary injunction can have effects which are not merely limited to the territory of the Member State in which the remedy has been granted. Cross-border European

the enforcement of EU *trademark* rights[470] and *design* rights[471] in which not only unitary rights exist, but there is also a certain form of common enforcement at a European level.[472]

Although over the decades nevertheless some convergence has taken place between the (courts of) EU Member States in their practices in the granting and denying of *both* preliminary and permanent injunctions in patent litigation,[473] differences between how courts handle these requests still exist. This is hardly surprising: as will be set out below the national courts have been given ample discretion in deciding on when and how to grant preliminary injunctions. This is precisely because the EU Enforcement Directive[474] and its subsequent interpretation by Member States have allowed them to do so.

§6.3.2. The EU Enforcement Directive (2004/48/EC)

Even after the conclusion of the TRIPS Agreement – to which all EU Member States at the time of enactment of the EU Enforcement Directive were signatory – the European Commission felt the need to conduct further harmonisation on a number

---

preliminary injunctions in patent litigation have been possible for some time now and this has been confirmed as being an acceptable practice by the Court of Justice of the European Union. See below at page 153 a.f. of this dissertation.

470 Council Regulation (EC) 207/2009 of February 26th, 2009 on the Community trademark right.

471 Council Regulation (EC) 6/2002 of December 12th, 2001 on Community design rights.

472 However, see: A. KUR, 'Enforcement of unitary intellectual property rights: international jurisdiction and applicable law' *Journal of Intellectual Property Law and Practice* 10, No. 6 (2015), pp. 468–480. Kur points out that with European trademarks and designs such unitary rights exist and the prosecution of infringement is facilitated by a common system. However, she notes that this system is not unitary in every aspect. The Community trademark courts and Community design courts in the individual Member States remain part of the national court system, which leads to problems with jurisdiction and certain gaps in substantive and procedural law. It is thus submitted by the present author of this dissertation, that this therefore differs from the envisaged Unified Patent Court. This court will be more supranational of nature, with a specialised and dedicated court system.

473 See: A. OHLY, 'Three principles of European IP enforcement law: Effectiveness, proportionality, dissuasiveness' in J. DREXL, R.M. HILTY *et al.* (eds). *Technology and Competition – Contributions in honour of Hanns Ullrich* (2009 Larcier), pp. 257–274.

474 Directive 2004/48/EC of the European Parliament and of The Council of 29th of April 2004 on the Enforcement of Intellectual Property Rights, as published in the Official Journal of the European Union, L 157, 30 April 2004.

of different aspects of intellectual property protection. This included provisional measures[475] as well as injunctions:

> "(...) despite the TRIPS Agreement, there are still major disparities as regards the means of enforcing intellectual property rights. For instance, the arrangements for applying provisional measures, which are used in particular to preserve evidence, the calculation of damages, **or the arrangements for applying injunctions**, vary widely from one Member State to another (...)"[476]

The disparities between Member States resulted, as the Commission stated, in an improper functioning of the European internal market and rights holders did not enjoy an equivalent level of protection throughout the Community. This in turn, hampered the free movement of goods and services and the level of competition.[477] Furthermore, the Commission warned that the situation could lead to a fragmentation of the internal market and the weakening of substantive law on intellectual property, ultimately leading to less confidence and less investment by businesses.[478] This resulted into the enactment of the Enforcement Directive with the aim of achieving a more homogeneous level of protection.[479] Whilst the early drafts of the Enforcement Directive were more ambitious and targeted specifically piracy and the counterfeiting of intellectual property by virtue of controversial and later deleted provisions on the applicability of criminal sanctions and technical protection measures,[480] the goal for the Commission was still to further approximate legislation. With respect to preliminary injunctions, the Commission stressed the perceived need to do so:

---

475 Please note that the terms 'provisional' or 'interim measures' in the context of the EU Enforcement Directive are wide concepts and encompass more than merely the remedy of the preliminary injunction as such but also cover other forms of interim relief. See the work of Heinze, in which he has researched the different definitions and descriptions of 'provisional measures' as formulated in international and EU Law and especially see his attempt to synthesise these into a unifying definition. See C. HEINZE, *Einstweiliger Rechtsschutz im europäischen Immaterialgüterrecht* (2007 Mohr Siebeck). See: pp. 126–129.

476 EU Enforcement Directive, 2004/48/EC, recital 7. Emphasis added.

477 Idem, at recital 8.

478 Idem, at recital 9.

479 These reasons are mentioned in the recitals of the Enforcement Directive and are elaborated on in the proposal of the Directive. EUROPEAN COMMISSION, *Proposal for a directive of the European Parliament and the Council on measures and procedures to ensure the enforcement of intellectual property rights.* (January 30th 2003) COM 2003 46 final. See: esp. pp. 4–12 of this proposal.

480 A. KUR, 'The Enforcement Directive – Rough Start, Happy Landing?' *International Review of Intellectual Property and Competition Law (IIC)* (2004), pp. 821–830. See: pp. 821–824.

> "It is also essential to provide for provisional measures for the immediate termination of infringements, without awaiting a decision on the substance of the case, while observing the rights of the defence, ensuring the proportionality of the provisional measures as appropriate to the characteristics of the case in question and providing the guarantees needed to cover the costs and the injury caused to the defendant by an unjustified request. Such measures are particularly justified where any delay would cause irreparable harm to the holder of an intellectual property right."[481]

However, the need to draft further European legislation in the area of enforcement has been frowned upon by some and the proposed Enforcement Directive was strongly criticised on many terms by a prominent group of intellectual property scholars.[482] This group was concerned for further European harmonisation of procedural and remedial law, including the grant of preliminary injunctions. They thereby pointed out the special nature of laws on remedies, which is influenced by national legal traditions as well as being of general nature, rather than specifically drafted for a particular legal field.

> "Who will keep control over the proceedings? Who will decide on the merits, who on the remedial consequences? In procedural law lie the real tests of how punitive, and therefore preventive, legal redress should be. The tests have evolved in different countries out of long experience with their own system, each with its virtues and idiosyncrasies. In large measure they apply to all types of claim, not just to particular fields, such as intellectual property, and that is a highly desirable presumption to be maintained."[483]

These valid points aside, it is submitted that from a legal point of view there were a number of compelling legal reasons for the drafting of further EU legislation in the area of enforcement,[484] despite that TRIPS already existed.

To begin with, TRIPS itself is inapplicable for truly domestic cases as for its application an *international element* of cross-border trade between WTO Member States should exist.[485] It was, at the time of enactment, a pending and open question whether the European Community and its Member States would be seen as one single WTO Member, in which case the application of TRIPS between Community Member States would be inapplicable. For the purpose of TRIPS, intra-community trade would then be seen as domestic trade. An EU extension of the

481 EU Enforcement Directive, 2004/48/EC, recital 22.

482 See the contribution of leading intellectual property academics on the proposed EU directive: W.R. CORNISH, J. DREXL, R.M. HILTY, A. KUR, 'Procedures and remedies for enforcing IPRs: The European Commission's proposed directive' *European Intellectual Property Review* 25, No. 10 (2003), pp. 447–449.

483 Idem, at p. 448.

484 M.P. WEBER, *Die Umsetzung der Enforcement Richtlinie ins deutsche Recht* (2010 Peter Lang GmbH). See: pp. 4–5.

485 Idem, at pp. 4–5.

TRIPS provisions, specifically targeted towards European intra-community trade could remedy this and provide more legal certainty to the signatories. A second reason is to be found in the different ways an international law treaty as TRIPS, and an EU directive, are implemented by Member States.[486] Lastly and importantly, in the case of an EU directive it should be noted that its implementation is also subject to the scrutiny and the jurisdiction of what is now the Court of Justice of the European Union (CJEU). The CJEU can then further harmonise specific aspects, based on the directive, and give clarification on the directive's interpretation. It does so by rendering case law which the (courts of) Member States should take into account.

This does not mean that the significance of the EU Enforcement Directive regarding preliminary injunctions is to be overstated when it comes to contributions of substantive nature. This is for two reasons. Firstly, rather than stipulating a more detailed legal test on how to decide on granting preliminary injunctions, the EU Enforcement Directive merely stipulates an EU minimum standard and a new legal basis. With respect to the articles on provisional measures, the wording of the EU Enforcement Directive is very similar to that of TRIPS, and in parts even identical. In terms of substance it thus does not offer much more than TRIPS did. Secondly, as Kur noted already in 2004, the harmonisation effect of a Directive should not be overstated. She points out that even before the implementation of the EU Enforcement Directive, all the then current EU Member States already offered *the possibility* for plaintiffs to request provisional measures of various kinds.[487] Despite this however, she argues that there were "conspicuous differences" that existed in the willingness of courts to provide preliminary injunctions in cases involving complex assessments, such as in patent law.[488] This resulted in a difference in the frequency that litigants made use of these provisions.[489] Kur continued, and this is something the present author agrees with, that "whilst legal deficiencies can be repaired from above by a Directive, the (un)willingness of the courts to actually grant remedies, can be a difficulty which is hard to overcome."[490] In other words, the Directive does not address the likely willingness, or unwillingness of the courts to provide interim relief and indeed, as will be seen, these differences still exist.

The core provisions governing preliminary injunctions in the Enforcement Directive are Art. 9 and a part of Art. 3. To begin with, Art. 9 states:

---

486 Ibidem.

487 A. KUR, 'The Enforcement Directive – Rough Start, Happy Landing?' *International Review of Intellectual Property and Competition Law (IIC)* (2004), pp. 821–830. See: p. 825.

488 Ibidem.

489 Ibidem.

490 Ibidem. Note that more or less the same is argued by P.B. HUGENHOLTZ, 'Een overbodige richtlijn' *IER* No. 4 (2004), pp. 247–248. Available at: http://www.ivir.nl/publicaties/download/951 (last accessed on 22 April 2017).

1. Member States shall ensure that **the judicial authorities may**, at the request of the applicant:

(a) issue against the alleged infringer an interlocutory injunction intended to prevent any imminent infringement of an intellectual property right, or to forbid, on a provisional basis and subject, where appropriate, to a recurring penalty payment where provided for by national law, the continuation of the alleged infringements of that right, or to make such continuation subject to the lodging of guarantees intended to ensure the compensation of the rightholder; an interlocutory injunction may also be issued, under the same conditions, against an intermediary whose services are being used by a third party to infringe an intellectual property right; injunctions against intermediaries whose services are used by a third party to infringe a copyright or a related right are covered by Directive 2001/29/EC;

(b) order the seizure or delivery up of the goods suspected of infringing an intellectual property right so as to prevent their entry into or movement within the channels of commerce.

2. (...) Omitted here

3. The judicial authorities shall, in respect of the measures referred to in paragraphs 1 and 2, have the authority to require the applicant **to provide any reasonably available evidence in order to satisfy themselves with a sufficient degree of certainty** that the applicant is the rightholder and that the applicant's right is being infringed, or that such infringement is imminent.

4. Member States shall ensure that the provisional measures referred to in paragraphs 1 and 2 may, in appropriate cases, be taken without the defendant having been heard, in particular where any delay would cause irreparable harm to the rightholder. In that event, the parties shall be so informed without delay after the execution of the measures at the latest. A review, including a right to be heard, shall take place upon request of the defendant with a view to deciding, within a reasonable time after notification of the measures, whether those measures shall be modified, revoked or confirmed.

5. (...) Omitted here

6. The competent judicial authorities may make the provisional measures referred to in paragraphs 1 and 2 subject to the lodging by the applicant **of adequate security or an equivalent assurance** intended to ensure compensation for any prejudice suffered by the defendant as provided for in paragraph 7.

7. Where the provisional measures are revoked or where they lapse due to any act or omission by the applicant, or where it is subsequently found that there has been no infringement or threat of infringement of an intellectual property right, the **judicial authorities shall have the authority to order the applicant, upon request of the defendant, to provide the defendant appropriate compensation for any injury caused by those measures.**[491]

491 Emphasis added.

As can be seen, the central elements which were at the heart of Art. 50 TRIPS also appear in Art. 9 of the Enforcement Directive. These include an acknowledgment of the objective of a preliminary injunction, as well as granting a high degree of discretion to a judicial authority.[492] The wording of the Article 9 also includes other similar elements of legislation, such as that the plaintiff should provide evidence that satisfies the court with a sufficient degree of certainty.[493] It also mentions the possibility of requiring from the applicant sufficient security for harm caused to the defendant, should the decision to grant a preliminary injunction prove to be wrong.[494] Finally, various safeguards for *ex parte* injunctions are mentioned,[495] and also there is the possibility for compensation to be ordered by the defendant to receive compensation when the preliminary injunction is revoked, or if the defendant is found not to be liable for infringement.[496]

Article 3 (2) of the EU Enforcement Directive is an equally important provision: measures implemented by the Member States in the context of this Directive should adhere to the following three principles:

> "3 (2.) Those measures, procedures and remedies shall also be **effective, proportionate and dissuasive** and shall be applied in such a manner as to avoid the creation of barriers to legitimate trade and to provide for safeguards against their abuse."[497]

In any case, when comparing the substance of Art. 9 Enforcement Directive with that Art. 50 TRIPS, one can see that not much was added in terms of further specifics on how the legal test governing the decision to grant or deny a preliminary injunction should be. And indeed, more than ten years after the introduction of the EU Enforcement Directive, the differences in legal culture that Kur referred to still exist. With respect to preliminary injunctions courts have not been spurred into action everywhere in similar degrees. As has already been pointed out by the findings in the *European Commission's Pharmaceutical Sector Inquiry*,[498] but as also will become clear in the next chapter, it is evident that in some Member States it is simply easier to obtain a preliminary injunction than in others. Likewise, the way courts decide upon granting or denying them differs considerably.

§6.3.3. Further comments on the EU Enforcement Directive

Ohly has made two interesting comments regarding the exact wording of Art. 9 of the Enforcement Directive. Firstly, he observes that "the Directive does not explicitly require interlocutory injunctions *to be necessary to avoid irreparable harm in*

---

492 EU Enforcement Directive, 2004/48/EC, Art. 9 (1).
493 Idem, at Art. 9 (3).
494 Idem, at Art. 9 (6).
495 Idem, at Art. 9 (4).
496 Idem, at Art. 9 (7).
497 Emphasis added.
498 See chapter 5 of this dissertation.

case of delay."[499] In contrast, Art. 9 (4) of the Directive does seem to grant this for *ex parte* injunctions. Ohly argues therefore that it seems that 'ordinary' interim injunctions which are not of an *ex parte* nature can be granted in cases in which damages would equally be sufficient.[500] This indeed seems to be the case, as was seen before in the context of TRIPS.[501] As is evident, Art. 50 (2) TRIPS is drafted in a very similar fashion. That provision too speaks of irreparable harm in case of delay and is only specifically mentioned with '*provisional measures inaudita altera parte*', the equivalent to *ex parte* injunctions in the Enforcement Directive. As was argued above, the words 'in particular' and 'in appropriate' of Art. 50 (2) seem to point to a sliding scale: the level of harm that is required for the grant of a preliminary injunction shifts upwards when the defendant is not heard. *Harm should then be of a more irreparable and more concrete nature.* Conversely, it then seems that for 'regular' preliminary injunctions, the irreparability of harm is *not* an absolute requirement. The present author does therefore not necessarily agree that the proportionality principle of Art. 3 (2) of the Enforcement Directive would per se prevent the grant of a preliminary injunction in cases that damages would suffice.[502] And indeed, as will be seen, courts in EU Member States in general do not investigate what the exact nature of the harm is and the irreparability or reparability of harm is often not even addressed in the national practice of many European courts when deciding on this.

A second comment that Ohly rightly makes is that Art. 9 (1) does not *prescribe* that the court should balance the interests of parties.[503] However, as he also argues this may not be an omission that is that serious in practice. Ohly firstly points out – as also will be seen later in this dissertation when looking at the legal frameworks and practices of EU Member States – that the balancing of interests of the involved parties *does however* take place in most national European jurisdictions.[504] Therefore, in practice this is something that the courts have allowed themselves to do, regardless of whether it is explicitly spelled out in the Enforcement Directive. Furthermore, as Ohly also submits,[505] the general 'proportionality' clause of the Enforcement Directive that is enshrined in Art. 3 (2), should also guarantee such a balancing

499 A. OHLY, 'Three principles of European IP enforcement law: Effectiveness, proportionality, dissuasiveness' in J. DREXL (ed). *Technology and Competition – Contributions in honour of Hanns Ullrich* (2009 Larcier), pp. 257–274. See: pp. 270–271.

500 Ibidem.

501 See the analysis in the context of TRIPS, in the footnotes and in the accompanying main text, at footnote 463 a.f. of this dissertation.

502 A. OHLY, 'Three principles of European IP enforcement law: Effectiveness, proportionality, dissuasiveness' in J. DREXL (ed). *Technology and Competition – Contributions in honour of Hanns Ullrich* (2009 Larcier), pp. 257–274. See: p. 271.

503 Ibidem.

504 Idem, at p. 270. However, it is submitted here that this refers to the *possibility* for a court to balance interests in deciding upon a preliminary injunction. In practice, many courts still do not do so, as will be seen, even although they are entitled to.

505 Idem, at p. 271.

exercise. This, even though when Art. 3 (2) is not directly applicable for litigants as this provision is directed to the Member States[506] and not always transposed.[507]

In addition to these two reasons, it is submitted here that a final reason why the omission of an explicit balancing of interests requirement in the Enforcement Directive is not that serious is because of the influence of the CJEU. Although outside the immediate and specific scope of preliminary injunctions and patent litigation, the CJEU has consistently made clear in a string of rulings, that national courts, in interpreting the provisions of the Enforcement Directive, should balance fundamental rights and interests against each other. Cases of the CJEU that have enshrined this principle are, amongst other decisions, that of *Promusicae v Telefónica, Scarlet v SABAM, L´Oréal v eBay and UPC Telekabel.*[508]

---

506 For more on the implementation of the EU Enforcement Directive in various Member States and the Directive's impact on the power of courts to issue injunctions, see M. MARFÉ, A. REETZ, C. PECNARD, R. FRUSCALZO AND R. VAN DER VELDEN, 'The power of national courts and the Unified Patent Court to grant injunctions: a comparative study' *Journal of Intellectual Property Law & Practice* 10, No. 3 (2015), pp. 180–190. See for Germany pp. 181–182, for The Netherlands p. 184 and for the United Kingdom pp. 184–186.

507 Ibidem.

508 Firstly, see the judgment in CJEU C-275/06, *Promusicae v Telefónica*, January 29 2008, ECLI:EU:C:2008:54, at par 72: "when transposing those directives, the Member States take care to rely on an interpretation of them which allows *a fair balance to be struck between the various fundamental rights protected by the Community legal order.* Further, when implementing the measures transposing those directives, the authorities and courts of the Member States must not only interpret their national law in a manner consistent with those directives but also make sure that they do not rely on an interpretation of them which would be in conflict with those fundamental rights or with the other general principles of Community law, such as the principle of proportionality." Emphasis added. Furthermore, see par. 65–68 of this ruling.
Secondly, see as an example the case of CJEU C-70/10, *Scarlet v SABAM,* November 24th 2011, ECLI:EU:C:2011:771, at par. 53: "Consequently, it must be held that, in adopting the injunction requiring the ISP to install the contested filtering system, the national court concerned would not be respecting the requirement *that a fair balance be struck between* the right to intellectual property, on the one hand, and the freedom to conduct business, the right to protection of personal data and the freedom to receive or impart information, on the other." Emphasis added.
Also in the context of trademarks, see the CJEU judgment of CJEU C-324/09, *L'Oréal v eBay,* July 12th 2011, ECLI:EU:C:2011:474, at par. 143: "The measures that are described (non-exhaustively) in the preceding paragraphs, as well as any other measure which may be imposed in the form of an injunction under the third sentence of Article 11 of Directive 2004/48, must *strike a fair balance between the various rights and interests* mentioned above." Emphasis added.
Lastly, see CJEU, C-314/12, *UPC Telekabel Wien v Constantin Film Verleih,* March 27th 2014, ECLI:EU:C:2014:192 at par. 64: "(..) the fundamental rights recognised

§6.3.4. *Art. 6 of the European Convention on Human Rights and Art. 47 of the Charter of Fundamental Rights of the EU*

Various authors, such as Petersen and Heinze, have discussed whether Art. 6 (1) of the European Convention on Human Rights (ECHR) could be seen as being applicable to preliminary injunction proceedings.[509] Art. 6 of the ECHR makes a direct reference to fairness, impartiality and the length of legal proceedings, stating that:

> "In the **determination of his civil rights** and obligations or of any criminal charge against him, everyone is entitled **to a fair and public hearing within a reasonable time** by an **independent and impartial** tribunal established by law. (...)"[510]

Both abovementioned authors have written – concurring with the common view at the time of publication on this[511] – that the influence of Art. 6 ECHR was deemed to be limited, since in general it was not seen as being directly applicable to preliminary injunction proceedings. This was because a granted preliminary injunction – at least in the area of intellectual property – was not considered as being an actual determination of civil rights, but merely a *temporary measure*

---

by EU law must be interpreted as not precluding a court injunction prohibiting an internet service provider from allowing its customers access to a website placing protected subject-matter online without the agreement of the rightholders when that injunction does not specify the measures which that access provider must take and when that access provider can avoid incurring coercive penalties for breach of that injunction by showing that it has taken all reasonable measures, *provided that (i) the measures taken do not unnecessarily deprive internet users of the possibility of lawfully accessing the information available and* (ii) that those measures have the effect of preventing unauthorised access to the protected subject-matter or, at least, of making it difficult to achieve and of seriously discouraging internet users who are using the services of the addressee of that injunction from accessing the subject-matter that has been made available to them in breach of the intellectual property right, that being a matter for the national authorities and courts to establish." Emphasis added.

509 See for instance the works of C.S. PETERSEN, *Immaterialrettigheder og foreløbige forbud* (2008 Jurist- og Økonomforbundets Forl.). See: pp. 41–43 and also C. HEINZE, *Einstweiliger Rechtsschutz im europäischen Immaterialgüterrecht* (2007 Mohr Siebeck). See: p. 41. For a wider perspective on the issue of human rights and interim measures, including that under the ECHR, see F.P. BOSTEDT, *Vorsorgliche und einstweilige Maßnahmen zum Schutz der Menschenrechte* (2009 Peter Lang Verlag).

510 The provision of Art. 6 (1) ECHR is only given in part here. Emphasis added.

511 See the report written by the EUROPEAN COURT OF HUMAN RIGHTS, RESEARCH DIVISION, *Guide on Article 6 – Right to a fair trial (civil limb)* (2013). See: esp. p. 10. Available at: http://www.echr.coe.int/Documents/Guide_Art_6_ENG.pdf (last accessed on 20 April 2017).

taken before and ahead of the actual decision on the merits.[512] The prevailing view was thus that Art. 6 ECHR did therefore *not constitute* a legal basis for preliminary injunction proceedings in the realm of patent litigation or wider intellectual property disputes.[513] This was even so when during preliminary injunctions proceedings in these areas a substantive assessment was made, along with a balancing of interests.[514]

Nevertheless, diverging from the main rule as stated above, there were exceptional circumstances that could lead to a different outcome and render that Art. 6 ECHR was in fact applicable to interim proceedings.[515] Furthermore, as Heinze correctly mentions, regardless of the status the ECHR had vis-à-vis preliminary injunction proceedings, the national courts in EU Member States were bound to Community fundamental rights and general principles of law, including the case law of the CJEU.[516] Since the latter sources of law touched upon the topics that Art. 6 ECHR covered, this guaranteed effective judicial protection through alternative ways than directly via the ECHR and the European Court of Human Rights (ECtHR).[517]

However, things have changed somewhat since the writings of Heinze and Petersen, meaning that Art. 6 ECHR is back in the picture again regarding its applicability when it comes to interim measures. Naturally, this also includes interim

512 C. HEINZE, *Einstweiliger Rechtsschutz im europäischen Immaterialgüterrecht* (2007 Mohr Siebeck). See: pp. 41–42.

513 Idem, at pp. 41–42.

514 Idem, at p. 42.

515 See C.S. PETERSEN, *Immaterialrettigheder og foreløbige forbud* (2008 Jurist- og Økonomforbundets Forl.). See: pp. 41–44. Also: C. HEINZE, *Einstweiliger Rechtsschutz im europäischen Immaterialgüterrecht* (2007 Mohr Siebeck). See: pp. 41–42 and see the paper of M. AICHINGER, W. PETRITZ, E. REICH, *Interim measures and the applicability of Article 6.* Available at: http://www.ejtn.eu/Documents/Themis%202012/Written%20paper%20Lisbon/Written_paper_%20Austria_1_%20Interpretation_and_application_of_article_5_and_6_of_the_ECHR%20.pdf (last accessed on 22 April 2017).
The much quoted example of an *exception to the norm* at the time is the case of *Markass* (ECthR, Grand Chamber, *Markass Car Hire Ltd. v Cyprus,* No. 51591/99). In the admissibility ruling to proceed before the Grand Chamber (of October 23rd 2001) the Court declared the application admissible and decided, that "in this respect, the Court cannot overlook the drastic character of the interim decision (..) The combined effect of the measure and its duration caused irreversible prejudice to the applicant's interests and drained to a substantial extent the final outcome of the proceedings of its significance. (..)." The violation of Art. 6 (1) ECHR was subsequently confirmed in the actual judgment of July 2nd 2002.

516 C. HEINZE, *Einstweiliger Rechtsschutz im europäischen Immaterialgüterrecht* (2007 Mohr Siebeck) See: pp. 43–49.

517 Ibidem.

injunctions in the area of intellectual property. This is based on two developments, both fuelled by the ECtHR case of *Micallef v Malta*.[518]

Firstly, in the judgment, the Grand Chamber of the ECthR held that the Court's previous view on interim measures was now *outdated*. Subsequently, the Grand Chamber rejected it altogether, thereby stressing the role preliminary injunction proceedings have *in practice* rather than considering their role and place in an enforcement system merely from a more theoretical perspective:[519]

> "The exclusion of interim measures from the ambit of Article 6 has so far been justified by the fact that they do not in principle determine civil rights and obligations. However, in circumstances where many Contracting States face considerable backlogs in their overburdened justice systems leading to excessively long proceedings, a judge's decision on an injunction will often be tantamount to a decision on the merits of the claim for a substantial period of time, even permanently in exceptional cases. It follows that, frequently, interim and main proceedings decide the same "civil rights or obligations" and have the same resulting long-lasting or permanent effects."[520]
> "Against this background, the Court no longer finds it justified to automatically characterise injunction proceedings as not determinative of civil rights or obligations."[521]

This definitely makes sense from the present author's point of view, since the above represents a much more practical view on the role preliminary measures have in reality. This is even more so because, as the ECtHR correctly pointed out, possible defects in these preliminary proceedings could often only be addressed with difficulty, if at all:

> "Nor is it convinced that a defect in such proceedings would necessarily be remedied at a later stage, namely, in proceedings on the merits governed by Article 6 since any prejudice suffered in the meantime may by then have become irreversible and with little realistic opportunity to redress the damage caused, except perhaps for the possibility of pecuniary compensation."[522]

---

518 European Court of Human Rights, Grand Chamber, *Micallef v Malta*, October 15th 2009, Application number 17056/06, ECLI:CE:ECHR:2009:1015JUD001705606.

519 Also see M. AICHINGER, W. PETRITZ, E. REICH, *Interim measures and the applicability of Article 6*. Available at: http://www.ejtn.eu/Documents/Themis%20 2012/Written%20paper%20Lisbon/Written_paper_%20Austria_1_%20Interpreta tion_and_application_of_article_5_and_6_of_the_ECHR%20.pdf (last accessed on 22 April 2017), p. 16.

520 European Court of Human Rights, Grand Chamber, *Micallef v Malta*, October 15th 2009, Application number 17056/06, ECLI:CE:ECHR:2009:1015JUD001705606. See par. 79. Emphasis added.

521 Idem, at par. 79 Emphasis added.

522 Idem, at par. 80. Emphasis added.

Secondly, having noted the downside of the old approach, the Grand Chamber of the ECtHR subsequently set out the *new approach* to be taken.[523] It held that interim measures fall under Art. 6 ECHR when two conditions are met. Firstly, the contested right in both the preliminary proceedings as at the trial on the merits should be of *civil nature* within the meaning of the Convention.[524] The second condition is that the *object, purpose and effect* of an interim measure should be considered by its nature: when this in practice determines the civil right at stake, this condition is fulfilled.[525] The (supposed) time an interim measure is then likely to be in force is no longer a key determinative factor.[526] When both these two conditions are satisfied, Art. 6 ECHR is in principle applicable to interim measures, including interim injunctions. However, as Aichinger writes, the Grand Chamber of the ECtHR also made an exception to the applicability of this Article: not all procedural requirements have to be complied with in an interim proceeding and for instance certain procedural rights are only applicable when they are compatible with the purpose of the interim proceedings.[527]

Practically speaking, the result of the ruling in *Micallef* is not likely to make a significant change to the common practice of the European courts regarding preliminary injunctions in patent cases. This said, however, Aichinger et al argue that it can for instance provide a guarantee to unreasonable delays taking place.[528, 529]

Beyond the two abovementioned developments connected to *Micallef*, there is another development that should be mentioned here. With the enactment of the Lisbon Treaty, the EU has incorporated *the rights and freedoms of the ECHR* – along

523 Idem, at par. 83–86.

524 EUROPEAN COURT OF HUMAN RIGHTS, RESEARCH DIVISION, *Guide on Article 6 – Right to a fair trial (civil limb)* (2013). See: p. 10. Available at: http://www.echr.coe.int/Documents/Guide_Art_6_ENG.pdf (last accessed on 20 April 2017).

525 Ibidem.

526 Ibidem.

527 M. AICHINGER, W. PETRITZ, E. REICH, *Interim measures and the applicability of Article 6.* Available at: http://www.ejtn.eu/Documents/Themis%202012/Written%20paper%20Lisbon/Written_paper_%20Austria_1_%20Interpretation_and_application_of_article_5_and_6_of_the_ECHR%20.pdf (last accessed on 22 April 2017). See: pp. 17 and 20. Also see the judgment of European Court of Human Rights, Grand Chamber, *Micallef v Malta*, October 15th 2009, Application number 17056/06, ECLI:CE:ECHR:2009:1015JUD001705606. At par. 86.

528 EUROPEAN COURT OF HUMAN RIGHTS, RESEARCH DIVISION, *Guide on Article 6 – Right to a fair trial (civil limb)* (2013). See: pp. 50–55. Available at: http://www.echr.coe.int/Documents/Guide_Art_6_ENG.pdf (last accessed on 20 April 2017).

529 M. AICHINGER, W. PETRITZ, E. REICH, *Interim measures and the applicability of Article 6.* See: p. 20. Available at: http://www.ejtn.eu/Documents/Themis%202012/Written%20paper%20Lisbon/Written_paper_%20Austria_1_%20Interpretation_and_application_of_article_5_and_6_of_the_ECHR%20.pdf (last accessed on 22 April 2017).

with the rights and freedoms stemming from CJEU case law and those which are common amongst the constitutions of the Member States – directly into the corpus of primary European Union law. It has done so with the addition of the Charter of Fundamental Rights of the European Union.[530, 531] Art. 47 of this Charter is similar, albeit slightly differently worded, to ECHR Art. 6.[532] This provision therefore also seems applicable as a direct legal basis for courts to ensure that effective preliminary injunction proceedings are also applicable for patent litigation.[533] After all, unlike the ECHR, intellectual property is something that is specifically mentioned in the Charter to be protected, namely in Art. 17 (2). Taken together, Art. 47 and Art. 17 (2) of the Charter constitute an alternative to the direct applicability of Art. 6 ECHR.

More importantly perhaps than the formal recognition of the applicability of these procedural guarantees, is the *reasoning* that is behind the new approach of the ECtHR. This recognises that:

- Preliminary proceedings and measures taken in these proceedings, such as injunctions, are often *final* in practice.
- Preliminary proceedings and measures taken in these proceedings, such as injunctions, *have effects that cannot be remedied later.*
- The importance of preliminary proceedings and measures taken in these proceedings, have been elevated due *to the overburdening of the justice system.* This results in longer litigation times and these delays form a threat for effective judicial protection.

530 CHARTER OF FUNDAMENTAL RIGHTS OF THE EUROPEAN UNION, Document 2012/C 326/02. Available at: http://eur-lex.europa.eu/legal-content/EN/TXT/PDF/?uri=CELEX:12012P/TXT&from=EN (last accessed on 22 April 2017).

531 See for more on the relationship between human rights and intellectual property rights in Europe in general, the work of A. OHLY, 'European Fundamental Rights and Intellectual Property' in A. OHLY, J. PILA, (eds) *The Europeanization of Intellectual Property Law; Towards a European Legal Methodology* (2013 Oxford University Press). See: pp. 145–163.

532 Art. 47 of the Charter of Fundamental Rights of the European Union, is worded as follows:
"Everyone *whose rights and freedoms guaranteed by the law of the Union are violated has the right to an effective remedy* before a tribunal in compliance with the conditions laid down in this Article.
Everyone is entitled to a fair and public hearing *within a reasonable time* by an independent and impartial tribunal previously established by law. Everyone shall have the possibility of being advised, defended and represented. (..)." Emphasis added. CHARTER OF FUNDAMENTAL RIGHTS OF THE EUROPEAN UNION, Document 2012/C 326/02. Available at: http://eur-lex.europa.eu/legal-content/EN/TXT/PDF/?uri=CELEX:12012P/TXT&from=EN (last accessed on 22 April 2017).

533 C. HEINZE, *Einstweiliger Rechtsschutz im europäischen Immaterialgüterrecht* (2007 Mohr Siebeck). See: p. 45.

As stated earlier in the preceding chapters, these three consequences are also apparent when it comes to preliminary injunctions in patent litigation.

§6.3.5. *The Brussels I Regulation*

Despite the fact that the EU has attempted to harmonise European litigation practices, this has only succeeded to a limited extent and litigation is still largely a national affair. Preliminary injunctions therefore remain to be national legal instruments that mainly have a domestic impact. However, due to the 2012 ruling from the CJEU in *Solvay v Honeywell,*[534] domestic preliminary injunctions having a cross-border effect are once again – to some extent – possible. This gives a European dimension to what are otherwise merely national decisions.

It is the *Brussels I Regulation* (BR),[535] regulating issues of jurisdiction and choice of law in Europe, that is applicable to present day European patent litigation and it is precisely this Regulation that has become central to the various CJEU judgments on cross-border preliminary injunctions. Note that International Private Law is a notoriously complicated area of law, so that only a brief account of the issues can be given here.

The landmark case of *Solvay* originated from The Netherlands, a country where it many years before the CJEU case at hand, had been made possible to grant (preliminary) injunctions with cross-border effects.[536]

The legality of this practice for patents was however doubted after two judgments by the CJEU, namely the cases of *Roche v Primus*[537] and *GAT v LuK.*[538] The former case of *Roche* established that a European patent was not to be seen as a unitary right, but instead as a bundle of national patent rights, that should be examined under national law. Therefore, *from a legal perspective*, there was not a risk for contradictory rulings when courts in different Member States would decide differently in disputes with respect to the same subject matter,[539] as the European patent could be seen as consisting of different national rights. This meant that the often-invoked

534 CJEU, C-616/10 *Solvay v Honeywell*, decision of 12 July 2012, ECLI:EU:C:2012:445.

535 Council Regulation (EC) No. 44/2001 of December 22nd 2000, on the jurisdiction, recognition and enforcement of judgments in civil and commercial matters ('Brussels I').

536 This was clearly stated by the highest court in The Netherlands, the Hoge Raad, in *Interlas v Lincoln,* November 24th 1989, NJ 1992, 404.

537 CJEU, C-539/03 *Roche v Primus,* July 13th 2006, ECLI:EU:C:2006:458.

538 CJEU, C-4/03 *GAT v LuK,* July 13th 2006, ECLI:EU:C:2006:457.

539 CJEU, C-539/03 *Roche v Primus,* July 13th 2006, ECLI:EU:C:2006:458. See: par. 30–32. It is noted that this is even the case when the factual situation is the same. This is, for example, when defendant companies belonging to the same group have acted in a similar manner due to for instance a common policy. Also then the legal situation differs, since a patent is not a unitary right and there is no risk of contradictory decisions. See: par. 34–35.

Art 6 (1) of the Brussels Regulation[540] would no longer be a suitable legal basis for the grant of a cross-border preliminary injunction to a plaintiff.[541]

The ruling in *GAT v LuK* was on the question of exclusivity of jurisdiction of the seized court in matters of patent validity, ex Art 22 (4) BR.[542] The CJEU held in that case that this Article is to be interpreted in such a manner that exclusive jurisdiction exists for the court of the country of patent registration when the proceedings *are concerned* with *the validity* of a patent right. This is regardless of whether a fully-fledged invalidity proceeding was started in the meantime or whether the issue of invalidity was raised by the defendant as a counterattack against the grant of a (preliminary) injunction.[543, 544] In either case, depending on the interpretation of this judgment, the foreign court that had been seized had either no jurisdiction at all (as for instance German courts believed)[545] or the court would have to suspend the infringement proceedings until the court in the country of registration of the contested patent right had ruled on its validity (as Dutch courts interpreted the ruling of the CJEU in *GAT v LuK*).[546]

---

540 Art. 6 (1) of the Brussels Regulation is on special jurisdiction, and reads:
"A person domiciled in a Member State may also be sued:
(1) where he is one of a number of defendants, in the courts for the place where any one of them is domiciled, provided the claims are so closely connected that it is expedient to hear and determine them together to avoid the risk of irreconcilable judgments resulting from separate proceedings."

541 X.E. KRAMER, 'Civiele sancties in het internationale geval in Europees perspectief' in A. VAN HOEK, R. KLOMP, M. LOOS, (eds), *Offerhauskring vijftig jaar* (2012 Boom Juridische Uitgevers), pp. 73–81. See: pp. 75–76.

542 Art 22 (4) of the Brussels Regulation – formerly Art. 16(4) of the Brussels Convention – is on exclusive jurisdiction of the seized Court:
"(4) in proceedings concerned with the registration or validity of patents, trade marks, designs, or other similar rights required to be deposited or registered, the courts of the Member State in which the deposit or registration has been applied for, has taken place or is under the terms of a Community instrument or an international convention deemed to have taken place.
Without prejudice to the jurisdiction of the European Patent Office under the [Munich Convention], the courts of each Member State shall have exclusive jurisdiction, regardless of domicile, in proceedings concerned with the registration or validity of any European patent granted for that State."

543 CJEU, *GAT v LuK*, par. 32. (..) "as meaning that the rule of exclusive jurisdiction laid down therein concerns all proceedings *relating to the registration or validity of a patent, irrespective of whether the issue is raised by way of an action or a plea in objection.*" Emphasis added.

544 See for the motivation for this, esp. par. 21–25 of CJEU's ruling in *GAT v LuK*.

545 W. PORS, 'Holland: cross border patent litigation revival 'Solvay v Honeywell'' (January 2013). Available at http://www.twobirds.com/en/news/articles/2012/holland-crossborder-patent-litigation-revival--solvay-honeywell-0113 (last accessed on 23 April 2017).

546 Ibidem.

Combined, these two cases resulted in some commentators speaking of a "serious blow" to the enforcement of foreign patents,[547] although the abovementioned cases were somewhat unsatisfactory in their argumentation and left much unclear.[548] Most importantly in the context of this dissertation however, is that with respect to preliminary injunctions, these cases left open the status of Art. 31 BR,[549] which enables jurisdiction *specifically* with respect to deciding on interim measures.[550, 551]

The case of *Solvay* provided more guidance by the CJEU on this. The CJEU argued that Article 22(4) BR "which concerns the jurisdiction as to substance, cannot, as a rule, be interpreted so as to derogate from Article 31 and, consequently, cause it to be disapplied."[552] This is because the preliminary injunction decision, which is of an interim nature, is seen as not impacting the decision on the merits, which includes the substantive issue of patent validity that Art. 22 (4) BR refers to.[553] The CJEU thus seems to have confidence in the court that decides upon the request for a preliminary injunction. This makes sense: if the preliminary injunction court has doubts about the patent validity, it is unlikely to grant the request for interim relief and therefore the chance on diverging judgments is reduced. Cross-border preliminary injunctions ex Art. 31 BR – as opposed to cross-border injunctions for cases held at trial on the merits – are therefore allowed and Art. 22 (4) does not stand in the way of this. However, the preliminary injunction court should not go too deep into the substance of the invalidity arguments since it would not have jurisdiction and

547 A. KUR, 'A farewell to cross-border injunctions? The ECJ Decisions GAT v. LuK and Roche Nederland v. Primus and Goldenberg' *International review of Intellectual Property and Competition Law (IIC)* 37, No. 7 (2006), pp. 844–855. See: p. 847. She notes that this practice was particularly apparent in The Netherlands and Germany.

548 Idem, at pp. 847–851.

549 Art. 31 of the Brussels Regulation reads as follows:
"Application may be made to the courts of a Member State for such provisional, including protective, measures as may be available under the law of that State, *even if, under this Regulation, the courts of another Member State have jurisdiction as to the substance of the matter.*" Emphasis added.

550 A. KUR, 'A farewell to cross-border injunctions? The ECJ Decisions GAT v. LuK and Roche Nederland v. Primus and Goldenberg' *International review of Intellectual Property and Competition Law (IIC)* 37, No. 7 (2006), pp. 844–855. See: pp. 852–853.

551 But only if there is *genuine link* between the requested measure and the court's jurisdiction, as set out by the CJEU in C-391/95, *Van Uden v Deco line*, November 17th, 1998, ECLI:EU:C:1998:543. See esp. par. 40.

552 CJEU, C-616/10, *Solvay v Honeywell*, 12 July 2012, ECLI:EU:C:2012:445. See: par. 40 and also par. 33–40.

553 Idem, at par. 49–50.

authority to do so.[554] As Kelkensberg and Bremer clearly write, the earlier *GAT-LuK* ruling on exclusivity ex Art. 22 (4) BR is thus not applicable when:

1) a plaintiff requests an interim measure against patent infringement in another Member State;
2) the defendant (alleged infringer), against this, questions the validity of the patent;
3) the requested interim measure is on the basis of Art. 31 BR; and
4) the seized court does not give a final decision, but interim relief, basing itself on the likelihood that the plaintiff will win on the merits. In doing so, the seized court will deny the requested interim measure when, in such a proceeding, there is a reasonable chance that the patent will be held as invalid."[555, 556]

Another issue that was addressed in *Solvay* was the status of Art. 6 BR, which had been questioned in *Roche v Primus*. With respect to the interpretation of Art. 6 BR, the CJEU in *Solvay* stated that it is for the court to assess whether there is a risk of irreconcilable judgments.[557] However, the CJEU stated that a situation that can result in this is when there is an overlapping connection between the defendants (i.e. subsidiaries) within the jurisdiction of the seized court, whereby each defendant is committing the infringing activities.[558]

---

554 R. EBBINK, 'Provisional cross-border jurisdiction in patent cases according to the CJEU in Solvay' (2013). Available at: https://www.boek9.nl/files/2013B9/Richard_Ebbink_-_Provisional_Cross-Border_Jurisdiction_in_Patent_Cases_according_to_the_CJEU_in_Solvay.pdf (last accessed on 23 April 2017).

555 L. KELKENSBERG, J. BREMER, 'Inbreuk v nietigheid in grensoverschrijdende gevallen; is de Nederlandse octrooirechter bevoegd?' *Berichten Industriële Eigendom* (October 2014), pp. 206–213. See: esp. p. 208 (paraphrased and translated by the present author from Dutch).

556 With respect to the third bullet, Ebbink seems to deduct from the *Solvay* ruling that "there is no doubt in the mind of the CJEU that when national courts are dealing with foreign invalidity defenses in cross-border PI proceedings, for jurisdiction they can rely *only* on Article 31<of the BR>." Emphasis added. R. EBBINK, 'Provisional cross-border jurisdiction in patent cases according to the CJEU in Solvay' (2013). See: p. 3. Available at: https://www.boek9.nl/files/2013B9/Richard_Ebbink_-_Provisional_Cross-Border_Jurisdiction_in_Patent_Cases_according_to_the_CJEU_in_Solvay.pdf (last accessed on 23 April 2017).

557 CJEU, C-616/10, *Solvay v Honeywell*, 12 July 2012, ECLI:EU:C:2012:445. See: par. 29–30. As the CJEU stated, this is because: "(…) potential divergences in the outcome of the proceedings are likely to arise in the same situation of fact and law, so that it is possible that they will culminate in irreconcilable judgments resulting from separate proceedings." At par. 27.

558 Idem, at par. 29–30.

Thus, the CJEU's *Solvay* decision has somewhat left the door open for cross-border preliminary injunctions ex Art. 31 BR, when certain requirements are fulfilled.[559] However, some unclarity remains after this decision, specifically with respect to the applicability of another legal basis to stool a cross-border preliminary injunction request upon, namely Art. 2 BR and Art. 5–24 BR in combination with Art. 22(4) BR.[560]

§6.4. Chapter conclusion

Preliminary injunctions have been stipulated and endorsed as an effective remedy in intellectual property protection by both international and European legislators (by virtue of TRIPS and the EU Enforcement Directive) as well as by the European courts (the ECtHR, recognising the lasting effects that they can have and the CJEU, in allowing their cross-border effects). However, it is still – given the importance and strong effects of the remedy – equally also clear that much has *not* been further specified by these entities. Whilst fundamental common minimums have been firmly anchored by the said efforts of legislators and courts, there is little or no clear guidance on *when* to grant such preliminary injunctions in the realm of patent law and *how* courts should assess a request for this remedy, thereby striving to provide swift and effective justice whilst dealing with complex and technical matters plus many uncertainties involved. We therefore now turn to those entities that have been traditionally more active in the field of enforcement: the (EU) nation states and the national courts. They have also done so with respect to preliminary injunctions in patent cases and have indeed provided further guidance and specifics on how to wield this power.

559 L. KELKENSBERG, J. BREMER, 'Inbreuk v nietigheid in grensoverschrijdende gevallen; is de Nederlandse octrooirechter bevoegd?' *Berichten Industriële Eigendom* (October 2014), pp. 206–213. See their examples of the interpretation of a number of Dutch cases after *Solvay* at pp. 210 a.f.

560 Idem, at p. 213.

Chapter 7: An Overview of National Legal Frameworks and the Practices and Issues Courts Encounter

The preceding chapter has made clear that obligations from international and European law have set certain minimum standards regarding the procedural and substantive aspects of the preliminary injunction proceedings and the remedy. Nevertheless, they do not stipulate any further how the legal test should be in order to decide on the granting or denying of such a measure. This is left up to the Treaty signatories and Member States of these international and European statutes. We will now look at four examples of these national practices. At first, a look is taken at The Netherlands and at Germany. Subsequently we will look at England and at the United States.

In doing so, the national legal framework governing preliminary injunctions will be reviewed, but also at how courts have interpreted these provisions *in practice*. Therefore, we will look specifically at patent case law in this chapter which features prohibitively-formulated preliminary injunctions. Most disputes concern either pharmaceutical patents or patents that are related to electronic industries. The cases that are referred to in this chapter are either: 1) cases that are considered to be exemplary of certain practices; 2) cases that are often cited; or 3) cases that form a certain exception to the rule.

§7.1. The Netherlands

§7.1.1. Introduction

In the Netherlands, interim relief is made available via the mechanism of a *kort geding* (a term which can be literally translated as 'short trial'). This can result into a *voorlopige voorziening* (interim measure) which can be prohibitory of nature. The *kort geding* procedure in The Netherlands has established itself as a widely accepted and much-used procedure in legal practice in almost all areas of law. This is no different with respect to patent litigation, even though the *accelerated patent proceedings on the merits* – the so-called 'vro regime' – is gaining more and more popularity in the realm of patents. To a certain extent this is now also used *instead* of kort geding proceedings. However, it is argued that both should be seen as complementary to each other, bearing in mind that they have different aims and timeframes.[561]

561 The *Versneld Regime in Octrooizaken (vro)* can literally be translated as 'accelerated regime in patent cases'. The vro embodies a procedure which is accelerated, summary and prioritised. Most importantly, it is a proceeding on the merits, in

Normally, patent proceedings on the merits takes about 18–24 months.[562] Here the strength of the Dutch *kort geding* proceedings is evident: a case is usually heard within 6 weeks, with a decision usually rendered two weeks later. If necessary, kort geding proceedings can also be held even quicker.[563]

The Dutch *kort geding* procedure has its roots directly in French law and practice, something still stemming from the beginning of the 19th century when Dutch territory was occupied by France.[564] Since 1838, with the enactment of the Dutch Civil Code, the legislative framework governing the *kort geding* has been virtually unchanged and the elements that were required for a preliminary measure at the time, are still required nowadays. What has changed significantly though, is that the procedure transformed from a barely used legal mechanism at first, to a very much applied legal form of relief nowadays. The *kort geding* has taken a huge flight, fuelled

---

contrary to a *kort geding* which always ends with a decision that is provisional of nature (at least on paper). It is a patent-specific procedure and not available for other forms of intellectual property. Although not designed for cases of the highest urgency – for which a kort geding is still a more suitable option – it is significantly quicker than normal proceedings on the merits. Instead of the normal period of 18–24 months until a trial of the merits is finished, an accelerated proceeding can be completed in 10–14 months. Largely this is accomplished by limiting time periods, setting a fixed and tight schedule of procedure in advance and by limiting the pleading rounds. A plaintiff who wants to have the case heard under the vro regime should request and gain approval from the judge ex. Art. 117 RV. The latest rules governing the vro regime are available (in Dutch) via the website of the Court of The Hague. This court has, as in other patent infringement and patent validity cases, sole jurisdiction in these matters:
COURT OF THE HAGUE, *Reglement VRO in octrooizaken* (2010). Available at: https://www.rechtspraak.nl/SiteCollectionDocuments/Reglement-versneld-regime-in-octrooizaken-VRO-reglement.pdf (last accessed on April 17th 2017).
There are now also experiments with a similar accelerated proceedings on appeal (*Versneld Innovatief Appel-procedure*). It should be noted here as well, that courts in other countries have also experimented with similar accelerated proceedings on the merits in patent litigation, as for instance in Germany, where the regional court of Munich did so. See for an article on this: J. STELZER, 'Münchener Verfahren – Patente – Deutlich verkürzter Prozess' *IHK Magazin 'Wirtschaft'* (August 2011).

562 W. HOYNG, F. EIJSVOGELS, chapter 'The Netherlands' in W. HOYNG, F. EIJSVOGELS (eds), *Global Patent litigation* (Kluwer Law Publishing, the Dutch supplement, updated as of December 2014). See: p. 92.

563 Idem, at p. 92.

564 See the seminal work of E.M. MEIJERS, *Het kort geding*, J. TH. VERMEULEN (ed), (1946 Second Edition, Tjeenk Willink Uitgeverij). For an elaborate historical analysis of the development of the *kort geding* in France, see especially the *first chapter* of the book of Meijers.

by three key developments.[565] These are, submitted, partly relevant for the popularity of preliminary injunctions in patent litigation, as well as for other areas of law:

a) a wider notion of tortious action; b) the possibility of demanding both mandatory and prohibitory type of (preliminary) measures (i.e. injunctions); c) the sanctioning of punitive payments to back up the effectiveness of a (preliminary) measures (like injunctions).[566]

It is important to mention here that specifically regarding *kort geding* cases in intellectual property disputes, there has been some doubt whether these were compliant with the TRIPS treaty. *Kort geding* proceedings, and the interim measures flowing from them, were (and still are) so frequent in Dutch intellectual property litigation, that in the past doubt emerged whether the *kort geding* proceedings genuinely were of an interim nature. This was reinforced by the observation that the outcome of a *kort geding* was in practice often regarded as a final decision,[567] instead of being regarded as a temporary measure that is in force until the trial on the merits was finished. Therefore, in the trademark case of *Hermés*[568] the following question was submitted to the CJEU for further clarification:

> "Does an interim measure, as, for example, provided for in Article 289 et seq. <these were the old provisions regulating the kort geding> of the Code of Civil Procedure, whereby an immediate, enforceable measure may be sought, fall within the scope of the expression "provisional measures" within the meaning of Article 50 of the Agreement on Trade-Related Aspects of Intellectual Property Rights?"[569]

The CJEU replied positively to this and confirmed that the Dutch *kort geding* proceedings were within the scope of the TRIPS provisions. It ruled that:

> "Any possible willingness of the parties to accept the interim judgment as a 'final' resolution of their dispute cannot alter the legal nature of a measure characterised as 'provisional' for the purposes of Article 50 of the TRIPS Agreement."[570]

According to the CJEU judges, the (outcome of a) Dutch *kort geding* therefore had *all the hallmarks* of a measure in the sense of Art. 50 TRIPS.

---

565 A.S. RUEB, E. GRAS, A.W. JONGBLOED, *Compendium van het Burgerlijk Procesrecht* (2015 20th edition, Kluwer Publishing). See: p. 311.

566 Ibidem.

567 As A.S. RUEB, E. GRAS, and A.W. JONGBLOED, *Compendium van het Burgerlijk Procesrecht* (2015 20th edition, Kluwer Publishing) write on p. 320, that according to an expert estimation, 95% of the cases in a *kort geding* (not limited to the field of intellectual property) do not continue on to a trial on the merits, simply because the litigants do not believe that the result will be different.

568 CJEU, C-53/96 *Hermés International v FHT Marketing Choice BV*, June 16th, 1998, ECLI:EU:C:1998:292. See especially par. 36–43 of this CJEU ruling.

569 Idem, at par. 21. The actual preliminary question asked is formulated in par. 34 of the decision.

570 Idem, at par. 44.

§7.1.2. Legal basis

Article 70 (1) of the *Rijksoctrooiwet* (ROW, the Dutch Patent Code),[571] states that the patentee can enforce its patent against anyone who infringes his exclusive rights. These rights are mentioned in Art. 53 (1) ROW.[572] As is argued by Verschuur and Van Dongen,[573] the Duch Supreme Court (*de Hoge Raad*) has pointed to the limited duration of the patent right and the effectiveness of a quick injunction in preventing further infringement and that the *kort geding* is an acceptable and important mechanism in which relief can be offered to rights holders in this.[574]

The *kort geding* is of a general purpose and its legal basis and core principles are not to be found in the ROW, but in Art. 254–259 of the *Wetboek Burgerlijke Rechtsvordering* (RV the Dutch Code of Civil Procedure). The provisions on the *kort geding* are short and rather general of nature. It is important to note here that in a Dutch preliminary injunction proceedings, there is always a single judge (the so-called *Voorzieningenrechter, Vzr.*) who decides on the preliminary injunction request.[575] The latter differs on appeal in *kort geding*.

---

571 Art. 70 (1) ROW: "De octrooihouder kan zijn octrooi handhaven jegens een ieder die, zonder daartoe gerechtigd te zijn, een der in artikel 53, eerste lid, genoemde handelingen verricht."
Note that this provision is directed towards *civil enforcement*, since a different article (namely Art. 79 ROW) opens the way for possible criminal enforcement against infringing parties.

572 Art. 53 (1) ROW: "Een octrooi geeft de octrooihouder, behoudens de bepalingen van de artikelen 53a tot en met 60, het uitsluitend recht: a. het geoctrooieerde voortbrengsel in of voor zijn bedrijf te vervaardigen, te gebruiken, in het verkeer te brengen of verder te verkopen, te verhuren, af te leveren of anderszins te verhandelen, dan wel voor een of ander aan te bieden, in te voeren of in voorraad te hebben; b. de geoctrooieerde werkwijze in of voor zijn bedrijf toe te passen of het voortbrengsel, dat rechtstreeks verkregen is door toepassing van die werkwijze, in of voor zijn bedrijf te gebruiken, in het verkeer te brengen of verder te verkopen, te verhuren, af te leveren of anderszins te verhandelen, dan wel voor een of ander aan te bieden, in te voeren of in voorraad te hebben."

573 A. VERSCHUUR, P. VAN DONGEN, 'Commentary on Art. 70 (1) ROW', pp. 612–615 in CH. GIELEN, D.J.G. VISSER (eds), *Tekst & Commentaar Intellectuele Eigendom* (2013 Wolters Kluwer).

574 Idem, citing the Dutch Supreme Court: Hoge Raad, *Vredo v Veenhuis,* June 4th 1993, NJ 1993/659.

575 See Art. 50 of the *Wet op Rechterlijke Organisatie* (Law on the Organisation of Judiciary). Here it is stated that this judge is called the 'Voorzieningenrechter' and is either the President of the Court, or one of the Vice Presidents.

Art. 254 (1) RV forms the main legal basis: it can be translated as follows:

"In all the cases where there is urgency, as regards to the interests of the parties, and this urgency requires an immediate decision, the presiding *kort geding* judge is entitled to provide interim relief."[576]

Figure 5. The Dutch preliminary injunction test (own image).

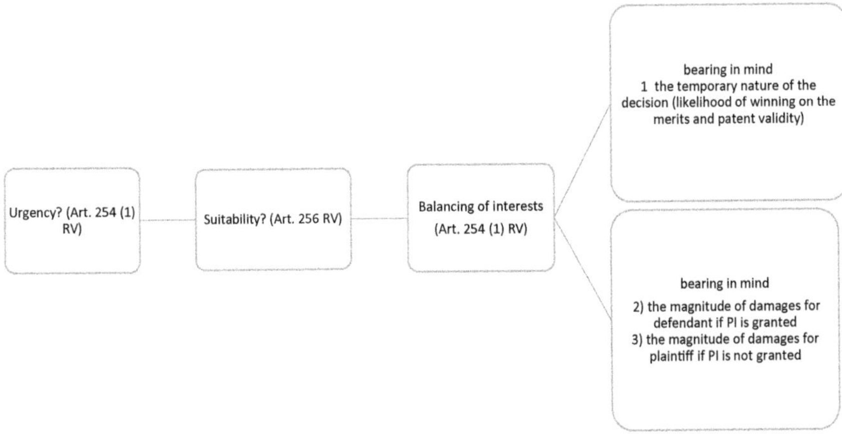

§7.1.3. *Urgency*

Urgency, is therefore the first principle that is required and is something that is firstly considered by the judge. It is to be interpreted as urgency in a *temporal sense* and not so much as the *need* for an injunction. Investigated is for instance whether the time period of simply waiting until the trial on the merits would be unacceptable. Also, it should just as well be clear that the plaintiff should not have waited too long with bringing a case before the court. As will be seen, the latter ground – to deny a preliminary injunction due to lack of urgency – is regularly invoked by the defendant and sometimes indeed accepted by the court. Kramer, one of the leading authors on the Dutch *kort geding*, raises the valid point that it is difficult to say much in general terms about how urgency is valued, because much about it revolves around the specific facts of the case and how this is assessed.[577]

576 The original wording of Art. 254 (1) RV is: "In alle spoedeisende zaken waarin, gelet op de belangen van partijen, een onmiddellijke voorziening bij voorraad wordt vereist, is de voorzieningenrechter bevoegd deze te geven." The other provisions of Art. 254 RV are mainly about procedural matters and on which specific court in The Netherlands can seize jurisdiction in this.

577 X.E. KRAMER, *Het kort geding in internationaal perspectief* (2001 Kluwer Uitgeverij). See: pp. 16–17.

However, she stresses that in practice in The Netherlands, urgency is not so much an issue regarding disputes concerning intellectual property infringement.[578] As she explains, due to the special nature of intellectual property rights, urgency is in practice easily assumed by the *kort geding* judge.[579]

And indeed, when looking at intellectual property case law, it is often stated that 'urgency follows *from the nature of the claims'* (or a similar wording) and then urgency does not have to be proven explicitly or separately.[580] However, as Kramer also submits, that whilst the urgency hurdle may not seem to be as stringent in practice as the law initially seems to require – at least for intellectual property infringement cases – it is certainly not to be seen as a dead-letter provision. A well-motivated argument by the defendant raising doubts about the urgency can turn the tables and lead the judge to reject a request for a preliminary injunction.[581]

Practice confirms this: a good example of this is depicted in the case of *Delaval v Boumatic Robotics*.[582] The defendant against the infringement allegation, Boumatic, tried to invoke a lack of urgency defence by pointing out that the plaintiff DeLaval knew well in advance about Boumatic's activities before it decided to launch a *kort geding*. Boumatic argued that both companies had presented on the same trade fairs and a video about the allegedly infringing machine of Boumatic was publicly available on YouTube.[583] The *kort geding* judge acknowledged these points, but however did not accept that they were sufficient. It held that DeLaval did not have to act immediately, as it first needed to make further investigations prior to going to court, such as checking for infringement with a customer of Boumatic.[584, 585] The urgency required for a preliminary injunction was still held to be pressing.[586]

---

578 Ibidem.

579 Ibidem.

580 See for example the cases of Vzr. Rechtbank Den Haag, *High Point SARL v Koninklijke KPN N.V. et al. and Ericsson Telecommunicatie B.V.*, May 26th 2009, KG ZA 09–157. Vzr. Rechtbank Den Haag, *SCA v MTS*, February 20th 2012, IEPT20120220 and Vzr. Rechtbank Den Haag, *Sirvis B.V. and Serrix B.V. v. Medical Brands B.V. and Progressare B.V*, February 13th 2014, KG ZA 13–1464. Also see W. TONKENS-GERKEMA in A.I.M. VAN MIERLO, C.J.J.C. VAN NISPEN, M.V. POLAK (eds) *Tekst & Commentaar Burgerlijke Rechtsvordering* (2008 Wolters Kluwer). See: p. 462.

581 Ibidem. Tonkens-Gerkema also mentions that the need for urgent relief should still exist at the time the actual decision (court order) is made.

582 Vzr. Rechbank Den Haag, *DeLaval Holding AB v Boumatic Robotics B.V*, December 7th 2012, KG-ZA 12–1165.

583 Idem, at par. 4.4.

584 Idem, at par. 4.5.

585 However, in for instance Gerechtshof Den Haag, *Boston Scientific v OrbusNeich*, March 13th 2012, IEPT20120313, it was ruled that the plaintiff had taken too long to commence with preliminary injunction proceedings after it had become clear that patent infringement had occurred.

586 Ibidem.

Another reason is given in *High Point Sarl v KPN / Ericsson* that was about the infringement of a patent for a *wireless access telephone-to-telephone network interface architecture.*[587] The defendant alleged that the plaintiff had waited for *too long* (namely seven months after the first use of the patented invention by the defendant) before requesting a preliminary injunction and this delay in taking action took away the necessary urgency. The court disagreed with this view, stating that the relevant moment in time that this period starts was to be seen differently, thereby also underlining the importance of *negotiations* instead of rushing to court:

> "swift actions <by the plaintiff> are expected at the moment it becomes clear to her that infringement is taking place **and that negotiations will not lead to a solution**. Furthermore, taking into account the **special complexity of this case**, as also acknowledged by KPN, one cannot argue that High Point has undertaken too little action to not be able to act in this procedure."[588]

Similarly, in *AstraZeneca v Sandoz,*[589] it was determined that *urgency* was *not taken away* when the patentee does not accept *earlier offers that are voluntarily made* by the generics company – this even when the first of such an offer is made a year prior to the start of a preliminary injunction proceedings.[590] With such an offer, the generics company, in order to avoid the (litigation) costs (the outcome of) a *kort geding* entails, offered to refrain from launching a generic product until the question of patent validity had been resolved on appeal in The Netherlands.[591] In return for this, the generics company required that the plaintiff-patentee would hold itself liable for its damages if the patent in the invalidity ruling is invalidated. Relevant here is that the *kort geding* judge ruled that the fact that *AstraZeneca could thus have prevented infringement at an earlier stage,* did not impact the urgency of the request.[592]

What also seems to matter in this respect, is the time that a patent is still valid at the moment of the preliminary injunction request. A patent expiration in the short term heightens the chance that urgency is presumed, as otherwise the outcome of

---

587 Vzr. Rechtbank Den Haag, *High Point SARL v Koninklijke KPN N.V. et al. and Ericsson Telecommunicatie B.V.,* May 26th 2009, KG ZA 09–157.

588 Idem, at par. 4.2. Own translation. Emphasis added. Original text: "Van de eisende partij mag als regel voortvarend handelen worden verwacht op het moment dat haar duidelijk is dat, naar zij meent, inbreuk op haar rechten wordt gemaakt en dat overleg niet tot een oplossing zal leiden. Gelet op de, ook door KPN aangevoerde, bijzondere complexiteit van het geschil kan echter niet worden geoordeeld dat High Point de inbreuk te veel op zijn beloop heeft gelaten om daar nog in deze procedure tegen op te treden."

589 Vzr. Rechtbank Den Haag, *AstraZeneca AB vs Sandoz B.V.* August 15th 2013, KG ZA 13–854.

590 Idem, at par. 4.2 and par. 4.3.

591 Idem, at par. 2.13 and par. 2.15.

592 Idem, at par. 4.3.

an alternative trial on the merits may well be after the moment patent protection has ended. However, this seems only to be so when the plaintiff himself also has made *sufficient efforts* into bringing his request for interim relief in time, so that a preliminary injunction is still of some use in the remaining lifetime of the patent.[593]

Urgency also plays a role, in practice, when infringement is *not yet occurring*: this is specifically the case with imminent infringement due to generic entry. This phenomenon brings unique questions along: is a plaintiff for a preliminary injunction for instance entitled to deduce that infringement is imminent from the fact that a) the infringer-defendant has received a marketing authorisation and b) at the same time refused to provide an undertaking to the patentee that it would not launch its product? No, said the court:

> "There is no general legal obligation to provide a written confirmation in which third parties (or competitors) are to confirm someone's absolute rights (something Eli Lilly appears to assume). **The refusal to do so does not result in an (urgent) interest** on which an injunction in kort geding can be based, **at least not without additional circumstances, which are perceived to be absent in this particular case.** This is why there cannot be an infringement of rights from Ratiopharm with respect to Lilly – or a specific threat of infringement to justify a preliminary injunction in kort geding."[594]

In doing so, the court held that such additional circumstances were not present and thus there was no case of imminent infringement, because:

- plaintiff Eli Lilly's argument that the defendant Ratiopharm had already commenced with invalidity proceedings in The Netherlands regarding Eli Lilly's patent was not to be seen as an additional (threatening) circumstance. Competitors are allowed to do so, and the fact that this particular competitor had already obtained marketing approval did not make a difference in this.[595]
- the fact that Ratiopharm *Germany* had earlier already entered the German market with a generic product, was not in itself seen as a telling precedent that should result in the grant of a preliminary injunction in The Netherlands. The *kort geding* judge noted that Ratiopharm Germany had only done so after the German *Bundespatentgericht* had held that Eli Lilly's patent was invalid and only then had Ratiopharm entered.[596]
- according to the 'sunset clause' in Directive 2001/83/EC, three years after the obtaining of marketing approval (as Ratiopharm had), a pharmaceutical should be launched on the market or otherwise the granted marketing approval expires.

593 See for instance Vzr. Rechtbank Den Haag, *Rhodia Chemie v PPG,* April 25th 2012, KG ZA 12–224.

594 Vzr. Rechtbank Den Haag, *Eli Lilly v Ratiopharm,* April 7th 2008, KG ZA 08–63. See par. 4.7. Own translation from Dutch. Emphasis added.

595 Idem, at par. 4.6.

596 Ibidem.

However, as the *kort geding* judge pointed out, this period commences *after* the patent has expired and this sunset period did not fall or end *within* Eli Lilly's patent lifetime of a remaining four years.[597] This too thus did not contribute to an additional (threatening) circumstance that justified the grant of a preliminary injunction.

- it was finally ruled that the fact that Ratiopharm had already obtained marketing approval a good *four years before the expiration of the patent*, without having apparent and specific plans of entering the market on short notice, was not something that was to be seen as suspicious or threatening in itself. This was perceived as being non-infringing behaviour by a competitor, as the outcome of invalidity proceedings may be positive for Ratiopharm, after which it could go to market swiftly.[598, 599] This too did not amount to imminent infringement.

A very similar case generic entry case, *Merck v Teva*,[600] had an almost identical factual situation as set out above. Here too, the *kort geding* judge reviewed (threatening) additional circumstances that warranted the conclusion that infringement is imminent:

- the fact that the defendant Teva, whilst maybe not having a spotlessly clean history when it came to launching its generic products was not deemed to be a factor that contributed to the need of urgent preliminary relief due to imminent infringement. Although Teva in the past may have launched a product 'at risk', the judge also observed that Teva could also point out many successful and non-infringing launches of generic pharmaceuticals.[601] A case-by-case assessment thus seemed warranted.
- in this light, it was also underlined by the *kort geding* judge that the defendant's interest in keeping its corporate information confidential (including the launch plans and schedules of its products) was of more weight than the plaintiff's interest in being warned on time.[602]

Instead, in practice in such generic entry cases, it is the moment that the defendant subscribes to the *G-Standaard* that is often seen as a definitive sign of imminent infringement, thereby triggering the required urgency that is one of the requirements

---

597 Ibidem.
598 Vzr. Rechtbank Den Haag, *Eli Lilly v Ratiopharm*, April 7th 2008, KG ZA 08–63. See: par. 4.8.
599 Vzr. Rechtbank Den Haag, *Novartis v Actavis*, July 8th 2009, KG ZA 09–611. See: par. 4.5.
600 Vzr. Rechtbank Den Haag, *Merck Sharp & Dohme v Teva Pharma B.V.*, March 27th 2012, KG ZA 12–138.
601 Idem, at par. 4.10.
602 Idem, at par. 4.11–4.12.

for the grant of a preliminary injunction.[603] The *G-Standaard* is a Dutch national database that is used by doctors, health insurance companies, hospitals and pharmacists, and includes a list of all pharmaceutical products which are allowed on the Dutch market, including their prices.

§7.1.4. Suitability

The second principle that is required by the law is *suitability*. With this, it is meant that the case should be fit to be decided on in the summary procedure of a *kort geding*. This does not only refer to 'suitability' in terms of (technical or legal) complexity but also means that the decision in *kort geding* is not solely of constitutive or declaratory nature. If a case is not suitable, Art. 256 RV gives the *kort geding* judge the possibility and authority to deny making a judgment on the request for an interim measure before him:

> "When the case is deemed to be unsuitable to be resolved in a kort geding, the judge will deny its judgment."[604]

At this point, a further provision should be mentioned that is connected to the issue of suitability. Art. 257 RV states that the *kort geding* has no bearing on the result of the trial on the merits.[605] As Rueb *et al.* explain, originally this meant that the judge could not give an interim ruling when this result could not be undone at the trial on the merits.[606] In those cases the request for an interim measure would not be seen as suitable.[607] The current view on this provision is that this article is not directed to the judge in *kort geding*, but rather to the court deciding at the trial on the merits. This means that the court is not bound in any way by the decision taken by the judge in the *kort geding* earlier.[608] It is submitted by some commentators, that the abovementioned current view of this provision has also largely contributed to the rise of the number of *kort geding* cases.[609]

---

603 See: Vzr. Rechtbank Den Haag, *Sanofi v Pharmachemie/Teva*, September 14th 2012, KG ZA 12–905, par. 2.14 and Vzr. Rechtbank Den Haag, provisioneel vonnis in *Sanofi v Pharmachemie/Teva*, September 3rd 2012, IEPT20120903. Also see Vzr. Rechtbank Den Haag, *The Wellcome Foundation & GSK v Mylan*, April 17th 2013, IEPT20130417. See: par. 4.2.

604 The original text of Art. 256 RV is: "Indien de voorzieningenrechter oordeelt dat de zaak niet geschikt is om in kort geding te worden beslist, weigert hij de voorziening."

605 Art. 257 RV: "De beslissingen bij voorraad brengen geen nadeel toe aan de zaak ten principale."

606 A.S. RUEB, E. GRAS, A.W. JONGBLOED, *Compendium van het Burgerlijk Procesrecht* (2015, 20th edition, Kluwer Publishing). See: pp. 313–314.

607 Ibidem.

608 Ibidem.

609 X.E. KRAMER, *Het kort geding in internationaal perspectief* (2001 Kluwer Uitgeverij). See: p. 14.

In any case, as was for instance pointed out in *Unilever v Procter & Gamble,*[610] the preliminary injunction judge should be very reluctant in applying Art. 256 RV and hold that a case is unsuitable for *kort geding* proceedings. This is even so when there are pending proceedings on the merits in other countries with respect to the same patent or when a decision on a patent's validity by the Boards of Appeal at the EPO is to be expected soon. Then as well, a *kort geding* is not likely to be held unsuitable. Nor is this the likely outcome when the potential damage of a possible erroneous decision in *kort geding* would be large.[611] Also in such a case, the *kort geding* judge is in principle considered of being up to the task of handling the case before him and in principle will give a substantive ruling on whether or not to grant a preliminary injunction.

§7.1.5. Balancing

Apart from the principles of *suitability* and *urgency,* the third core principle that is prescribed in the law is that Dutch *kort geding* judges should also undertake a *balancing test* regarding the interests of the parties (*belangenafweging*). Although this is not something that is explicitly and clearly stipulated as such, this is read into the wording of Art. 254 (1) that speak of "*as regards to the interests of the parties.*" Note that *interests* and *parties* are given in the plural form and this is to be interpreted as meaning that the judge shall have regard to more than just the interests of the plaintiff alone.[612] This will in any case include the interests of the defendant. This balancing of interests encompasses a 'likelihood of success test', in which the *kort geding* judge makes an assessment of the legal merits of the plaintiff's request. This is a critical part of the *belangenafweging*. Furthermore, the balancing of interests can encompass an assessment of other interests and harms parties face, in the case a preliminary injunction is denied or granted.

Rueb *et al.,*[613] Kramer,[614] and Tonkens-Gerkema[615] point out that the first element of the *belangenafweging* is that the judge should have the confidence that the

---

Also see the book of F. SCHNEIDER, *Die Leistungsverfügung im Niederländischen, Deutschen und Europäischen Zivilprozessrecht* (2013 Mohr Siebeck). See: pp. 146–149.

610 Vzr. Rechtbank Den Haag, *Unilever N.V. v. Procter & Gamble Nederland B.V. et al,* December 19th 2013, KG ZA 13–1038.

611 Idem, at par. 4.13–4.14.

612 Also see, E.M. MEIJERS, *Het kort geding,* J. TH. VERMEULEN (ed), (1946 Second Edition, Tjeenk Willink Uitgeverij). See: p. 103.

613 A.S. RUEB, E. GRAS, A.W. JONGBLOED, *Compendium van het Burgerlijk Procesrecht* (2015 20th edition, Kluwer Publishing). See: p. 314.

614 X.E. KRAMER, *Het kort geding in internationaal perspectief* (2001 Kluwer Uitgeverij). See: p. 19.

615 W. TONKENS-GERKEMA in A.I.M. VAN MIERLO, C.J.J.C. VAN NISPEN, M.V. POLAK (eds) *Tekst & Commentaar Burgerlijke Rechtsvordering* (2008 Wolters Kluwer). See: p. 462.

outcome of a *kort geding* will be the same as on the later trial on the merits.[616] In this sense, the notion of what in other countries and in the bulk of the literature is dubbed as the '*likelihood of success*', in The Netherlands is *incorporated* as part of the *belangenafweging* test. To a certain extent this is somewhat confusing as in some countries, like the United States, the likelihood of success and balancing of interests tests are separate.

The 'likelihood of success' in patent litigation includes issues of patent validity and infringement. This proves to be the most critical part of a preliminary injunction request in The Netherlands and in practice these issues are often the only real subject of debate.[617]

With respect to (likely) *infringement*, the court will in general review the arguments made by the plaintiff on whom, in principle, lies the burden of proof to convince the judge that his patent is infringed by the defendant and that therefore a preliminary injunction is necessary.[618] In doing so, the court can both look at infringement in a literal sense and at infringement falling within the scope of the *Doctrine of Equivalence*.[619]

Regarding *patent validity*, it is to be observed that the Dutch preliminary injunction doctrine features no legal requirement that the patent should have been tested before in earlier legal proceedings, in order to warrant a preliminary injunction. This means that the *kort geding* judge can just as well grant a preliminary injunction to a patent that has survived prior invalidity and revocation proceedings, as it can grant a preliminary injunction to a patent that has not gone yet through such proceedings prior to the request for interim relief. In both cases, the *kort geding*

---

616 A.S. RUEB, E. GRAS, A.W. JONGBLOED, *Compendium van het Burgerlijk Procesrecht* (2015 20th edition, Kluwer Publishing). See: p. 314.

617 See for instance, Vzr. Rechtbank Den Haag, *Global Factories B.V. v ZIUZ*, December 3rd 2010, KG ZA10–1216.

618 According to the general principles of Dutch laws on civil procedure, Art. 150 RV.

619 In general, this follows from Art. 69 EPC and *the Protocol on its Interpretation.* Recent cases on this from the Dutch Supreme Court are that of Hoge Raad, *AGA v Occlutech*, May 25th 2012, ECLI:NL:HR:2012:BV3680, and Hoge Raad, *Medinol v Abbott*, April 4th 2015, ECLI:NL:HR:2014:816. These cases, along with other rulings, confirm that numerous issues are to be taken account in establishing the equivalence: the literal wording of the claims, common knowledge, the nature of the patent, the granting file of the patent office, the description in the patent application, the debate between parties at trial and in opposition proceedings etc. For an example of a preliminary injunction case where the plaintiff fails to meet this burden and prove equivalence: Vzr. Rechtbank Den Haag, *Matador v Bick*, April 22nd 2015 KG ZA 14–754. See par. 4.12: "Therefore, there is a considerable chance that also in a trial on the merits no infringement, not even in the sense of equivalence, will be accepted." Own translation.

judge anticipates the issue of patent validity (afresh).[620] Nor is there, with respect to pharmaceuticals in a generic entry setting, *a special presumption* that protects these type of patents more than other categories of patents, in the sense that patent infringement and validity are easier assumed. A similar presumption, as will be seen, sometimes exists in other countries.

In practice the only situation when the *kort geding* judge will not accept the 'likelihood of success' of a plaintiff's request for interim relief, is when he has doubts about the validity of the patent. These doubts are then to such an extent that the judge believes that there is a considerable chance ('*gerede kans*') that subsequently this patent may be invalidated at the trial on the merits,[621] or that infringement will not be proven at that stage.

Upon reading *kort geding* decisions, it becomes clear that the Dutch preliminary injunction court in principle is prepared to relatively deeply engage on the issues of patent infringement and validity. With respect to patent validity, the legal debate will concentrate on new arguments questioning the validity which are brought by the defendant, as well as the arguments in favour submitted by the plaintiff. The focus will be less on invalidity arguments that have been brought forward during the *granting process* of the patent in question.[622] This is notably different from the role a judge has during the trial on the merits, in which a judge should conduct a more independent and thorough analysis of *all* the aspects concerning validity of the disputed patent.[623]

It is furthermore clear that when an earlier ruling on a patent's validity has taken place, the preliminary injunction judge should in principle take into account the previous decision by a Dutch court on a patent's validity and follow this ruling (so-called 'attuning'). It was held for instance in *AstraZeneca v Sandoz*, that a *kort geding was not the place to redo the work* of the trial court on the issue of validity of a patent, but that nevertheless exceptions to this remained possible and could impact the decision to grant a preliminary injunction:

> "In principle, there is no place in a kort geding to (again) investigate the validity of a patent that has been held valid in a regular proceedings on the merits, nor to estimate the chance of success of an invalidity request at the court of appeal. This is different in

---

620 See for instance: Vzr. Rechtbank Den Haag, *Novartis v Alvogen & Focus Farma*, 23 December 2013, KG ZA 13–1160. The decision was confirmed on appeal in Gerechtshof Den Haag, *Novartis v Alvogen & Focus Farma*, November 18th 2014, ECLI: NL:GHDHA:2014:36.

621 A. VERSCHUUR, P. VAN DONGEN, 'Commentary on Art. 70 (1) ROW' in CH. GIELEN, D.J.G. VISSER (eds), *Tekst & Commentaar Intellectuele Eigendom* (2013 Wolters Kluwer). See: p. 618, citing Hoge Raad, *Tetra Laval Food Koppens v Meyn Machinefabrieken*, October 26 2001, ECLI:NL:HR:2001:AB2774. See: par. 3.4.2.

622 J.L.R.A. HUYDECOPER, C.J.J.C. VAN NISPEN (eds), *Industriële eigendom, deel 1, bescherming van technische innovatie* (2002 Kluwer Publishing). See: p. 173.

623 Ibidem.

> the case of obvious errors, or when circumstances arise after the ruling of the court, that would have had an influence on its decision, would they have been known at the time."[624]

This is in line with what Van den Broek wrote, on this 'attunement rule' (*afstemmingsregel*). He states that the bar for not following such a previous court decision on patent validity is *very high.*[625] This is either so whether the patent has been upheld or has been invalidated. Van den Broek states that this is different in the case of an 'obvious error', or in other words when there is a "so clearly visible error in law and fact, that in relation there can be no reasonable doubt, without further investigation."[626]

The latter was for instance not deemed to be the case in the *kort geding* of *AstraZeneca-Sandoz.* Sandoz argued in vain that a Dutch court had made 'obvious errors' in an earlier invalidity ruling, in which the patent was held to be valid. These were, Sandoz argued, firstly that the court previously had not applied the *Problem Solution Approach* correctly and secondly that the earlier court had made errors with its view on the *first pass metabolism rate* and the *PH-dependent solvability* of quetiapine.[627] The *kort geding* court refused to accept either argument, pointing out that these were complicated issues to which there were various views and that in any case it was not clear if one of these other perspectives would have been followed, this would have resulted into a different decision. It held that these points did certainly not qualify as 'obvious errors' and were not sufficient to set aside an earlier invalidity judgment of a Dutch court in the pending *kort geding.*[628, 629] Subsequently,

---

624 Own translation. See: Vzr. Rechtbank Den Haag, *AstraZeneca AB v Sandoz B.V.* August 15th 2013, KG ZA 13–854 at par. 4.7. "Er is in beginsel geen ruimte in kort geding (opnieuw) de geldigheid te onderzoeken van een octrooi dat door de bodemrechter reeds geldig is geacht, dan wel om de kans van slagen van een hoger beroep van een dergelijk vonnis in te schatten. Dit is evenwel anders als de bodemrechter kennelijke misslagen heeft begaan of wanneer omstandigheden die zich hebben voorgedaan na het oordeel van de bodemrechter het oordeel ten gronde hadden beïnvloed als deze daar kennis van had genomen." Citing the Dutch Supreme Court in: Hoge Raad, *Yukos v Rosneft*, January 7th 2011, ECLI:NL:HR:2011:BP0015. Also see par. 4.11 of the abovementioned case of Vzr. Rechtbank Den Haag, *AstraZeneca AB v Sandoz B.V.* August 15th 2013, KG ZA 13–854.

625 B. VAN DEN BROEK, 'The Lundbeck Saga' in *Liber Amicorum Willem Hoyng* (2013 Uitgeverij deLex), pp. 64–87. See: pp. 82 -83.

626 Ibidem.

627 Vzr. Rechtbank Den Haag, *AstraZeneca AB v Sandoz B.V.* August 15th 2013, KG ZA 13–854. See: par. 4.8.

628 Idem, at par. 4.9–4.12.

629 Idem in Vzr. Rechtbank Den Haag, *Novartis v Actavis*, July 8th 2009, KG ZA 09-611. Also here, the prior court's decision on the merits was not seen as containing 'obvious errors' and the preliminary injunction judge thus had to follow the earlier decision that the disputed patent was invalid. Therefore, the preliminary injunction was denied. See: par. 4.13.

the preliminary injunction was granted due to the plaintiff's likelihood of success on the merits. It is therefore clear that, also here, the threshold for the court to set aside an earlier ruling on (in)validity is high and an 'obvious error' should be so clear in law and in fact that reasonable doubt exists, without further investigation on the clarity of this error being necessary.

As Van den Broek notes, this high standard seems to be at odds with the situation of when preliminary injunctive relief is requested following a decision of the EPO in Opposition in first instance.[630] Should Dutch courts rely on this result pending an appeal made to the Boards of Appeal at the EPO? With respect to this, the Dutch *Hoge Raad* has established on multiple occasions that what matters in these cases is what the preliminary injunction court *believes what will happen* on appeal and whether there is a *serious chance* that the outcome will be different. As one can see, this is thus not limited to situations of 'obvious errors'.[631] This thus results, as Van den Broek argues, with a high threshold and higher respect for Dutch court decisions on the merits regarding patent validity than for EPO first instance decisions.[632] Thus for instance, in *Coloplast v Medical4you*,[633] it is also shown that despite an earlier EPO Opposition decision which ruled that the contested patent was valid, the preliminary injunction judge nevertheless made its own assessment and held that it was nevertheless still *likely* that the patent would be held invalid at the Boards of Appeal of the EPO or in national patent invalidity proceedings, due to a probable lack of inventive step.[634]

Another issue that is also interesting, is that Dutch courts have regularly taken prior foreign judgments on validity and infringement into account, when deciding on whether or not to grant a preliminary injunction. They have not always felt bound to them. Rather, such judgments are cited when they are perceived as similar enough and when it is believed that the foreign judicial review has been conducted in a proper manner. Thus, in the case of *Novartis AG v Sun Pharmaceutical Industries*[635] a preliminary injunction was *not* granted after the Dutch judge concluded that there was a 'serious chance' that the patent would not likely be held valid at

630 B. VAN DEN BROEK, 'The Lundbeck Saga' in *Liber Amicorum Willem Hoyng* (2013 Uitgeverij deLex) pp. 64–87. See: pp. 83–84.

631 Idem, at p. 84. Cited are the Dutch Supreme Court cases in Hoge Raad, *Meyn v Tetra* October 26 2001, thereby rejecting the earlier view on this issue from Hoge Raad, *Boehringer Mannheim v Kirin Amgen*, 21 April 1995, where it was stated that EPO Opposition proceedings can be equated to Dutch proceedings on the merits.

632 Idem, at p. 84.

633 Vzr.Rechtbank Den Haag, *Coloplast A/S v Medical4you B.V.*, August 14th 2015, KG ZA 15–9.

634 Idem, see par. 4.31, par. 4.33 and par. 4.25–4.31. It was held that it was likely that the 'Person Skilled in the Art' would have come to the same insight as was in the claimed embodiment.

635 Vzr. Rechtbank Den Haag, *Novartis AG v Sun Pharmaceutical Industries (Europe) B.V.*, 12 mei 2014, KG ZA 14–185.

trial, due to lack of novelty. In doing so, the court noted that it was strengthened in this view because the invalidity of the patent had been concluded twice before by an English court *after* a trial on the merits.[636] This had been on similar concerns as well as after a thorough hearing of experts in those cases.[637] Because of the high likelihood of invalidity, the preliminary injunction judge did not go into the issue of infringement anymore itself.[638, 639]

This is not to say, that the judgments of foreign courts are always followed and much depends on how confident the preliminary injunction judge is of the similarity of facts between the cases and on the quality of the analysis that has been undertaken by the foreign courts. This was for instance made clear in *Novartis v Alvogen*.[640, 641] Equally interesting is the decision of the court in *Novartis v*

636 Idem, par. 4.10. "That there is a serious chance that a court at a trial on the merits will declare claim 7 of the Dutch part of the patent as being invalid, on the grounds mentioned above, is stressed by the fact that the English court, at trial on the merits, in two instances has ruled that the similarly worded claim 7 of the English part of the patent is not valid. The judgments of these English courts are based on similar grounds as those mentioned above and also are supported by an elaborate cross-examination of experts." Own translation.

637 Idem, at par. 4.10.

638 Idem, at par. 4.11.

639 However, this ruling of the *kort geding* judge was overturned on appeal eight months later, in Gerechtshof Den Haag, *Novartis AG v Sun Pharmaceutical Industries (Europe)*, January 27th 2015, KG ZA 14–185. *Inter alia*, in contrast to the two English courts and the Dutch preliminary injunction judgment, the Dutch Court of Appeal held that the patentee could rely on the priority of a US patent, due to new insights in reading the priority document and new arguments of the parties. See: par. 4.3. Therefore, the patent of Novartis should be seen as valid. Infringement was also proven.

640 Gerechtshof Den Haag, *Novartis AG v Alvogen*, November 18th, 2014, KG ZA 13–1160. The earlier refusal happened in Vzr. Rechtbank Den Haag, *Novartis v Alvogen & Focus Farma*, 23 December 2013, KG ZA 13–1160. The court observed that with respect to both the issues of validity and infringement, the Dutch view differed from that of various European courts that gave diverging decisions in the same case. However, the Gerechtshof believed that the court could differ from most of its European counterparts. It was explicitly mentioned that the court was entitled to do so since the earlier foreign decisions were not satisfactory from a quality point of view. It was noted that for instance the Italian and Romanian courts had not looked at the issue of patent validity in depth and neither had the Danish and Austrian courts done so in a sufficiently proper manner. Only the German court (LG Düsseldorf) ruled against the grant of an *einstweilige Verfügung* for Novartis, this due to the patent's likely invalidity.

641 Similarly, a case noting the grant of a preliminary injunction in Germany but nevertheless denying a preliminary injunction in the Dutch situation is Vzr. Rechtbank Den Haag, *Global Factories B.V. v ZIUZ*, December 3rd, 2010, KG ZA10–1216.

Actavis[642] in which the court dealt with a situation that there was an earlier Dutch ruling on invalidity as well as conflicting decisions from abroad. The preliminary injunction court then held that whilst it was bound to follow an earlier invalidity decision of a Dutch court – save 'obvious errors' – a diverging decision from abroad, such as from the *Bundespatentgericht*, was then not to be followed, as the Dutch preliminary injunction judge should attune its decision to the earlier Dutch findings.[643]

However, there is more to *belangenafweging* than just the 'likelihood of success' test. Commentators point out that the legal issue underpinning the interests and the corresponding question of 'likelihood of success' is not always determinative in practice in a preliminary injunction court's decision to grant or deny interim relief.[644] These commentators refer to the Supreme Court cases of *Panhonlibco*[645] and especially *Procter & Gamble v Kimberly-Clark*.[646] These rulings have given the *kort geding* judge wide discretion on this issue of *belangenafweging*, and have provided more factors, of a less legal nature, to consider. In its latter decision, the Supreme Court indicated that in deciding whether to actually grant the preliminary injunction, a *kort geding* judge should, when undertaking the exercise of *belangenafweging*, bear the following factors in mind.[647]

---

642 Vzr. Rechtbank Den Haag, *Novartis v Actavis*, July 8th 2009, KG ZA 09–611.

643 Idem, at par. 4.3. "The kort geding judge has to, after all, work under Dutch Civil Procedural Law." Own translation.

644 A.S. RUEB, E. GRAS, A.W. JONGBLOED, *Compendium van het Burgerlijk Procesrecht* (2015 20th edition, Kluwer Publishing), see: p. 314. Also see: W. TONKENS-GERKEMA in A.I.M. VAN MIERLO, C.J.J.C. VAN NISPEN, M.V. POLAK (eds) *Tekst & Commentaar Burgerlijke Rechtsvordering* (2008 Wolters Kluwer), see: p. 462. Finally, see: A. VERSCHUUR & P. VAN DONGEN, 'Commentary on Art. 70 (1) ROW', pp. 612–615 in CH. GIELEN, D.J.G. VISSER (eds), *Tekst & Commentaar Intellectuele Eigendom* (2013 Wolters Kluwer). See: p. 614.

645 X.E. KRAMER, *Het kort geding in internationaal perspectief* (2001 Kluwer Uitgeverij). See: p. 19. She cites the judgment of the Hoge Raad, *Panhonlibco*, January 15th, 1960, NJ 1960 84. This case was about the right of dockworkers to strike. Workers refused the unloading of cargo ships from Panama, Honduras, Liberia and Costa Rica (hence the name Panhonlibco). The Hoge Raad commented in the *obiter dictum* that even despite the question of lawfulness or unlawfulness of the strike action, the question could be raised whether it was for the *kort geding* judge to intervene with a judicial ruling in this matter. From this, the strong discretionary powers of the judge, including sidestepping the legal issue and relying on other interests and efficiency concerns, can be deduced. Also see: pp. 373–375 of C.J.J.C. VAN NISPEN, *Rechterlijk verbod en bevel* (1978 Kluwer) for more on this decision, and for a critical commentary on the case.

646 Hoge Raad, *Procter & Gamble v Kimberley-Clark*, December 15th, 1995, *Bijblad Industrieele Eigendom* No. 12, 1996.

647 See par. 3.4 of *Procter & Gamble v Kimberley-Clark* of the Hoge Raad. "The nature of the kort geding brings along that, in the preliminary view of the *kort*

- The temporary and interim nature of the interim decision to be taken, and what is clear from the interim proceedings so far. Note that this point forms the basis of the 'likelihood of success' test.
- The consequences and magnitude of damages for the defendant when the preliminary injunction is granted.
- The consequences and magnitude of damages for the plaintiff when a preliminary injunction is *not* granted.

It is thus clear that, along with the 'likelihood of success', the preliminary injunction court has more factors which it can take into account in the context of the *belangenafweging*. In practice however, strikingly, these other factors do not play a significant role, at least when it concerns prohibitive preliminary injunctions in patent cases. In fact, in *none* of the recent Dutch patent cases which has been cited in this chapter was an explicit balancing test with respect to other interests than the 'likelihood of success' undertaken. Urgency, the likelihood of patent infringement and the likelihood of patent validity thus form the main battlefields in a preliminary injunction proceeding. Once these have been positively determined, a preliminary injunction is in principle granted by the *kort geding* judge.

The case of *Sanofi v Teva* is an exception to the picture painted above.[648] Here, the defendant Teva argued that a preliminary injunction should not be granted because if it later occurred that Teva, with hindsight, had indeed infringed Sanofi's SPC, it would be much easier for Teva to financially compensate Sanofi then. This in contrast with Sanofi compensating the defendant Teva for the 'missed market access chances' when it turned out that a granted preliminary injunction was granted erroneously. However, the *kort geding* judge refused to go along with Teva's view, reiterating again that because it was likely that the SPC of Sanofi

---

geding judge, the defendant is under the obligation to refrain from certain activities (..) and that such a requested injunction depends on a *balancing exercise. On the one hand, the temporary nature of the court's judgment in kort geding and the impact of the consequences of a possible injunction for the defendant should be taken into account. On the other hand, the damages that the plaintiff faces, also due to the possibility of repeated infringement, when a preliminary injunction is denied, are to be considered.* Such a balancing act, in the case that the kort geding judge rules that the activities are indeed infringing, will likely be in favour of the requested injunction, especially when a continuation of those activities is likely. This does not take away the possibility that a *kort geding* judge can nevertheless, in certain circumstances, deny the requested preliminary injunction, *for example when it is of the view that the interests of the plaintiff are or can be met in a different manner.*" Own translation, slightly edited for readability, emphasis added.

648 Vzr. Rechtbank Den Haag, *Sanofi v Pharmachemie/Teva*, September 14th, 2012, KG ZA 12–905.

would hold at trial, there was little reason to follow Teva in this line of argument.[649] The difficulty of the calculation of compensation in the case of an erroneous preliminary injunction decision was therefore not something that tipped the scales in a different direction.

The abovementioned example thus confirms that even when infringement is found and it is likely that this will be the same result as on trial, the *kort geding* judge is however not under *the obligation* to grant a preliminary injunction and at least will *consider* not granting it, *based on the other parties' interests*.[650] Instead, as the literature also points out, the preliminary injunction court may decide otherwise when this is justified on for instance the grounds of balancing the (various) interests against each other, or on the grounds of efficiency.[651] This is, as Verschuur and Van Dongen point out, in stark contrast with the very limited discretion a judge has in The Netherlands when deciding in a trial on the merits.[652] With respect to this, they argue that Art. 3:296 (1) *Burgerlijk Wetboek* (BW, Dutch Civil Code) opposes judicial discretion at a trial on the merits, and this limits the possibility of denying a *permanent* injunction when infringement is found, unless residual discretion is explicitly provided for in the Law.[653] Examples of the latter would be in cases of overriding major societal interests (Art. 6:168 BW)[654] or when there has been a misuse of powers (Art. 3:13 BW). Both grounds are rarely invoked successfully.

However, despite this given judicial discretion to look at a multitude of factors in the *belangenafweging* stage of a *kort geding*, as said, an explicit review of the parties' other interests rarely take place when deciding on a preliminary injunction in patent litigation and it in practice are the legal merits of a case – the likelihood of patent infringement and patent validity- along with urgency, that determine

---

649 Idem, at par. 4.36.

650 See par. 3.4 of Vzr. Rechtbank Den Haag, *Sanofi v Pharmachemie/Teva*, September 14th, 2012, KG ZA 12–905.

651 Ibidem.

652 A. VERSCHUUR, P. VAN DONGEN, 'Commentary on Art. 70 (1) ROW', pp. 612–615 in CH. GIELEN, D.J.G. VISSER (eds), *Tekst & Commentaar Intellectuele Eigendom* (2013 Wolters Kluwer). See: p. 614. Furthermore, see Hoge Raad, *Procter & Gamble v Kimberley Clark*, par. 3.3, in which it is stated that the court can decide to deny a preliminary injunction when there are other ways to temporarily aid the plaintiff and provide him relief.

653 Ibidem.

654 Ibidem. The text of 6:168 BW is worth noting here: "The judge can deny a request, aiming to enjoin an unlawful activity, on the basis that this activity, because of very important societal interests, should be endured. The harmed party has a right to compensation of the damages (..)." Own translation.

the outcome.[655] Nevertheless, sometimes the court still balances other interests at *different prongs* than the actual *belangenafweging* stage. The court did so for instance under the *urgency* heading in *Apple v Samsung*.[656] There the court noted that the patents central to this dispute were on Computer-Implemented Inventions and it would therefore be *relatively easy and little work* for Samsung to alter the software in its products in such a manner that the products would no longer be infringing. Because of this, the court was willing to easier accept the aspect of urgency, that the plaintiff, Apple, had put forward.

Finally, it should be mentioned that the court can somewhat balance the effects of its decision with respect to the *scope and nature of the preliminary injunction itself*. As commentators note, the preliminary injunction should be proportionate and effective and the grant can be subject to certain conditions or a time limit.[657] In principle, the plaintiff can formulate the scope of the preliminary injunction as he desires, although the preliminary injunction court has a wide discretion to amend this.[658] The court can use this for instance to *tailor its result*, something that happened in the abovementioned *Apple v Samsung* case. Here it ruled that it would provide for a six-weeks delay before the preliminary injunction would become effective. By doing so, the grant of the interim injunction would not directly hamper the ongoing negotiations between the two companies on providing licenses to each other: a preliminary injunction with immediate effect would put these negotiations under direct pressure.[659]

§7.1.6. *Security and compensation*

In general, there is no obligation under the Dutch *kort geding* system, at least when it comes to patent disputes, which requires the plaintiff-applicant to post upfront security, i.e. in the form of a bond, the moment when a preliminary injunction is granted. Rarely indeed is the plaintiff requested to do so in patent cases.

However, Dutch legislation *does* foresee in the plaintiff-applicant providing compensation in the form of damages, in the case of an erroneous *kort geding* decision. The mechanism through which this happens is the general civil law mechanism of liability for damages (*aansprakelijkheid voor een onrechtmatige*

---

655 See on more on this X.E. KRAMER, *Het kort geding in internationaal perspectief* (2001 Kluwer Uitgeverij). See: p. 21 and also p. 25.

656 Vzr. Rechtbank Den Haag, *Apple v Samsung*, August 24th 2011, KG -ZA 11–730. See: par. 4.2–4.4.

657 W. TONKENS-GERKEMA in A.I.M. VAN MIERLO, C.J.J.C. VAN NISPEN, M.V. POLAK (eds) *Tekst & Commentaar Burgerlijke Rechtsvordering* (2008 Wolters Kluwer). See: pp. 464–465.

658 Ibidem.

659 Vzr. Rechtbank Den Haag, *Apple v Samsung*, 24 August 2011, KG ZA 11–730. See: par. 4.2–4.4.

daad) as stipulated in the Dutch Civil Code in Art. 6:162 BW.[660] As is written by Rueb *et al.*,[661] it is the provision of Art. 6:162 (3) BW and case law of the Dutch Supreme Court[662] that activates the liability for the plaintiff-applicant in a situation like this.[663] This is because the plaintiff-applicant should be aware of the provisional nature of the *kort geding* remedy before it decides to enforce the granted preliminary injunction against another party. When it does do so, it thereby also takes the risk that the final result of a case may later turn out to be different. By taking this risk, the plaintiff consequentially assumes liability under 6:162 BW when the decision indeed turns out to have been granted wrongly. Similarly, in the same line of reasoning and although this is doctrinally much less clear,[664] the litigation costs of a preliminary injunction proceedings can, in the event of an overturned *kort geding* decision, likely be demanded to be compensated by the party that eventually triumphs on the merits.[665]

§7.1.7. Intermediate conclusion

In conclusion, Dutch *kort geding* proceedings in patent cases are relatively straightforward affairs and can be more or less seen as a 'mini-trial'. There are relatively few special exceptions or unique procedures for preliminary injunction proceedings vis-à-vis normal (patent) infringement proceedings. There are no artificial or doctrinal constructs and strict presumptions to be dealt with, regarding patent validity or irreparable harm, as is sometimes the case in other jurisdictions. Critical in practice is the judge's view on whether patent infringement and validity are likely to be upheld at a later trial on the merits. This 'likelihood of success' is, in a strictly doctrinal sense, part of the court's *belangenafweging*. Other issues rarely seem to be ground of much dispute or debate, and are often largely unaddressed by both court and parties. Urgency is relatively easily assumed for intellectual property cases, as is the suitability of a case for *kort geding* proceedings. The balancing of other (economic) interests and factors in the context of the *belangenafweging* (beyond the 'likelihood

660 The main gist of Art. 6:162 is to be found in paragraph (1): "He that commits an unlawful act against another party, which can be attributed to him, is under the obligation to compensate the damages of the other party." Own translation.

661 A.S. RUEB, E. GRAS, A.W. JONGBLOED, *Compendium van het Burgerlijk Procesrecht* (2015, 20th edition, Kluwer Publishing). See: pp. 320–321.

662 Hoge Raad, *Ciba Geigy v Voorbraak*, 16 of November 1984, NJ 1985, 547.

663 Art. 6:162 (3) BW: "An unlawful act can be attributed to the perpetrator, if this is his fault, or is due to a cause that because of statute or views in common practice, can be seen as his responsibility." Own translation.

664 I. WERTS, W. MAAS, 'Wat te doen met proceskosten uit kort geding na een andersluidend bodemvonnis?' *IE Forum* (2015). Available at: http://www.ie-forum.nl/artikelen/wat-te-doen-met-de-proceskosten-uit-kort-geding-na-een-andersluidend-bodemvonnis (last accessed on 23 April 2017).

665 Ibidem.

of success') is not something that – although possible – seems to be invoked often by parties or the court. Finally, it is noteworthy that judges in The Netherlands do not require a bond to be posted by the plaintiff-applicant, as a condition for the preliminary injunction to become granted.

§7.2. Germany

§7.2.1. Introduction

Germany is by far the most popular patent litigation country in Europe.[666] This is partly due to the economic importance of the German market, but also because its litigation system is characterised by reliable proceedings, along with reasonable costs. Regarding the speed of proceedings, which at the trial on the merits is bifurcated, there is a significant discrepancy between the time that infringement proceedings and invalidity proceedings take.[667] Whilst in general, infringement proceedings can be undertaken in 8–12 months at first instance and 9–12 months on appeal, an invalidity procedure of a patent can take 12–18 months at first instance and a lengthy 24–36 months on appeal.[668] From this point of view, there is clearly a role for interim relief. This is known in German as the '*Einstweilige Verfügung*' (preliminary measure), and these requests are normally dealt with in 2–4 months at first instance and 3–5 months on appeal.[669, 670]

666 K. CREMERS, M. ERNICKE, F. GAESSLER, D. HARHOFF, ET AL, 'Patent litigation in Europe' *Zentrum für Europäische Wirtschaftsforschung, Discussion Paper* (2013), No. 13–072. See: p. 3.

667 For more on bifurcation, see page 193 of this dissertation. The German patent infringement courts are *Landgerichte* (LG), *Oberlandesgerichte* (OLG) and ultimately the *Budesgerichtshof* (BGH) in Karlsruhe. For patent validity matters, the *Bundespatentgericht* (BPatG) in Munich and the *Bundesgerichtshof* are entitled.

668 J. BÜHLING, chapter 'Germany' in W. HOYNG, F. EIJSVOGELS (eds), *Global Patent litigation* (Kluwer Law Publishing, the German supplement as updated on January 2015). See: p. 72.

669 Ibidem.

670 As Cotter and Golden note, the data on the number of applications for preliminary injunctions in patent cases in Germany is scarce and contains gaps. For a general impression though, note that they write that research has shown that in the period of 1996–2000 there were over 100 preliminary injunction applications per year. See: T.F. COTTER, J.M. GOLDEN, 'Empirical Studies relating to Patents – Remedies' *University of Minnesota Law School Legal Studies Research Paper Series* (2015) Research Paper No. 15–31. See: p. 21, footnote 33, thereby citing and basing themselves on a prior study undertaken by Von Falck. See: A. VON FALCK, 'Einstweilige Verfügungen in Patent und Gebrauchsmustersachen' *Mitteilungen der deutschen Patentanwälte* (2002), pp. 429–438.

§7.2.2. *The legal basis*

The substantive legal basis for a preliminary injunction with respect to patent infringement in Germany is Paragraph 140 (b) (7) PatG (*Patentgesetz*, German Patent Act).[671] This in turn refers to the relevant procedural provisions that form the legal basis for the *Einstweilige Vefügung*. These are to be found in Paragraphs 935 to 945 ZPO (*Zivilprozessordnung*, German Act on Civil Procedure).

Paragraph 935 ZPO:

> "Injunctions regarding the subject matter of the litigation are an available remedy **given the concern that a change of the status quo might frustrate** the realisation of the right enjoyed by a party, or might make **its realisation significantly more difficult**."[672]

And paragraph 940 ZPO:

> "Injunctions are **also admissible** for the purpose of providing for **a temporary status concerning a legal relationship that is in dispute**, to the extent this provision is deemed to be necessary in order to avert significant disadvantages, to prevent impending force, or for other reasons, in particular in the case of legal relationships of a long-term nature existing."[673]

Doctrinally, things in Germany at first sight seem to be rather complicated because there are three types of interim relief that fall under the umbrella term of *Einstweilige Verfügung*: the *Sicherungsverfügung*, the *Regelungsverfügung* and the *Leistungsverfügung*.

---

671 This provision states that a preliminary injunction can be granted in cases of patent infringement. The original German text of Art. 140 (b) (7) PatG reads: "In Fällen offensichtlicher Rechtsverletzung kann die Verpflichtung zur Erteilung der Auskunft im Wege der einstweiligen Verfügung nach den §§ 935 bis 945 der Zivilprozessordnung angeordnet werden."

672 This translation of the ZPO here (with emphasis added by the present author) is from the hand of C. VON SCHÖNING and was made on request of the German Ministry of Justice. To be found at: http://www.gesetze-im-internet.de/englisch_zpo/englisch_zpo.html (last accessed on 26 April 2017). The original German text of par. 935 ZPO states: "Einstweilige Verfügungen in Bezug auf den Streitgegenstand sind zulässig, wenn zu besorgen ist, dass durch eine Veränderung des bestehenden Zustandes die Verwirklichung des Rechts einer Partei vereitelt oder wesentlich erschwert werden könnte."

673 Emphasis added. The orginal German text of par. 940 ZPO reads: "Einstweilige Verfügungen sind auch zum Zwecke der Regelung eines einstweiligen Zustandes in Bezug auf ein streitiges Rechtsverhältnis zulässig, sofern diese Regelung, insbesondere bei dauernden Rechtsverhältnissen zur Abwendung wesentlicher Nachteile oder zur Verhinderung drohender Gewalt oder aus anderen Gründen nötig erscheint."

Figure 6. Three classes of Einstweilige Verfügung (own image).

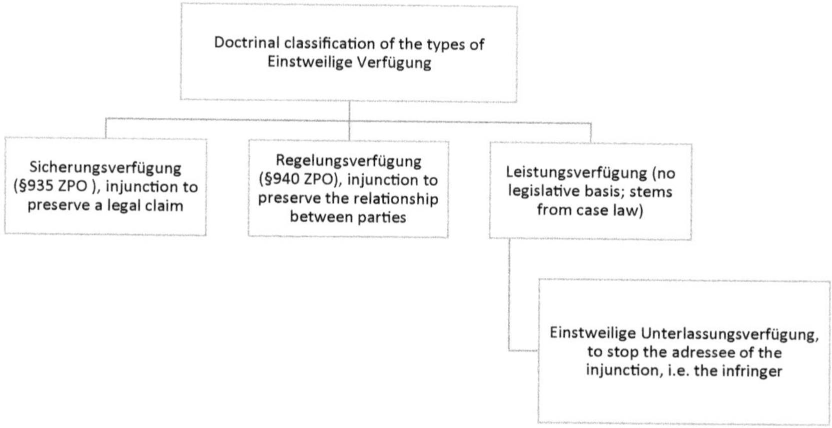

The *Sicherungsverfügung* (doctrinally regulated by §935 ZPO) attempts to secure certain future legal claims of a non-monetary nature (i.e. preventing measures that make the delivery of a good impossible). The *Regelungsverfügung* (doctrinally regulated by §940 ZPO), attempts to offer an interim regulation of the relationship between the involved parties in order to prevent significant disadvantages from occurring.[674] The *Leistungsverfügung* is the third doctrinal type of *Einstweilige Verfügung.*[675] Whilst the *Leistungsverfügung* is not explicitly regulated by a legislative provision in the ZPO, it is indirectly based on the provisions §935 and §940 ZPO and is a creature of *case law* and *legal practice.*[676] Because the remedy of *Leistungsverfügung* has been developed beyond what the German legislator intended, the requirements to obtain one are – theoretically – stricter to meet than the requirements that should be met in order to obtain a *Sicherungsverfügung* or *Regelungsverfügung.*[677] Thus, whilst the *Sicherungsverfügung* and *Regelungsverfügung* merely tend to *preserve* legal claims for the plaintiff for future litigation or to maintain a certain and specific legal relationship between parties, the *Leistungsverfügung* directly attempts to provide to the plaintiff interim relief at a more substantial level: i.e. by

674 X.E. KRAMER, *Het kort geding in internationaal perspectief* (2001 Kluwer Uitgeverij). See: pp. 61–63.
675 Idem, at pp. 62–63.
676 S.K. EHRENZELLER, *Der vorläufige Rechtsschutz im internationalen Verhältnis* (2005 Mohr Siebeck), pp. 96–100. See: p. 99. Also see F. SCHNEIDER, *Die Leistungsverfügung im Niederländischen, Deutschen und europäischen Zivilprozessrecht* (2013 Mohr Siebeck). See: p. 59.
677 Idem, at p. 29.

temporary prohibiting or positively prescribing certain acts.[678] The most relevant type of *Leistungsverfügung* in patent infringement cases is the negatively formulated *Unterlassungsverfügung*. Doctrinally, it is submitted that this is the closest to what in Common Law is known as the *prohibitory* preliminary injunction and in The Netherlands known as the voorlopige (*verbods*)voorziening na *kort geding*.

However, regardless of the doctrinal differences between the three types of *einstweilige Verfügung* as set out above, the distinction between the three is not as clear cut as it may seem to be on first sight[679] and in the practice of patent litigation these doctrinal differences exist even less, resulting into the situation that the same legal provisions[680] apply to all three main types of *einstweilige Verfügung*.[681] Pansch therefore speaks about the provisions of §935-§940 ZPO as (now) being a *unified provision of general nature* and as something that has transcended beyond the German legislator's initially neatly divided framework.[682] Therefore, a plaintiff wanting to stop the infringement of a patent and obtain an *einstweilige Unterlassungverfügung* (although doctrinally a type of *Leistungsverfügung*) will base its application on *both* §935 and §940 ZPO. The plaintiff should subsequently prove that it has a claim (*Verfügungsanspruch*) and a *ground* (*Verfügungsgrund*) for the requested preliminary injunction. It are these to which we turn now.

---

678 X.E. KRAMER, *Het kort geding in internationaal perspectief* (2001 Kluwer Uitgeverij). See: pp. 61–63. Also S.K. EHRENZELLER, *Der vorläufige Rechtsschutz im internationalen Verhältnis* (2005 Mohr Siebeck). See: p. 99. She writes: "Das Merkmal der Leistungsverfügung liegt darin, dass sie –im Gegensatz zu den übrigen einstweiligen Maßnahmen – nicht nur zu einer Sicherung, sondern darüber hinaus zu einer *Befriedigung* führt."

679 SCHNEIDER submits, for instance, that doctrinally Leistungsverfügungen are clearly demarcated from Sicherungsverfügungen, but are not so distinct with respect to Regelungsverfügungen. The same also applies between both the Sicherungsverfügungen and the Regelungsverfügungen. See F. SCHNEIDER, *Die Leistungsverfügung im Niederländischen, Deutschen und europäischen Zivilprozessrecht* (2013 Mohr Siebeck). See: p. 59. Furthermore, see X.E. KRAMER, *Het kort geding in internationaal perspectief* (2001 Kluwer Uitgeverij). See: p. 63. She comments that there is no sharp distinction between §935 and §940 ZPO and that the remedies that these provide are practically interchangeable.

680 See: §935-§945 ZPO.

681 S.K. EHRENZELLER, *Der vorläufige Rechtsschutz im internationalen Verhältnis* (2005 Mohr Siebeck). See: p. 111.

682 R. PANSCH, *Die einstweilige Verfügung zum Schutze des geistigen Eigentums im grenzüberschreitenden Verkehr* (2003 Carl Heymanns Verlag). See: pp. 87 and 88: "Die Deutsche Regelung der einstweiligen Verfügung in §935 and §940 ZPO ist, abweichend vom Erscheinungsbild der gesetzlichen Regelung, ebenfalls zu einer einheitlichen Generalklausel geworden. Handfeste Abgrenzungskriterien zwischen Regelungs-und Sicheringsverfügung haben sich nicht durchgesetzt. Die Institute ergänzen sich, und überdies werden Maßnahmen zugelassen, etwa die Leistungsverfügung, die den Rahmen des gesetzlich Vorgesehenen überschreiten."

Figure 7. The German preliminary injunction test (own image).

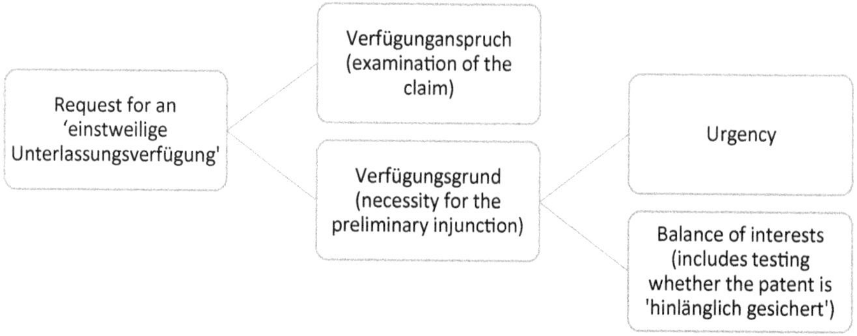

It should finally be mentioned that in Germany it is not possible for parties in interim cases (including decisions on preliminary injunctions) to make an appeal to the Supreme Court (*Bundesgerichtshof*). Consequently, the case law of (regional) lower courts and Courts of Appeals differs somewhat on certain aspects, as will be mentioned below. Secondly, it means that the various Courts of Appeal are the final arbitrator with respect to preliminary injunction cases.

§7.2.3. *Verfügungsanspruch*

The *Verfügungsanspruch* refers to a summary examination of the plaintiff's claim.[683] Under the German tradition, a plaintiff has to have a claim to a right, for which it turns to the court to receive judicial protection. In this manuscript, the desired protection is in the form of a preliminary injunction. After the plaintiff has submitted his claim of infringement of the patent, the court then, in a summary manner, examines whether the alleged *infringement* (*Verletzungstatbestand*) of the patent has indeed occurred under Par. 9 or 10 PatG[684] in combination with Par. 139 (1) PatG. The latter prescribes[685] that there should be either a danger of repetition of

683 C. RADEMACHER, *Die gerichtliche Durchsetzung von Patent-und Markenrechten in Deutschland, Japan und den USA* (2010 Nomos). See: pp. 92–94.

684 §9 PatG prohibits direct patent infringement and §10 PatG prohibits indirect patent infringement.

685 Pat. 139 PatG (1) reads: "Any person who uses a patented invention in contravention of sections 9 through 13 <of the PatG> may, *if there is a danger of repetition*, be sued by the injured party for injunctive relief. The claim shall also apply if there is a *danger of first preparation*' Emphasis added. The English translation above is from the WIPO website, available at: http://www.wipo.int/wipolex/en/text.jsp?file_id=238776 (last accessed on 21 April 2017). The original German text reads: "Wer entgegen den §§ 9 bis 13 eine patentierte Erfindung benutzt, kann von dem Verletzten bei Wiederholungsgefahr auf Unterlassung

the infringing activities (*Wiederholungsgefahr*) or either a risk of an (imminent) infringement (*Erstmalige Zuwiderhandlung*). The plaintiff's claim does not have to be proven with absolute certainty, but the claim should be deemed credible to the preliminary injunction court.[686] This demonstration of the credibility of the claim can occur with any evidence possible,[687] a relaxation of the strict requirements related to evidence as is normally the case in German Civil proceedings. In other words, it should be unlikely that at the trial on the merits a different result will be reached.[688] This does not mean that such an infringement analysis is extremely superficial of nature. Legal practice points to the contrary and the court is prepared to go rather deep into arguments regarding the (technical) subject matter of the case, thereby not only looking at literal infringement of the patent[689] but also, if relevant, at infringement on the basis of the Doctrine of Equivalence.[690] However, this said of course, given the summary nature of the proceedings, there is a more reduced possibility for legal debate and investigation compared to normal proceedings on the merits.

Imminent infringement – Under the German preliminary injunction doctrine it is also possible to obtain this type of relief against infringement that may occur in the future. The case of '*HIV-Medikament*' is a good example of what constitutes imminent infringement[691] and shows the typical issues that are discussed before the courts well. In this case, the OLG Düsseldorf established that the LG had not erred in *denying* the plaintiff a preliminary injunction against the conduct of a generic company[692] and neither did the OLG Düsseldorf honour the request for preliminary relief as there was no *Verfügungsanspruch*.[693] In casu, the protected medication was used in the treatment of HIV-1 patients and the contested patent would expire about

---

in Anspruch genommen werden. Der Anspruch besteht auch dann, wenn eine Zuwiderhandlung erstmalig droht."

686 See §920 (2) ZPO, in combination with the enabling §936 ZPO. Together they require that the claim on which the application for a preliminary injunction is based, should be demonstrated *to the satisfaction of the court*. See W. BERNEKE, E. SCHÜTTPELZ, *Die einstweilige Verfügung in Wettbewerbsachen* (2014 NJW Praxis / C.H. Beck). See: p. 228.

687 Note that the term '*Glaubhaftmachung*' is defined in §294 ZPO.

688 C. RADEMACHER, *Die gerichtliche Durchsetzung von Patent-und Markenrechten in Deutschland, Japan und den USA* (2010 Nomos Verlagsgesellschaft). See: p. 94.

689 As shown in for instance OLG Düseldorf, December 18th, 2014, Az. I-2 U 60/14.

690 See for instance the cases such as OLG Düsseldorf, *Drospirenon* September 13th 2013, Az. I-2 U 26/13 and OLG München, *Apple v Samsung*, July 26th, 2012, Az. 6 U 1260/12.

691 OLG Düsseldorf, *HIV Medikament*, September 20th 2012, Az. I-2 U 44/12. Also: GRUR RR (2013) at pp. 241–246.

692 LG Düsseldorf, April 12th, 2012, Az. 4a O 16/12.

693 OLG Düsseldorf, *HIV Medikament*, September 20th 2012, Az. I-2 U 44/12. Also: GRUR RR (2013) at pp. 241–246. See: "Die Verfügungskl. haben keine Tatsachen glaubhaft zu machen vermocht, auf Grund derer *ein Verfügungsanspruch* aus Art. 64 I EPÜ, § 139 I 2 in Verbindung mit §139IS. 1 PatG (i. V. mit § 16 a II PatG)

1,5 years after the request for a preliminary injunction was made. To give a good idea of the motivation of the court in such cases, the following factors were found relevant and held to be persuasive:

- The OLG came to the conclusion that the LG had not erred, as the alleged infringement consisted merely of the generic company obtaining regulatory approval and this was not imminent enough to warrant a preliminary injunction. This was deemed particularly so, bearing in mind that receiving the approval did not mean the defendant had to launch imminently in order for the approval not to be revoked:

> "(..) it has been established in case law that neither the application for regulatory approval of patented medicines, nor the obtaining of the actual approval, are by themselves suitable grounds to assume **imminent infringement** on (..) This is also confirmed for the pharmaceutical field, by the ratio of §11 Nr 2b PatG **(the so-called Bolar Exemption)** which allows generic companies to prepare for regulatory application and approval, prior to the expiration of the patent. **There has to be much more than these purely preparatory acts, to justify preliminary judicial protection.**"[694]

- The fact that it was still *more than a year* before the patent expired and the fact that other generic companies had not yet applied for obtaining this regulatory approval did not change this view of the OLG either.[695]
- The fact that the defendant (although not yet selling any HIV medication in Germany) had internationally already built up a broad portfolio of HIV medication and had threatened to launch a generic version of a still patented medication in the United Kingdom, could not lead to the deduction that it was about to imminently launch a generic HIV medicine in Germany as well.[696] Firstly, because it could not be assumed that all such HIV medication would indeed be infringing of nature. Secondly, the (infringing) marketing actions by the

---

zu bejahen wäre. *Zu Recht hat das LG deshalb mangels einer „Erstbegehungsgefahr "einen Verfügungsanspruch verneint.*" Emphasis added.

694 OLG Düsseldorf, *HIV Medikament,* September 20th 2012, Az. I-2 U 44/12. Also: GRUR RR (2013) at pp. 241–246. See: pp. 242–243. Emphasis added. Original text, with internal references omitted: "(..) Insofern ist es zu Recht anerkannt, dass weder ein Antrag auf eine arzneimittelrechtliche Zulassung patentgeschützter Medikamente noch die Erteilung der Zulassung allein geeignet sind, eine „Erstbegehungsgefahr' zu begründen, (..) Dies wird für den Bereich der Pharmazie letztlich auch durch die ratio des § 11 Nr. 2b PatG (so genannte Roche Bolar-Regel) bestätigt, der es Generikaherstellern ermöglichen soll, eine arzneimittelrechtliche Zulassung/Genehmigung schon vor Ablauf eines Patents vorzubereiten. (..) Es müssen vielmehr über diese bloße Vorbereitung hinausgehende Anhaltspunkte gegeben sein, die einen vorbeugenden Rechtsschutz rechtfertigen, (..)."

695 OLG Düsseldorf, *HIV Medikament,* September 20th 2012, Az. I-2 U 44/12. Also: GRUR RR (2013) at pp. 241–246. See: p. 243.

696 Idem, at p. 245.

defendant in another EU Member State could not lead to the deduction that it would act unlawfully within Germany. This would not only be against principles of corporate law,[697] but would also be against the notion of the territoriality of patent rights, as enshrined in Art. 3 EPC. The latter implies that the court should only focus on the activities happening in the country where it has jurisdiction.[698] Otherwise, an infringement of an European patent in one Member State would automatically amount to infringement in another Member State.[699]

- Furthermore, it was held that although the generic company remained silent to the plaintiff's request to give an undertaking – in which it would pledge to wait with launching a generic product until the plaintiff's patent had expired – this did not amount to a valid deduction that infringement was imminent.[700] Since there is no statutory obligation for a (generic) company to reply to such a request, such a conclusion cannot be deducted from that company remaining silent.[701] The value of such an undertaking was also disputed anyhow: the court noted that the pharmaceutical market was very transparent and that the plaintiff should instead keep an eye on the market and start proceedings when generic entry was *really imminent*:

> "Convincingly, the defendants have pointed out that on the basis of publications on market access, **it is very easy to monitor the market,** by regularly undertaking database research (with respect to example the *Lauer Taxe*, that often is published before the actual list). **From this point of view, the pharmaceutical market is especially transparent.**"[702]

---

697 This, as the defendant's foreign activities concerned *a different corporate entity* within the same holding structure.

698 OLG Düsseldorf, *HIV Medikament,* September 20th 2012, Az. I-2 U 44/12. Also: GRUR RR (2013) at pp. 241–246. See: at 245. "Es obliegt ihnen aufzuzeigen, dass und warum dies nicht anzunehmen sein sollte. Mit Rücksicht auf den Territorialitätsgrundsatz, der – wie Art. 3 EPÜ zeigt – auch für europäische Patente gilt und nicht etwa durchbrochen ist (...), muss auch die Frage nach einer Erstbegehungsgefahr grundsätzlich *allein anhand auf das Inland* bezogener Handlungen/Erklärungen beantwortet werden." Emphasis added, internal literature reference omitted.

699 Ibidem.

700 OLG Düsseldorf, *HIV Medikament,* September 20th 2012, Az. I-2 U 44/12. Also: GRUR RR (2013) at pp. 241–246. See: 244.

701 Ibidem. "Schweigen kommt im Rechtsverkehr nur dann ein Erklärungswert zu, wenn eine Verpflichtung zur Äußerung besteht. Wer schweigt, bringt grundsätzlich weder Zustimmung noch Ablehnung zum Ausdruck."

702 OLG Düsseldorf, *HIV Medikament,* September 20th 2012, Az. I-2 U 44/12. Also: GRUR RR (2013) at pp. 241–246. See: pp. 244–245. Emphasis added. Original text: "Überzeugend haben die Verfügungsbekl. darauf hingewiesen, dass auf Grund der Veröffentlichung eines Marktzutritts es gerade hier besonders leicht möglich ist, den Markt durch regelmäßige Datenbankrecherchen (z. B. der Lauer-Taxe, die

It is submitted that this case shows well that although legislators have allowed the possibility for a plaintiff to obtain a preliminary injunction against imminent infringement, this bar is set high and infringement should indeed be genuinely deemed to be imminent.

§7.2.4. *Verfügungsgrund*

In establishing the *Verfügungsgrund*, the preliminary injunction court looks at the *necessity* for a preliminary injunction. In doing so, it looks at the elements of urgency, the balancing of interests and it will attempt to make an assessment of patent validity in this context.

Urgency

Urgency (*Dringlichkeit*) is an element that plays a key role in German preliminary injunction proceedings and this is no different when it comes to patent infringement. Proven should be that the course of normal infringement proceedings cannot be awaited *with respect to time*, thus that a preliminary injunction is therefore necessary. In contrast to under German Unfair Competition Law (codified in the UWG),[703] the urgency for a preliminary injunction *is not presumed* in cases of patent infringement,[704] as is also the case regarding most other intellectual property rights.[705] The reason that patent rights are not subject to this presumption from Unfair Competition Law is because the issues of patent validity and infringement generally require a more thorough review than the issues in Unfair Competition Law cases. Furthermore, this is also due to the (technical) complexity of the subject-matter and because of the potentially large consequences for the defendant when

---

häufig noch vor der tatsächlichen Liste vorangekündigt wird) zu über wachen. Insofern zeichnet sich der Arzneimittelmarkt durch eine besondere Transparenz aus." It should be noted here that the *Lauer Taxe*, similar to the Dutch *G-Standaard*, is a database with price and product information of all pharmaceuticals on the German market. It is designed for pharmacies, insurers, hospitals etc.

703 See for this presumption: § 12(2) UWG (*Gesetz gegen den unlauteren Wettbewerb*, the German Act against Unfair Competition).

704 D. CREUTZFELDT, *Die Dringlichkeit der einstweiligen Verfügung im gewerblichen Rechtsschutz und im Urheberrecht* (2010 Peter Lang). See: p. 21.

705 C. RADEMACHER, *Die gerichtliche Durchsetzung von Patent-und Markenrechten in Deutschland, Japan und den USA* (2010 Nomos Verlagsgesellschaft). See: pp. 94–95. He writes that such an analogy to §12 UWG is more likely, though controversial, with respect to trademark infringement (pp. 95–96). But also see on this the view of Berneke and Schüttpelz: "Ganz überwiegend abgelehnt wird deshalb auch die Anwendung des §12 Abs. UWG auf Unterlassungsanprüche wegen Verletzung von Patent-und Gebrauchsmusterrechten, Designrechten sowie Urheberrechten." W. BERNEKE, E. SCHÜTTPELZ, *Die einstweilige Verfügung in Wettbewerbsachen* (2014 NJW Praxis / C.H. Beck). See: Randnummer 129.

enjoined.[706] Also doctrinally this seems to be justified; Creutzfeldt points out, that patent litigation is not about (unfair) competition and therefore an application of this presumption by analogy falls outside of the scope of the UWG.[707] This is also because patent litigation does originally not concern public interests, but private interests of the litigants.[708]

In any case, the burden of persuasively demonstrating that there is no time to wait for a ruling in the trial on the merits (*Hauptsache*) is therefore on the plaintiff.[709] Urgency is then not accepted, when it is clear that the applicant has waited before starting proceedings (delay).[710] Negligence, as a result of simply overlooking the infringement, is usually deemed as less culpable, since there is mostly no general duty for the plaintiff to observe the market.[711] The permitted time from the learning of the infringement to the filing of a request for an preliminary injunction depends on the preliminary injunction court that rules and on the constellation of facts of the case at hand but, as practice proves, this period is about a month.[712] Thus for instance the plaintiff in *Fernwärmeübergabestation* acted too late, since it had all the knowledge to file for a preliminary injunction, but failed to act immediately.[713] Equally, although this is not a case of the plaintiff-applicant acting too passively, in *VA-LCD*,[714] it was deemed as 'urgency-destroying' that the patentee-plaintiff and the defendant had conducted licensing negotiations in advance. Whilst maybe not

---

706 Ibidem.

707 D. CREUTZFELDT, *Die Dringlichkeit der einstweiligen Verfügung im gewerblichen Rechtsschutz und im Urheberrecht* (2010 Peter Lang). See: pp. 21 and 24.

708 Ibidem.

709 A. DEUTSCH, 'Preliminary injunction proceedings in German intellectual property disputes' *Journal of Intellectual Property Law & Practice* 8, No. 2 (2013), pp. 136–145. See: p. 139. Furthermore, see: C. RADEMACHER, *Die gerichtliche Durchsetzung von Patent-und Markenrechten in Deutschland, Japan und den USA* (2010 Nomos Verlagsgesellschaft). See: pp. 95–98.

710 A. DEUTSCH, 'Preliminary injunction proceedings in German intellectual property disputes' *Journal of Intellectual Property Law & Practice* 8, No. 2 (2013), pp. 136–145. See: p. 139.

711 Ibidem. But note that there are nevertheless multiple views on this issue, see: D. CREUTZFELDT, *Die Dringlichkeit der einstweiligen Verfügung im gewerblichen Rechtsschutz und im Urheberrecht* (2010 Peter Lang). See: pp. 29–47.

712 C. RADEMACHER, *Die gerichtliche Durchsetzung von Patent-und Markenrechten in Deutschland, Japan und den USA* (2010 Nomos Verlagsgesellschaft). See: pp. 96–97. Also see D. CREUTZFELDT, *Die Dringlichkeit der einstweiligen Verfügung im gewerblichen Rechtsschutz und im Urheberrecht* (2010 Peter Lang). See: pp. 46 a.f. He notes here that there is no real unity on this between courts. The author also argues that it depends on the nature of the case and that he considers this period to be normally around 1 month, exceptionally longer, but no more than 6 months.

713 LG Düsseldorf, *Fenrwärmeübergabestation*, September 4th 2012, Az. 4a O 83/12. Here the court also mentioned a period of one month time.

714 OLG Karlsruhe, *VA LCD*, July 8th 2009, Az. 6 U 61/09. See: par. 72.

always 'urgency destroying' as such, in this case it resulted into the court's conviction that a preliminary injunction was not necessary from an urgency point of view.[715] At least, it was not considered as urgent enough for this remedy to be acceptable. Some courts, although this is disputed in the literature,[716] have even assumed that urgency can be taken away if the plaintiff has knowledge of the infringement but does not act with sufficient speed or decisiveness towards *third parties* that are related to the infringer, i.e. to an infringing sister company belonging to the same corporation as the later defendant or an infringing manufacturer of components to that defendant.[717]

In this context, it is necessary to mention the case of *Flupurtin-Maleat*.[718] Here was again a classic originator-generic entry scenario, with the plaintiff seeking a preliminary injunction to prevent a generic company from entering the market before its monopoly right had expired. Tellingly, the OLG Düsseldorf held that the question of *Dringlichkeit* is not about whether the plaintiff undertook action as fast and as promptly as possible, but much more relevant is the question whether – from an objective point of view – the plaintiff has been dwindling and too hesitant in bringing a preliminary injunction action.[719] However, as has been pointed out by the court, this does not imply that the plaintiff has instead to take a litigation risk

---

715 Ibidem.

716 See on this the insightful article of Hoppe-Jänisch, in which he describes this aspect of urgency in more detail. D. HOPPE-JÄNISCH, 'Das Zögern zu Gunsten Dritter', GRUR (2015), pp. 1075–1082.

717 Ibidem. Citing various cases, including the recent one of: KG Berlin, February 20th 2015, Az. 5 U 150/14. Here it was held that it was 'urgency destroying' that the plaintiff had not acted towards an earlier patent infringement of a sister company of the firm it seeked to enjoin a year later.

718 OLG Düsseldorf, *Flupirtin-Maleat*, March 17th 2013, GRUR RR (2013), at pp. 236–241. In first instance, on the 6th of November 2012, the LG Düsseldorf had denied the request for a preliminary injunction. The OLG disagreed and a preliminary injunction was issued.

719 OLG Düsseldorf, *Flupirtin-Maleat*, January 17th 2013, Az. I-2 U 87/12. Also: GRUR RR (2013) pp. 236–241. See: p. 238. "Das gilt insbesondere für die Dringlichkeit, deren Vorliegen das LG rechtsfehlerhaft verneint hat. Der Verfügungskl. braucht sich bei der Vorbereitung des Verfahrens und der Beschaffung der Glaubhaftmachungsmittel nicht der vom LG geforderten 'besonderen Eile' zu befleißigen. Er muss nicht die größtmögliche Schnelligkeit walten lassen – jede einzelne Maßnahme lässt sich im Zweifel immer noch weiter beschleunigen. Vielmehr verhält es sich genau umgekehrt: Die maßgebliche Frage ist, ob sich der Verletzte bei der Verfolgung seiner Ansprüche wegen Patentverletzung in einer solchen Weise nachlässig und zögerlich verhalten hat, dass aus objektiver Sicht der Schluss geboten ist, dem Verletzten sei an einer zügigen Durchsetzung, seiner Rechte nicht gelegen, weswegen es auch nicht angemessen ist, ihm die Inanspruchnahme vorläufigen Rechtsschutzes zu gestatten."

(*Prozessrisiko*) by making a premature request for a preliminary injunction.[720] The plaintiff should be convinced first that it can win the litigation.[721]

In casu, it was deemed by the court to be acceptable that the plaintiff had not acted immediately and that it had taken longer than he *could have done*, because the party did so in order to elaborately prepare the litigation. Thus:

- the extra time that the plaintiff took, about a month, to conduct further in-house laboratory tests to establish the infringing use of the defendant's product (inter alia this included X-Ray diffraction analysis[722] instead of simply merely relying on publicly documented information such as the *Lauer Taxe* database)[723] was deemed as completely understandable by the court. This because in the upcoming litigation, the plaintiff should be able to as adequately as possible rebut the defendant's analysis that his product is not infringing and be able to present this to the court.[724] This is deemed especially important in preliminary injunction proceedings; the OLG Düsseldorf noted that in these type of proceedings the court itself has no third-party experts to its disposal.[725]
- the fact that the plaintiff had asked an independent expert ('*ein externes Gutachten bei Prof. Dr. X*') to conduct further tests on the issue of equivalence and infringement, was perceived by the court as understandable too. Although costing time, this was not deemed to amount to unreasonable delay of litigation, taking away urgency.[726] The court acknowledged that the impartiality of the prior tests undertaken in-house might become an issue at trial and also stressed the use of the expert's opinion in clarifying the infringement question, since the first test results were not completely clear-cut.[727]
- In line with that point of view, it has been held as well on multiple occasions that it is not *urgency destroying* that a plaintiff waits for the (positive) outcome

720 OLG Düsseldorf, *Flupirtin-Maleat*, January 17th 2013, Az. I-2 U 87/12. Also: GRUR RR (2013) pp. 236–241. See: p. 238.

721 Ibidem.

722 OLG Düsseldorf, *Flupirtin-Maleat*, January 17th 2013, Az. I-2 U 87/12. Also: GRUR RR (2013) pp. 236–241. See: p. 237. X-Ray Diffraction is a method used in particle analysis, in order to estalish the crystallinity of a compound.

723 OLG Düsseldorf, *Flupirtin-Maleat*, January 17th 2013, Az. I-2 U 87/12. Also: GRUR RR (2013) pp. 236–241. See: p. 238.

724 Idem, at p. 239. "(..) musste sich die Verfügungskl.darauf einrichten, dass es in einem gerichtlichen Verfahren darauf ankommen würde, die von der Gegenseite präsentierten Analysebefunde nicht nur zu entkräften, sondern in einer Weise zu widerlegen, dass sich das Gericht ohne eigene sachverständige Beratung (die im Verfahren des einstweiligen Rechtsschutzes untersagt ist) in der Lage sieht, den Benutzungssachverhalt als hinreichend glaubhaft gemacht anzusehen."

725 OLG Düsseldorf, *Flupirtin-Maleat*, January 17th 2013, Az. I-2 U 87/12. Also: GRUR RR (2013) pp. 236–241. See: p. 239.

726 Ibidem.

727 Ibidem.

of a pending (EPO) opposition proceeding or the outcome of an invalidity proceeding.[728] This makes sense, since as we will see in the next paragraph it is in Germany a de facto requirement that a patent has survived such proceedings. Being strict on the issue of urgency and delay at this point would not make things easier for the court then. It is submitted that it also makes sense since in both opposition and invalidity proceedings, a patent can be limited in scope.[729] This may thus have important consequences for the infringement issue in a preliminary injunction proceeding.

In this context, it should be noted that also *after* bringing the request for a preliminary injunction but still prior to the moment that a decision on this has been taken, a plaintiff can risk losing the notion of urgency that drives his claim when he unreasonably delays the pending case. The latter could for instance be done in order to win time for certain litigation tactics.[730]

Finally, it should be mentioned that the case law between the various German lower courts and the appeal courts is not homogeneous on the point of urgency. Perspectives differ somewhat on which period of time is acceptable for a plaintiff to rely on.[731] As was pointed out before, the fact that there is no recourse to the Supreme Court (BGH) in interim matters does not help in this.

§7.2.5. Interessenabwägung

§7.2.5.1. The issue of patent validity

In the context of patent litigation cases, the balancing of interests *(Interessenabwägung)* will also play a potentially important role in deciding whether or not to grant a patent in the decisionmaking of the court.[732] This is a major difference compared to the German practice with respect to *permanent injunctions* in patent litigation, where courts do not have this discretion and an injunction should in principle be

728 As for instance in: OLG Karlsruhe, September 23rd 2015, Az. 6 U 52/15. See: par. 76. Also see the case of OLG Düsseldorf, January 21st 2016, Az. I-2 U 49/15. See: par. 162 and 164.

729 OLG Düsseldorf, January 21st 2016, Az. I-2 U 49/15. See: par. 165.

730 In much detail, this topic is covered by D. CREUTZFELDT, *Die Dringlichkeit der einstweiligen Verfügung im gewerblichen Rechtsschutz und im Urheberrecht* (2010 Peter Lang). See: pp. 75–122.

731 A. DEUTSCH, 'Preliminary injunction proceedings in German intellectual property disputes' *Journal of Intellectual Property Law & Practice* 8, No. 2 (2013), pp. 136–145. See: at p. 139. "The time frame from the moment the applicant first became aware of the infringement until filing of the court request varies among the different German court districts."

732 C. RADEMACHER, *Die gerichtliche Durchsetzung von Patent-und Markenrechten in Deutschland, Japan und den USA* (2010 Nomos Verlagsgesellschaft). See: p. 97.

granted upon the finding of infringement.[733] At the stage of *Interessenabwägung* the court can look at circumstances and interests mitigating the issues of validity and harms, as well as look at any wider interests of parties.

The issue of patent *validity* is a patent-specific problem that doctrinally also pops up at the *Interessenabwägung* stage. The preliminary injunction court will here anticipate the risk that the disputed patent turns out to be invalid after a preliminary injunction is granted. Though this is a common exercise for judges in many countries, in the German legal system this is something less straightforward then it looks on first sight. After all, as is well known, the German patent litigation system is bifurcated of nature.[734] Bifurcation entails that the infringement proceedings and invalidity proceedings are (strictly) separated proceedings and are also held in different courts. This is generally seen as enhancing the quality of the invalidity decisions, due to heightened specialisation of the validity court. In patent proceedings on the merits (thus not related to interim proceedings), the infringement court[735] can then decide to stay the proceedings until the invalidity court, the *Bundespatentgericht*,[736] has taken a decision on the validity issue. Alternatively, as is often the case in practice, the infringement court, when it is inclined to believe the patent will ultimately be held valid can decide to grant the permanent injunction

---

733 M. MARFÉ, A. REETZ, C. PECNARD, R. FRUSCALZO AND R. VAN DER VELDEN, 'The power of national courts and the Unified Patent Court to grant injunctions: a comparative study' *Journal of Intellectual Property Law & Practice*. 10, No. 3 (2015), pp. 180–190. See: p. 181.
In the same light, but then looking more at the EU and International Law roots of *final injunctions* (Art. 44 TRIPS and Art 11 Enforcement Directive), rather than at the *national implementation* of final injunctions, is the work of Von Mühlendahl. He argues that the wording of the legal provisions in TRIPS and the Enforcement Directive both stipulate that the national courts should have the *power* (which hints to the *availability*, not the obligation) to grant injunctive relief in these cases. However, there seems to be a preferred tendency of the CJEU to *oblige* European national courts to grant a permanent injunction after the finding of infringement, unless there are circumstances specific to the case which would allow a conclusion that further infringement will not occur. See: A. VON MÜHLENDAHL, 'Enforcement of Intellectual Property Rights – Is injunctive relief mandatory?' *IIC* (2007), pp. 377–379. See: p. 379.

734 However, on the terminology and concept of *Bifurkation*, see the article of P. MEIER BECK, 'Bifurkation und Trennung; Überlegungen zum Übereinkommen über ein Einheitliches Patentgericht und zur Zukunft des Trennungsprinzips in Deutschland' *GRUR* (2015), pp. 929–936. Beck points out that the German system is actually not bifurcated at all, but simply split ("getrennt") and the Unified Patent Court will be the first and only court in the world to be truly bifurcated.

735 These are the *Landgerichte* and *Oberlandesgerichte*.

736 For patent validity matters, the *Bundespatentgericht* and the *Bundesgerichtshof* are entitled to decide on this.

provisionally, the so-called *vorläufige Vollstreckbarkeit*,[737] thereby mitigating the strictness of bifurcation.[738]

With respect to preliminary injunctions proceedings concerning patents, the separation due to bifurcation is not the case anyhow and the court *will always* anticipate the validity and infringement of a patent simultaneously. In doing so, the court will attempt to make an assessment of the 'likelihood of success' for the plaintiff to win on both issues at trial. Otherwise the inevitable delays that bifurcation involves would not lead to a procedure that is in line with Art. 50 (1) TRIPS and Art. 9 of the Enforcement Directive.[739] This said, the preliminary injunction court will essentially look at both infringement and validity in a summary way and it remains a challenging task for it to assess these points, especially regarding the limited preparatory time the court has and the fast pace of proceedings.[740] Nevertheless, it seems that the preliminary injunctions courts are up to this task, with Böhler arguing that the rise of preliminary injunctions in patent cases in Germany is also partly due to the high specialisation and technical expertise of the courts.[741]

---

737 This has already been commented on before, in footnote 28 of this dissertation, and the reader is kindly referred to this. In short, it was submitted that a difference between an injunction taken with *vorläufige Volstreckbarkeit* and that of a preliminary injunction – although both are temporary measures to bridge the interval until the final decision is made on *all* aspects of the case – is that with the former, a higher degree of scrutiny has taken place, namely with respect to infringement. Since the court in the case of *Vorlaüfige Vollstreckbarkeit* has also had more time, it also may be in a better situation to anticipate the (in)validity of the patent.

738 As has been stated in footnote 28 of this dissertation as well, this can lead to the paradoxical situation of a later invalidated patent that can be legally enforced. See for empirical work confirming this problem: D. HARHOFF, K. CREMERS, F. GAESSLER, C. HELMERS, 'Invalid but infringed? An analysis of Germany's bifurcated patent litigation system' *Zentrum für Europäische Wirtschaftsforschung. Discussion Paper* (2014), No. 14–072.

739 OLG Düsseldorf, *Leflunomid/Teriflunomid II*, November 10th 2011, Az. 2 U 41/11. "Mit dem Gebot eines *effektiven* vorläufigen Rechtsschutzes in Patentsachen (Art. 50 Abs. 1 TRIPS, Art. 9 Abs. 1a Enforcement-Richtlinie) *wäre es nicht zu vereinbaren*, wenn das Verletzungsgericht, bevor es einstweilige Maßnahmen zum Schutz des im Verfügungspatent verkörperten geistigen Eigentums anordnet, stets den rechtskräftigen Abschluss des Einspruchs- oder Nichtigkeitsverfahrens abwarten würde." Emphasis added.

740 OLG Düsseldorf, *Harnkatheterset*, April 29th 2010, Az. I-2U 126/09. See: par. 53. "Gerade hier ergeben sich regelmaßig besondere Schwierigkeiten daraus, die Schutzfähigkeit bzw. Rechtsbeständigkeit des Antagsschutzrechtes *innerhalb kurzer Zeit und ohne eine dem Verfahren der Hauptsache entsprechende schriftsätzliche Vorbereitung sachgerecht zu beurteilen.*" Emphasis added.

741 R. BÖHLER, 'Einstweilige Verfügungen in Patentsachen' GRUR (2011), pp. 965–977. See: p. 965.

At this point, two important cases should be mentioned which have made their mark on the strict Düsseldorf court's practice regarding patent validity during preliminary injunction proceedings. These are the cases of *Harnkatheterset* and *Olanzapin*, and they will both be set out below. Whilst other preliminary injunction courts in Germany, i.e. Hamburg or München, may at times be less doctrinally strict than Düsseldorf with respect to the requirements to patent validity,[742] we will on this aspect focus on the latter court. This for two key reasons: 1) the importance of the Düsseldorf court with respect to patent litigation,[743] and 2) the strict standard set by the Düsseldorf court differs with that of other courts in Europe, which makes this highly interesting for comparative purposes and may result into a potential 'best practice' for the UPC to follow. Finally, it should be acknowledged that the Düsseldorf court's approach has at times also been adopted by other regional German preliminary injunction courts.[744]

Whilst, as written, differences between the various regional German courts exist in the degree of strictness that they impose on a patent's validity, the bottom line across the regional German preliminary injunction courts however is that the preliminary injunction court should be convinced of the likelihood of patent validity. The court should be convinced that the disputed patent will thus likely be able to survive a trial on the merits and should therefore be sufficiently strong and this is something that will be assessed. In other words, the patent should be *hinlänglich gesichert.* Thus whilst the Munich *Landesgericht* in the case of *Apple-Samsung* for instance explicitly did not follow the strict Düsseldorf approach that will be set out below, the court refused to grant a preliminary injunction nevertheless as it had doubts about the chances of the patent to survive an opposition proceeding, esp. regarding lack of novelty.[745] Obviously there is also a pivotal role for the defendant here: the defendant who can raise sufficient doubt about the patent's validity may successfully prevent the preliminary injunction from being granted.[746]

Back to the OLG Düsseldorf's strict approach: Whilst the *Harnkatheterset*[747] itself was an interesting preliminary injunction case by itself, it is especially known for

---

742 W. BERNEKE, E. SCHÜTTPELZ, *Die einstweilige Verfügung in Wettbewerbsachen* (2014 NJW Praxis / C.H. Beck). See: Randnummer 772.

743 According to Cremers et al, the Düsseldorf court for instance hears more than seven times as many patent cases as the Munich regional court and more than double the amount of Mannheim. K. CREMERS, M. ERNICKE, F. GAESSLER, D. HARHOFF, ET AL, 'Patent litigation in Europe' *Zentrum für Europäische Wirtschaftsforschung, Discussion Paper* (2013), No. 13–072. See: p. 4 and pp 43–44.

744 For instance: OLG Karlsruhe, September 23rd 2015, Az. 6 U 52/15. See: par. 62.

745 LG München, February 1st 2012, Az. 21 O 26022/11.

746 W. BERNEKE, E. SCHÜTTPELZ, *Die einstweilige Verfügung in Wettbewerbsachen* (2014 NJW Praxis / C.H. Beck). See: Randnummer 773.

747 OLG Düsseldorf, *Harnkatheterset*, April 29th 2010, Az. I-2U 126/09.

its teaching on the relationship between *preliminary* injunctions and patent validity and it clarified pre-existing case law.[748]

The main rule, whilst acknowledging that Art. 50 (1) TRIPS prescribes that preliminary relief should be available,[749] is that a preliminary injunction can *only* be granted if both patent infringement and patent validity are clearly established and likely to hold at the trial on the merits:

> "(..) that the grant of a preliminary injunction, **specifically regarding the prohibition of a particular act**, will **only be considered** in the case when the question of **patent enforceability** and **patent infringement** are clearly to be answered in favour of the plaintiff **and that an erroneous, to be revised decision** in a trial on the merits **is not to be expected**."[750]

As is apparent, the court here mentions patent infringement *and* patent validity in one breath, implying the equal importance of both. It has been submitted that the German rules on patent validity can be regarded as the most critical element to be determined in practice and the highest hurdle for the plaintiff to clear.[751] As pointed out before, the disputed patent should thus likely be able to survive a trial on the merits and should therefore be sufficiently strong. In other words, it should be *hinlänglich gesichert*.[752] To a certain extent, it is submitted that this approach in the preliminary injunction doctrine is in line with the aims and spirit of bifurcation in normal patent proceedings, since then too, the bifurcation system also aims to be as certain as possible on the issue of validity when confronted with a disputed patent.

---

748 See for instance for a 'pre-Harnkatheterset' decision, the case of OLG Düsseldorf, *Kleinleistungsschalter*, March 1st 2007, Az. 2 U 98/06. Also: GRUR RR (20079 pp. 219–221. In this case it was held that it was not required that the contested patent was beyond all doubt, but that instead it was about the likelihood that the patent would be held valid at trial: "Prüfungsmaßstab ist, ob das angerufene Gericht, hätte es über den Patentverletzungsvorwurf als erstinstantzliches Gericht im Klageverfahren zu entscheiden, den Patentverletzungsrechtsstreit aussetzen würde" at p. 220, citing the case of OLG Düsseldorf, *Catopril*, Mitt 1996, 87.

749 OLG Düsseldorf, *Harnkatheterset*, April 29th 2010, Az. I-2U 126/09. See: par. 54.

750 Idem, par. 51. Emphasis added, own translation. The original German text is worded as follows: "(..) dass der Erlass einer einstweiligen Verfügung insbesondere auf Unterlassung nur in Betracht kommt, wenn sowohl der Bestand des Verfügungspatents als auch die Frage der Patentverletzung im Ergebnis so eindeutig zugunsten des Antragstellers zu beantworten sind, dass eine fehlerhafte, in einem etwa nachfolgenden Hauptsacheverfahren zu revidierende Entscheidung nicht ernstlich zu erwarten ist. (..)."

751 R. BÖHLER, 'Einstweilige Verfügungen in Patentsachen' GRUR (2011), pp. 965–977 "(...) dass die Rechtsbeständigkeit des Verfügungspatents hinlänglich gesichert ist. Hierin liegt häufig die für den Rechtsinhaber größte zu überwindende Hürde." See: p. 967.

752 OLG Düsseldorf, *Harnkatheterset*, April 29th 2010, Az. I-2U 126/09. See: par. 54

The OLG Düsseldorf in *Harnkatheterset* has provided a number of guiding principles (*Beurteilungskriterien*) that it took into account when looking at validity when deciding on a preliminary injunction request. These have become the main yardstick of the Düsseldorf court to gauge the validity question of a preliminary injunction request against. The case of *Harnkatheterset* has been oft cited in subsequent case law – of the Düsseldorf courts, but also of other regional German preliminary injunction courts which sometimes follow the set principles – and it is submitted that it can be seen as an important decision. It is again underlined here that in interim cases there is no further appeal possible for parties to the *Bundesgerichtshof.*

According to the teaching of *Harnkatheterset*, the preliminary injunction court should thereby look, *inter alia*, at whether the patent has already survived being challenged on invalidity grounds – either at the EPO or Deutsches Patent und Markenamt (DPMA) in opposition proceedings, or at an invalidity proceedings at the *Bundespatentgericht*. There are three likely scenarios;[753]

- Firstly, if a patent is challenged and has been subsequently revoked or held to be invalid, the default rule is that enforceability of the patent after a trial on the merits will be so uncertain, that the grant of a preliminary injunction is *not* warranted and therefore in principle will be denied.[754] This is only different in the case an evident error (*erkennbar fehlerhaft*) was made in the proceeding in which the validity of the patent was challenged and this is an error of such a nature that it can be corrected in further litigation.[755] This is a direct result due to the *Olanzapin* case, which is a decision that will be described below subsequently. As will be seen there, the invalidity of the patent should stem only from this error and the party requesting a preliminary injunction should furthermore suffer an exceptional disadvantage when it, because of the earlier and erroneous invalidity ruling, cannot obtain the requested preliminary injunction. This exceptional disadvantage should also be substantiated and made likely to the court.[756]

---

753 Apart from the wording of the decision of the OLG Düsseldorf, also see the article of R. BÖHLER, 'Einstweilige Verfügungen in Patentsachen' GRUR (2011), pp. 965–977. Here, he covers this case in an excellent manner and in a similar way.

754 OLG Düsseldorf, *Harnkatheterset*, April 29th 2010, Az. I-2U 126/09. See: par. 63.

755 Ibidem. "Anderes gilt von Verfassungs wegen nur dann, wenn die Entscheidung über die Vernichtung des Verfügungspatents erkennbar fehlerhaft ist und deswegen sicher abgesehen werden kann, dass sie im nächsten Rechtszug aufgehoben werden wird. Dies verlangt nicht nur die Feststellung, dass die für die Vernichtung gegebene Begründung offenkundig fehlerhaft ist, sondern darüber hinaus die verlässliche Erkenntnis des Verletzungsgerichts, dass auch kein anderer Grund für eine Vernichtung des Verfügungspatents eingreift."

756 OLG Düsseldorf, *Harnkatheterset*, April 29th 2010, Az. I-2U 126/09. See: par. 63. "(..) Hinzukommen zur evidenten Unrichtigkeit der Vernichtungsentscheidung muss ferner, dass dem Patentinhaber ein außergewöhnlicher Nachteil droht, wenn er bis zur Rechtsmittelentscheidung im Rechtsbestandsverfahren daran gehindert

- Secondly, if the disputed patent has been challenged before, but this challenge has not resulted in the patent's invalidation or revocation, a preliminary injunction is in principle allowable, because the patent is likely to survive a closer inspection at the later trial on the merits. In other words, the patent is in principle *hinlänglich gesichert.*[757] Later cases have made clear that the fact that even if during the invalidation or revocation proceedings the party who contested the patent stopped halfway and did not further pursue the invalidation, a patent is nevertheless deemed to have survived these proceedings when there has been a verdict on the validity, even though this is then, strictly speaking, taken in an unilateral proceeding.[758] However, in such a case, the arguments against the patent's validity should have already been reviewed and tested.[759]
- However, even when a patent has survived earlier opposition or invalidity proceedings, it may still not always been deemed as being *hinlänglich gesichert* for the purpose of a preliminary injunction: newly found prior art can for instance result into a second attempt to invalidate the patent. In such a situation the preliminary injunction court, pending the outcome of those (second) invalidity proceedings, cannot blindly rely on the patent's survival of the first revocation proceedings. Instead, it should deny granting this if such a second attempt may be successful.[760]
- It is noted that foreign judgments on a patent's validity can also play a role in this, but although they can be influential, the German preliminary injunction court is of course not bound to them; much depends on the facts and confidence the German preliminary injunction court has in the foreign court's judgment. In *Mundipharma* for instance, the court looked at foreign judicial fora and noted that the upholding of parallel oxycodone patents by various courts in the United Kingdom and in The Netherlands. This contributed to the court's view on the German situation; it ruled that it would be unlikely that the patent would later be regarded as invalid.[761]

---

wird, seine Verbietungsrechte durchzusetzen. Dies kann sich – wie beispielsweise bei einem patentierten Arzneimittel und dem Auftreten von Generikaherstellern – von selbst verstehen und bedarf ansonsten eines substantiierten Sachvortrages und der Glaubhaftmachung durch den Antragsteller."

757 OLG Düsseldorf, *Harnkatheterset*, April 29th 2010, Az. I-2U 126/09. See: par. 54.

758 OLG Düsseldorf, February 19th 2016, Az. I-2 U 54/15. See: par. 57–58.

759 Ibidem.

760 OLG Düsseldorf, *Gleisattelscheibenbremse II*, September 30th 2010, Az. 2-U 47/10. See: par. II.3.a,b.

761 LG Düsseldorf, *Mundipharma*, March 30th 2010, Az. 4a O 13–10. "Wird dann noch berücksichtigt, dass sich auch der High Court of Justice, Patents Court und der Supreme Court of Judicature, Court of Appeal (Civil Division) in Großbritannien und die Rechtbank, s-Gravenhage in den Niederlanden mit dem Rechtbestand paralleler Patente, in denen ähnliche Einwände gegen die Schutzfähigkeit wie im vorliegenden Verfahren erhoben wurden, auseinandergesetzt und für nicht

- The third scenario is *when no prior decision* on the validity of the patent has taken place yet. For instance, if a revocation or invalidity action has not yet taken place, or when this has commenced, but the proceedings are still pending.[762] In principle a preliminary injunction will, in such a situation, not be granted,[763] although certain indicative circumstances can warrant an exception (*Sonderfall*) to this.[764] This is, when validity is likely for instance when there is a considerable number of licensees for the patent. It can also be that the objections of the defendant against the patent's validity seem to be *prima facie* groundless, or that there are exceptional circumstances (*außergewöhnliche Umstände*) that make waiting for a decision on the validity issue unreasonable.[765] These exceptional circumstances are treated in an *Interessenabwägung* context, and will be dealt with below.[766] As has become clear, these exceptional circumstances can only make the de facto requirement of a positive prior decision on patent validity unnecessary, but they do not 'repair' any doubts that there are regarding the validity of a patent: in such cases, no matter the number of licensees a patent has, validity is then deemed as insufficient for the grant of a preliminary injunction to be based on.[767]

> "In any case, when a patent revocation action has already been initiated, or is imminent to begin soon, *the burden of proof* shifts from the defendant to the plaintiff-patentee, to substantiate before the court that the patent is or will remain valid, and that therefore a grant of a preliminary injunction is possible after all."[768]

Finally, it was held in *Harnkatheterset* that the defendant in a preliminary injunction proceeding cannot simply state its objections to the patent's validity during the preliminary injunction proceedings: this is not enough. Instead, the defendant has to have undertaken actions of a more specific nature, for instance in opposition at

---

durchgreifend erachtet haben, ist es *zumindest unwarscheinlich, dass der Rechtsbestand des Verfügungspatents im vorliegenden Fall zu Unrecht als gesicheret angeshen wird.*" Emphasis added. See: p. 48 of the judgement.

762 For instance: LG Mannheim, February 27th 2009, Az. 7 O 29/09.

763 OLG Düsseldorf, *Harnkatheterset*, April 29th 2010, Az. I-2U 126/09. See: par. 61.

764 Ibidem.

765 Ibidem.

766 See page 202 a.f. of this dissertation.

767 OLG Düsseldorf, December 18th 2015, Az. I-2 U 35/15. See: par. 66.

768 OLG Düsseldorf, *Harnkatheterset*, April 29th 2010, Az. I-2U 126/09. See: par. 58. "Sobald das Verfügungspatent in seinem Rechtsbestand angegriffen oder ein bevorstehender Angriff hinreichend absehbar ist, steht es zur Glaubhaftmachungslast des Antragstellers, der den vorläufigen Rechtsschutz für sich in Anspruch nimmt, das Verletzungsgericht davon zu überzeugen, dass die gegen das Verfügungspatent vorgebrachten Einwendungen unberechtigt sind und das Verfügungspatent mit Sicherheit das laufende (oder avisierte) Rechtsbestandsverfahren überstehen wird. (..)."

the EPO or at the DPMA, or in invalidity proceedings at the Bundespatentgericht.[769] Equally, it was held that the national court in preliminary injunction proceeding cannot simply rely its insights on validity on the work done by the (national or European) patent office in granting a patent, but it should base its decision about the patent's validity on its own and independent assessment thereby mainly relying on the arguments of the defendant.[770] The court should then assess whether these arguments highlight validity problems that may obstruct a preliminary injunction to be given.

In the end however, the exact standard to asses patent validity that is to be used by a German court in a preliminary injunction proceeding is provided for in the following citation:

> "**The <patent's> invalidation** should, based on the **objections of the defendant**, and from the viewpoint of the infringement court **not be imperative, nor should it be highly likely,** but on the basis of the conclusive, reasonable and non-dismissible argumentation of the defendants should this **be possible**, in order to **withhold the grant of a preliminary injunction**."[771]

It is submitted that this citation highlights both the active role the defendant should have in this, as well as the discretion of the court. Furthermore, as is clear from the wording 'be possible' in combination with the *Beurteilungskriterien* given before, this seems to imply *a very high standard* to obtain a preliminary injunction.[772] It is clear that the defendant can quite easily render this unattainable, and the court is likely to deny a request at the moment when even a little doubt emerges.

Concluding on the case of *Harnkatheterset*, it is argued that the strict approach of the Düsseldorf courts to rely on a patent having gone through prior revocation or invalidity proceedings is a good one: as has been set out and described in case

769 OLG Düsseldorf, *Harnkatheterset*, April 29th 2010, Az. I-2U 126/09. See: par. 56.

770 Idem, at par. 54. "(..) Die Einschätzung der Rechtsbeständigkeit muss das Verletzungsgericht in eigener Verantwortung vornehmen. (...) Es kann sich also nicht kurzerhand auf den Erteilungsakt verlassen, sondern hat selbständig zu klären, ob angesichts des Sachvortrages des Antragsgegners ernstzunehmende Anhaltspunkte dafür bestehen, dass das Verfügungspatent ggf. keinen Bestand haben wird. (...)."

771 OLG Düsseldorf, *Harnkatheterset*, April 29th 2010, Az. I-2U 126/09. See: par. 54. Emphasis added. "(..) Seine Vernichtung muss als Folge der Einwendungen des Antragsgegners aus Sicht des Verletzungsgerichts nicht zwingend und sie muss auch nicht überwiegend wahrscheinlich, aber aufgrund einer in sich schlüssigen, vertretbaren und letztlich nicht von der Hand zu weisenden Argumentation des Antragsgegners möglich sein, um einem Verfügungsantrag den Erfolg versagen zu können."

772 This is in agreement with R. BÖHLER, 'Einstweilige Verfügungen in Patentsachen' GRUR (2011), pp. 965–977. See: p. 969. He also adds that the clear guidelines given in *Harnkatheterset*, despite setting the bar highly, also made legal practice more predictable.

law,[773] this way, a second and critical look can be taken at the validity of the patent, by a technically skilled body, that thereby bases themselves on the research and arguments of those who know the product and market (including the prior art) well: a patentee's competitors.[774] This way, the chance of granting a preliminary injunction to protect a later invalidated patent, (an erroneous decision) is greatly reduced, as the viability and strength of a patent is now examined from a different perspective than solely from the perspective of patent examiners when deciding on the grant of a patent.

Lastly a few remarks on that other important case regarding patent validity, *Olanzapine*. As stated before, in principle a court is, when deciding on a preliminary injunction, bound to follow an earlier decision of either the DPMA, the EPO or the German Bundespatentgericht on patent validity. An exception to this is given in the case of *Olanzapine,* which was an handed down by the OLG Düsseldorf.[775] This ruling confirmed that even if there has been a prior ruling rendering the patent invalid, the preliminary injunction court is still in the position to put this decision on patent validity aside if it believes the other court was wrong in this invalidity ruling.

The case at hand concerned a request for a preliminary injunction enforcing a disputed patent – 'the olanzapine patent' – that covered the fabrication of an antipsychotic medicine against schizophrenia and bipolar disorders. This patent had, at an earlier stage, been held as invalid by the Bundespatentgericht on the grounds that the patent was not novel, and an appeal against this at the Bundesgerichtshof was pending.[776] In the meantime, the main issue was whether the OLG Düsseldorf, that reconsidered a request for a preliminary injunction, could *disregard* this prior ruling of the Bundespatentgericht, by nevertheless still granting a preliminary injunction.[777] After all, one of the conditions for a preliminary injunction – namely to have no doubts regarding the validity of the patent – was not met at the time of the request for a preliminary injunction, due to the prior invalidity decision. As Barth and Zimmer argue, in normal proceedings when there are doubts with respect

773 OLG Düsseldorf, February 19th 2015, Az. I-2 U 54/15. See: par. 57.

774 Ibidem.

775 OLG Düsseldorf, *Olanzapin*, May 29th 2008, Az. I-2, W 47/07.
For an excellent English-language article on the Olanzapine case, see G. BARTH, F.J. ZIMMER 'The Olanzapine patent dispute: German court grants a preliminary injunction on a patent invalidated by the first instance Federal Court' (2008). Available at: http://www.grunecker.de/files/olanzapine_article.pdf (last accessed on 24 April 2017).

776 OLG Düsseldorf, *Olanzapin*, May 29th 2008, Az. I-2, W 47/07. See: par. 28.

777 It should be noted here that the Bundesgerichtshof did indeed, half a year after the OLG Düsseldorf's decision, declare that the disputed 'Olanzapin patent' was valid. After this, competitors – the generic companies – had to wait again until the patent (in fact the SPC) had expired in 2011. See: BGH, December 16th 2008, Az. X ZR 89/07. Also: GRUR (2009) pp. 382–389.

to the validity of the patent, bifurcation applies and this would likely result in the staying of the infringement procedure. However, they argue here that such a stay would be inconsistent with the character of a preliminary injunction proceeding, which is designed to do 'swift justice', and they note that normally when the validity of the patent is in doubt, the request for a preliminary injunction would be denied.[778] The OLG Düsseldorf in this case however took the ground-breaking step to hold that the Bundespatentgericht was evidently wrong (*evident unrichtig*) in its invalidity decision, and the OLG considered that it had the freedom to consider the validity itself and, if infringement was found as well, to indeed be entitled to grant the requested preliminary injunction.[779, 780]

§7.2.5.2. The balancing of interests as part of the Interessenabwägung

We have seen above that strong emphasis is put on patent validity in Germany and that especially according to the strict Düsseldorf court's approach the survival of opposition or invalidity proceedings is seen as a de facto requirement to obtain a preliminary injunction. Nevertheless, German preliminary injunction courts, under the *Interessenabwägung* prong, have the opportunity to look at special circumstances, interests and harms of the parties, and this way offer a less rigid and strict approach to the issues of validity, but also of parties' interests and harm that are impacting the outcome of a request and which otherwise may have swung the result in a different direction.

---

778 G. BARTH, F.J. ZIMMER 'The Olanzapine patent dispute: German court grants a preliminary injunction on a patent invalidated by the first instance Federal Court' (2008). Available at: http://www.grunecker.de/files/olanzapine_article.pdf (last accessed on 24 April 2017). See: p. 4.

779 OLG Düsseldorf, *Olanzapin*, May 29th 2008, Az. I-2, W 47/07. See: par. 72. "*Eine Ausnahme* von dem prinzipiellen Vorrang der erstinstanzlichen Einspruchs- oder Nichtigkeitsentscheidung ist von Verfassungs wegen (Art. 2 Abs. 1 GG i.V.m. dem Rechtsstaatsprinzip) allerdings dort zwingend geboten, wo der Widerruf oder die Nichtigerklärung *evident unrichtig* ist und das selbst nicht fachkundig besetzte Verletzungsgericht diese Unrichtigkeit verlässlich erkennen kann, (..) so dass dem Schutzrechtsinhaber seine – trotz erstinstanzlicher Vernichtung fortbestehenden – gesetzlichen Verbietungsrechte für die Dauer einer Aussetzung des Hauptsacheverfahrens bzw. einer Verweigerung vorläufigen Rechtsschutzes endgültig und unwiederbringlich genommen werden.' (Emphasis added). And at Par. 74: 'Bei Anwendung dieser Grundsätze überwiegen im Streitfall die Interessen der Antragstellerin die Belange der Antragsgegnerin. Für letztere streitet zwar vordergründig, dass das Bundespatentgericht das Verfügungspatent für nichtig erklärt hat. Es ist jedoch mit Sicherheit zu erwarten, dass das Nichtigkeitsurteil im Berufungsverfahren keinen Bestand haben wird, (..)."

780 And this was exactly what happened. In doing so, the OLG Düsseldorf went through a rather long novelty analysis, to support its view that the Bundespatentgericht had erred in its assessment on validity, because it was precisely because of a perceived lack of novelty that the latter had held the patent to be invalid.

A first important example, is that case law[781] has recognised that pharmaceutical patents facing generic entry are worthy of a *special position*, and such a patent does not have to have undergone and survived prior opposition or invalidity proceedings, in order for a plaintiff to be able to obtain preliminary relief. Normally, a lack of such proceedings would be weighing heavily against the grant of a preliminary injunction, but a generic entry is seen as one of the 'exceptional circumstances' (*ausßergewöhnliche Umstände)* mentioned in *Harnkatheterset.*[782] The reason for this is that the consequences for the patentee, when generic entry occurs, are very significant. They are also difficult to undo when an erroneous decision occurs, and another factor here is the notion that the patentee deserves extra protection because the generic company is not taking a real economic risk in bringing a product to the market, but mostly relying on the work done by the patentee.[783] Clearly therefore, it are commercial considerations recognising the special nature of these patents, that are backing this bespoke treatment.

It is stressed however, that this does not mean that this special position for patentees against generic entry trumps any doubts that may exist about a patent's validity. It only addresses the principle that a patent should have been re-examined in opposition or invalidity proceedings prior to considering a preliminary injunction request, and is thus an exception to the rule. The preliminary injunction court should still examine the validity itself, and be convinced that the patent is likely to be held valid when it comes to later examination.[784] It is also clear, that this exception to the rule only applies to genuine generic entry situations, in which the generic pharmaceutical is considerably cheaper than that of the originator, and enters the market at the end of the patent's lifetime. Ergo, a pharmaceutical that simply targeted the same market and the same medical indication, even though it was partly based on the originator's clinical trials and mentioned the originator in its advertising,[785] was deemed not to be a true generic threat, but a *Konkurrenzprodukt,* so that the plaintiff could not benefit from this special exception.[786]

Apart from the exception for generic entry cases to forego a prior invalidity challenge, there is more to be mentioned on validity. A few cases can well show the *typical arguments* that are considered, when deciding on the issue of validity in the balancing prong.

---

781 See *inter alia*: OLG Düsseldorf, *Flupirtin-Maleat,* January 17th 2013, Az. I-2 U 87/12. Also: GRUR RR (2013) pp. 236 – 241. Furthermore, see OLG Düsseldorf, *Desogestrel,* November 7th 2013, Az. I-2 U 94/12. See: par. 32 and par. 36.

782 OLG Düsseldorf, *Harnkatheterset,* April 29th 2010, Az. I-2U 126/09. See: par. 61.

783 OLG Düsseldorf, *Desogestrel,* November 7th 2013, Az. I-2 U 94/12. See: par. 32.

784 OLG Düsseldorf, December 18th 2015, Az. I-2 U 35/15, and OLG Düsseldorf, *Desogestrel,* November 7th 2013, Az. I-2 U 94/12. See: par. 32.

785 LG Düsseldorf, October 24th 2013, Az. 4c O 84/13. See: par. 82–87.

786 Ibidem.

An exemplary case is the *Interessenabwägung* that takes place in the decision of *Motoneurons*. After having found that the patent had not yet been tested for validity in an opposition or invalidity proceeding, this would normally be weighing against the grant of a preliminary injunction to the plaintiff. However, citing the *Harnkatheterset* case, the court submitted that it can divert from this, but only if exceptional circumstances are present (*außergewöhnliche Umstände*).[787] Subsequently, the court went into whether indeed the circumstances were exceptional in this particular case, and most importantly considered the following:

- It noted that the defendant has had ample time (namely more than three years, since it received regulatory approval) to attack the plaintiff's patent to prepare market entry.[788]
- It then stressed the *extraordinary sensitivity* of the market of pharmaceuticals. This is exemplified in the effects of a delay in market access of generics, and also the difficulty of recapturing of market shares by the plaintiff, and the price drop the patented product experiences after generic entry.[789]
- In the immediate balancing of the interests of both parties, the court looked at *consequences* for both parties of granting a preliminary injunction: the fact that the plaintiff had allowed a generics company *that is part of the same concern as the patentee*, to prepare a generic launch, did not take away the need for a preliminary injunction against other parties. The patentee has the freedom to choose the licensee it wants, and in this view a preliminary injunction is also an acceptable tool in order to secure a market share for a preferred generics company, against another party (i.e. other generic companies). This is even so, although a preliminary injunction would then have (market) effects beyond the life of the patent.[790]

787 LG Düsseldorf, *Motoneurons*, October 19th 2012, Az. 4b O 135/12. See: par. 49.

788 Idem, at par. 50. "Ihnen wäre es daher ohne weiteres möglich gewesen, um den Markteintreitt hinreichend absuzichern, den Rechtsbestand des Verfügungspatentes durch eine Nichtigkeitsklage überprüfen zu lassen."

789 LG Düsseldorf, *Motoneurons*, October 19th 2012, Az. 4b O 135/12. See: par. 51.

790 Idem, at par. 52. "Es liegt indes im Rahmen der Entscheidungsfreiheit eines Patentinhabers, Lizenzen, im vorliegenden Fall für den Vertrieb eines Generikums, gegen Zahlung einer Lizenzgebühr zu vergeben, um so bereits kurz vor Ablauf eines Patentes ein Generikum auf dem Markt zu etablieren. Zwar mag in einem solchen Fall der Zweck eines Antrags auf Erlass einer einstweiligen Verfügung auch der Einrichtung und Sicherung einer Marktposition im Bereich der Generika im Sinne eines firstentries dienen. *Auch ein solches Ansinnen des Patentinhabers ist gerechtfertigt und Ausfluss der effektiven Durchsetzung des Patentschutzes durch den Patentinhaber.* Dieses mag zwar auch Auswirkungen über den Ablauf des Patentschutzes hinaus entfalten. Solches ist indes hinzunehmen." *Sic.* Emphasis added.

- It also was noted, and taken into account, that in this context, the defendant could have requested a license from the plaintiff, but had not done so, at least not until after the preliminary injunction proceedings had started.[791]
- The preliminary injunction itself was only meant to be in place for a relatively short time as it was not that long anymore until the patent expired: merely one month. Although this of course meant that the generic product of the firm that belonged to the same concern as the plaintiff would already be on the market the moment the patent expired, the court did not follow the defendant in his argumentation that with the grant of a preliminary injunction, there would no longer be anymore room on the market for the defendant's generic product.[792]
- The court also observed, and took into account, that the contested patent had been respected by competitors for more than 15 years, and that this was now being attacked at the end of the patent's lifetime.[793] It also observed that a decision on its validity could not be made during the patent's lifetime.[794] Bearing this in mind, simply having doubts on a patent's validity was not enough: there should be concrete evidence against this, evidence that in casu was not deemed to be established.

These above mentioned grounds in the *Interessenabwägung* led the court to, despite that the patent had not been tested before for validity in neither opposition or invalidity proceedings, to nevertheless decide in favour of a preliminary injunction to be granted to the plaintiff.

Similarly, as the court held in *Mundipharma*[795] that even if the patent's validity was not completely certain, the requirements to this should not be exaggerated when looking at the 'total picture'. Therefore, the *interests* of the plaintiff in obtaining a preliminary injunction should also be taken into account. In casu, they outweighed the interests mitigating against preliminary relief,[796] namely:

---

791 LG Düsseldorf, *Motoneurons*, October 19th 2012, Az. 4b O 135/12. See: par. 52.

792 Ibidem. "Dass sich bis zum 22. Oktober 2012 die Marktposition im Bereich der Generika schon so weit zugunsten der Verfügungsklägerin auf Grund der Lizenzvergabe an die F Arzneimittel GmbH verfestigt haben könnte, dass nach Ablauf des Verfügungspatentes dieses ausschließliche Wirkungen in der Weise zeigt, *dass für weitere Generikahersteller kein Raum mehr ist, ist weder zu erkennen noch von den Verfügungsbeklagten behauptet worden.*" Emphasis added.

793 LG Düsseldorf, *Motoneurons*, October 19th 2012, Az. 4b O 135/12. See: par. 54.

794 Ibidem.

795 LG Düsseldorf, *Mundipharma*, March 30th 2010, Az. 4a O 13–10. The preliminary injunction was confirmed on appeal in OLG Düsseldorf, January 20th 2011, Az. I-2 U 55/10.

796 LG Düsseldorf, *Mundipharma*, March 30th 2010, Az. 4a O 13–10. See: p. 49.

- Firstly, the court noted that that the patent had already been in force for almost two decades and would expire in 1,5 years' time.[797]
- In this light, if a preliminary injunction was to be denied, there would be little remaining time for the patentee to still benefit from the exclusivity of the patent, considering that it would likely be a year before the trial on the merits would take place.
- Thirdly, the court acknowledged the well-known argument of loss of market share and a revenue drop (due to the lower price and less sales) that would occur due to the infringer's actions. Also, specifically relevant for this type of pharmaceutical litigation is that infringement may have consequences for the pricing of a pharmaceutical within the German health system. If a preliminary injunction was not granted, the availability of a cheaper generic product would influence the height of the *Festbetrag*.[798] This is the maximum price of a pharmaceutical that is reimbursed by health insurers.[799]
- Taking into account the interests of the defendant, the court noted that if a preliminary injunction was granted, the economic consequences for the generic company would be severe and could possibly not be repaired anymore.[800] Nevertheless, the court held that making the grant of the preliminary injunction conditional on a *Sicherheitsleistung*, which could offer compensation to the defendant, would be sufficient to deal with this concern.[801, 802]

---

797 Ibidem.

798 LG Düsseldorf, *Mundipharma*, March 30th 2010, Az. 4a O 13–10. See: p. 49–50. Own translation. Original tekst: "In Arzeinmittelbereich besteht aber abweichend von sonstigen Patentverletzungen zudem die Gefahr, dass der Patentinhaber aufgrund der Bildung einer Festbetragsgruppe reglmäßig gezwungen ist, sein Produkte dauerhaft unter den von ihm kalkulierten Verkaufspreisen anzubieten, weil die Festbeträge aufgrund einer Durchschnittsbetrachtung der Preise aller Arzneimittel mit vergleichbarem Wirkstoff festgesezt werden. (..)"

799 Although not explicitly stated in the judgment, it is submitted that the logic behind the raising of this argument by the plaintiff-originator is that a reducement of the *Festbetrag*, would be something that would be difficult to undo if it later turned out, at the trial on the merits, that the generic firm's actions were not infringing.

800 LG Düsseldorf, *Mundipharma*, March 30th 2010, Az. 4a O 13–10. See: p. 50.

801 Ibidem.

802 Similarly, see LG Düsseldorf, August 15th 2012, Az. 4a 0 109/12. There, the court held that the grounds for an injunction were met in accordance of §935 ZPO, and the plaintiff's interest in enforcement of its rights via injunctive relief, resulting into preventing market entry by the defendant, was deemed as being more important than the defendant's interest in immediate and first access to the market as a generic company. It was also decided the defendant is suffciently protected against an erreneous decision by the obligation for the plaintiff to provide financial security.

Other interests can as well play a pivotal role in the process of the *Interessenabwägung*:

As is apparent from another decision, a factor weighing against the grant of a preliminary injunction is when a patentee does *not use the patent itself*, as this impacts the notion of irreparable harm and thus the necessity for a preliminary injunction.[803, 804] Equally, such a preliminary injunction was denied after the *Interessenabwägung* in *VA LCD*.[805] There it was held that the plaintiff's likelihood of success on the merits was not large and this, together with the fact that it merely was just a few weeks away until the trial on the merits would take place, meant that the plaintiff would not be withheld for long, by this decision of the preliminary injunction court, from a (next) possibility to enforce his rights.[806] Therefore, interim relief was regarded as not being necessary.

Heading in the other direction, namely in favour of a preliminary injunction, was for instance the decision[807] that the infringing party only had a small part (1.9%) of the total market share. Nevertheless, it was held by the court that a plaintiff was also entitled to enforce its rights against a 'small infringer' with such a minor market share and that even with such a small market presence there was a considerable risk for the patentee to experience a drop in revenue.[808] Another factor that has been taken along by courts in the *Interessenabwägung* is for instance that of solvability. A preliminary injunction may be difficult to withhold when there are doubts about the defendant's ability to pay future damages, which may be awarded to the patentee after a trial on the merits.[809]

The case of the OLG Düsseldorf in *Lungengefäßverengung*[810] is another notable example of factors that can be taken along in the *Interessenabwägung* as *specifically* the interests of patients were taken into account, although they did not prove to be decisive in this case. In casu, the court explicitly considered whether the grant of a preliminary injunction, prohibiting the infringing device, would lead to *problems with the supply of adequate medication to patients requiring* the *product of the infringer* (a so-called '*Versorgungslücke*'). Because of this, the court investigated

---

803 LG Düsseldorf, October 24th 2013, Az. 4c O 84/13. See: par. 120.

804 See the examples given in C. RADEMACHER, *Die gerichtliche Durchsetzung von Patent-und Markenrechten in Deutschland, Japan und den USA* (2010 Nomos Verlagsgesellschaft). See: p. 97.

805 OLG Düsseldorf, *VA LCD*, July 8th 2009, Az. 6 U 61/09.

806 Ibidem.

807 OLG Düsseldorf, January 21st 2016, Az. I-2 U 49/15.

808 Idem, at par. 159.

809 Examples in C. RADEMACHER, *Die gerichtliche Durchsetzung von Patent-und Markenrechten in Deutschland, Japan und den USA* (2010 Nomos Verlagsgesellschaft). See: p. 98.

810 OLG Düsseldorf, *Lungengefäßverengung*, February 14th 2013, Az. 4b O 187/12. See: III.2.

whether therefore a preliminary injunction should perhaps better not be granted. The court still allowed the request for a preliminary injunction however, as it was convinced that a preliminary injunction would not lead to problems of this nature. In the same case, the preliminary injunction court also rejected the notion made by the defendant that the product prices of the patentee were too high – and that therefore more competition should be allowed – as the court held that the research of originators benefitted the public.[811]

Nevertheless, whilst grounds concerning patent *validity* are regularly explicitly balanced in the *Interessenabwägung*, this is not nearly always the case with other (commercial) interests, as was stated clearly in *Leflunomid/Teriflunomid II*.[812] Here, the court ruled that the balancing of hardships, thereby taking into account market circumstances and economic interests, is not an obligation to be met and *certainly not when both validity and infringement are established clearly in favour of the patentee* as in such situations a preliminary injunction was deemed to be in place.[813, 814]

Finally, as we have also seen in The Netherlands, it is proper to mention at this point that a German court can grant a preliminary injunction under the condition

811 Ibidem.

812 OLG Düsseldorf, *Leflunomid/Teriflunomid II*, November 10th 2011, Az. 2 U 41/11.

813 Idem, at II.4. "Nachdem somit feststeht, dass die angegriffenen Präparate der Beklagten das Verfügungspatent wortsinngemäß verletzen und dieses darüber hinaus zumindest erstinstanzlich ein streitiges Rechtsbestandsverfahren überstanden hat, wobei die gegen die Aufrechterhaltung des Verfügungspatents gerichteten Angriffe keine nennenswerte Erfolgsaussicht bieten, *gibt es ungeachtet der bestehenden Marktverhältnisse und der jeweils betroffenen wirtschaftlichen Interessen beider Parteien keinen Grund, der Klägerin eine Durchsetzung ihres Unterlassungsanspruchs im Verfahren des einstweiligen Rechtsschutzes zu verweigern* und damit der Beklagten eine Fortsetzung ihres rechtswidrigen Verhaltens zu ermöglichen.*Zu widersprechen ist der Verfügungsbeklagten in ihrer Auffassung, es habe in jedem Fall eine Interessenabwägung stattzufinden, wobei sich die Notwendigkeit der Gewährung einstweiligen Rechtsschutzes nicht schon aus der Patentverletzung als solcher ergeben könne.* Sind die Verletzungsfrage und der Rechtsbestand klar zugunsten des Schutzrechtsinhabers zu beantworten, so begründet schon die Eindeutigkeit der Rechtslage für sich die Notwendigkeit, dem deliktischen Verhalten des Verletzers mithilfe des vorläufigen Rechtsschutzes Einhalt zu gebieten." Emphasis added.

814 Although the court in the decision of OLG Düsseldorf, January 21st 2016, Az. I-2 U 49/15 still considers the defendant's arguments, it stated that the principle it takes into consideration here, is as follows: "Ist sowohl die Frage der Patentbenutzung als auch die des Bestands des Verfügungspatents im Ergebnis eindeutig zugunsten des Verfügungsklägers zu beurteilen, *überwiegen grundsätzlich seine Interessen gegenüber denjenigen des Verfügungsbeklagten.*" Emphasis added. See: par. 158.

that it only becomes effective after a certain time, i.e. in three weeks after the ruling of the court. This is the *Aufbrauchfrist.* This way, whilst prohibiting infringement on the longer term, the effect of an enjoining order for the defendant/infringer is somewhat softened in the immediate sense, at it can better adjust to the changed situation. This is again another example of one of the possibilities to offer a balanced remedy. It should be noted here that also the *Bundesgerichtshof* in the case of *Wärmetauscher*[815] has confirmed in a decision that this practice is something that court can decide on in disproportionate situations, as in case the infringed patent was on a small but highly important part of a complex machine for which it is difficult to find alternatives.[816] The court thereby balances the interests of parties.[817] However, delay in the effects of the enjoinment is not something that the defendant/infringer is entitled to by default. The norm remains to be strict with providing this, allowing an *Aufbrauchfrist* only under certain circumstances.[818]

§7.2.6. Sicherheitsleistung and damages

Germany differs from other European countries such as The Netherlands and England in requesting security. It is common practice that a preliminary injunction in a patent case will only be enforceable if the plaintiff posts a bond, *a Sicherheitsleistung*. This is with an eye on the possibility that the court at the trial

---

815 BGH, *Wärmetauscher*, May 10th 2016, Az. X ZR 114/13.

816 Idem, at par. 60. "(...) Dabei wird insbesondere Raum für eine ausnahmsweise zu bewilligende Aufbrauchfrist gesehen, wenn der Verletzungsgegenstand nur einen kleinen, aber funktionswesentlichen Bestandteil eines technisch komplexen Geräts betrifft und nicht in zumutbarer Zeit durch ein patentfreies oder lizenzierbares Produkt ersetzt werden kann. (...)."

817 Idem, at par. 58: "Eine Aufbrauchfrist kommt nach der Rechtsprechung des Bundesgerichtshof im Allgemeinen, beispielsweise in Wettbewerbsstreitigkeiten, unter dem Gesichtspunkt von Treu und Glauben (§ 242 BGB) in Betracht, wenn der unterlassungspflichtigen Partei bei sofortiger Wirkung des Untersagungsgebots unverhältnismäßige Nachteile entstünden und die befristete Fortsetzung des angegriffenen Verhaltens für den Verletzten keine unzumutbaren Beeinträchtigungen mit sich bringt (..)."

818 Idem, at par. 61: "Die Gewährung einer Aufbrauchfrist kommt im Falle einer Patentverletzung aus in der Natur der Beeinträchtigung liegenden Gründen nur unter engen Voraussetzungen in Betracht. (..) Eine Einschränkung der Wirkung des Patents durch Gewährung einer Aufbrauchfrist ist deshalb nur dann zu rechtfertigen, wenn die wirtschaftlichen Folgen der sofortigen Befolgung des Unterlassungsgebots den Verletzer im Einzelfall aufgrund besonderer Umstände über die mit seinem Ausspruch bestimmungsgemäß einhergehenden Beeinträchtigungen hinaus in einem Maße treffen und benachteiligen, das die unbedingte Untersagung als unzumutbar erscheinen lässt."

on the merits could decide otherwise. The preliminary injunction court has sole discretion in establishing the amount that is required for this *Sicherheitsleistung* to be deemed sufficient.[819]

Additionally, the plaintiff assumes a no-fault liability to pay the defendant's damages in the case a preliminary injunction is eventually overturned because it was granted erroneously.[820] This is regulated in §945 ZPO and this provision also applies to decisions that are temporarily enforceable (*vorläufige Vollstreckbarkeit).*[821] The liability covers the situation of that when a preliminary injunction should not have been granted in the first place.[822] However the situation in which changed circumstances that afterwards have made a preliminary injunction unjustified, does not trigger this liability.[823] In order to gain compensation, the defendant should start a separate proceedings (*Schadenersatzprozess*) to obtain a decision that the granted preliminary injunction was indeed unjustified. If the latter has not been confirmed yet in an earlier legal ruling, (i.e. a trial on the merits), the court dealing with the request for damages is itself entitled to examine whether a preliminary injunction was granted erroneously or not.[824] The plaintiff for the preliminary injunction can then still escape liability when it demonstrates that there was indeed a genuine claim for preliminary relief.[825] The amount of damages that is ordered under the heading of §945 ZPO can cover the consequences of a prohibitive preliminary injunction from the moment the injunction has been enforced and in principle encompasses all direct

---

819 See: §108 ZPO.

820 C. HEATH, 'Wrongful patent enforcement – Threats and post-infringement invalidity in comparative perspective' *IIC* No. 3 (2008), pp. 307–322. See: pp. 321–322.

821 §945 ZPO reads: "Should the order of a seizure or an injunction prove to have been unfounded from the start, or should the measure directed be repealed pursuant to section 926 subsection (2) or section 942 (3), *the party that has obtained the order is under obligation to compensate the opponent for the damages* that he has suffered as a result of the measure directed having been enforced, or as a result of the opponent having provided security in order to avert the enforcement or to obtain the repeal of the measure." This translation of the ZPO – with emphasis added by the present author – is from the hand of C. VON SCHÖNING, and is made for the German Ministry of Justice. Available at: http://www.gesetze-im-internet.de/englisch_zpo/englisch_zpo.html (last accessed on 26 April 2017).

822 W. BERNEKE, E. SCHÜTTPELZ, *Die einstweilige Verfügung in Wettbewerbsachen* (2014 NJW Praxis / C.H. Beck). See: p. 214, RN 725.

823 Ibidem.

824 C. RADEMACHER, *Die gerichtliche Durchsetzung von Patent-und Markenrechten in Deutschland, Japan und den USA* (2010 Nomos Verlagsgesellschaft). See: pp. 100–101.

825 Ibidem.

and indirect damages as a result of the enjoinment.[826] However, it should be stated here that despite this strongly drafted statutory liability, it is often difficult to gain compensation in actual practice. As Heath states, when writing on this subject, this is especially the case with a defendant's loss in production and decline in market share as a result of being enjoined by the court, as these are both difficult issues to prove and get compensated for.[827]

§7.2.7. *Intermediate conclusion*

It has been observed that the German preliminary injunction doctrine is characterised by a cautious approach to the use of the remedy in patent litigation. Whilst in principle these are allowed and regularly granted, much is undertaken to prevent erroneous decisions from being made. The influential and important Düsseldorf court in particular upholds relatively strict requirements with respect to the likelihood of a patent being held valid before enjoining (thereby requiring a patent in principle to have survived a prior opposition or invalidity challenge) and also critically look at the issue of patent infringement. In line with other European jurisdictions, but different with the domestic presumption under Unfair Competition Laws, the *Dringlichkeit* of a preliminary injunction is something that is not presumed. Things are therefore not necessarily made easy for the plaintiff-applicant, that also has to prove urgency. At the same time, it has also been demonstrated that courts in Germany are not over-rigid and they allow themselves to tailor and balance an otherwise unjust result. With respect to *Dringlichkeit*, for instance, it has been made clear that the plaintiff does not have to take a *Prozessrisiko*. In the context of *Interessenabwägung*, firstly, the principle that a patent should have survived a prior opposition or invalidity challenge can be mitigated somewhat when certain exceptional conditions are both present and met. This can even be the case for an entire class of patents, namely when pharmaceutical patentees are facing generic entry by competitors. Furthermore, the courts also do indeed sometimes address other (commercial or economic) interests and hardships of parties under the heading of the *Interessenabwägung*, although it seems that these have only limited influence and the main emphasis of the German preliminary injunction doctrine remains to be the 'likelihood of prevailing on the merits' aspect. With respect to security, in contrast with other European countries, German preliminary injunction courts usually require a *Sicherheitsleistung* to be posted and an erroneous decision can open the way for the defendant to claim (non-statutory capped) damages for which the plaintiff for the request of a preliminary injunction can be held liable.

826 Following §249 BGB.

827 C. HEATH, 'Wrongful patent enforcement – Threats and post-infringement invalidity in comparative perspective' *IIC* No. 3 (2008), pp. 307–322. See: p. 331.

§7.3. England

§7.3.1. Introduction

The subsequent paragraph will focus on the legal situation as it exists in England, home to the key patent cases in the United Kingdom.[828] Within Europe, England is a frequently used venue for patent litigation, despite the relatively high costs of (patent) litigation.[829] Different than in Germany, a trial on the merits is not bifurcated of nature.

§7.3.2. The legal basis and guiding principles: Equity and American Cyanamid

As is well-known, both the United States and England base the remedy of injunctive (interim) relief on the principles of equity.[830] In England, the historic roots of injunctive (interim) relief can be traced centuries back to the emergence of the Chancery Court in England and the growing role of equity instead of Common Law.[831] The rigid nature of early Common Law courts and the fact that they did not have injunctive powers to prevent wrongs resulted into the Chancery becoming a more and more important and effective forum to provide legal justice.[832] Whilst over time equity became more developed into a stable system of law (based on principles and precedents) injunctive relief itself remained in its infancy. As Leubsdorf writes, in the 18th century *neither a general standard* for interlocutory injunctions had developed, nor did interlocutory injunctions require a special justification:

> "It is also likely that the interlocutory injunction was not yet regarded as an extraordinary decree requiring special justification. Chancery proceedings were so slow that, in almost all cases, injunctive relief had to be granted preliminarily if it was to be of any use. The typical injunction was therefore an interlocutory decree granted either by

---

828 At this point it should be mentioned that the law for Wales is the same as in England. The Scottish proceedings and test, which differ somewhat from that of England and Wales, is not covered in this dissertation. It is nevertheless submitted it can be assumed that the bulk of *the most important patent litigation* takes part in the English (London) courts.

829 R. WILLOUGHBY, chapter 'The United Kingdom' in W. HOYNG, F. EIJSVOGELS (eds), *Global Patent litigation* (Kluwer Law Publishing, the United Kingdom supplement as updated in August 2014), p. 75.

830 For more on the history of the emergence of equity, see G. SAMUEL, *A short introduction to the Common Law* (2013 Edward Elgar). See: pp. 13–15 and 60.

831 D.W. RAACK, 'A history of injunctions in England before 1700' *Indiana Law Journal* 64. No. 4 (1986), pp. 539–592. See: esp. pp. 591–592. He points out that with the Act of the King in 1616, the Chancery's role in granting injunctions was sanctioned and after this the Chancellors developed equity as a stable system of precedents.

832 Idem, at p. 554.

> default or on motion supported by affidavits. The cases concentrated on the availability of injunctive relief, not whether it should be preliminary or final."[833]

At the end of the 19th century, Leubsdorf writes, the abovementioned changed and the belief gradually emerged that there should be *one general,* uniform standard, across all areas of law, for interlocutory relief.[834] Key elements of standards that we know today slowly started to develop. Courts began to focus on 'the strength of a plaintiff's case', 'irreparable injury', the 'balancing of convenience' and also the preservation of the 'status quo'.[835] Despite the emergence of these key elements, which were independently used in many different individual cases, uncertainty how to deal with interim relief remained until deep in the 20th century, especially with respect to how to deal with the issue of 'prima facie' nature of a case.

Indeed, a true unified standard did not emerge for a long time. It took until the mid 1970's before the House of Lords gave a judgment with the *American Cyanamid v Ethicon* case,[836] that – as we know with the benefit of hindsight – would become very much decisive in the fixture of a single standard and it still provides the guiding principles of the test used today. It also was a major change with respect to the House of Lords' previous line of authority.[837]

The core of interim relief in England is thus to be found in the court's equitable powers and not in legal statute. Nevertheless, there is one source of legislation that is worth mentioning in the context of interim injunctions and that is that of the *Civil Procedure Rules* (CPR). Procedurally, patent litigation in England and Wales is regulated by the CPR and the relevant provisions for interim injunctions are to be found in Rule 25 CPR.[838] The provisions enacted in the CPR first of all allow the court to grant interim remedies in general, including the granting of interim injunctions.[839, 840] Furthermore, the CPR provisions stipulate various procedural

833 J. LEUBSDORF, 'The standard for preliminary injunctions' *Harvard Law Review* 91, No. 3 (1978), pp. 525–566. See: p. 528. Emphasis added.

834 Idem, at p. 528. Also see R.G. HAMMOND, 'Interlocutory injunctions: time for a new model?' *The University of Toronto Law Journal* 30, No. 3 (1980), pp. 240–282. See: esp. pp. 242–243 and 249.

835 J. LEUBSDORF, 'The standard for preliminary injunctions' *Harvard Law Review* 91, No. 3 (1978), pp. 525–566. See: p. 528.

836 House of Lords, *American Cyanamid v Ethicon,* 1975, AC 396.

837 A. GORE, 'Interlocutory injunctions. A final judgment' *The Modern Law Review* 38, No. 6 (1975), pp. 672–679. See: p. 675.

838 The Civil Procedure Rules (CPR) are effective since April 1999 and the latest version can be found at the website of the UK Ministry of Justice: https://www.justice.gov.uk/courts/procedure-rules/civil/rules/part25 (last accessed on 17 April 2017).

839 CPR Rule 25 (1) (a).

840 There are other statutes too, that confirm that the court has the power to grant interim injunctions. See for instance Section 37 of the *Senior Courts Act* (formerly known as *the Supreme Court Act*): "The High Court may by order (whether

matters – i.e. how and in what manner to apply for an interim order[841] – and provisions that foresee in the matter of costs.[842] Even more practical guidance on these issues is provided for in the *Practice Directions on Interim Injunctions* which is a supplement to Rule 25 CPR.[843]

These procedural provisions aside however, the CPR does not provide much in terms of substance on how to decide on a request for interim relief. Nor does it form a legal basis as such: this legal basis has always been that of equity and the guiding principles that the court should bear in mind when using its equitable powers when deciding whether or not to grant an interim injunction have been clearly set out in case law. Indeed, it is the *American Cyanamid* case that is the dominant ruling in this respect. This 1975 House of Lords patent case was about a dispute concerning a patent on the use of absorbable surgical sutures of filaments made of a specific kind of chain polymer. Despite its patents origins, the case has been tremendously influential and its application stretches beyond that of patent law alone. Until the day of today, it remains the leading case giving guidance for interim injunction requests in England and Wales, in all areas of law.[844, 845]

Before a look is taken at this decision in more detail, it is good to point out that Lord Diplock (the judge that drafted the decision)[846] clearly drew the main boundaries that the court deciding on the request for an interim injunction has to adhere to:

> "It is no part of the court's function **at this stage** of the litigation to try to resolve conflicts of evidence on affidavit as to facts on which the claims of either party may ultimately depend **nor to decide difficult questions of law which call for detailed argument** and mature considerations. **These are matters to be dealt with at the trial**."[847]

Instead, when deciding whether to grant an interim injunction, the court should assess the request bearing in mind three questions, which are listed below. Because the judge's wording in the ruling is very insightful in order to understand the intended role of interim injunctions, it is deemed as useful to give various fragments

interlocutory or final) grant an injunction or appoint a receiver in all cases in which it appears to the court to be just and convenient to do so."

841 CPR Rule 25.3.

842 CPR Rule 25.12–25.15.

843 Available at the website of the Ministry of Justice, *Practice Direction 25A – Interim Injunctions*: https://www.justice.gov.uk/courts/procedure-rules/civil/rules/part25/pd_part25a (last accessed on 17 April 2017).

844 Save a few exceptions to this, such as for disputes concerning defamation.

845 Also see H. MACQUEEN, C. WAELDE, G. LAURIE and A. BROWN, *Contemporary Intellectual Property: Law & Policy* (2011 Oxford University Press). See: pp. 963–965.

846 The other Lords appointed to this case all fully agreed with the opinion of Lord Diplock.

847 House of Lords, *American Cyanamid v Ethicon*,1975, AC 396. See: p. 4. Emphasis added.

of the judgment in full.[848] This also contributes to a better comprehension of the questions that should be raised by a preliminary injunction court in examination of the plaintiff's request.

Figure 8. The English preliminary injunction test (own image).

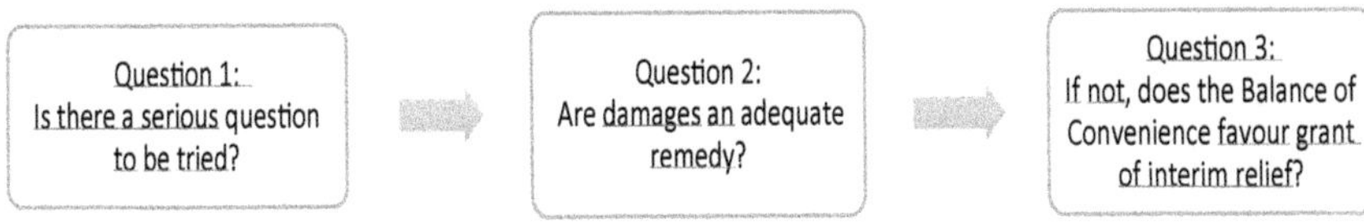

§7.3.2.1 Is there a serious question to be tried?

The first question which should be raised by the court dealing with a request for an interim injunction, is whether the dispute that is before the trial judge is *serious.* A genuine issue must be at stake and brought before the court. Sometimes this is also worded as a case to be 'non-frivolous'. As Mei writes,[849] Lord Diplock with this judgment recognised that judicial unclarity had emerged in earlier case law on interim injunctions on exactly how courts should assess the strength of the plaintiff's case with respect to prevailing on the merits. With his ruling, Lord Diplock attempted to address this. No longer was it after *American Cyanamid* required that a case *prima facie* had to favour the plaintiff. With this was meant that initially, the plaintiff had to show that he had reasonably good prospects of success at trial, in order to obtain interim relief.[850] However, the House of Lords recognised that the burden of proving a good prospect of success entailed (especially in patent cases) multiple difficult questions, i.e. that of infringement and validity. The House of Lords was of the view that these issues should not be dealt with in interim injunction proceedings which over time had increasingly resulted into mini-trials.[851] It was argued:

> "the use of such expressions as 'a probability' **a 'prima facie case' or 'a strong prima facie case'** in the context of the exercise of a discretionary power to grant an interlocutory injunction **leads to confusion** as to the object sought to be achieved by this form of temporary relief. The court no doubt must be satisfied that the claim **is not frivolous or vexatious; in other words, that there is a serious question to be tried.**"[852]

848 Furthermore, the most important elements of the citations are highlighted in bold.
849 G. MEI, 'Interlocutory injunctions in IP Infringement actions in England and Wales and in Ireland – *American Cyanamid* revisited' *International Review of Intellectual Property and Competition Law* 46, No. 2 (2015), pp. 175–202. See: p 177.
850 Idem, at p. 177.
851 Idem, at p. 177.
852 House of Lords, *American Cyanamid v Ethicon,* 1975, AC 396. See: p. 4. Emphasis added.

Thus in other words, now, when the plaintiff has a *genuine* prospect of winning, the court can move on to the second question of the test. Even if a case is weak, a plaintiff can still pass this hurdle as long as there is sufficient merit to convince the court that there is a genuine prospect.[853] Although at first glance the wording of *American Cyanamid* seems to be completely discouraging any look at the merits – thus precluding the court to form an opinion on the strength of the case – this view was watered down by subsequent case law such as in *Series 5 Software v Clarke ltd.*[854] This is another much cited and important case in the context of interim relief. It clearly points out that to a certain extent the strength of a case should be taken along in the assessment of the court;

> "(..) Lord Diplock <in American Cyanamid> did not intend by the last quoted passage **to exclude consideration of the strength of the cases** in most applications for interlocutory relief. It appears to me that what is intended is that the court should not attempt to solve difficult issues of fact or law on an application for interlocutory relief, if, **on the other hand the court is able to come to a view as to the strength of the parties' cases on the credible evidence, then it can do so.**"[855]

This is also the view of the authors Cumming, Freudenthal and Janal.[856] They also submit that whilst *American Cyanamid* is sometimes interpreted as precluding the consideration of the merits, the authors submit that Lord Diplock's statement was primarily "to remove a fetter which appears to have been imposed in certain previous cases viz. That a party seeking an interlocutory injunction had to establish a prima facie case for substantive relief."[857] Because of this, the principles of *American Cyanamid* are in line with the spirit of what is stated in Art. 9 (3) of the EU Enforcement Directive.[858]

---

853 G. MEI, 'Interlocutory injunctions in IP Infringement actions in England and Wales and in Ireland – *American Cyanamid* revisited' *International Review of Intellectual Property and Competition Law* 46, No. 2 (2015), pp. 175–202. See: p. 185.

854 EWCA, *Series 5 Software v Clarke ltd.*, 1996, 1 ALL ER 853.

855 Laddie J. in EWCA *Series 5 Software v Clarke ltd.*, 1996, 1 ALL ER 853. In support of this view, Laddie J also states, in the *Series 5 Software* case that: "If it is apparent from that material <namely, the documents and evidence presented at trial> *that one party's case is much stronger than the others, then that is a matter that the court should not ignore.* To suggest otherwise would be to exclude from consideration an important factor and such exclusion would fly in the face of the flexibility advocated earlier in American Cyanamid." Emphasis added.

856 G. CUMMING, M. FREUDENTHAL, R. JANAL, *Enforcement of Intellectual Property rights in Dutch, English and German civil procedure* (2008 Wolters Kluwer Publishing). See: pp. 163–165.

857 Ibidem, citing Lord Goff.

858 On first glance there seems to be tension between the *American Cyanamid* principles and the wording of the EU Enforcement Directive. This is an interesting issue, that has proven to be unproblematic in practice. The doubt occurs mainly because of Art. 9 (3) Enforcement Directive. There it is stated that the court should

All this means that in answering the first question from *American Cyanamid*, a preliminary injunction court can – *to a limited extent* – look at the merits of the request. This in order to obtain a better view of the likelihood of success of the plaintiff on infringement and for the likelihood of success of the defendant's arguments on non-infringement and – if relevant – on the issue of patent validity.[859] However, as Mei writes, the court's observations on the strength of the case can, at least in theory, only be used during this first question and not at the other stages of the analysis that has been set out in *American Cyanamid*.[860] These observations may thus not be used during questions on the adequacy of harm (the second question of the test) and the balancing of convenience (the third question).

The case of *Novartis v Dexcel*,[861] is a good example of that a 'serious question' is not always something that should easily be taken for granted and the court in the case does indeed look at the merits of the plaintiff's claim nevertheless. This case also shows that this can be a difficult issue to deal with for the court at this stage and in this manner. Firstly, Judge Floyd considered each of the patent's claim features and the position of the evidence in turn.[862] He thereby made various references to the differences with the earlier judgment in *Novartis v Ivax*, a case the defendant relied on. Quite elaborately, bearing in mind the specific nature of a preliminary injunction proceedings (something that he explicitly stressed),[863] Judge Floyd examined rather technical and substantial issues. For instance, assuming that ethyl lactate and tricaprin are miscible, he went into the issue whether or not there are separately identifiable phases in the pre-concentrate.[864] In the end of his analysis, Floyd was convinced that Novartis' case on the 'miscibility point' was *seriously arguable* and was sufficient to pass this hurdle of *American Cyanamid*.[865] At the same

---

satisfy itself with a 'sufficient degree of certainty' of (imminent) infringement of the applicant's rights. As is clear from the judgment above, one can interpret the *American Cyanamid* decision as a rejection of going into the merits of the case to assess the strength of the plaintiff's requests, beyond looking at whether the question is 'non-frivolous'. However, in light of later case law, especially *Series 5 Software*, this view is more nuanced and English practice is in line with the Enforcement Directive.

859 For instance, EWHC, *BASF SE v Sipcam UK Ltd*, September 12th 2013, EWHC 2863 (Pat.). See: par. 17.

860 G. MEI, 'Interlocutory injunctions in IP Infringement actions in England and Wales and in Ireland – *American Cyanamid* revisited' *International Review of Intellectual Property and Competition Law* 46, No. 2 (2015), pp. 175–202. See: p. 178.

861 EWHC, *Novartis AG v Dexcel Pharma Limited*, June 10th 2008, EWHC 1266 (Pat.).

862 Idem, at par. 26 a.f.

863 Idem, at par. 24. "In deciding whether there is a serious issue to be tried, I should not embark on anything approaching a mini-trial on the basis of expert statements without cross-examination."

864 Idem, at par. 30.

865 Idem, at par. 40, 44, 45.

time, he acknowledged that these issues in this case were very complex indeed.[866] Another example can be found in the *Cephalon* case.[867] Here, because the evidence on a specific issue (relating to particle size) was deemed to be weak, it was further investigated whether the plaintiff's request made the first prong. Finally, the court concluded that it had: "In the end, and not without difficulty, I have concluded that the evidence *just about clears the threshold of establishing that there is a serious question to be tried.*"[868] This, however was different in the *Protomed* case, where the judge failed to see how infringement should be proven in the context of the given patent, resulting into the finding that a 'serious question' was not established.[869]

Under the 'serious question' heading, one can also include the issue of not yet occurring but nevertheless *imminent* infringement. Interim injunctions against this type of conduct can indeed be given in England and the questions that the court should deal with are of the same nature as we have seen before in other jurisdictions. Most notable are 1) *what* can be determined from previous infringing conduct and 2) *what can be deduced* from a competitor not willing to provide an undertaking not to launch a possibly infringing product before the expiry of the patent? The

---

866 Idem, see for instance par. 44. "Even if Mr Thorley <one of Dexcel's lawyers> is right, and there is a series of further sub-requirements of a micro-emulsion, I am *not persuaded that Novartis has failed to demonstrate an arguable case* in relation to any of them. (..) In any case, *the evidence would require expert interpretation* (Novartis says it is translucent and Dexcel says opaque) and there is a dispute about how far one should dilute. Mr Thorley had other criticisms of the evidence on spontaneous formation of the micro-emulsion and stability: *but all this is plainly in issue and I could not fairly resolve it now.*" Emphasis added.

867 EWHC, *Cephalon & Ors v Orchid & Anor, trading as Mylan,* November 19th 2010, EWHC 2945 (pat.). See: par. 16–35.

868 Idem, at par. 35.

869 EWHC, *Protomed Ltd v Medication Systems Ltd,* December 10th 2012, EWHC 3726 (Ch). See: par. 26; "It therefore seems to me that, on the material and arguments placed before me at the hearing of the application, the claimant's arguments on infringement are wrong and the defendants' arguments are right. That, however, by itself might not be sufficient to enable the defendants to succeed. *The question is whether I am satisfied that the defendants are so right that there is no arguable case against them on infringement.* I consider that that is indeed the case. *This is not a complicated patent. There is no real prospect* that any relevant evidence or other material would be adduced at a trial which would assist in the exercise of construing Claim 1. The exercise of construing it so as to judge the infringing nature, or otherwise, of the defendants' product is sufficiently straightforward to allow me to reach a clear view on the material that I have. *My clear view is that the claimant does not have an arguable case on infringement.* In those circumstances, the claimant does not get over the first hurdle in American Cyanamid and is therefore not entitled to an interim injunction." Emphasis added.

case of *Merck Sharp Dohme Corp and BMS v Teva Pharma BV*,[870] is a good example of how the English judiciary responded to what type of conduct amounted to an actionable threat of imminent infringement. If this threat is indeed deemed to be sufficiently grave, an interim injunction – doctrinally known in the Common Law as a *quia timet interim injunction* – can be granted; this is done when it is feared that a wrong *will be committed*.[871]

In casu, the plaintiff for a preliminary injunction, BMS, is the owner of a patent and an SPC related to efavirenz, an anti-retroviral compound in a drug used in the treatment of HIV/AIDS. Both the patent and the SPC would expire mid 2013, about 1,5 years after the request for an interim injunction. Until the expiry, BMS demanded from Teva (which had just received marketing authorisation) an undertaking setting out its intentions regarding the launch of a competing product.[872] Teva remained silent to BMS' request. Additionally, the plaintiff had concerns about previous behaviour of Teva – that had launched a generic version of a patented drug (*atorvastatin)* whilst the patent was still pending – and therefore BMS felt it needed to take pre-emptive action and requested an interim injunction.

With respect to the silence of Teva, the interim injunction court held that this should be seen in the context of the marketing authorisation that Teva had received.[873] Although the court held that the obtaining of a market authorisation in itself was not enough to warrant an interim injunction, it could however be *indicative* of a launch soon and this was especially so if a marketing authorisation was requested *well before the expiry of the patent*.[874]

> "The simple fact of obtaining a marketing authorisation only supports an inference that the applicant will launch the product once the marketing authorisation has been granted. **Considered in isolation it does not support an inference as to the timing of the launch. However, one can draw inferences** from the timing of the marketing authorisation application. (..)"[875]

870 EWHC, *Merck Sharp Dohme Corp and BMS v Teva Pharma BV*, March 15th 2012, EWHC 627 (Pat). Appointed Judge: Birss QC. The validity of the grant of the interim injunction in this case was confirmed at the trial on the merits. EWHC, *Merck Sharp Dohme Corp and BMS v Teva Pharma BV*, 2013, EWHC 1958 (Pat).

871 EWHC, *Merck Sharp Dohme Corp and BMS v Teva Pharma BV*, March 15th 2012, EWHC 627 (Pat). See: par. 30–42.

872 Idem, at par. 64.

873 Ibidem. "It is not unreasonable for BMS to infer from the marketing authorisation for generic efavirenz coming 22 months before the expiry of their patent rights in the compound efavirenz that Teva intend to launch generic efavirenz before expiry."

874 Idem, at par. 79.

875 Ibidem. Emphasis added.

As a justification for its non-responsiveness, Teva pointed out the risk of valuable commercial secrets becoming public information to both the plaintiff (BMS) and to other generic companies. Teva therefore claimed confidentiality as being the reason behind its decision not to share any information on this with BMS. The court acknowledged this consequence, but argued that this not took away the fact that the preliminary injunction action was nevertheless well founded and that Teva's explanation did not take away BMS' concerns of Teva launching before the patent expired.[876] The court also held that making such an inference from Teva's silence was allowable.[877]

As to the *previous infringing conduct* of Teva in a similar case, namely with respect to the drug *atorvastatin*, the court acknowledged Teva's argument that in 2011 it had introduced 36 products and had only launched 1 product (namely *atorvastatin*) in the face of a compound patent.[878] Justice Birss nevertheless submitted that:

> "In my judgment atorvastatin does not lead to an inference that Teva has a policy of always launching at risk of infringement in the face of a compound patent. However, it does show that Teva are prepared to do it if they choose to and it does place into context any prior assurances they may have given. (..)."[879]

All in all, the court here deemed that the abovementioned inferences amounted to a threat of imminent infringement[880] and from this perspective an interim

---

876 EWHC, *Merck Sharp Dohme Corp and BMS v Teva Pharma BV*, March 15th 2012, EWHC 627 (Pat). See: par. 68. "I agree and accept that if Teva intend to launch in advance of expiry of the SPC then the date on which they intend to do so is a valuable commercial secret which would be of value to Teva's competitors – including BMS and other generics. *However self evidently if Teva are going to launch before expiry then this action is entirely well founded.* If it is really Teva's case that the patent is invalid, they can and should bring a claim for revocation. While in the abstract it may have been premature to expect that claim to be brought 2 years in advance of expiry, it is not premature to expect that claim to be commenced now that Teva has this marketing authorisation." Emphasis added.

877 Idem, at par. 65: "Civil courts regularly draw inferences from silence and this situation is no exception. The key in my judgment is that it is not silence without more nor is it drawing an inference from nothing more than an unwillingness to offer an undertaking. The existence and timing of the marketing authorisation is critical. Moreover, since this action is properly constituted in any event, if Teva choose to defend it on the basis that they have no such intention, disclosure will be given and the Court can decide about their intentions. *At this interim stage, it is entirely fair to draw inferences from silence.*" Emphasis added. Also: "To justify an order for interim relief one does not need to know precisely when Teva intend to launch, *all one needs to know is that they intend to launch before expiry and before a full trial could be heard.*" See: par. 71. Emphasis added.

878 Idem, at par. 60.

879 Idem, at par. 61.

880 Idem, at par. 81.

injunction was warranted.[881] It is thus clear that English courts are prepared to consider a 'serious question' and eventually give an interim injunction *before* infringement actually takes place. Equally, it is evident that courts are prepared to draw inferences from a constellation of facts, even when hard evidence for specific conduct is perhaps lacking.

Another interesting aspect with respect to whether there is a 'serious question' is when the *infringement issue*[882] has been dealt with before. This was so in the dispute of *Novartis v Dexcel,*[883] which was on a clylosporin-based patent, designed to prevent the rejection of tissue after transplantation had taken place. Novartis was the proprietor of the patent and aimed to restrain Dexcel in marketing a product that allegedly would infringe its patent. Crucial here is that the contested patent had been subject of earlier litigation. In the earlier litigation, the patent was found to be valid, but under the claim construction made then, the formulation of Ivax was *not found to be infringing.*[884] Dexcel, in its defence, now argued the same. Basing itself on the claim construction that was arrived at in the earlier decision, it held that *there was no serious question about infringement* here.[885] The interim injunction court held that whilst in principle an English court is bound on questions of law, the presented evidence on infringement – in both the present case as on a previous case – can make the difference[886] to how far such a decision is followed and to whether this impacts the 'serious question' principle.[887]

> "For present purposes – this is an interim application after all – all I need say is that I regard it as seriously arguable that a subsequent court is not bound by a previous court's conclusion as to the correct construction of a patent specification if that

881 Idem, at par. 86: "In considering the claim for interim relief, I infer from all the circumstances including but not limited to Teva's silence on the question of their intentions that Teva are not prepared to commit themselves to waiting for the conclusion of these proceedings before launching their generic product. If they were prepared to wait until the proceedings are over, they could readily have said so."

882 Note that this is not about an earlier decision of *patent validity*, see for this the case of *Hospira* at page 233 a.f. of this dissertation.

883 EWHC, *Novartis AG v Dexcel Pharma Limited,* June 10th 2008, EWHC 1266 (Pat.).

884 EWHC, *Novartis v Ivax,* October 16th 2006, EWHC 2506 Pat, October 16th, 2006. Also the case of EWCA, *Novartis v Ivax*, October 18th 2007, EWCA Civ 971.

885 EWHC, *Novartis AG v Dexcel Pharma Limited,* June 10th 2008, EWHC 1266 (Pat.). See: par.1 and par. 5.

886 As was the case here.

887 EWHC, *Novartis AG v Dexcel Pharma Limited,* June 10th 2008, EWHC 1266 (Pat.). See: par. 22: "(..) But if the evidence on which the legal conclusion is founded is different in a relevant way, one may ask legitimately, why should subsequent litigants be bound by the evidence adduced in a previous action? The point of law to be decided once the evidence is different is itself different. I think this comes within what Jacob LJ had in mind in *SKB v Apotex* when he said that the subsequent court is not bound by the previous court's decision "so far as it turned on evidence."

> conclusion **turns in a material respect on evidence which was either lacking in the previous case or which is materially different in the present one**.
> In the context of a patent case the evidence must be sufficiently precise to enable the court to come to a view that **there is a serious prospect that the patentee will be able to show** that each of the features of the claim is present in the alleged infringement."[888]

Finally, although Rule 25.2 (1) CPR states that an order for an interim remedy can be made at any time, it is also clear that Rule 25.2 (2)(b)(i) CPR stresses that the matter should be *urgent*. Further specifications are not given in the legislation and it also seems from the case law that this is a factor which is not heavily considered in practice.[889] However, the issue of *delay* for instance, can in theory be taken along in the first question of the legal test, but this is more common as a factor of influence under the third *American Cyanamid* question, namely that of the balance of convenience.

§7.3.2.2. Are damages an adequate remedy?

The second question that the court should ask itself when deciding on the request for an interim injunction, is whether damages are an adequate remedy. In answering this question, both the positions of the plaintiff and the defendant are to be considered.

With respect to this, Lord Diplock ruled that if damages were to be considered as adequate *and* the *defendant* would have no problem in paying these damages – in the case the plaintiff would later win at the trial on the merits – the court should in principle deny the request for an interim injunction.

> "As to that, the governing principle is that the court should first **consider** whether if the plaintiff were to succeed at the trial in establishing his right to a permanent injunction **he would be adequately compensated by an award of damages for the loss he would have sustained as a result of the defendant's continuing to do what was sought to be enjoined between the time of the application and the time of the trial.** If damages in the measure recoverable at common law **would be adequate remedy and the defendant would be in a financial position** to pay them, no interlocutory injunction should normally be granted, however strong the plaintiff's claim appeared to be at that stage."[890]

The inverse is true as well: when damages are *not* an adequate remedy for the plaintiff, the court should grant an interim injunction as a matter of principle.

---

888 Idem, at par. 25.

889 X.E. KRAMER, *Het kort geding in internationaal perspectief* (2001 Kluwer Uitgeverij). See: p. 89.

890 House of Lords, *American Cyanamid v Ethicon,* 1975, AC 396, at p. 5. Emphasis added.

Again, only on the condition that damages would suffice for the other party (here the defendant) and that the plaintiff would be in the position to pay, in case the decision turned out to be incorrect.

> "If, on the other hand, damages would not provide an adequate remedy for the plaintiff in the event of his succeeding at the trial, the court should then consider whether, on the contrary hypothesis that the defendant were to succeed at the trial in establishing his right to do that which was sought to be enjoined, he would be adequately compensated under the plaintiff's undertaking as to damages for the loss he would have sustained by being prevented from doing so between the time of the application and the time of the trial. If damages in the measure recoverable under such an undertaking would be an adequate remedy and the plaintiff would be in a financial position to pay them, there would be no reason upon this ground to refuse an interlocutory injunction."[891]

As pointed out before, in principle the strength of a plaintiff's case plays no role when considering the adequacy of damages.[892] As will be seen too, it is also not always a prong that is dealt with directly and explicitly[893] even though it is a stage prescribed by the *American Cyanamid* doctrine.[894] In practice often, instead of first looking at harms explicitly, the court seems to assume that both parties will suffer harm, and will directly focus on the hardships and convenience of an interim injunction for the parties instead and base its decision on this.[895]

The issue of adequacy of damages however was clearly addressed in *Leo Pharma v Sandoz*[896] where, also on appeal, an earlier given interim injunction was upheld.[897] The patent itself covered calcipotriol monohydrate which was used in a pharmaceutical cream by Leo. The alleged-infringer, Sandoz, had launched a generic

891 Ibidem. Emphasis added.

892 G. MEI, 'Interlocutory injunctions in IP Infringement actions in England and Wales and in Ireland – *American Cyanamid* revisited' *International Review of Intellectual Property and Competition Law* 46, No. 2 (2015), pp. 175–202. See: p. 179.

893 As for instance happened in EWHC, *Merck Sharp Dohme Corp and BMS v Teva Pharma BV*, March 15th 2012, EWHC 627 (Pat). See: par. 53. Furthermore, see that of EWHC, *Novartis AG v Dexcel Pharma Limited*, June 10th 2008, EWHC 1266 (Pat.). See: par. 24.

894 On this, note that Mei writes that there has been confusion whether the 'adequacy of damages' stage is really a separate prong, or simply part of a wider and more general 'balance of convenience' exercise which is undertaken straight after the 'serious question' prong. G. MEI, 'Interlocutory injunctions in IP Infringement actions in England and Wales and in Ireland – *American Cyanamid* revisited' *International Review of Intellectual Property and Competition Law* 46, No. 2 (2015), pp. 175–202. See: pp. 178–180.

895 Ibidem.

896 EWCA, *Leo Pharma A/S & ANR v Sandoz Ltd*, June 25th 2008, EWCA Civ 850.

897 EWHC, *Leo Pharma A/S and Leo Laboratories Limited v Sandoz Limited*, March 17th 2008, EWHC 541 (Pat.).

calcipotriol cream but – and that is important to stress – had done so *on an unusually small scale for a generics company.*[898] Equally important is to underline that Sandoz' selling price was of the same order of Leo's selling price was.[899] The question was then, whether these two particular factors *contributed to the inadequacy of damages,* or that Leo would not genuinely be harmed by the conduct of Sandoz.[900] In other words: *how likely had the interim injunction court in first instance been in presuming that a price drop indeed would occur,* because of the entry of the generic drug of Sandoz?

> "(..)It would be right for a judge conducting this exercise to disregard any possibility which is fanciful. But if there is a possibility which is more than fanciful then, as it seems to me, the judge is entitled to go on and say, as Mann J did, that **there is doubt as to the adequacy of "the respective remedies and damages"** to use Lord Diplock's words. **So the question here is whether there is a realistic possibility of there being a price cut.**"[901]

The heart of the debate was then how realistic a price cut was, bearing in mind that at that point the launch of Sandoz was very modest in scale and Sandoz had not priced the generic version of calcipotriol monohydrate very differently than Leo had done. As LJ Jacob stated, there was of course no guarantee that Sandoz would keep that price and neither was there a guarantee that it would not put more products on the market.[902] The court ruling on the request for an interim injunction at first instance had therefore been correct in assuming that there was a risk that Sandoz would do either and that this amounted to a 'non-fanciful possibility'.[903] Similarly, it had been clear that Leo's response to a price cut would be speculative and clouded by uncertainty; Leo's response would also depend on the magnitude of the price cut and how much of the market would be taken by Sandoz.[904] Citing *Peaudouce v Kimberley-Clark,*[905] the EWCA held persuasively:

> "(..) The real point is that Leo currently have a monopoly price. If Sandoz come in with their considerable marketing powers, as a substantial company, and were to lower their price, the consequences of working out the financial damage to Leo go beyond merely difficult to being incalculable.

---

898 EWCA, *Leo Pharma A/S & ANR v Sandoz Ltd,* June 25th 2008, EWCA Civ 850. See: par. 5.
899 Ibidem.
900 Idem, par. 6, thereby citing EWHC, *Leo Pharma A/S and Leo Laboratories Limited v Sandoz Limited,* March 17th 2008, EWHC 541 (Pat.) at par. 38 and par. 41.
901 EWCA, *Leo Pharma A/S & ANR v Sandoz Ltd,* June 25th 2008, EWCA Civ 850. See: par. 9–10. Emphasis added.
902 Ibidem.
903 Ibidem.
904 Idem, at par. 16–18.
905 *Peaudouce SA v Kimberley-Clark Ltd and Others,* 1996, FSR 680

> Walker J, as he then was, in *Peaudouce v Kimberley-Clark [1996] FSR 680, at page 699,* said: "The test is whether damages are an adequate remedy, not a perfect remedy." And later on he referred to damages being "as adequate as possible in an imperfect world." **But there comes a point when the uncertainty is too great to regard damages as adequate even on that basis."**[906]
> "Here Mann J was considering what might happen if there was a price cut. Once he got to the point of considering that was a realistic possibility then one was moving not simply to whether the remedy of damages was adequate but whether damages were reasonably calculable at all."[907]

When damages are perceived as not being adequate or when the court does not explicitly address this issue,[908] it is the final step of the *American Cyanamid* analysis that the court will proceed with, in order to come to a decision.

§7.3.2.3. *If damages are not adequate, taking into account the position of both the plaintiff and the defendant, does the balance of convenience favour the injunction?*

The third and last step for the court to take, when deciding on an interim injunction, is to see in which direction the balance of convenience tips. At this stage, it is obvious that one or both of the parties will suffer a certain degree of irreparable harm. It is now up to the court to compare the magnitudes of harm for both the parties and look at other factors that may impact the strength of the plaintiff's or defendant's case, either in favour or against the grant of interim relief:

> "It is where there is doubt as to the adequacy of the respective remedies in **damages available to either party or to both**, that the question of **balance of convenience** arises."[909]

Apart from the issue of comparing the irreparable harms with each other, something that, as Mei states should receive priority,[910] the somewhat thorny issue of the strength of the merits can also reappear again at this stage.[911] The merits of a case should be taken into account when the relevant irreparable harms do not differ widely from each other:

---

906 EWCA, *Leo Pharma A/S & ANR v Sandoz Ltd,* June 25th 2008, EWCA Civ 850. See: par. 22–23.
907 Idem, at par. 24.
908 See footnote 894 of this dissertation.
909 House of Lords, *American Cyanamid v Ethicon,* 1975, AC 396. See: p. 5. Emphasis added.
910 Also see G. MEI, 'Interlocutory injunctions in IP Infringement actions in England and Wales and in Ireland – *American Cyanamid* revisited' *International Review of Intellectual Property and Competition Law* 46, No. 2 (2015), pp. 175–202. See: p. 180.
911 Ibidem.

> "The extent to which the disadvantages to each party would be incapable of being **compensated in damages** in the event of his succeeding at the trial is **always a significant factor in assessing where the balance of convenience lies**; and if the extent of the uncompensatable disadvantage **to each party would not differ widely**, it may **not be improper to take into account** in tipping the balance the **relative strength of each party's case** as revealed by the affidavit evidence adduced on the hearing of the application."[912]

With respect to the latter, the court is however limited to those substantive issues to which there is no real question mark hovering above it. In doing so, the court should not hold a mini-trial of any kind; this is, as we have seen, something that the House of Lords in their decision in *American Cyanamid* attempted to rid itself of.[913]

Finally, in those situations when also the overall balancing exercise does not tip the case decisively towards one of the parties, this would point towards maintaining the status quo.[914] Maintaining the current state of affairs is here not seen as an end in itself,[915] but rather as a likely indicator to avoid the greater injury.[916] In the context of a request for a prohibitory preliminary injunction in patent litigation, this would thus for instance be the maintaining of a patentee's monopoly position, by preventing market entry by competitors until a decision on the merits has been taken. Maintaining the status quo is here not to be seen as an independent factor as such.[917]

Lord Diplock was clear that the court has very wide discretion with the factors it takes into the balance of convenience analysis:

> **"It would be unwise to attempt even to list all the various matters** which may need to be taken into consideration in deciding where the balance lies, let alone to suggest the **relative weight** to be attached to them. **These will vary from case to case**."[918]

---

912 House of Lords, *American Cyanamid v Ethicon,* 1975, AC 396. See: p. 5. Emphasis added.

913 Idem, at p. 6. "This, however, should be done only where it is apparent upon the facts disclosed by evidence as to which there is no credible dispute that the strength of one party's case is disproportionate to that of the other party. *The court is not justified in embarking upon anything resembling a trial* of the action upon conflicting affidavits *in order to evaluate the strength of either party's case.*" Emphasis added.

914 Ibidem.

915 See page 54 a.f. of this dissertation.

916 G. MEI, 'Interlocutory injunctions in IP Infringement actions in England and Wales and in Ireland – *American Cyanamid* revisited' *International Review of Intellectual Property and Competition Law* 46, No. 2 (2015), pp. 175–202. See: p. 182.

917 Idem, p. 181. But as Mei, convincingly writes on p. 197, the confusing element of the 'status-quo' sometimes still plays this role and can serve as a cover to reach a certain result in the decision.

918 House of Lords, *American Cyanamid v Ethicon,* 1975, AC 396. See: p 5. Emphasis added.

Whilst the latter is more than true, it is good to point out a few interesting examples and issues of this balancing exercise. The first is that of 'clearing the way'. This has proven itself to be a decisive element with respect to interim injunctions, predominantly in the pharmaceutical industry. Secondly, there are other factors, as will be seen,[919] that can also play a decisive role.

§7.3.2.3.1. Balancing – 'clearing the way'

Over the last decade, the English courts have shown a willingness to protect the interests of patentees in pharmaceutical patent litigation, by granting interim injunctions against generic competitors attempting to enter the market. This approach has not always been the case, but was particularly established after the authorative *Apotex* cases. It was in these judgments, that the English courts lowered the threshold for originator companies to obtain an interim injunction against a generic competitor. In doing so, a clear link was made between the efforts that were undertaken by generic competitor against the patent, in deciding whether or not to grant an interim injunction. This approach entails that an entrant should have used the strategy of 'clearing the way' vis-à-vis the originator's patent, by either seeking a declaratory judgment of non-infringement or by attempting to revoke or invalidate the patent. If these steps have not been taken, a launch of the generic's product on the market is at the defendant's *own risk* and an interim injunction is then highly likely to be granted. Whilst this approach may appear to be strict, it in fact does recognise the special nature of pharmaceuticals and the risk of irreparable harm a patentee in this specific industry can suffer (i.e. in the form of an irreversible price drop and in losing a certain regulatory position) when they face generic competition.[920] Competition, which at a trial on the merits may prove to have been infringing the rights of the patentee.

In the first *Apotex* case, Justice Jacob granted an interim injunction at first instance,[921] thereby pointing out that it was the defendant's responsibility to 'clear the way' before it launched its product:

> "I see no question of principle involved here of any sort. It is purely commercial common sense. **If there may be an obstacle in your way, clear it out.** To my mind, this is a case where the retention of the status quo is a rational thing to do. It was something that could have been avoided by the defendants; **they chose not do it**."[922]
>
> "I remain of the same opinion that I was in the *Generics* case. Where litigation is bound to ensue if the defendant introduces his product he can avoid all the problems of an

919 See: page 229 a.f. of this dissertation.

920 See: page 104 of this dissertation.

921 EWHC, *SmithKline Beecham PLC & GlaxoSmithKline (UK) Ltd v Apotex Europe Limited et al*, November 28th 2002, EWHC 2556 (pat).

922 Idem, at par. 63.

interlocutory injunction if he clears the way first. That is what the procedures for **revocation and declaration for non-infringement** are for."[923]

The defendants appealed the granted preliminary injunction,[924] but the EWCA saw no fault with the prior approach taken by Arnold J.[925] On the issue of the approach of 'clearing the way' by the generic entrant, the EWCA ruled without reservations and put the burden of responsibility firmly on the shoulders of the defendant.[926] Whilst after the *Apotex* decisions, the *de facto* obligation for the defendant to 'clear the way' appears to have become the dominant approach in England, the approach is not entirely rigid.

Firstly, it has become clear that a defendant has to *expect that litigation is bound*, before it is required to 'clear the way'. This means that when a patentee has essentially tolerated infringement in another EU Member State, it cannot be expected that the defendant clears the way in England, because the defendant should not have known that litigation was inevitable.[927]

More important is what the case of *Cephalon v Ors v Orchid & Anor (Mylan)* showed.[928] In casu, the EWHC held that a failure to not 'clear the way' should not always trump other factors:

> "These <arguments justifying the 'clearing away approach'> are certainly considerations which, depending on the evidence, may be material in particular cases. **There is a danger however in treating them as principles of law. Whether they apply at all in any given case and whether, if they do, they outweigh other factors is to be decided on the evidence.**"[929]

923 Idem, at par. 65.

924 EWCA, *SmithKline Beecham PLC & GlaxoSmithKline (UK) Ltd v Apotex Europe Limited et al*, February 14th 2003, EWCA Civ 137.

925 Idem, at par. 41.

926 Idem, at par. 39: "Apotex *rightly submitted that there was no obligation* on a potential defendant to start proceedings. However, this was a case where Apotex intended to come on to the market with their product and they must have realised, back in November 2001, that SB would be likely to seek an interlocutory injunction if there was an arguable case of infringement. It was Apotex *who knew the process that was to be used* and when they intended to launch their product, but they refrained from telling SB until the late autumn of 2002. *If they had wanted to, they could have had the issue of infringement and validity decided before launch. They chose not to do so with the result that there was potential injustice whichever way the court decides.*" Emphasis added.

927 EWHC, *BASF SE v Sipcam UK Ltd*, September 12th 2013, EWHC 2863 (Pat.). See: par. 46.

928 EWHC, *Cephalon & Ors v Orchid & Anor, trading as Mylan,* November 19th 2010, EWHC 2945 (pat.).

929 Idem, at par. 51. Emphasis and text between brackets added.

> "I must take this factor into account, but I am not obliged to give it so much weight that it necessarily swamps all the others. Here, I do not think it does."[930]

It is submitted however, that this is a useful case and other factors should indeed always play a role. The court should keep an open mind for other circumstances as well, apart from merely verifying whether the defendant-infringer has indeed 'cleared the way'. As is stated in the European Commission's *Pharmaceutical Sector Inquiry*, there are indeed downsides to an over-strict 'clearing the way' policy for generic companies.[931] Firstly, a generic company may not yet have finished the rather lengthy revocation procedure or obtained a declaration of non-infringement before it has the opportunity to launch. Secondly, if a generic company believes it may not (be likely to) infringe the patent, it would nevertheless still be forced to go through a lengthy procedure in order to obtain a declaration of non-infringement.

§7.3.2.3.2. Balancing – other factors

Amongst the other factors that can be taken along in the balancing of convenience exercise – apart from 'clearing the way'- are furthermore that of *magnitude of harms* and factors *such as the remaining duration of a patent's lifetime* and the *nature of competition*. A number of cases illustrate this.

Regarding the *harms to the parties*, Justice Floyd made clear in the *Cephalon v Mylan* case, that whilst the patentee Cephalon would be exposed to generic competition that would lead to a price drop, he did not believe that the impact of competition would have as a result that Cephalon would be forced to divert resources from R&D activities, due to the short period remaining between the interim injunction proceedings and the trial on the merits.[932] Furthermore, Cephalon believed that entry would result into an irreversible price drop,[933] as it would be prevented from raising its price again to original level. Even if Cephalon eventually would win the litigation at the trial on the merits, damage would be done, the plaintiff argued. It held: 1) that consumers would be unsympathetic to paying more again (resulting in loss of goodwill); 2) that other generic competitors would then meanwhile have entered the market, and 3) when Cephalon modafinil would be placed in another *National Health Service* (NHS) drug category, the restoration of the price would be difficult.[934]

---

930 Idem, at par. 72.

931 EUROPEAN COMMISSION, *Pharmaceutical Sector Inquiry Final Report* (2009). Available at: http://ec.europa.eu/competition/sectors/pharmaceuticals/inquiry/staff_working_paper_part1.pdf (last accessed on 20 April 2017). See: pp. 459–460.

932 EWHC, *Cephalon & Ors v Orchid & Anor, trading as Mylan*, November 19th 2010, EWHC 2945 (Pat.). See: par. 54.

933 Idem, at par. 59.

934 Idem, at par. 58. Cephalon's fear was that, after a generic entry occurred, its version of modafinil would be relegated from the NHS drug pricing category 'A' to

Justice Birss mostly disagreed with the likelihood of the *nature of these harms* however and held that price restoration would be possible for the plaintiff.[935] Neither did he believe that in the period until the trial on the merits, parallel imports would rise.[936] He held this as unlikely due to increased competition because of the entry of a generic competitor.[937]

Justice Birss subsequently considered the nature of the harms of the defendant if a preliminary injunction *was* to be granted. Mylan firstly claimed that their loss would consist of being deprived of the advantage resulting from a *First Mover Advantage*, something which resembled a unique business opportunity. To have to wait until the moment after a trial on the merits had taken place would take this opportunity away. Additionally, Mylan argued that it had a competitive edge vis-à-vis other entrants, in the race to become the first generic on the market. It believed that this would not be the case anymore after a trial on the merits.[938]

The court's response to this is particularly interesting to read. It first held that both the parties faced unquantifiable losses. Subsequently, it pointed out that the market of modafinil is a relatively mature one *and thus more calculable* than the nature of the defendant's possible losses, which seemed to represent a larger unknown variable.

> "(i) **Both sides are able to identify heads of unquantifiable loss.** On the claimants' side there is a risk that there will be some damage to their goodwill when prices come back to their former levels, as I believe they are likely to do if the claimants succeed at trial. On the defendants' side, if they are injuncted and win at the trial, there is a strong likelihood that they will lose the position of being the first generic to market – the loss of a unique market opportunity.
>
> (ii) **The market for modafinil is a relatively mature one**, allowing one to assess at the inquiry as to damages what profits the claimants would have made absent competition. By contrast one has no yardstick by which to judge how much of that market the defendants would have taken if allowed to compete instead of being enjoined.
>
> (iii) I am not persuaded the damage to the claimants is on this evidence likely to be greater and more unquantifiable than that to the defendants, the conclusion reached in the line of cases I have referred to above. In the present case **I think the evidence establishes that the loss to the defendants is the more likely to occur, the more likely to be substantial and will be the more difficult to quantify**."[939]

category 'M'. The latter is characterised by a lower tariff for purchase and reimbursement and is thus less attractive for (originator) pharmaceutical companies.

935 Idem, at par. 61.
936 Idem, at par. 67.
937 Ibidem.
938 Idem, at par. 68–69.
939 Idem, at par. 70. Emphasis added.

Instead of granting an interim injunction, the court decided that an *expedited trial* about five months later would be more suitable than providing immediate interim relief. This time would allow the defendants to take advantage of their entry into the market, but the short period until conclusion of the expedited trial would not lead to injustice. This because, in the eyes of the court, a change in the price category – one of Cephalon's main fears – would occur in about six months.[940]

Arriving to a different conclusion, namely in *granting* a preliminary injunction, was the interim injunction court after the balancing exercise in the case of *Novartis v Dexcel.* Here, other factors – the remaining duration of the patent's life and the exact nature of the product and the competition – played a decisive role in the court's decision.[941] On the balance of convenience, Justice Floyd explicitly stated that he would examine the likely losses if he would be 'wrong'.[942] He therefore went into the question of how Novartis would be hurt by a generic entry of Dexcel. It was held that a generic entry would lead to a downward price spiral and/or a significant loss of market share for the product and result into the decision for Novartis to either reduce prices or lose market share.[943] However, Novartis admitted, bearing in mind the nature of the particular pharmaceutical in this case, that the losses would be less severe than otherwise normally would be the case, due to the nature of the drug (cyclosporin).[944] Physicians would show a reluctance to change a patient from one drug to another for such a serious condition as transplant surgery rehabilitation.[945] Also, it was noted that pharmacists can dispense Novartis' drug even when a generic version existed, as it was a branded prescription drug.[946] Notwithstanding, Novartis contended that if its request for interim relief was refused but it would later prevail at the trial on the merits, it would still suffer loss in goodwill in an attempt to

---

940 Idem, at par. 73–75.

941 Similarly, see: EWHC, *BASF SE v Sipcam UK Ltd*, September 12th 2013, EWHC 2863 (Pat.). There the court held at par. 44: "I have decided that I should grant an interim injunction in this case essentially for the following reasons. First, it would cause harm to both sides but I think the harm to BASF if I refuse the injunction (when in fact the patent is infringed) will be more significant than the harm to the defendant if I grant the injunction (when in fact they do not infringe). That is because of the irredeemable price depression which will cause a permanent change to the market. If I grant an injunction against Sipcam but, in fact, should not have done because the patent is not infringed, and order a speedy trial as both sides say I should, then they will be kept out of the market for a season or perhaps two. They will be able to sell again and those sales will be a guide as to what would have been sold before. That mitigates any problems of assessment on a cross-undertaking, if that should prove necessary."

942 EWHC, *Novartis AG v Dexcel Pharma Limited*, June 10th 2008, EWHC 1266 (Pat.). See: par. 52.

943 Idem, at par. 54.

944 Ibidem.

945 Ibidem.

946 Idem, at par. 55.

recapture the market segment consisting of those patients that would have started treatment with Dexcel's generic version. Also it added that a refusal of an interim injunction would lead to unlawful competition of other generic companies attempting to launch their products (for which there was some evidence) resulting in the start of a price war. Both Novartis' considerations held some merit, Justice Floyd found.[947] Opposed to this was the view of the harms presented by the defendant: Dexcel claimed the strategic importance of its generic launch and the necessity for the company to achieve a First Mover Advantage. This was especially so, because Dexcel believed that another generic competitor (*Ivax*) was also poised to enter the market and if it did so, business for Dexcel would be lower for many years compared to the situation if it would have been allowed to launch immediately.[948]

Dexcel's arguments however were not enough to change the mind of Justice Floyd in granting the interim injunction.[949] Having directly compared both party's harms with each other, he pointed out that both parties would have unquantifiable losses if the 'wrong order' was made. He also pointed out the fact that Dexcel had not 'cleared the way' and he referred to maintaining the status quo as the goal of the preliminary injunction. Finally, Justice Floyd pointed out the court should, as a principle, grant a preliminary injunction in case of doubt on the balance of convenience:

> "Both sides recognise that the other will suffer a measure of unquantifiable loss if I make the "wrong order". **Balancing the risk of injustice is made very difficult by the uncertainty as to whether Ivax will launch**. On the whole I think there is more to put in the scales on Novartis' side than on Dexcel's. Moreover, I am impressed by the fact that Dexcel had it within its power to clear its product in time for its launch and neglected to do so. The fact that it claims the product to be a strategic and important one makes its strategy all the more surprising."[950]
> "**Weighing all these factors, I consider the balance of convenience to favour Novartis.** It seems to me that even if I were not persuaded that the balance of justice were in favour of Novartis, and that it was more or less evenly balanced, I would nevertheless have thought this an appropriate case in which to preserve the status quo. The status quo is that there is no infringing product on the market. I do not feel able, on the necessarily incomplete evidence before me, to come to a sufficiently clear view on the merits as disclosed in the witness statements to allow that to influence the result."[951]

Apart from this, some other factors that can influence the outcome of the balance of convenience prong have already been described. These are *inter alia* the availability to speed up a decision on the merits with an early or expedited trial and the factor

947 Idem, at par. 56–57.
948 Idem, at par. 59.
949 Idem, at par. 60–61.
950 Idem, at par. 60. Emphasis added.
951 Idem, at par. 61. Emphasis added.

of unreasonable delay, in bringing the application for an interim injunction.[952] The latter is then based on the principle of acquiescence by silence. Other factors are familiar too, such as the risk that an interim injunction puts a party out of business and the relative size of the companies involved, with a factor being that in a dispute between a smaller company versus a large company, the former is more vulnerable to being enjoined.[953]

Whilst an overriding *public interest* can in in principle be invoked in order to *not* grant an interim injunction[954] – i.e. with respect to public health – [955] it seems rather exceptional in the context of interim injunctive relief to do so in practice.[956]

§7.3.3. Previous decisions on patent validity

Having looked at the general English test for deciding on interim injunctions, it is now time to zoom in on some other related issues.

The English case of *Hospira*[957] is on a request for an interim injunction, *pending the appeal of an invalidated patent at first instance.* This is somewhat similar to the *Olanzapin* case in Germany,[958] although there the earlier invalidation was made and complicated due to the context of bifurcation. *Hospira* established a Common Law

952 G. MEI, 'Interlocutory injunctions in IP Infringement actions in England and Wales and in Ireland – *American Cyanamid* revisited' *International Review of Intellectual Property and Competition Law* 46, No. 2 (2015), pp. 175–202. See: pp. 190–192.

953 H. NORMAN, *Intellectual Property Law – Directions* (2014, Second Edition, Oxford University Press). See: p. 40.

954 I.C.F. SPRY, *Equitable Remedies* (1990 Sweet & Maxwell). See: p. 464. "Similar principles apply where the hardship that would be caused by the grant of relief would be caused to a third person, or to members of the public, rather to the defendant This consideration also is taken into account by the court in determining whether it is just that an interlocutory injunction should be issued (..) In principle the interests of third persons and of the public are no less material in interlocutory applications than in applications for final relief."

955 H. NORMAN, *Intellectual Property Law – Directions* (2014, Second Edition, Oxford University Press). See: p. 40, and G. MEI, 'Interlocutory injunctions in IP Infringement actions in England and Wales and in Ireland – *American Cyanamid* revisited' *International Review of Intellectual Property and Competition Law* 46, No. 2 (2015), pp. 175–202. See: p. 192. Both sources cite the case of *Roussel-Uclaf v. G D Searle*, 1977, FSR 125 (Ch).

956 On this point, see: R.C. BERNIERI, 'Ex-post liability rules: a solution for the biomedical anti-commons' in A. FLANAGAN, M.L. MONTAGNANI (eds), *Intellectual Property Law: Economic and Social Justice Perspectives* (2010 Edward Elgar Publishing) at pp. 93–111. See: pp. 109–110. There, Bernieri cites a judge who suggests that the public interest is in general best served by 'the good working rule' that after infringement an injunction is given, and that the public is protected through the exceptions in the Patent Act.

957 EWCA, *Novartis AG v Hospira UK Ltd,* May 22nd 2013, EWCA Civ 583.

958 *Supra* at footnote 775 a.f. of this dissertation.

precedent[959] that also pending an appeal of an invalidated patent at first instance, English interim injunction courts can still nevertheless grant interim relief to the plaintiff, based on this patent.

The case at hand was about a generic company, Hospira, that in its effort to launch a new generic product on the market, had started revocation proceedings of two of Novartis' European patents that were valid until 2021. The revocated patents in question were for the treatment of osteoporosis using zoledronic acid. A third invention, now protected by an SPC, was on zoledronic acid itself and was to expire in 2013. Before the SPC had expired, the two patents, on Hospira's request, were indeed deemed by the first instance court to be invalid on grounds of non-priority and insufficiently formulated claims.[960] Against these decisions, Novartis appealed. Since Hospira's strategy was to launch a generic version of zoledronic acid as soon as the (valid) SPC expired, Novartis requested an interim injunction to prevent Hospira from launching, at least as long as the appeal against the prior invalidity decision of the two patents was still pending.

This interim injunction was initially refused, by Birss J.[961] He first reviewed the principles for (interim) injunctive relief pending appeal as he saw them at the time. He acknowledged that normally he would likely have granted the requested interim injunction to Novartis,[962] but this was different in casu, since a trial on the merits had already taken place. This affected the balance of convenience.

Shortly later, the case was heard on an urgent basis by the EWCA. Lord Justice Floyd, who drafted the judgment, did not agree with Birss J that the first instance court's invalidity ruling should indeed affect the balance of convenience in the manner it did in Birss J's opinion.[963] It is submitted that this again shows the troublesome and artificial treatment of the merits of the case, under the *American Cyanamid* doctrine. Floyd LJ:

> "I do **not** think that the approach adopted by the judge was correct. **Once he was satisfied that the appeal had real prospects of success,** he should, on the facts of the present case, **have gone on to consider the balance of hardships** in accordance with the principles I have set out above. **He should not have put a weight into the**

959 R. BATEMAN, 'Novartis v Hospira – Interim injunction granted pending appeal when patent found invalid' *Lexology* (2013). Available at: http://www.lexology.com/library/detail.aspx?g=f3655785-7f52-49b3-a104-4072195242e4 (last accessed on 24 April 2017).

960 EWCA, *Novartis AG v Hospira UK Ltd,* May 22nd 2013, EWCA Civ 583. See: par. 14.

961 EWHC, *Novartis AG v Hospira UK Ltd,* May 14th 2013, EWHC 1285 Pat.

962 Idem, at par. 36. "If this case was at the outset of proceedings months or even a year before trial, then as long as all I could say about the merits was what I can now say about the merits of the appeal, I would probably grant the interlocutory injunction."

963 EWCA, *Novartis AG v Hospira UK Ltd,* May 22nd 2013, EWCA Civ 583. See: par. 41. Also see par. 30–40 of this judgment for an extensive analysis of the English case law on this.

> **scales against Novartis merely because they could not satisfy some higher threshold on the merits.** Further, for reasons I explain in relation to the second ground, I do not think that this is a case where it could be said that there is substantial unfairness in declining to give Hospira the right to rely on their judgment pending appeal if the other considerations of unquantifiable loss to each side would otherwise justify an injunction."[964]

Applying its discretion in an 'afresh manner'[965] and thereby *disregarding* the merits introduced in the earlier invalidity ruling, thus *restricting* himself to hearing the arguments presented at the proceeding for an interim injunction,[966] Floyd LJ decided to grant the interim injunction pending the appeal. Hospira was indeed enjoined from launching its generic product ahead of the appeal and had to wait.

From this case, it can be deducted that even pending an appeal due to an earlier patent invalidity ruling, an interim injunction is possible in English courts. What is important to stress, is that there should be a *reasonable prospect of success on appeal* for the plaintiff, so merely arguing the possible validity of patent cannot always be invoked.[967]

§7.3.4. *Cross-undertaking in damages*

Whilst in England the posting of a bond is not required, instead it is not unusual for a cross-undertaking to be required from the plaintiff. This is to be provided to the court, in anticipation of the possible event that an interim injunction turns out to be granted in error.[968] The court however has a discretion in requiring this. A cross-undertaking is a legal promise by the plaintiff-applicant to the court, that the addressee of the injunction (the defendant) will be made whole for any losses it suffers

---

964 Idem, at par. 47.

965 Idem, at par. 56.

966 Floyd LJ held that the unquantifiable damage to Novartis was likely to be graver than that of Hospira. This due to the significant price drop in the period pending the appeal and because the public interest arguments that Hospira submitted – inter alia based on the fact that the *National Health Service* could not fully recover its extra costs if it could not use generic products – were not seen as persuasive. Neither was it held to be convincing that Hospira would lose its unique First Mover Advantage.

967 This was different in the case of *Les Laboratoires Servier & Anr v Apotex* in which it was explicitly held that the interim injunction against the generic manufacturer pending appeal could not be extended, since no reasonable prospect of success existed. See: EWCA, *Les Laboratoires Servier & Anr v Apotex,* July 9th 2007, EWCA Civ 783.

968 On this see, C. RENNIE-SMITH, 'Patent Enforcement in the United Kingdom' in C. HEATH (editor) *Patent Enforcement Worldwide: Writings in honour of Dieter Stauder* (2015, Third Edition, Hart Publishing), pp. 81–110. See: p. 93.

due to it being enjoined. If the plaintiff-applicant for the interim injunction declines to give this undertaking, the court can decide to not grant an interim injunction.

When an interim injunction indeed turns out to be wrongly granted – i.e. the patent was later ruled to be invalid or infringement was not confirmed at the trial on the merits – the defendant can turn to the court and ask the court to request the plaintiff to pay damages. This then should be assessed by the court. The level of compensation is supposed to be compensatory of nature and not punitive. Furthermore, this estimation should be made according to the principles of a breach of contract.[969] This is not an easy task to complete and this may involve the investigation of different (counterfactual) scenarios and different interpretations of facts and hypotheses.[970]

As was made clear in a commentary on the *Astrazeneca v KRKA appeal,* the court can be *liberal* in awarding such damages. In casu this was for the defendant losing its first mover advantage due to it being – as later emerged – wrongfully enjoined by the preliminary injunction:[971]

> "(..) the Court of Appeal has made clear that a claimant who obtains interim relief in a process involving a limited consideration of the merits should similarly expect a "liberal assessment" of damages under any cross-undertaking, in the event that it is unsuccessful in its substantive claim. Further, where any 'wrongful' behaviour is identified in the claimant's enforcement of its patent, restitution damages may, potentially, be available. For several years, the courts were relatively sympathetic to requests for interim injunctions in pharmaceutical patent claims, and there seemed relatively little exposure for patentees protecting a monopoly market in a high value pharmaceutical. The law, and the sympathies, have perhaps developed. Patentees can no longer take for granted profits made during the term of interim injunctive relief, irrespective of the outcome of the substantive claim."[972]

---

969 EWCA, *Astrazeneca v KRKA*, May 21st 2015, EWCA Civ 484. See: par. 12. Appeal to the decision taken in EWHC, *Astrazeneca v KRKA,* Janaury 24th 2014, EWHC 84 (Pat).

970 As was stated in, EWCA, *Astrazeneca v KRKA*, May 21st 2015, EWCA Civ 484: "The conventional method of undertaking this exercise is to assess damages on a particular hypothesis and then to adjust the award by reference to the percentage chance of the hypothesis occurring. In many cases, it is sufficient to postulate one hypothesis and make one discount: but there is no reason in principle why one should not say that either Scenario 1 or Scenario 2 would have occurred and to discount them by different percentages."

971 Building on the case of EWHC, *Les Laboratoires Servier v Apotex*, October 9th 2008, EWHC 2347 (Ch). See: par. 9.

972 P. INMAN, A. CARTER, 'When the biter gets bit: Cross-undertakings in damages' *The IPKat weblog* (Blogpost of May 22nd 2015); available at: http://ipkitten.blogspot.nl/2015/05/when-biter-gets-bit-cross-undertakings.html (last accessed on 24 April 2017).

It is submitted that this 'liberal assessment' of the wrongfully enjoined party's damages makes sense: this party has to prove that the damages are partly based on a hypothetical situation (namely on the premises of what when the interim injunction was not granted) and therefore a liberal assessment is warranted. It also makes sense from the perspective of justice. After all, a defendant would otherwise be victim of flawed justice twice: firstly, by being enjoined by the wrongfully-granted interim injunction, and secondly by the challenge of passing a high hurdle in obtaining compensatory damages. Instead, with this 'liberal assessment', according to Rennie-Smith, a cross-undertaking in damages can fulfil a role of deterring a doubtful application for a preliminary injunction.[973] This would be a request which, although first may be seen as arguable, is actually aimed towards shutting down the defendant's activity.[974]

Lastly, it should be mentioned that a cross-undertaking can in principle also cover the damages of *another party* than just that of the direct defendant in the preliminary injunction proceedings.[975] This can for instance be other companies in the same corporate group as the defendant; however, the wording of the cross-undertaking should then not be (formulated) too open and too vague: a cross-undertaking for '(potential) customers' is not adequately defined enough to pass that hurdle.[976] This said, an entity as *the National Health Service (NHS)* for instance – being a significant customer of generic medicines which can be hardly hit by a wrongfully-granted interim injunction – can sometimes be deemed as being an entity that is both relevant and specific enough to be covered by such an cross-undertaking in damages.[977]

---

973 C. RENNIE-SMITH, 'Patent Enforcement in the United Kingdom' in C. HEATH (editor) *Patent Enforcement Worldwide: Writings in honour of Dieter Stauder* (2015, Third Edition, Hart Publishing), pp. 81–110. See: esp. p. 93.

974 Ibidem.

975 In line with the CPR Practice Directive 25A, See Par. 5.1A: "When the court makes an order for an injunction, it should consider whether to require an undertaking by the applicant to pay any damages sustained by a person other than the respondent, including another party to the proceedings or any other person who may suffer loss as a consequence of the order."

976 EWHC, *Actavis v Boehringer Ingelheim*, September 23rd 2013, EWHC 2927 (Pat). See esp. par. 32–42. At par. 35 it was written: "A cross-undertaking has been called the price of an injunction and, in the end, it seems to me that the person paying that price needs to know with reasonable certainty what it is. It could be, in a given case, that the price demanded would be too high. A party seeking an interim injunction, or accepting undertakings in lieu of an interim injunction, is entitled to be wary of an indeterminate and open-ended cross-undertaking in favour of persons unknown."

977 Idem, at par. 39. Also see for instance: EWHC, *Warner Lambert v Actavis, NHS, Teva and others*, March 2nd 2015, EWHC 485 (Pat.).

§7.3.5. *Intermediate conclusion*

Concluding, one can argue that the prescribed guidelines and practices stemming from *American Cyanamid* result in a rather different approach of deciding on preliminary injunctions than that is taken by other European courts such as The Netherlands and Germany. In England, there is a relatively large focus on the harms of the parties and what the (commercial) consequences of granting or withholding the interim injunction are likely to be. This, instead of an approach with emphasis on the likelihood of the plaintiff-applicant winning at trial and on the issues of infringement and validity. Whilst in practice, the court can be more flexible to take along the strength of a case than it would first seem after reading *American Cyanamid*, this does not take away that the interpretation of the decision has resulted in a rather difficult and artificial way of dealing with the merits of the case.[978]

Unsurprisingly therefore, that House of Lords decision, although setting a unified standard for interim injunctions, can be seen as a judgment that is regularly misunderstood and misapplied.[979] Furthermore, the judicial emphasis on a practice of 'clearing the way', which has become dominant after the *Apotex* cases, is also deemed as being somewhat problematic and rigid, although it is consistent with the general approach set by *American Cyanamid*. From that point of view the *Cephalon* case, arguing for more flexibility on this issue, is a valuable court ruling.

Equally, it is positive development to see that it has now been held possible for the court to provide an interim injunction pending the appeal of an earlier invalidated patent, when there is a *reasonable chance* that this invalidation may be corrected at the appeal. Lastly, it is deemed as being a positive development that courts have ruled that there should be a 'liberal assessment' of injuries in the context of a cross-undertaking for damages. This in order to sufficiently compensate a party that has been wrongfully enjoined by an erroneously granted interim injunction.

---

978 The present author agrees with Mei. As Mei writes, the fact that the *American Cyanamid* guidelines, by de-emphasising the role of the merits, essentially allow a party that has a relatively weak, but arguable case, to have a just as large chance of winning at the interlocutory level than a party with a strong defence. This is aggravated by the legal fiction in intellectual property cases, that nevertheless justice will be done at the trial on the merits. The latter disregards the fact that in patent cases this stage is often not reached and after the interim injunction proceedings the defendant might abandon its activities or opt for an alternative product or process. See G. MEI, 'Interlocutory injunctions in IP Infringement actions in England and Wales and in Ireland – *American Cyanamid* revisited' *International Review of Intellectual Property and Competition Law* 46, No. 2 (2015), pp. 175–202. See: p. 178 and pp. 194–196.

979 Idem, at p. 194.

§7.4. The United States

§7.4.1. Introduction

The classic Supreme Court case of *Marbury v Madison* already specified that where there is a right, there is a remedy.[980] And since the foundation of the United States, it has been clear that equity played a significant role in providing this remedy. Less clear for centuries has been what the standard was that governed this wide judicial discretion in the realm of (preliminary) injunctions. Lee for instance remarked that differing practices had resulted into a "rift between US Federal Circuit courts"[981] and Vaughn noted that problems and confusion had arisen due to the inability to predict what legal test was to be used in order to wield this remedy.[982] Even more famous has become the wording of Leubsdorf. He stated that the unclarity had led to a "dizzying diversity of formulations" used by the courts,[983] He also sharply criticised the lack of a doctrinal basis for preliminary relief:

> "The various standards articulated by courts and treatises rest **on no coherent theory about the purpose** of preliminary relief. Each of the factors usually cited implies certain goals, but the courts rarely discuss how these goals relate to each other or to some unified view."[984]

Unsurprisingly therefore, the development of the standard of (preliminary) injunctions has been a topic of considerable interest in American academic literature, with commentators attempting to find the 'right' legal standard for preliminary injunctions, often with an eye to its historic origins.[985]

---

980 US Supreme Court, *Marbury v Madison*, February 24th, 1803, U.S. 163. "The very essence of civil liberty certainly consists in the right of every individual to claim the protection of the laws whenever he receives an injury. One of the first duties of government is to afford that protection."

981 T. R. LEE, 'Preliminary injunctions and the status quo' *Washington Law Review* 58 (2001), pp. 109–166. Also see footnote 112 of this dissertation.

982 L.B. VAUGHN, 'A need for clarity: toward a new standard for preliminary injunctions' *Oregon Law Review* 68 (1989), pp. 839–884. See: p. 840.

983 J. LEUBSDORF, 'The standard for preliminary injunctions' *Harvard Law Review* 91, No. 3 (1978), pp. 525–566. See: p. 526.

984 Ibidem. Emphasis added.

985 To a large extent, this interest is about the remedy of preliminary injunctions in general, rather than its application specifically to patent litigation. Besides the works of LEE, VAUGHN and LEUBSDORF mentioned directly in the footnotes above, also see: R.G. HAMMOND, 'Interlocutory injunctions: time for a new model?' *The University of Toronto Law Journal* 30, No. 3 (1980), pp. 240–282. See: p. 247. S.H. BLACK, 'A new look at preliminary injunctions: can principles from the past offer any guidelines to decisionmakers in the future?' *Alabama Law Review* 36, No. 1 (1984), pp. 1–49. A. DISARRO, 'Freeze Frame: The Supreme Court's reaffirmation of the substantive principles of preliminary injunctions'

It is obvious however that the legal standard underpinning the remedy has been in considerable flux. Hammond points out that whilst earlier cases were expressed in little strict terms,[986] slowly, especially through the second half of the 19th century, the requirements that courts set in order to issue a preliminary injunction became more firm.[987] Steadily, the modern-day elements such as 'likelihood of prevailing on the merits', 'irreparable injury', a 'balancing of convenience examination' and the 'preservation of the status-quo' became more and more prevalent in general preliminary injunction litigation. In parallel, also since the 1850s, additional elements *more specific to patent litigation* emerged in the legal test of the courts. Examples are the 'likelihood of patent infringement', 'patent validity' and 'title', within the preliminary injunction context.[988]

As the exact interpretation of the abovementioned elements in the 20th century has been prone to different and constantly changing interpretations, both per judicial circuit and temporally, a detailed analysis of this process and evolution is out of scope of this dissertation.[989] Instead, a look is taken to a number of Supreme Court and Federal Circuit cases, from the early 2000s. All have been doctrinally important in *shaping* the remedy of preliminary injunction, specifically with regard to patent cases, to what it is now.

§7.4.2. *The legal basis and test*

The modern day statutory basis for preliminary injunctions against patent infringement in the United States is *equal* to that of permanent injunctions and is to be found in Title 35 of the United States Code (U.S.C.), at §283.[990] Procedural aspects of

---

Gonzaga Law Review 47, No. 1 (2011–2012), pp. 51–98. See: pp. 52–72. S.E. SHAPIRO, 'Preliminary injunction motions in patent litigation' *IDEA: The Journal of Law and Technology* (1992–1993), pp. 323–348. H.F. SCHWARTZ, 'Injunctive relief in patent infringement suits' *University of Pennsylvania Law Review* 112 (1964), pp. 1025–1048. Finally, see J.J. FOSTER, 'The preliminary injunction – a 'new' and potent weapon in patent litigation' *Journal of the Patent and Trademark Office Society* (1986) p. 281–291 and M. DENLOW, 'The Motion for a Preliminary Injunction: Time for a Uniform Federal Standard' *The Review of Litigation* 22, No. 3 (2003), pp. 495–539.

986 HAMMOND, R.G., 'Interlocutory injunctions: time for a new model?' *The University of Toronto Law Journal* 30, No. 3 (1980), pp. 240–282. See: p. 247.

987 Ibidem.

988 H.F. SCHWARTZ, 'Injunctive relief in patent infringement suits' *University of Pennsylvania Law Review* 112 (1964), pp. 1025–1048. See: p. 1027 a.f.

989 But see the work done by BLACK, HAMMOND, LEUBSDORF and LEE. All mentioned in footnote 985 *supra* of this dissertation.

990 Title 35 U.S.C. § 283 reads: "The several courts having jurisdiction of cases under this title may grant injunctions *in accordance with the principles of equity* to prevent the violation of any right secured by patent, on such terms as the court deems reasonable." Emphasis added.

the preliminary injunction proceedings are found in the Federal Rules of Civil Procedure, at Rule 65.[991] Beyond these two statutory provisions, the decision whether and when to grant a requested preliminary injunction has been completely left to decide upon by the courts. These have traditionally based the large discretion that they have in their decision-making on the principles of equity. It is on how the courts harness these powers in the context of preliminary injunctions in patent cases to which we will turn.

Two points remain to be made prior to this: firstly, reviewing the principles on which US doctrine is based seems confusing *prima facie*, as many cases refer to different precedents. Below we will therefore review the often-recurring cases. Secondly, as will be seen, cases involving requests for *permanent* injunctions have had a precedential value in shaping the remedy of the preliminary injunction.

The Federal Circuit cases of *HyrbridTech v Abbot*[992] and especially *Amazon v Barnesandnoble*[993] are rulings that are often cited in later patent cases as clearly having set out the standard that a plaintiff should fulfil in order to obtain a preliminary injunction. This standard is that the plaintiff can succeed in showing (1) a 'likelihood of success' on the merits; (2) that he will suffer irreparable harm when an injunction is *not* granted; (3) a balance of hardships that is in his favour; (4) a positive outcome regarding the public interest. Subsequent Supreme Court cases such as *eBay*[994] and *Winter*[995] have not only used and *reconfirmed* a *similar test* as the standard for equitable injunctive relief – the former with respect to permanent injunctions in a patent case and the latter with respect to preliminary injunctions (although in a non-patent case) – but these decisions also have impacted the notion of what constitutes *irreparable harm*. The latter, key issue, will be considered after initially reviewing the first prong of the current preliminary injunction test, which is 'the likelihood of success'.

---

991 Rule 65 (a) (1) of the Federal Rules of Civil Procedure states: "The court may issue a preliminary injunction only on notice to the adverse party." Other provisions of Rule 65 merely go into further procedural issues such as that security can be ordered by the court from the plaintiff for the defendant – Rule 65 (c) – and on the form (content and scope) that a preliminary injunction order has to adhere to; Rule 65 (d).

992 Federal Circuit, *Hybritech Incorporated, v. Abbott Laboratories*, June 16th 1988, 849 F.2d 1446.

993 Federal Circuit, *Amazon.com v Barnesandnoble.com*, February 14th 2001, 239 F.3d 1343 LEXIS 2163.

994 US Supreme Court, *eBay Inc et al. v. MercExchange L.L.C.*, May 15th 2006, No. 05–130.

995 US Supreme Court, *Winter, Secretary of the Navy et al. v. Natural Resources Defence Council, Inc et al.*, November 12th 2008, No. 7–1239. Herein the Court stated: "A plaintiff seeking a preliminary injunction must establish that he is (1) likely to succeed on the merits, (2) that he is likely to suffer irreparable harm in the absence of preliminary relief, (3) that the balance of equities tips in his favour, (4) and that an injunction is in the public interest."

Figure 9. The US preliminary injunction test (own image).

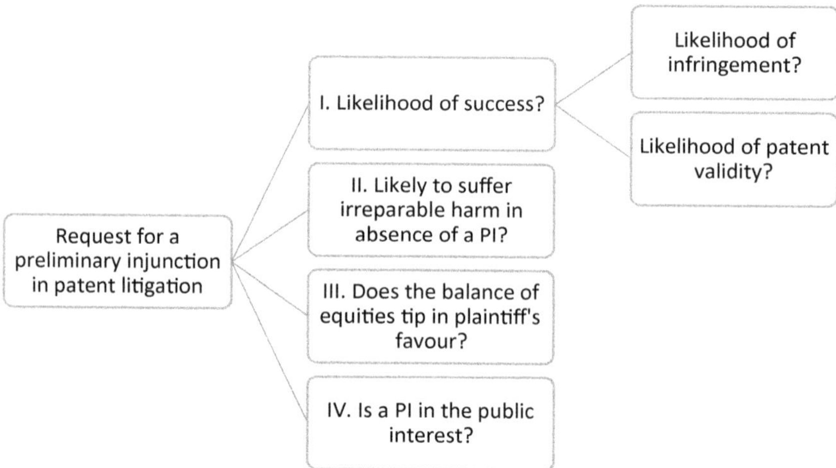

§7.4.3. Likelihood of success

The first factor of 'likelihood of success' is critical for the grant of preliminary injunctions in patent litigation and this prong carries significant weight. Along with proving irreparable harm – now a more significant hurdle due to the abandoning of the irreparable harm presumption[996] – proving the 'likelihood of success' continues to be the most important hurdle for plaintiffs, especially in patent litigation. A much-cited case in this context, clearly pointing out which actions the court should take, is the decision in *Titan Tire Corp v New Holland*.[997] This ruling is actually regarding a design-patent, but is just as valid for patents in general. It clearly shows that the 'likelihood of success' can be split in a 'likelihood of success' on the patent infringement issue and in a 'likelihood of success' on the patent validity issue.

It should be stressed at this point that the preliminary injunction court, unlike a court at the trial on the merits, does not (attempt to) resolve the issue of patent infringement or patent validity; the court should here only make *an assessment of*

996 As will be seen, this was clearly stated in the case of US Supreme Court, *eBay Inc et al. v. MercExchange L.L.C.*, May 15th 2006, No. 05–130 and US Supreme Court, *Winter, Secretary of the Navy et al. v. Natural Resources Defence Council, Inc et al.*, November 12th, 2008, No. 7–1239 and in *Bosch*: Federal Circuit, US Court of Appeals, *Robert Bosch LLC v Pylon Manufacturing Corp*, October 13th 2011, F.3D 1142.

997 Federal Circuit, *Titan Tire Corp v New Holland Inc*, June 3rd 2009, 566 F.3D 1372.

persuasiveness on these points, thereby at the same time recognising that it does so without knowing all the evidence that may come out at trial.[998]

Regarding *infringement*, the plaintiff should demonstrate a need for a preliminary injunction, namely that the defendant infringes *one or more* of the patentee's patent *claims*.[999] Again, what should be proven here is a 'likelihood of success' on this issue, not absolute certainty.

With respect to the point of patent *validity*, it should be noted that in the United States there is a firm statutory presumption – 35 U.S.C. §282 (a) – that a granted patent is valid.[1000] Based on this presumption, the validity does not have to be proven by the plaintiff when it is not challenged by the alleged infringer-defendant.[1001] There is no principle that a patent should have per se survived an earlier opposition or invalidity challenge, in order for a preliminary injunction to be issued. However, if the defendant challenges the validity of the patent with reasonable arguments or evidence (i.e. lack of substantial merit),[1002] the plaintiff has to respond to this and should attempt to convince the court otherwise, in order to obtain the desired interim relief.[1003] In the end, it is the preliminary injunction court that assesses whether "it is more likely than not that the challenger will be able to prove at trial, by clear and convincing evidence, that the patent is invalid."[1004]

A good example of the issues at this prong is the case of *Heart Imaging*.[1005] Here, the patent in question was a software patent aimed at 'medical image conversion and management technology' and the plaintiff (Heart) sought to enjoin future sales by Merge, a company with a similar product. The preliminary injunction court conducted a thorough analysis of the 'likelihood of success' prong, by

998 Idem, at 1377.

999 Federal Circuit, *Abbot Labs v Andrx Pharms*, January 5th 2007, 473 F.3d 1196. See: 1201: "In order to establish the first preliminary injunction factor, Abbott must show that it will likely prove that Andrx infringes *at least one valid and enforceable* patent claim." Emphasis added.

1000 This presumption of patent validity under US Law is enshrined in 35 U.S.C. §282 (a) and is worded as follows: "A patent shall be presumed valid. Each claim of a patent (whether in independent, dependent, or multiple dependent form) shall be presumed valid independently of the validity of other claims; dependent or multiple dependent claims shall be presumed valid even though dependent upon an invalid claim. The burden of establishing invalidity of a patent or any claim thereof shall rest on the party asserting such invalidity."

1001 Federal Circuit, *Titan Tire Corp v New Holland Inc*, June 3rd 2009, 566 F.3D 1372. See: 1377.

1002 Idem, at 1377 and 1378.

1003 Idem, at 1377.

1004 Idem, at 1379.

1005 United States District Court for the Middle District of North Carolina, *Heart Imaging Technologies, LLC v Merge Healthcare Inc*, August 14th 2013, U.S. Dist. Lexis 114679.

making an elaborate claim construction[1006] and an equally thorough infringement analysis,[1007] before looking at arguments in the context of patent validity.[1008] Whilst the preliminary injunction court agreed with Heart's claim construction as being the most appropriate, it was not convinced of the 'likelihood of success' for Heart regarding the issues of patent infringement and patent validity. Based on this, the court was not prepared to issue a preliminary injunction as Heart Imaging had requested.

That passing the 'likelihood of success' prong can prove to be a hurdle for plaintiffs, is for instance further demonstrated in the cases of *Asus v Exotablet,*[1009] *Celgard v LG Chem*[1010] and *BitTitan v SkyKick.*[1011]

§7.4.4. Irreparable harm

Traditionally, *irreparable harm* has been one of the most crucial requirements for obtaining injunctive (interim) relief in the United States.[1012] However, as Laycock has already shown in his extensive research from 1990,[1013] the level of harm that is required to satisfy this requirement has been in considerable flux in the last few decades and this is not something that has changed in the period after his research, as more recent cases have also shown. Laycock wrote at the time that, with respect to injunctive relief, it was clear to him that the 'irreparable injury rule'[1014] – namely the rule that states *that equity will not act if there is no irreparable injury* – was in fact 'dead'.[1015] According to Laycock, courts had eliminated the irreparable injury

1006 Idem, at 13–22.
1007 Idem, at 33–40.
1008 Idem, at 41–53.
1009 United States District Court for the Northern District of California, *Asus Computers Intnl. et al. v. Exotablet Ltd.,* August 12th 2014, U.S. Dist. Lexis 111843.
1010 United States Court of Appeals for the Federal Circuit, *Celgard, LLC v. LG Chem America Inc,* August 12th 2015, U.S. App. Lexis 14079 (non-precedential).
1011 United States District Court for the Western District of Washington, *BitTitan Inc, v SkyKick Inc,* August 27th 2015) U.S. Dist. Lexis 114082.
1012 See D. LAYCOCK 'The death of the irreparable injury rule' *Harvard Law Review* 103, No. 3 (1990), pp. 687–771.
1013 Ibidem.
1014 Idem, at p. 689.
1015 Idem, at p. 689. Laycock also writes, at p. 692: "I conclude that the irreparable injury rule is dead. It does not describe what the cases do, and it cannot account for the results. *Injunctions are routine, and damages are never adequate unless the court wants them to be.* Courts can freely turn to the precedents granting injunctions or the precedents denying injunctions, depending on whether they want to hold the legal remedy adequate or inadequate. Whether they want to hold the legal remedy adequate depends on whether they have some other reason to deny the equitable remedy, and it is these other reasons that drive the decisions." Emphasis added.

rule in actual practice, with as result that meeting the requirement of 'irreparable harm' had become more and more easily to satisfy.[1016] Sometimes courts 'escaped' this rule by holding the rule inapplicable, but more often, Laycock found, courts worked *within the rule*, finding (other) legal remedies – such as damages – to be inadequate.[1017] Laycock commented in his work that only with respect to preliminary injunctions the rule did still have some teeth.[1018]

A good example of Laycock's conclusion in the 1990s that the irreparable injury rule was dead, could be seen in the area of intellectual property infringement.[1019] More specifically, this is clear in patent infringement cases with the creation of a

---

1016 Ibidem.

1017 Ibidem, and at p. 701.

1018 Idem, at p. 691. Furthermore, Laycock writes at p. 732: "It is universally true that courts are more willing to grant permanent injunctions than preliminary injunctions, and a common way to explain the results is to find no or insufficient irreparable injury at the preliminary injunction stage. (..) *The irreparable injury rule has teeth at the preliminary injunction stage because it still serves a purpose there.* At the preliminary injunction stage, the merits are unresolved, plaintiff may be undeserving, and it is still possible that plaintiff will not get any remedy at all. Defendant has legitimate interests in a full hearing and in freedom to act in ways not yet shown to be unlawful. *These interests coincide with the court's interest in avoiding error and being fair to both sides.* These interests may also coincide with less savory interests, such as defendant's desire to force a cheap settlement by means of delay and litigation costs. Unfortunately, the court may not be able to screen out such interests until it hears the merits. At the permanent injunction stage, the merits are resolved, defendant is a known wrongdoer, and the court has eliminated the option of no remedy at all. *Now the choice is between damages and injunctions, and in most cases, neither the court nor the defendant prefers a damage remedy.* Moreover, the court has heard the merits and is now in a position to assess the legitimacy of any reasons defendant does offer for preferring damages." Emphasis added.

1019 The strong belief that infringement of intellectual property rights leads to irreparable harm, something that has dominated intellectual property injunction cases for a long time, is not restricted only to patent litigation. It is also very apparent with respect to copyright injunctions. Samuelson and Bebenek for instance have argued that even after the *eBay* case, in the context of copyright, harm is too often considered as irreparable. This practice of courts has, in their view, become 'lamentably common' and cannot be squared with the traditional principles of equity. See: P. SAMUELSON, K. BEBENEK, 'Why plaintiffs should have to prove irreparable harm in copyright preliminary injunction cases' *I/S: A Journal of Law and Policy* 6, No. 1 (2010), pp. 67–94. For another interesting article on the effects of *eBay* on copyright injunctions in the US, see J. PHILLIPS, 'eBay's effect on copyright injunctions: when property rules give way to liability rules' *Berkley Technology Law Journal* 24, No. 1 (2009) pp. 405–435. Available at: http://scholarship.law.berkeley.edu/cgi/viewcontent.cgi?article=1780&context=btlj (last accessed on 24 April 2017).

presumption of irreparable harm in patent litigation that existed after the Federal Circuit case of *Smith International v Hughes Tool co.*[1020, 1021] This ruling changed a situation of preceding unclarity[1022] and firmly established the presumption of irreparable harm, creating a *de facto* situation that when patent infringement and validity were found (to be likely), irreparable harm was assumed, paving the way for injunctive relief. This was a long and dominant view, until a string of relatively recent cases emerged challenging this perspective.

The first is the case of *eBay v MercExchange*, handed down by the Supreme Court.[1023] This case was specifically on *permanent* injunctions and held in a patent

---

1020 Federal Circuit, *Smith International Inc. v Hughes Tool Co*, October 6th 1983, 718 F.2d 1573. See: 1581: "The very nature of the patent right is the right to exclude others. Once the patentee's patents have been held to be valid and infringed, he should be entitled to the full enjoyment and protection of his patent rights. The infringer should not be allowed to continue his infringement in the face of such a holding. A court should not be reluctant to use its equity powers once a party has so clearly established his patent rights. We hold that where validity and continuing infringement have been clearly established, as in this case, immediate irreparable harm is presumed. To hold otherwise would be contrary to the public policy underlying the patent laws." Also see D. LAYCOCK 'The death of the irreparable injury rule' *Harvard Law Review* 103, No. 3 (1990), pp. 687–771. See: p. 713.

1021 C. GRIFFITH TOWLE, R. ZARCO, 'Proving irreparable harm, have the standards changed?' (2012) *American Bar Association. 35th Annual Forum on Franchising*, pp. 1–33. See: p. 7. Available at: http://zarcolaw.com/wp-content/uploads/2014/11/Proving-Irreparable-Harm-Have-the-Standards-Changed-ABA-2012.pdf (last accessed on 24 April 2017).

1022 See R.C. DORR, B.J. DUFT, 'Patent preliminary injunctive relief' (1978) *Journal of the Patent Office Society*. 60, No. 10 (1978), pp. 597–635. See: p 605 a.f. Dorr and Duft wrote in 1978, that "All circuits universally recognize that a patent duly issued by the United States Patent and Trademark Office is presumptively valid. This presumption is explicitly mandated in 35 U.S.C. §282. *The weight accorded this presumption, however, varies substantially from circuit to circuit*." Emphasis added. The authors, in their article, subsequently go into these differences between circuits.

1023 US Supreme Court, *eBay Inc et al. v. MercExchange L.L.C.*, May 15th 2006, No. 05–130. For an interesting background article to the eBay case, see D.B. CONRAD, 'Mining the patent thicket: the Supreme Court's rejection of the automatic injunction rule in eBay v MercExchange' *The Review of Litigation* 26, No. 1 (2007), pp. 119–154. Equally, see the contribution of S. SURABRAMNIAN, 'Different rules for different owners – Does a Non-competing patentee have a right to exclude? A study of post-eBay cases' *IIC* (2008), pp. 419–451. Here Surabramnian cites the immediate aftermath of the eBay case, before the *Winter* case (below), when it was *unclear whether eBay was applicable to preliminary injunctions or not.* As Surabramnian demonstrates the lower courts were first divided on this and their opinion ranged from 'the standard for preliminary

litigation context. The case is considered to be a landmark ruling since it was a decisive break with decades of Federal precedent that, as pointed out above, was based on the presumption that an injunction was justified when infringement in a patent litigation case was found.[1024] The Federal Circuit reasoned, until the *eBay* decision, that it was precisely because of the very nature of patents – granting their owners the right to exclude unlicensed firms from making, selling or using their inventions – that justified a general rule that injunctions should be issued upon a finding of patent infringement.[1025] In other words, an injunction indirectly supported the core business of a patentee by allowing it to rely on the exclusivity offered by the patent, and there was thus a direct link between the grant of the remedy and the infringement of the right. This link was challenged with *eBay*.[1026] It is submitted here that this was rightly so since, as Justice Kennedy put it, a new industry had emerged, in which patents were no longer the basis for selling and producing goods but were sometimes seen merely as tools to obtain license fees.[1027] Justice Kennedy wrote in his concurring opinion that, in that light, there was a particular risk that had emerged with a (quasi)-automatic injunction rule: "Where the threat of an injunction is employed simply for undue leverage in negotiations, legal damages may well be sufficient to compensate for the infringement, and an injunction may not serve the public interests."[1028] As Sterk commented, this strongly suggests that monetary damages should suffice in those cases where uncertainty is most pervasive and where the removal costs of the defendant (thereby giving leverage to the patent holder) are high.[1029]

---

injunctions is essentially the same' to 'eBay addressed the proper analysis only for permanent injunctive relief' and even 'the court's reasoning likely applies with even greater force at the preliminary injunction stage'. See: page 443.

1024 As Darch writes on p. 110, the Supreme Court in eBay rejected a categorical approach, *both for providing injunctive relief and for denying it* and instead the plaintiff must satisfy the four-factor test, which is derived on equitable principles. See: M.C. DARCH, 'The Presumption of Irreparable Harm in Patent Infringement Litigation: A Critique of Robert Bosch LLC v. Pylon Manufacturing Corp.' *Northwestern Journal of Technology and Intellectual Property* 11, No. 2 (2013), pp. 103–119.

1025 P. SAMUELSON, K. BEBENEK, 'Why plaintiffs should have to prove irreparable harm in copyright preliminary injunction cases' *I/S: A Journal of Law and Policy* 6, No. 1 (2010), pp. 67–94. See: esp. p. 70.

1026 Ibidem.

1027 Justice Kennedy in US Supreme Court, *eBay Inc et al. v. MercExchange L.L.C.*, May 15th 2006, No. 05–130. See: 1842.

1028 Ibidem.

1029 S.E. STERK, 'Property rights, liability rules and uncertainty about property rights' *Cardozo School of Law Working Paper* No. 205, (2007). See: p. 51. Available at: http://papers.ssrn.com/sol3/papers.cfm?abstract_id=1016168 (last accessed on 17 april 2017).

A similar finding, namely that irreparable harm does not follow automatically after having proven the likelihood of prevailing on the merits, has also been made with respect to preliminary injunctions in the Supreme Court case of *Winter.*[1030] This ruling was issued a few years after eBay.[1031] This was not a case on the subject of patents or even intellectual property, but on the issue of environmental (wildlife) protection.[1032] The legal dispute was started by an environmental group against the United States Navy, who had as their objective to have the court enjoin the use of sonar during Navy training exercises because of the harm these activities caused to marine mammals. Here as well, the Supreme Court confirmed that *also a preliminary injunction* is to be seen as an extraordinary remedy, never given quasi-automatically as of right: instead, it is the plaintiff that has to convince the court of the necessity of a preliminary injunction.[1033] This means that a preliminary injunction does not only flow from the likelihood of success on the merits, but the plaintiff has to succeed on the hurdles of likelihood and irreparable harm.[1034] The mere *possibility* of irreparable harm is thus not deemed any longer as being sufficient enough to warrant the grant of a preliminary injunction.[1035]

Taken together, *eBay* and *Winter* made clear that for preliminary injunctions in patent litigation 1) an automatic injury rule was off the table; 2) equity was at the

1030 US Supreme Court, *Winter v Natural Resources Defense Council*, November 12th 2008, 129 S. Ct. 365.

1031 This also took away the uncertainty whether a similar finding of *eBay* was applicable to preliminary injunctions. See on this: S. SURABRAMNIAN, 'Different rules for different owners – Does a Non-competing patentee have a right to exclude? A study of post-eBay cases' *IIC* (2008), pp. 419–451.

1032 The request for a preliminary injunction was granted by the District Court and later confirmed by the Ninth Circuit. The Supreme Court however disagreed with this, and reversed the decision made earlier by the Ninth Circuit and vacated the granted preliminary injunction. For a good background article to the *Winter* case, see B. NARODICK, 'Winter v. National Resources Defense Council: going into the belly of the whale of preliminary injunctions and environmental law' *Boston University Journal of Science and Technology Law* Vol. 15 (2009), pp. 332–347.

1033 US Supreme Court, *Winter v Natural Resources Defense Council*, November 12th 2008, 129 S. Ct. 365. See: 365–366. "Issuing a preliminary injunction based only *on a possibility* of irreparable harm is inconsistent with our characterization of injunctive relief as an extraordinary remedy that may only be awarded upon a clear showing that the plaintiff is entitled to such relief." The Supreme Court thereby thus disagreed with the earlier decisions of the District Court and the Federal Courts of Appeals.

1034 Also: A. DISARRO, 'Freeze Frame: The Supreme Court's reaffirmation of the substantive principles of preliminary injunctions' *Gonzaga Law Review* 47, No. 1 (2011–2012), pp. 51–98. See: p. 83 a.f.

1035 Note that in order to obtain a *permanent* injunction, the plaintiff should actually *succeed* on the merits of the case, instead of showing the mere likelihood.

heart of (interim) injunctive relief;[1036] and 3) the plaintiff's (likely) irreparable harm had to be proven. These points were again reconfirmed in *Bosch*, with respect to *patent infringement*.[1037] The Federal Circuit ruled in the latter:

> "We take this opportunity to put the question to rest and confirm that eBay jettisoned the presumption of irreparable harm as it applies to determining the appropriateness of injunctive relief."[1038]

Irreparable harm should thus be proven by the plaintiff and it should be demonstrated that any loss and damages due to such harm cannot be compensated by monetary damages later.[1039] Examples of what constitutes irreparable harm, were given in *Bosch* too.[1040] Factors that are taken into account mentioned in *Bosch* which can indicate irreparable harm to the plaintiff – and thus favour the grant of a preliminary injunction – are that of:

1036 Empirical research by Gupta and Kesan looks at the effect of the eBay ruling on the use of both preliminary and permanent injunctions. Their research suggests that – thereby using a comprehensive dataset with thousands of patents both before and after the ruling – that the eBay decision has rather dramatically reduced the rate of which injunctions are sought, as well as the rate at which they are granted by the courts after being sought. This effect is particularly strong with respect to preliminary injunctions. See: K. GUPTA, J.P. KESAN, 'Studying the impact of *eBay* on injunctive relief in patent cases' *University of Illinois College of Law Legal Studies Research Paper* No. 17–03 (2015).

1037 Federal Circuit, *Robert Bosch LLC v Pylon Manufacturing Corp*, October 13th 2011, F.3D 1142. Also see on this case the interesting analysis of Darch, who is critical of the reading of *eBay* by the Federal Circuit in *Bosch* and argues that there should be more focus on the exclusivity function of a patent: "While equitable principles, including the balance of hardships test, should control the grant of an injunction, *the loss of the right to exclude is certainly a harm that does not have a monetary value*. Thus, following a showing of infringement, irreparable harm should be presumed in patent infringement cases." M.C. DARCH, 'The Presumption of Irreparable Harm in Patent Infringement Litigation: A Critique of Robert Bosch LLC v.Pylon Manufacturing Corp.' *Northwestern Journal of Technology and Intellectual Property* 11, No. 2 (2013), pp. 103–119. See: p. 118. Emphasis added.

1038 Federal Circuit, *Robert Bosch LLC v Pylon Manufacturing Corp*, October 13th 2011, 2011 F.3D 1142. See: 1149.

1039 As stated explicitly in Federal Circuit, *Automated Merchandising Systems Inc. v. Crane and Co.*, December 16th 2009, LEXIS 27667. "The burden is now on the patentee to demonstrate that its potential losses cannot be compensated by monetary damages. The proof of lost market share and lost sales cited by the district court here was insufficient to meet this standard." See: 301.

1040 Federal Circuit, *Robert Bosch LLC v Pylon Manufacturing Corp*, October 13th 2011, 2011 F.3D 1142. See: heading C at 1152–1156.

- direct competition in certain markets or market segments;[1041]
- the loss of market share;
- price erosion;
- whether there is damage to the patentee's reputation;
- the financial situation of the defendant resulting in the possible inability to pay;

Other 'irreparable harm' factors that have been listed elsewhere,[1042] are:

- whether the issuance of an injunction will deter other existing or potential infringers;
- whether the defendant's continuing infringement will interfere with the plaintiff's ability to control the use and licensing of the patented technology;
- whether the patent expires in less than two years;

Thus, despite that *eBay, Winter and Bosch* can be regarded as decisively letting go of the presumption of irreparable harm in patent litigation, the function of (preliminary) injunctions in offering patentees exclusivity, is still clearly articulated by the Federal Circuit as for instance in the case of *Douglas Dynamics.*[1043, 1044] This is especially when there is direct competition between the plaintiff and the defendant:

> "Lastly, the evidence shows that Douglas <the patentee> had never licensed the infringed patents, and intentionally chose not to, so that it could maintain market exclusivity. **Exclusivity is closely related to the fundamental nature of patents as property rights.** It is an intangible asset that is part of a company's reputation, and here, Douglas' **exclusive right to make, use, and sell the patented inventions** is under attack by Buyers' infringement. **Where two companies are in competition**

1041 Also see for instance the US District Court for the Northern District of California, *Open Text v Box*, April 9th 2014, 2014 36 F.Supp.3d 885, at 906, citing the case of Federal Circuit, *i4i Ltd. Partnership v. Microsoft Corp.*, 2010, 598 F.3d 831, where such a situation occurred: "In a market where only two parties are directly competing, the potential harm in allowing the defendant to continue its infringing conduct is probably at its greatest."

1042 See the factors given in D.W. MARTENS, J.B. SGANGA Jr., *Pre-litigation patent enforcement* (2013–2014 Thomson Reuters) at p. 579. Also provided in K.A. MOORE, T.R. HOLBROOK, J.F. MURPHY, *Patent litigation and strategy* (2013, Fourth edition, West Academic Publishing). See: p. 877.

1043 Federal Circuit, *Douglas Dynamics LLC v Buyers Products Company*, May 21st 2013, 717 F.3d 1336. Note that this case was on a request for a permanent injunction.

1044 See the analysis of *Darch* on this: M.C. DARCH, 'The Presumption of Irreparable Harm in Patent Infringement Litigation: A Critique of Robert Bosch LLC v. Pylon Manufacturing Corp.' *Northwestern Journal of Technology and Intellectual Property* 11, No. 2 (2013), pp. 103–119.

against one another, the patentee suffers the harm—often irreparable—of being forced to compete against products that incorporate and infringe its own patented inventions."[1045]

This abovementioned practical approach would likely be in line with the view of Millard who,[1046] whilst acknowledging that the Supreme Court in *eBay* was correct to recognize that in some situations a denial of injunctive relief would be appropriate, proposed that in the aftermath of that case the courts "should be mindful of this country's long history of protecting patent rights and of the goals that the patent system is designed to promote."[1047]

At this point it is interesting, by way of example, to make the concept of irreparable harm more tangible and specific and for instance to see what are commonly accepted sources of irreparable harm in the pharmaceutical industry regarding generic entry.[1048] In the United States, a loss of revenue and a drop in sales in this sector is generally not seen as sufficiently irreparable because these harms can be quantified fairly well and therefore are able to be compensated by monetary damages.[1049] This is due to the transparency of the market and the nature of the infringement, where there is a clear moment of entry by the other party. However other sources of harm are in fact deemed by the courts as being irreparable. As Cameron writes, these can be grouped under five headings, given below.[1050]

- A reduction in overall R&D budgets and activities
- Curtailments in brand-specific R&D and brand-specific marketing investments
- Health insurance related harms such as formulary displacement
- Loss of goodwill
- Other sources of irreparable harm

1045 Federal Circuit, *Douglas Dynamics LLC v Buyers Products Company*, May 21st 2013, 717 F.3d 1336. See: 1345.

1046 E.E. MILLARD, 'Injunctive relief in patent infringement cases: should courts apply a rebuttable presumption of irreparable harm after eBay Inc. v Mercexchange?' *St. Louis Law Journal* 52 (2008), pp. 985–1035.

1047 Idem, at p. 1035. Millard proposed in her 2008 article – written before *Bosch* – that a rebuttable presumption of irreparable harm should be factored into the equitable balancing act set by *eBay*. This way, the exclusive rights of the patentee would be safeguarded, whilst at the same time adding more predictability to the system of when a preliminary injunction would be granted.

1048 For these sources, see the paper of L.J. CAMERON, 'Preliminary injunctions in pharmaceutical litigation: the economics of irreparable harm' *Discussion Paper The Brattle Group* (February 2011). Available at: http://www.brattle.com/system/publications/pdfs/000/004/959/original/Preliminary_Injunctions_in_Pharmaceutical_Litigation_Feb_2011.pdf?1384877054 (last accessed on 24 April 2017).

1049 Idem, at p. 2.

1050 Idem, at pp. 4–7.

The first and fourth heading have already been referred to in preceding chapters: the former refers to *less available budget that can be invested into Research and Development* activities, resulting into less opportunities to develop new drugs or therapeutic applications of existing drugs, as well as a slowing down of the pace of innovation. The latter, *loss in goodwill,* occurs when the generic company that launched at risk, has to withdraw from the market in the case the plaintiff prevails at a trial on the merits. Due to generic entry, the status quo has changed however and not all will be again as it was; patients will not be pleased that they have to (co)pay more again for the same drug and may decide to switch completely to another brand, if this is possible within their specific drug and treatment combination.

The category of *curtailments in brand-specific R&D and brand-specific marketing investments,*[1051] refers, Cameron explains, to how originator pharmaceutical firms build further upon their branded drugs and market this. Unexpected (and possibly unlawful) generic entry hampers further innovation somewhat, it is then argued, in the sense that the branded company now forgoes specific R&D related to the particular drug, i.e. finding new indications and therapies based on its product. This is because the fruits of developments in this area can also be reaped by the generic entrant. In the same line of argument, free-riding can then also occur with the originator's marketing investments in promoting new indications of the branded drugs; the target group of the promotion is not the patients but those deciding *for them,* namely doctors or pharmacists who this way learn about (new) therapeutic options in comparison to other drugs. After generic entry, the marketing efforts for branded products will be greatly reduced, because of the potential free-riding by generic versions. Because it is difficult to estimate how doctors and patients would have reacted *if they would have known about (for instance) new indications,* this harm is difficult to estimate.

Formulary displacement, Cameron points out, refers to a specific trait of the American healthcare system, but is also featured in other countries in different forms. A crucial determinant for the value of a (prescription) pharmaceutical is in which specific 'tier' a pharmacy dispensed prescription drug is in. Out of the three tiers that determine the level of co-payments to be made by patients (and thus the price for the consumer of the drug) a firm with a branded drug would ideally be positioned in Tier 2, due to a favourable co-payment rate.[1052] Often there are various branded drugs treating the same therapeutic condition on the market, leading to intense competition to obtain and hold Tier 2 status.[1053] This position could become under threat when a generic version of a specific branded drug enters the market, as maintaining the branded version of the drug on Tier 2 is less defendable when a cheaper generic equivalent exists. When a branded drug loses its Tier 2 position, a later restoration, in the event that the generic entry proves to be unlawful and has

1051 Idem, at p. 5.
1052 Idem, at p. 6.
1053 Ibidem.

to be pulled back from the market again, will be difficult and it is this where the irreparability comes from.[1054]

Finally, the heading of *other sources* refers to harms such as a loss of jobs. Due to the generic entry, the originator will be forced to scale back production and this will result into the loss of jobs or loss of scientific talent for the company. Cameron provides examples of pharmaceutical companies slashing 1800 or 5000 jobs when faced with unexpected generic competition.[1055] These harms may also be found by the preliminary injunction court to be irreparable because their magnitude is difficult to estimate, let alone to undo.

As Cameron points out, illustrative cases citing these harms are for instance *Sanofi Synthelabo v Apotex Inc*,[1056] *Eli Lilly and Co v Teva*,[1057] and *Eisai v Teva*.[1058]

Obviously, both in pharmaceutical related disputes, as with other type of non-pharmaceutical disputes, irreparable harms should not only be claimed but should also be made probable and substantiated, as far as possible.[1059] Thus when in *PPC Broadband* the plaintiff claimed irreparable harm consisting of price erosion, damages to goodwill and finally the layoffs of employees, the preliminary injunction court, taking into account the market conditions and factual circumstances, found this to be *too speculative*, thereby also pointedly stating that "granting preliminary injunctions on the basis of speculative loss of market share would result in granting preliminary injunction in every patent case where the patentee practices the invention."[1060] A plaintiff cannot thus merely use economic arguments as a rhetorical device, but should substantiate the claims it makes as far as possible.[1061]

1054 Idem, at p. 6. Here, Cameron provides the example that other (current or new) branded competitors may then have already taken over the Tier 2 formulary position.

1055 Idem, at p. 7.

1056 Federal Circuit *Sanofi-Synthelabo v Apotex Inc.*, December 8th 2006, 470 F. 3d 1368.

1057 United States District Court of New Jersey, *Eisa Co v Teva Pharmaceuticals*, 2008, No. 05–05727.

1058 Federal Circuit, *Eli Lilly v Teva Pharmaceuticals*, 2009, 557 F.3d 1346.,

1059 As Resis wrote, on p. 28: "A movant should be prepared to present evidence of irreparable harm, as a court will likely find argument alone insufficient" thererby citing *Automated Merchandising v Crane*, see footnote 1039 of this dissertation. R.H. RESIS, *Preliminary relief in patent infringement disputes* (2011 American Bar Association Publishing).

1060 United States District Court for the Northern District of New York, *PPC Broadband, Inc. v Corning Gilbert Inc.*, June 5th 2014, LEXIS 76462, at 9.

1061 Also see the comments made by Cameron: "In addition, it found that Sanofi had *provided independent evidence* of irreparable harm arising from several adverse effects of "at risk" generic entry, including irreversible price erosion associated with formulary displacement and loss of goodwill from customers who would become accustomed to lower generic prices." and, in another case, "it found that Purdue *had provided supportive evidence of irreparable harm* from (a) future effects of price erosion, (b) loss of experienced staff resulting from cuts required by the

Another specific issue related to irreparable harm that seems to be making headway, is the *causal nexus requirement*, which, it is submitted, can significantly complicate the obtaining of a preliminary injunction in products with many (patented) features or components.

In *Apple I*,[1062] the Federal Circuit held that there should be a causal nexus between the irreparable harm of lost market share for Apple and the (alleged) infringement by Samsung. In first instance, Apple's motion for a preliminary injunction[1063] was denied by the District Court. In doing so, the District Court used the causal nexus test to establish whether Apple had suffered irreparable harm due to Samsung's conduct and whether because of this a preliminary injunction was justified. This causal nexus test essentially encompasses that a patentee should show a 1) link between the infringement and the harm caused and 2) that this is considered irreparable enough. To meet this requirement, the patentee should therefore now demonstrate that *the particular (infringed) patented feature or component is a driver of consumer demand of the product.*[1064]

It should thus be shown that consumers purchase the product for the (infringed) patented component or feature, in order to claim irreparable harm which could warrant preliminary injunctive relief. On appeal, this prescribed *use* of the causal nexus test was confirmed by the Federal Circuit – stating even that there should be a 'sufficiently strong' causal nexus – but also here it was established that the 'bounce back patent' of Apple[1065] was not something sufficient enough to prove the causal nexus between infringement and loss of sales for Apple. In both instances, it was thus considered that consumers would not base their purchasing decision on

loss of revenue, (c) disruption to Purdue's sales force from having to respond to the introduction of the generic at issue, and (d) lost allocation of revenues to further R&D, together with the consequent lost future opportunities in the marketplace." Emphasis added. L.J. CAMERON, 'Preliminary injunctions in pharmaceutical litigation: the economics of irreparable harm' *Discussion Paper The Brattle Group* (February 2011). See: p. 8. Available at: http://www.brattle.com/system/publications/pdfs/000/004/959/original/Preliminary_Injunctions_in_Pharmaceutical_Litigation_Feb_2011.pdf?1384877054 (last accessed on 24 April 2017).

1062 Federal Circuit, *Apple Inc. v Samsung Electronics Co (Apple I)*, May 14th 2012, 678 F.3d 1314. LEXIS 2012 U.S. App. 9720.

1063 This litigation concerned, along with a design patent, various utility patents covering software features concerning the user-interface. Amongst them were patents on the 'bounce back' effect when the user is unable to scroll further on the screen, multi-touch gestures and a 'double touch to zoom' feature.

1064 Federal Circuit, *Apple Inc. v Samsung Electronics Co (Apple I)*, May 14th 2012, 678 F.3d 1314. LEXIS 2012 U.S. App. 9720 at 1321 and 1324. Also, at 1324: "If the patented feature does not drive the demand for the product, sales would be lost even if the offending feature were absent from the accused product."

1065 Which was the only utility patent to be considered on appeal.

the presence of a 'bounce back' element in the phone's user interface.[1066] A similar scenario unfolded in *Apple II*.[1067] Also here, a requested preliminary injunction was denied to Apple, this time with respect to a patent for a 'unified, heuristic search feature'.[1068] Once again, this was for the plaintiff not meeting the causal nexus requirement.[1069]

Taken together, these two Apple cases[1070] made several things clear, Brean writes. Firstly, it clarified that the causal nexus requirement is indeed a requirement that should be demonstrated in such cases and the courts did not err in asking for this. Secondly, Brean states, it is now clear that the plaintiff should affirmatively prove that the patented feature or component for which it seeks (preliminary) injunctive relief actually drives consumer demand. Insufficient for this purpose is the notion that the absence of the patented feature leads to a decrease in sales.[1071]

According to Brean, this causal nexus approach reflects the Federal Circuit's concept and language on damages[1072] and then especially on the *Entire Market Value Rule*.[1073] Brean argues that in the case of established patent infringement, it is clear that plaintiffs are entitled to receive a minimum of reasonable royalty damages.[1074] The complex issue in multi-component products is establishing the correct royalty-base,[1075] as it is often unclear what the magnitude and value is of the single

---

1066 Federal Circuit, *Apple Inc. v Samsung Electronics Co (Apple I)*, May 14th 2012, 678 F.3d 1314. LEXIS 2012 U.S. App. 9720, at 1327.

1067 Federal Circuit, *Apple Inc v. Samsung Electronics Co* (*Apple II*), October 11th 2012, 695 F.3d. 1370. U.S. App. LEXIS 21085.

1068 Idem, at 1373.

1069 Idem, at 1375–1377.

1070 Not much later, The Federal Circuit gave a *third* ruling in another Apple-Samsung case (*Apple III*). This case again was on the nexus, but this time regarding permanent relief. The court confirmed that the nexus requirement mentioned in the preliminary injunction cases was also valid for permanent injunctions in multi-component cases. However, the court found that in casu Apple had not satisfied this requirement and declined to grant the permanent injunction. See: United States Court of Appeals for the Federal Circuit, *Apple Inc. v Samsung Electronics Co, (Apple III)*, November 18th 2013, 735 F.3D 1352. Subsequently, in Federal Circuit, *Apple Inc. v Samsung Electronics Co* (*Apple IV*), December 16th 2015, No. 2014–1802, the Federal Circuit confirmed the use of the causal nexus requirement again, thereby stating its applicability to both preliminary and permanent injunctions. This time though, the court stated that Apple had satisfied the nexus requirement.

1071 D.H. BREAN, 'Will the "Nexus" requirement of Apple v. Samsung preclude the injunctive relief in the majority of patent cases? Echoes of the Entire Market Value Rule' *San Diego Law Review* 51 (2014), pp. 153–207. See: p. 163.

1072 Idem, at p. 167.

1073 Idem, at p. 168.

1074 Ibidem.

1075 On this, also see the article of M. LEMLEY, C. SHAPIRO, 'Patent holdup and royalty stacking' *Texas Law Review* 85 (2008), pp. 1991–2049. See: pp. 2023–2035, where the

(infringed) feature or component with respect to a certain percentage of the total value of the product.[1076] A royalty-based damage calculation on the latter may lead to overcompensation of the patentee.[1077] To prevent this, damages are therefore then calculated on the basis of a smaller component: if a patent covers a laptop battery, the rate is then calculated from the battery and not from the laptop as such.[1078] But, and this is the *Entire Market Value Rule*, when a component or feature is considered to be so vital that it creates *substantial value* of the component parts, in the sense that it becomes the basis of consumer demand, the royalty base from which damages are calculated can then be the product as a whole.[1079]

It is submitted that the causal nexus requirement certainly has merits, since it is arguable that this limits hold-up situations. That the requirement may be beneficial was also something that was stated in *Apple III*:

> "The causal nexus requirement ensures that an injunction is only entered against a defendant on account of a harm resulting from the defendant's wrongful conduct, not some other reason. For example, it ensures that an injunction is not entered on account of irreparable harm caused by otherwise lawful competition."[1080]

On the other hand, the requirement complicates the preliminary injunction proceedings a lot, due to the challenge to obtain evidence. In some situations it may simply prove to be too difficult for a plaintiff to obtain preliminary injunctive relief, as a result of insufficient evidence (either in quantitative or qualitative terms) that is required in order to substantiate the nexus. The case of *Rudolph Technologies v Camtek*[1081] is an example: the court cited *Apple I, II* and *III* cases and pointed to

---

authors point out that a problem in establishing this value is that "it is not clear that the parties have either the ability or the incentive to introduce evidence that *other* patented components contribute to a product's success. Certainly, we rarely see such evidence introduced in actual cases. The patentee will not introduce such evidence because it would only reduce the royalty rate. The accused infringer often will not introduce it because that firm does not want to admit that it might be infringing other patented inventions. Even if the accused infringer tries to do so, courts do not want to admit such evidence because it will require collateral litigation (..)."

1076 D.H. BREAN, 'Will the "Nexus" requirement of Apple v. Samsung preclude the injunctive relief in the majority of patent cases? Echoes of the Entire Market Value Rule' *San Diego Law Review* 51 (2014), pp. 153–207. See: p. 168.

1077 Ibidem.

1078 Idem, at p. 169.

1079 Idem, at p. 169. The author cites two Federal Circuit cases as examples of this practice: Federal Circuit, *Lucent v Gateway*, 2009, 580 F.3d 1301, 1336 and Federal Circuit, *LaserDynamics Inc. v Quanta Computers*, 2012, 694 F.3d 51, 56–57.

1080 Federal Circuit, *Apple Inc. v Samsung Electronics Co, (Apple III)*, November 18th 2013, 735 F.3D 1352, at 1361.

1081 United States District Court for the District of Minnesota, *Rudolph Technologies, Inc. v. Camtek, Ltd.*, August 26th 2015, LEXIS 113007.

the differences between Rudolph's machinery and Camtek's competing product (named 'Eagle') and subsequently held that the plaintiff did not satisfy the causal nexus requirement:

> "In Apple III, the Federal Circuit remanded the nexus question to the district court for **consideration of survey evidence** that showed that customers were willing to pay a premium price for a product that included certain utility patents. (..) **Here however, no such evidence exists, the only source of evidence is Rudolph's own expert.** Moreover, the products at issue are highly complex machines performing an incredibly technical task of extreme precision. As evidenced by the Eagle's operational manual and promotional materials, **these systems have numerous features permitting inspection of increasingly smaller components. Because of this complexity, the causal nexus requirement is not easily satisfied.** ("[T]he causal nexus requirement applies regardless of the complexity of the products. It just may be more easily satisfied (indeed, perhaps even conceded) for relatively 'simple' products.")."[1082]

In the same line of argument, rejecting the causal nexus requirement in *Rudolph* but also showing the complicated nature of such an analysis, the court in *Rudolph* also noted that *a price difference* can also drive consumer demand; instead of going for the main feature of Rudolph's machine, it may be price that plays a significant role in a consumer's purchasing decision and this thus may go against the causal nexus that Rudolph attempted to make.[1083]

A final issue to be considered under the prong of *irreparable harm* is when the plaintiff has waited too long in filing the request for a preliminary injunction. As has been seen in other jurisdictions, *urgency* is a factor to be taken along in considering a request for a preliminary injunction, even when it not (as in the US) explicitly spelled out in the legal test. However, also in the US, it is a factor to be considered, since it can take away the extraordinary nature of a preliminary injunction[1084] and it can impact the notion of irreparable harm.[1085] The research of the authors Webster

---

1082 Idem, at 39. Emphasis added.

1083 Idem, at 40. "Also cutting against Rudolph's causal nexus arguments is the sizable *price difference* of the Eagle and Rudolph systems. (..) While price always influences purchasing decisions, the sizeable disparity here suggests *price difference would play a significant role* in the purchase decision." Emphasis added.

1084 B.E. WEBSTER, S. WALMLEY, 'Unclean hands and preliminary injunctions: the effects of delay in bringing patent infringement cases' *Journal of the Patent and Trademark Office Society* (2002), pp. 291–309. At p. 297, they cite: Federal Circuit, United States Court of Appeals, *Polymer Techs. v. Bridwell and Westmark,* 1996, F.3d 970, LEXIS 33384.

1085 B.E. WEBSTER, S. WALMLEY, 'Unclean hands and preliminary injunctions: the effects of delay in bringing patent infringement cases' *Journal of the Patent and Trademark Office Society* (2002), pp. 291–309. See: p. 297, thereby citing the case of Federal Circuit, *High Tech Medical Instrumentation Inc. v. New Image Industries,* 1995, F.3d 1551, LEXIS 4290.

and Walmley has shown[1086] that US courts have regularly struck down a request for a preliminary injunction due to delay,[1087] although court practices vary widely of what is seen as *culpable* delay.[1088] [1089] It therefore is wise for a plaintiff to move as quickly as possible, even though courts, as the authors show, do take into account the circumstances behind the delay as well as the length of time of this.[1090] [1091] Webster and Walmley conclude on this:

> "**Specifically, the courts have excused delays** in the following circumstances: (1) where the parties were attempting to negotiate a settlement, (2) where the defendant has misled the patent holder to believe that it would cease the infringing conduct (fraud by the defendant), (3) when the patent holder could not obtain actual evidence of infringement, (4) examination proceedings at the Patent and Trademark Office, and (5) council's awareness of court calendar congestion. **These circumstances illustrate that the courts tend to excuse delay when the patent holder is actively**

As is apparent, this case stated at 1557: "Finally, as the district court found, HTMI delayed bringing this action for almost 17 months after the issuance of the re-examination certificate for the '001 patent. This court has recognized that delay in seeking a remedy is an important factor bearing on the need for a preliminary injunction. (..) absent a good explanation, not offered or found here, 17 months is a substantial period of delay that militates against the issuance of a preliminary injunction by demonstrating that there is no apparent urgency to the request for injunctive relief. While the period of delay may not have been enough, standing alone, to demonstrate the absence of irreparable harm, it did not stand alone in this case. (..)."

1086 B.E. WEBSTER, S. WALMLEY, 'Unclean hands and preliminary injunctions: the effects of delay in bringing patent infringement cases' *Journal of the Patent and Trademark Office Society* (2002), pp. 291–309- See: pp. 297–298.

1087 Idem, at p. 298 and at p. 303. Furthermore, see the extensive survey of cases that is undertaken by the authors, at pp. 305–309.

1088 Ibidem.

1089 Similarly, but not restricted to patent cases, is the conclusion of K. STOLL-DE BELL, N.L. DEMPSEY, B.E. DEMPSEY, *Injunctive relief; Temporary Restraining Orders and Preliminary Injunctions* (2009 American Bar Association). See: pp. 176–180. The authors state that in general one month delay should be not seen as unreasonable and courts have recognised the need for a plaintiff to prepare a request.

1090 B.E. WEBSTER, S. WALMLEY, 'Unclean hands and preliminary injunctions: the effects of delay in bringing patent infringement cases' *Journal of the Patent and Trademark Office Society* (2002), pp. 291–309. See: pp. 305–309.

1091 Thus, as shown in *Open Text v Box*, a dispute on various software patents, the defendant invoked delay. The court examined the facts of the case and agreed that the plaintiff had failed to move on time. This weighed against the plaintiff's argument that it would suffer irreparable harm if a preliminary injunction was denied. US District Court for the Northern District of California, *Open Text v Box*, April 9th, 2014, 36 F.Supp.3d 885, at 909.

protecting his right to exclude others or when she is unaware (either by lack of knowledge or fraud perpetrated by the defendant) of defendant's infringement.
Alternatively, the courts have not excused delays in the following circumstances: (1) where the movant put forth no evidence to justify delay, (2) movant should have known of infringement and took no action, (3) the movant's financial problems and litigation burden, (4) speculative expert testimony, and (5) licensing practices of plaintiff. (...)
In general, it can be concluded that a patent holder has to vigilant in identifying potential infringers and in preparing to file suit with a motion for a preliminary injunction at the first sign of infringing activity. Simply put, the cases indicate that courts favour proactive plaintiffs that do not sit on their rights."[1092]

§7.4.5. Balance of convenience

Under the balance of convenience prong, the preliminary injunction court is entitled to look at interests mitigating the decision to grant or deny the preliminary relief. A similar exercise is done under the public interest test. The Federal Circuit has stressed that these two factors are of less importance than the likelihood of harms and the notion of irreparable harm.[1093] However, unlike other jurisdictions that we have looked at, these prongs are *not only prescribed* by the legal test, but *in principle also explicitly considered* as well by the court, when deciding on a preliminary injunction.

As Resis writes, the plaintiff's hardships are usually extracted from the prong of irreparable harm, after which the countervailing harms of the other party (the defendant) are compared to.[1094] Most notably, these harms for the defendant are for instance that a preliminary injunction will put a company out of business or that a preliminary injunction may upset relationships with important clients.[1095] Importantly, as Resis writes, in such a case a preliminary injunction court will stress the relationship between a substantial hardship for the defendant and a corresponding non-speculative benefit to the plaintiff.[1096] Thus in the case of *OpenText v Box*,

---

1092 B.E. WEBSTER, S. WALMLEY, 'Unclean hands and preliminary injunctions: the effects of delay in bringing patent infringement cases' *Journal of the Patent and Trademark Office Society* (2002), pp. 291–309. See: p. 303. Internal references omitted and emphasis added.

1093 Federal Circuit, *Qingdao Taifa Group v United States*, September 28th 2009, 581 F.3D 1375. Here it was held: "The third and fourth factors, *while less consequential than the first two* (..)". Emphasis added.

1094 R.H. RESIS, *Preliminary relief in patent infringement disputes* (2011 American Bar Association Publishing). See: p. 28.

1095 Idem, at p. 29.

1096 Ibidem. This was for instance, as Resis writes, held to be the case in United States District Court of the Southern District of New York, *Novo Nordisk A/S v Pfizer*, December 16th 2006, LEXIS 90387, where it was held that Pfizer had already invested a lot in the product and this would be an investment that otherwise would

the court concluded: "Open Text's showing of loss of market share is speculative, whereas an injunction would exclude Box from selling in the market where a majority of its revenue is derived."[1097]

Equally, this would also mean that the balance would normally favour the defendant if this puts him out of business when enjoined and when the plaintiff would survive the rejection of the request of the preliminary injunction.[1098]

§7.4.6. *Public interest*

At the public interest prong, a court can consider the consequences of a preliminary injunction that *stretch beyond the consequences for the litigating parties.* This makes sense, because lawsuits are indeed, as Stein writes, "no bipolar affairs that affect only two private parties".[1099] This way, a preliminary injunction court can attempt to minimise irreparable injury for the wider society.[1100] Another reason to do so is a matter of *fairness*: it could be considered as unfair if these wider harms were not taken along.[1101]

The public interest in favour or against a preliminary injunction can be formulated and framed in *general terms*, or they can be more *articulated* harms, directly referring to specific public interest harms of non-parties.[1102] Regardless of how they

---

be frozen pending trial proceedings. This was balanced with Novo's hardships; this firm had not yet entered the US market, and accordingly would thus not lose revenue if it later became clear that Pfizer had indeed infringed the patent. Equally, Resis cites the case of the United States District Court of the Southern District of Texas, *Ascend Geo v OyoGeospaceCorp*, November 4th 2009, LEXIS 104129, where it was held that if the defendant was enjoined, other parties in the same market were also likely to make sales benefitting from the absence of the defendant, thus this would not result into a non-speculative benefit that would be strong enough to offset the negative consequences for the defendant.

1097 US District Court for the Northern District of California, *Open Text v Box*, April 9th, 2014, 36 F.Supp.3d 885, at 911.

1098 D.W. MARTENS, J.B. SGANGA Jr., *Pre-litigation patent enforcement* (2013–2014). See: p. 580.

1099 L.W. STEIN, 'The Court and the Community: why non-party interests should count in preliminary injunction actions' *The Review of Litigation* 16 (1997), pp. 27–63 See: p. 63.

1100 Idem, at pp. 48–49. Here, at p. 32, Stein states that "Preliminary injunction proceedings are fraught with the risk of error' and that therefore non-party harms should be taken along: 'There is great appeal to giving weight to non-party interests in preliminary injunction proceedings."

1101 Idem, at p. 49. In more general terms, see S.A. ALLEN, 'Justifying 'the public interest' in patent litigation' *Indiana Law Journal* 88, No. 3 (2013), pp. 1047–1088.

1102 R.H. RESIS, *Preliminary relief in patent infringement disputes* (2011 American Bar Association Publishing). See: p. 29. In American practice, non-party harms can and are taken along under the public interest prong and it is then considered whether the grant or denial will harm these. But note that Stein points out that amongst

are framed, these harms can be diverse of nature, but mostly courts consider public interest arguments relating to 1) the value of patents for society and the role of litigation; 2) health-related arguments; and 3) safety-related arguments. All these can have a bearing on the decision whether or not to grant a preliminary injunction. The American preliminary injunction test is unique in specifically prescribing that such a public interest investigation should be carried out and courts indeed regularly look into this issue. That being said, the fact that there is a separate prong for public interests however, does not mean that public interests are indeed guaranteed to be clearly addressed in practice and this fourth factor of the preliminary injunction test is not embraced as useful by everyone.[1103]

As stated, a classic public interest in favour of granting a preliminary injunction, is the valuable role patents are perceived to have in society.[1104] This was also for instance reiterated in the *Celsis* case,[1105] in which the established and in this context much cited cases of *Sanofi-Synthelabo v Apotex*[1106] and *Abbot v Sandoz*[1107] were mentioned, in which the importance to of patents in society was underlined:

> "**The public interest favours the enforcement of Celsis' patent rights here**. See *Sanofi-Synthelabo v. Apotex, Inc.*, ("We have long acknowledged the importance of the patent system in encouraging innovation."). **Such investment in drug research and development must be encouraged and protected by the exclusionary rights conveyed in valid patents.** *See Abbott Labs. v. Sandoz, Inc.* That incentive would be

some commentators there is debate whether from a doctrinal perspective, there should be limits on the range of non-party harms that the court should consider when looking at a preliminary injunction. L.W. STEIN, 'The Court and the Community: why non-party interests should count in preliminary injunction actions' *The Review of Litigation* 16 (1997), pp. 27–63. See: pp. 30–31.

1103 See for example: O.H. LEWIS, 'The wild card that is the public interest: putting a new face on the fourth preliminary injunction factor' *Texas Law Review* (1994), pp. 849–892. Lewis has equated the practical significance of the public interest prong in the United States to what in game of cards is known as a 'wildcard'; an unknown entity that can be played as anything the wielder desires and, due to the fact that the public interest factor is not judicially limited, in practice it is often near meaningless. He argues, at p. 853, that in practice there is little scope for independent factors of *extrinsic* policy that have not yet been addressed before. Lewis therefore, at the conclusion of his work, proposes that the test for a preliminary injunction in the US should be modified with the public interest prong removed (at p. 891) and that instead the balance of hardships should focus, *when relevant*, on particularised non-party harms.

1104 D.W. MARTENS, J.B. SGANGA Jr., *Pre-litigation patent enforcement* (2013–2014). See: p. 581.

1105 Federal Circuit, *Celsis in Vitro v Cellzdirect*, January 9th 2012, 664 F.3d 922, at heading VI.

1106 Federal Circuit, *Sanofi-Synthelabo v Apotex*, December 8th 2006, F.3d 1368.

1107 Federal Circuit, *Abbott Laboratories v Sandoz*, October 21st 2008, 544 F. 3d. 1341, LEXIS 21880, at 1362.

> adversely affected by taking market benefits away from the patentee and giving them to the accused infringer in this case."[1108]

On the other hand, this does not mean that a public interest in strong patent protection always trumps other interests: sometimes it is exactly *the value of competition* that is invoked at this prong, arguing *against* the grant of a preliminary injunction. Then it is the prevention of monopolistic practices that serves the public interest best.[1109]

Apart from the perceived role that patents should have in society, another much cited public interest is that of *health* concerns. As Rachlin points out,[1110] this was for instance the case in *Edwards Lifesciences AG v CoreValve Inc & Medtronic.*[1111] It is submitted that this case is a good example of that a first instance preliminary injunction court can look at the issue of public interest in rather great detail, if it wishes. An extensive analysis of this prong is thus not something that only happens in practice on appeal. In *Edwards Lifesciences*, the District Court assessed the public interest issue extensively and looked at whether the defendant's infringing product – the patented invention was on artificial heart valves – was better suited to deal with certain types of patients than the patentee's invention. It was held by the court that the submitted expert testimony suggested that with respect to patients with small vessel sizes this might not be the case, however with respect to patients with large annulus sizes, the defendant's product seemed to perform better than the patentee's.[1112] Overall the court held that the defendant's product might be a *safer product.*[1113] However, medical experts that testified in this case, warned the court of interfering too much with medical practice, something that was not in the public interest:

1108 Federal Circuit, *Celsis in Vitro v Cellzdirect,* January 9th 2012, 664 F.3d 922, at heading VI at the consideration of the public interest.

1109 This was for instance decided under the public interest prong in United States District Court for the District of Minnesota, *Rudolph Technologies, Inc. v. Camtek, Ltd.*, August 26th 2015, LEXIS 113007.

1110 M. RACHLIN, 'Developments in injunctive relief in health care patent cases' *Intellectual Property Litigation Committee Articles* (Published on October 16th 2014). Available at the website of the American Bar Association at: http://apps.americanbar.org/litigation/committees/intellectual/articles/fall2014-0914-recent-developmentss-in-injunctive-relief.html (last accessed on 24 April 2017).

1111 United States District Court of Delaware, *Edwards LifeSciences v CoreValve and Medtronic*, April 15th 2014, LEXIS 51778.

1112 Idem, at 39. And at 27–31.

1113 Idem, at 39. "The expert testimony suggests that patients with large annulus sizes must be allowed ongoing access to the CoreValve Generation 3. The testimony also indicates that the CoreValve Generation 3 may be to some degree the safer, better option for most patients. (..)"

> "As <one expert> passionately emphasized, "these valves are not interchangeable" and some room must be made for doctors **to choose from both devices** in determining which one is most suitable for each patient. (Explaining regarding the possibility of banning the CoreValve Generation 3 that "**I think by eliminating the physician, and tying their arm behind their back in deliverance of care, I think that is a huge mistake for the patient population out there that is being treated.**")"[1114]

The court acknowledged the latter[1115] and concluded that overall the public interest was likely to be best served by at least *permitting a certain number* of the infringing products on the market. But was the above enough to prevent the grant of a preliminary injunction enjoining the defendant? No, because the court also held *that strong enforcement of patents rights was of vital importance in the public interest* and this was even more so because it held that the defendant had wilfully infringed the patent ('egregious conduct') and denying a preliminary injunction could be interpreted as a reward for this behaviour, possibly inducing others to infringe as well.[1116] Therefore, again acting in the public interest it saw best, the court *granted but tailored* the preliminary injunction; the enjoined defendant was allowed to sell a restricted number of the infringing products to those patients that could not be helped by the patentee's products.[1117] Although the preliminary injunction was granted, a month later the parties reached a global settlement on the issue with Edwards reportedly receiving compensation.[1118] [1119]

1114 Idem, at 39. Internal references omitted.

1115 Idem, at 40.

1116 Idem, at 41.

1117 Ibidem. The preliminary injunction order, at number 4, stated that the parties should immediately enter into discussions to jointly determine a mechanism by which a sufficient number of the defendant's products could be provided to hospitals and clinics already using this. It is submitted, that although the court did not explicitly state this, it is likely that such a mechanism would also include an agreement on financial compensation for the patentee for each device that would be provided by the defendant.

1118 As Rachlin writes on p. 3, this case was not exactly written on a blank slate. M. RACHLIN, 'Developments in injunctive relief in health care patent cases' *Intellectual Property Litigation Committee Articles* (Published on October 16th 2014). Available at the website of the American Bar Association at: http://apps.americanbar.org/litigation/committees/intellectual/articles/fall2014–0914-recent-developmentss-in-injunctive-relief.html (last accessed on 24 April 2017). For more on this, see: L. WYATT, 'Rebuttable presumption of public interest in protecting the public health – the necessity for denying injunctive relief in medically related patent infringement cases after eBay v Mercexchange' *Chicago-Kent Journal of Intellectual Property* 13 (2013), pp. 298–326.

1119 See the comments of Rachlin on pp. 3–4. M. RACHLIN, 'Developments in injunctive relief in health care patent cases' *Intellectual Property Litigation Committee Articles* (Published on October 16th 2014). Available at the website of the American

An example of a *public safety* argument, another regularly invoked public interest ground, is to be found in the *Nest Labs* case.[1120] Here, the contested patent was part of an electronic home alarm system that detects hazardous gasses and – crucially – which could communicate wirelessly to and with other alarms. The court – who's opinion was drafted by Richard Posner – already questioned the irreparable harm that the plaintiff alleged and it was also not certain of the likelihood that the plaintiff would win the case at trial. However, what was perceived to be decisive in the end was the public interest. The court refused to enjoin the defendant Nest Labs from selling its detection alarms because doing so would deprive the public of a product that was aimed at enhancing the public safety. This would be hard to justify in the public interest and therefore the court denied the preliminary injunction to the plaintiff. Judge Posner argued as follows on the fourth prong:

> "In these circumstances, to enjoin Nest from selling its product, thus depriving the consuming public of a premium product, particularly one directed toward ensuring public safety, without as yet evidence of infringement of a valid patent, would be unconscionable. (..)"[1121] [1122]

Finally, it should be noted that when a patent covers a not particularly crucial application and an injunction would have limited effects to the public, the public interest consideration has been held to be of little relevance.[1123]

§7.4.7. *Bond and damages*

Under the Federal Rules of Civil Procedure, Rule 65 (c), a granted preliminary injunction is subject to the condition that the plaintiff provides sufficient financial security to pay costs and compensation to the enjoined party, in the case that the grant of the preliminary injunction proves to be erroneously made.[1124] In practice, this security is

---

Bar Association at: http://apps.americanbar.org/litigation/committees/intellectual/articles/fall2014-0914-recent-developmentss-in-injunctive-relief.html (last accessed on 24 April 2017).

1120 United States District Court for the Northern District of Illinois, Eastern Division, *BRK Brands, Inc and Gary J. Morris v Nest Labs Inc.*, March 19th, 2014, LEXIS 41375.

1121 Idem, at footnote 13–14 of the ruling.

1122 However, for a case where a safety argument was raised, but this not held as being pressing enough to swing the pendulum the other way, see United District Court for the District of New Jersey, *Power Survey, LLC v Premier Utility Services, LLC et al.*, November 21st 2014, LEXIS 163288.

1123 Federal Circuit, *Trebro Manufacturing v Firefly Equipment et al*, April 9th 2014, No. 2013–1437. It was held at heading VII: "Finally, as to the public interest, there is scant evidence on this record showing that an injunction would harm the public. The patent deals with sod harvesting and covers a small market that may not have a broadreaching effect."

1124 Rule 65 (c): "The court may issue a preliminary injunction or a temporary restraining order only if the movant gives security in an amount that the court considers

given by the plaintiff in the form of a *bond*. Whilst the Federal Rule seems to consist of an absolute obligation, in practice the actual need and the amount of the bond is solely up to the court at which preliminary injunction proceedings are held, that thereby bases itself on the facts of the case. It is established case law that the court has full discretion to set the height of a bond at a level that it deems to be fit.[1125]

An important, and it is submitted rather critical difference with other countries as Germany and The Netherlands, is that the set bond *caps the damages that are available to the wrongly enjoined defendant*, thereby (unless a very high bond is requested) potentially limiting the liability of the plaintiff and greatly aggravating the consequences of an erroneously granted preliminary injunction.[1126] [1127]

§7.4.8. Intermediate conclusion

As we have seen, the American preliminary injunction test differs from its European counterparts in a few important aspects: It is clear that from the combined rulings of *Bosch*, *Winter*, *eBay* and the *Apple* cases, it is the issue of 'irreparable harm' that in practice arguably is the most important hurdle to be cleared by the plaintiff, in order to obtain a preliminary injunction. It is also evident that this is not only a rhetorical exercise, it is not always an easy aspect to prove for the plaintiff and from that point of view it can be seen as an extra barrier to overcome in comparison with for instance Germany and The Netherlands, where this is not an explicit issue to be proven by the plaintiff. The issue of the 'causal nexus' has, in the author's view, complicated this issue even further.

On the other hand, whilst the likelihood to prevail on the merits (the first prong) should be demonstrated (and this includes the issues of likely patent infringement and likely patent validity) there is not a *de facto* requirement that a patent should

---

proper to pay the costs and damages sustained by any party found to have been wrongfully enjoined or restrained. The United States, its officers, and its agencies are not required to give security."

1125 This large discretion of the court is clearly stated in *inter alia* the following cases: Federal Circuit, United States, Court of Appeal, *Sanofi-Synthelabo v Apotex,* December 8th 2006, F.3d 1368, at 1385. Federal Circuit, United States Court of Appeal, *Celsis in Vitro v Cellzdirect,* January 9th 2012, F.3d 922, at 931. The case of Federal Circuit, *Doctor's Associates Inc. v Distajo,* February 24th 1997, F.3d 126. at 36 serves as an example that a bond may not be necessary at all, although this was not a patent case.

1126 O. GROSSKOPF, B. MEDINA, 'Remedies for Wrongfully-Issued Preliminary Injunctions: The Case for the Disgorgement of Profits' *Seattle University Law Review* 32 (2009), pp. 903–941. See: p. 925, footnote 25.

1127 P. MAROTTA, 'The injunction bond in high technology litigation: the need for reform' *Santa Clara High Technology Law Journal* 4, No. 1 (1988), pp. 19–47. At p. 47 it is noted that: "Since an entire company can potentially be destroyed by an injunction, a rule which limits the recovery for a wrongfully enjoined party to the amount of a bond, is archaic."

have survived prior opposition or invalidity proceedings, as is the case in Germany. This is a hurdle less for the plaintiff to be taken. The balance of convenience and public interest factors are rather valuable in the United States in the sense that, unlike sometimes in other jurisdictions, these are not only prescribed but in practice mostly also explicitly considered by the court in its decisionmaking process. Finally, it should be noted that although a bond is usually requested by the preliminary injunction court from the plaintiff, it is a worrying observation that under American doctrine the height of the bond essentially caps the damages that a wrongfully-enjoined defendant can obtain from the plaintiff, in the case an erroneously granted preliminary injunction is taken.

§7.5. Concluding discussion, thereby relating to earlier findings

Despite different origins and different legal systems, it is clear that both the function and necessity of preliminary injunctive relief, as well as the risks that preliminary injunctions can entail, have been recognised in the four covered jurisdictions. Having now looked at The Netherlands, Germany, England and the United States, certain patterns have become rather clear and it is interesting to see how these findings connect to the findings of preceding chapters.

§7.5.1. Key commonalities

Key elements that the abovementioned jurisdictions have *in common* are:

- The preliminary injunction courts that have been covered are all vested with a relatively large amount of discretion compared to what a judge at the trial on the merits has. This discretion is for instance clear in dealing with the question of patent validity, in assessing irreparable harm and in the setting of a bond.
- The courts in the covered jurisdictions have (accommodated themselves) an *opportunity* to balance interests. This is also the cases within civil law countries where equity does not form the basis of preliminary injunctive relief;
- The same applies with respect to *urgency* and delay in bringing an preliminary injunction application. In the four covered jurisdictions this is a factor that can be incorporated at some part of the test governing the grant of the remedy.
- The preliminary injunction courts in the four covered jurisdictions allow themselves to look at the merits of a case. This is, to a certain degree, also the case in England, despite the judgment of *American Cyanamid* of which the wording was sometimes interpreted as preventing this.
- Preliminary injunctions preventing *imminent* infringement are in general possible and a preliminary injunction can also be granted with respect to a previously invalidated patent, when it is likely that this invalidation may be corrected at a later instance.

§7.5.2. *Key differences*

However, from the national legal practices covered in this chapter, a number of key *differences* have also become clear:

- In Germany and The Netherlands, the emphasis of the court in practice is on the plaintiff's likelihood of success at trial: the issues of infringement and patent validity therefore play a significant role. In England and the United States it are however the issues of the irreparability of harm and the balance of convenience that are the more prominent features in actual practice.
- Courts differ in the way they deal with the issue of patent validity when deciding to grant a preliminary injunction: this can range from a strict approach which in principle requires that a patent has to have survived a prior opposition or invalidity proceeding (as is held by some German courts, i.e. Düsseldorf), or a policy that requires the defendant-infringer to 'clear the way' in advance (as in England with respect to pharmaceutical generic entry). Furthermore, there is a doctrinally more neutral approach that has less strong patent validity presumptions in favour or against a preliminary injunction, as is the case in practice in The Netherlands and in The United States.
- National courts seem to differ in how actively they indeed balance hardships and look at the public interest in practice, let alone be influenced by them. Where this is for instance relatively uncommon in The Netherlands, it is more common and routine in the United States, England and to a limited extent Germany.
- There are different practices between courts when it comes to demanding a form of security; whilst in some countries a bond is required before a preliminary injunction is granted or can become effective, courts in other jurisdictions only seldom ask for a bond. A cross-undertaking is yet another alternative that can be chosen for.

§7.5.3. *How do national practices tie in with preceding chapters?*

Having given these commonalities and differences between the jurisdictions, how do these observations connect to what has been learned in earlier chapters of this work?

Before,[1128] it has been demonstrated that there are strong economic justifications to grant preliminary injunctions. Amongst others, these are most notably that the remedy can be a very effective manner to prevent irreparable harm from occurring and to prevent delay in providing relief, otherwise rendering patent rights meaningless. Also, it was pointed out that the remedy can have positive

1128 See Chapter 2 of this work.

effects on innovation and on investment.[1129] Equally,[1130] it has been demonstrated that there are (potential) economic risks attached to issuing preliminary injunctions for alleged patent infringement too soon and too easily. It has been shown that the remedy can potentially lead to hold-up problems and can be used to put companies under financial pressure. Most serious was the observation that there is a significant risk that preliminary injunctions can be issued wrongly and that the preliminary injunctions proceedings often form the final stage of litigation in practice. In the latter case, a proper examination of the facts at a trial on the merits is then not held. Finally, it has also been written that relying on bonds or cross-damages is not an ideal solution. This notion too is something that should be considered by the court, as a warning signal to maybe not grant a preliminary injunction too easy.

The findings above show why the preliminary injunction court can feel stuck between a rock and a hard place. A preliminary injunction may be the only real effective remedy in a given situation, but the potential economic costs attached to the grant can (turn out to) be significant. The cloud of uncertainty which surrounds a case complicates the work of the court even more.[1131] The preceding pages in this chapter nevertheless show that in the four countries covered, the courts are prepared to grant preliminary injunction when this seems warranted and at the same time are focussed on preventing erroneous decisions or granting 'flimsy' applications. As is clear from the language of the courts given in the citations provided in this chapter, it seems that the court is often aware of the tricky position it is in. The legal and economic advantages and risks of preliminary injunctions are also regularly acknowledged by courts and legislators. Sometimes these are explicitly addressed in individual judgements but also in and via the way the national legal standards are formulated and have developed, as well as the checks and balances that are in place in the national legal tests.

Earlier as well,[1132] an account has been given on how various Law & Economics theories deal with preliminary injunctions. It has been demonstrated that theoretical approaches differ on core elements such as of the role of the court, the influence of the merits of the case and the notion of irreparable harm. It was also deducted

1129 Regarding investment, also recall the findings of chapter 4 of this work, which show that preliminary injunctions are granted relatively frequently in the pharmaceutical industry, in order to protect originator companies. This way, originator pharamceutical companies can finance their innovative activites, by offering protection to those patented inventions that are highly profitable. With these profits, orginator companies also finance those R&D investments that have been made, but that have not resulted into further development or an actual product.

1130 See Chapter 3 of this work.

1131 See Chapter 1, paragraph 3 of this work.

1132 See Chapter 5 of this work.

from the majority of the teachings of these theoretical approaches, that it is vital that the legal system ensures – at an *absolute minimum* – that:

- The judge is central to decisionmaking and has discretion to grant or deny a preliminary injunction.
- The judge is key, in order to balance interests of litigating parties and third parties, and filter for abusive practices.
- The merits of a case should play a role in this decisionmaking process.

It is safe to say that the national legal frameworks and legal practices of The Netherlands, Germany, England and the United States result in meeting the minimum principles set above. That said, differences amongst national legal frameworks and practices exist, reflecting the different approaches existing in the Law and Economics theories.

§7.5.4. Improving the court's information position

Preliminary injunction courts in different countries have thus found ways to cope with a request for preliminary injunctive relief. However, it is submitted that the courts could potentially do more. Courts should therefore – where possible and only if necessary – attempt to maximise their information position in order to gain a better perspective on whether or not to grant the requested preliminary injunctive relief. In other words, courts should be able to obtain more (independent) technical expertise (to help with patent validity and infringement issues) and economic and business expertise (to help understand the adequacy of damages and the irreparability of harm) when *they think it would be beneficial in a specific case to do so.* This may be because the preliminary injunction court is uncomfortable about certain issues that it faces or because the stakes of a specific case are very high. Such an approach can contribute to lifting the cloud of uncertainty somewhat, which ultimately may result in less erroneously granted decisions. This suggestion is by no means meant as criticism of the current work done by the courts – which are facing a difficult job. Instead, it is a recognition of the observation that the degree of information on which the preliminary injunction court bases its decision is often suboptimal.

As the information position of the court is so dependent on the specific circumstances of the case, it is difficult to make comments of a general nature on when this should be undertaken, other than that the preliminary injunction court itself is in the *best position* to know when more information would be required in order to make a well, or better-informed decision. It is therefore submitted that the preliminary injunction court should therefore self-assess its further need for more information. It is proposed that if the court should decide that the uncertainty in a specific case is very high, it should be able to take measures to reduce the uncertainty to more acceptable levels.

One of these measures could be that the court can delay its decision on whether to grant interim relief somewhat and invite *amici curiae* to submit briefs.[1133] In the majority of patent cases it is submitted that a little extra time for this would not make a significant difference,[1134] whilst it could improve the information position of the court and the quality of decisionmaking considerably. This invitation will mean that the court will take a more active role in affairs. The preliminary injunction court should hereby attempt to improve and expand its information position instead of mainly relying on the information and arguments provided by the parties.

As always, there are caveats to be made: firstly, it is submitted that the above should not result in preliminary injunction proceedings becoming more like a fully-fledged trial. In other words, the preliminary injunction should not be robbed of its function to prevent swift and temporary relief until a trial on the merits takes place, as this is precisely the reason for the remedy's existence. This means that inviting *amici curiae* to present briefs should thus only be done should the court feel it is both *necessary* as well as *beneficial.* Secondly, the above should be limited to those situations when there is adequate manoeuvring room, i.e. when there is sufficient time for it. Whilst obtaining more information can contribute to better

---

1133 The 'information theory' is one of the main reasons behind *amici curiae* briefs. Chien has written an interesting article on briefs regarding patents matters in the US – mainly Federal Circuit and Supreme Court, not specifically preliminary injunctions cases. She writes on the information function of these briefs as follows: "Under the "information" theory, briefs are useful for bringing to the courts' attention legal arguments or factual information not already on the record. Some of the most successful briefs, for example, have detailed the implications of a ruling for a particular constituency. (..) Former Supreme Court clerks have stated that "amicus briefs were most helpful in cases involving highly technical and specialized areas of law. Patent law would seem to fit this description, although the patent bar is well-funded and the parties tend to be sophisticated." (..) Patent amici can also provide novel arguments or facts that the parties may not have thought of or are not in a position to make.' However, she also warns that not all briefs are as neutral as they may seem: "Still, briefs that add "new information" can be a hindrance to the courts. In attempting to influence the courts, amici, who are generally presumed to be more neutral than the parties themselves as to the specific outcome of a case, may nonetheless present information in a biased way or exaggerate the impact of a potential ruling." C.V. CHIEN, 'Patent amicus briefs: what the court's friends can teach us about the patent system' *UC Irvine Law Review* 1, No. 2 (2011), pp. 397–433. See: pp. 405–407. Note that these briefs do not have to be restricted to legal arguments alone. So-called *Brandeis briefs* are an example of a special form of briefs which are used in US litigation (though often at an appellate level) and these focus less on providing legal arguments, but more on presenting scientific and economic data and policy arguments to the court.

1134 One should bear in mind that a delay of a couple of weeks for instance would often be much faster than the start, trial and verdict of a proceedings on the merits in most cases could take place.

judicial decisionmaking, it is submitted that the decisionmaking should not be too much delayed because of it. It is therefore of no help in cases where highly urgent preliminary relief is needed. Lastly, it is unrealistic to expect that all uncertainties connected to the question whether or not to grant a preliminary injunction will be resolved by gaining more information. Certain uncertainties can only be resolved over time for instance, or will become only clear after an actual decision is taken.

As has been demonstrated in this chapter, there is not one universal preliminary injunction test, and key elements differ between countries. We will now look at how these elements are likely to play out under the upcoming UPC.

Part III: A Look into the Future

Chapter 8: Preliminary Injunctions under the Unified Patent Court; What is known and to be Expected

§8.1. Introduction

After the entry into force has been delayed multiple times, the Unified Patent Court is now poised to commence its operations in early 2018.[1135] Despite a slow ratification process and the uncertainty that the 'Brexit' has on the coming-to-life of the UPC, the project that has been on the drawing board for so long finally seems to become reality. With respect to the consequences of the 'Brexit', there seem to be no legal obstacles for the United Kingdom to be on-board[1136] and even if the United Kingdom decides to stay at the sidelines at first, the project may still commence, albeit in a different constellation.

Although at the time of writing the exact working and the initial popularity of the Unified Patent Court (UPC) amongst litigants taking this route of dispute resolution is still unclear, the preparatory procedure and corresponding academic debate is long underway. Whilst more and more of details have emerged over the years, nevertheless, it should be said that this chapter is sometimes characterised by a certain degree of speculation with respect to the design and future working of the system.

1135 UNIFIED PATENT COURT: "Final Preparatory Committee Signals State of Readiness – 15 March 2017" https://www.unified-patent-court.org/news/final-preparatory-committee-signals-state-readiness-15-march-2017 (Last accessed April 13th 2017).
Note that at the time that this dissertation is being *published*, it has become clear that this date of early 2018 has not been met and that for the next step of the project the outcome of a legal challenge pending before the German Constitutional Court is awaited, even though organizational and technical preparations and the ratification process have continued.

1136 On this, see the article of Ohly and Streinz, in which it is argued that the UK can remain a member to the UPC also after it has formally left the EU. The authors write that after ratifcation of the UPC Agreement, there will be no need for additional treaties to be drafted between the EU and the UK once the Brexit has taken place, in order for the latter to remain subject to CJEU jurisdiction concerning UPC matters. They also point out that the current UPC Agreement should then only be amended in a very limited manner. A. OHLY, R. STREINZ, 'Can the UK stay in the UPC system after Brexit?' *GRUR Int.* (2017) pp. 1–11.

§8.2. Background

Whilst a partial and limited degree of European harmonisation of patent rights has already been achieved in the early 1970's with respect to the *granting procedure* of patents rights under the flag of the EPO, the actual patent right itself remained a national creature: the EPO grant resulted in a bundle of national patent rights and also the enforcement of these rights remained solely in the hands of national courts. For the last decades, 'Europe' – acting in various constellations, namely under leadership of EPO, the EU and its predecessor in the form of the European Community – has attempted to harmonise patent rights and patent enforcement procedures, because this for has long been seen as a desirable goal. History shows that this has not been an easy process though, and there are quite a few failed attempts to illustrate this: The 1970's Community Patent Convention,[1137] the 1989 Agreement,[1138] the Community Patent Regulation of the early 2000s[1139] and the European Patent Litigation Agreement (EPLA).[1140] As Jaeger notes correctly, the main challenges that the enactment of the system has historically faced and to a certain extent still faces today, are *inter alia* territorial fragmentation between EU Member States and those outside the EU, as well territorial fragmentation between the EU and EPO system.[1141] Therefore there has been legal opposition from

1137 The *Convention for the European Patent for the common market* was signed at Luxembourg in 1975, and Members would be all the European Community Member States. The project never materialised since ratification proved to be an obstacle.

1138 The *1989 Luxembourg Agreement relating to Community patents* was similar to the Convention for the European Patent for the common market from 1975, but again failed to pass the ratification stage with various key countries not ratifying.

1139 The Community Patent Regulation was a proposal to streamline the work of the EPO, especially regarding translation. In short, a patent would be valid in the EPO area if the application was published in one of the three official EPO languages, with translation of the claims in the other two. There would also be a dedicated EU court, in order to decide on validity issues for the whole EU (but not rule on infringement). The project failed, since the translation issue was deemed to be problematic for some Member States.

1140 The attempt to reach a European Patent Litigation Agreement (EPLA), aiming specifically at the issue of enforcement, proposed a central EPO-wide court system that was competent to rule on infringement and revocation issues, both in first instance and in appeal, and the attempt was led by the EPO. Whilst supported by many legal professionals, it eventually did not grow into something viable, particularly because of competence problems between EU Members States and the European Community.

1141 T. JAEGER, 'What's in the unitary patent package?' *Max Planck Institute for Innovation and Competition Research Paper* No. 14–08 (2014). See: pp. 10–11.

various Member States towards the UPC.[1142] Furthermore, there are the tricky issues of keeping the harmonised patent system accessible for users despite changes stemming from costs, languages and decentralisation[1143] and preventing mistrust by the established national courts vis-à-vis a proposed central court, such as the UPC aims to be.[1144] Secondly, Jaeger is more than right in highlighting the effect of EPLA: in spite of the lack of success for EPLA, this attempt was particularly valuable – most certainly from the perspective of this dissertation – as it helped shift the debate within the EU from the focus on the unified patent right as such, to a focus more on the issue of *central enforcement*, thereby, highlighting the importance of the relationship between the EPO and the EU in making progress on this matter.[1145]

This is not the place to venture further into the history of the previous attempts to come to a single European patent and a unified litigation system, as space does not allow to do so and others have done so already in a very fine manner.[1146] Instead

1142 As for instance by Italy and especially Spain that legally challenged the UPC: this hurdle was however cleared in CJEU, C-146/13 & C-147/13, *Kingdom of Spain v European Parliament and Council of the European Union*, May 5th 2015, ECLI:EU:C:2015:298.

1143 T. JAEGER, 'What's in the unitary patent package?'*Max Planck Institute for Innovation and Competition Research Paper* No. 14–08 (2014). See: pp. 10–11.

1144 Idem, at p. 10.

1145 T. JAEGER, 'What's in the unitary patent package?'*Max Planck Institute for Innovation and Competition Research Paper* No. 14–08 (2014). Jaeger points out the difficult relationship that existed between the EPO and the EU: "EPLA showed that the EPO system urgently required a more effective litigation structure to better exploit the economic value and legal potential of EPO patents. That need for reform of the EPO patent litigation system was in principle separate from the discussion on the creation of an EU patent right. So, while the EU might be threatened by EPO plans to improve, the EPO had nothing to gain from an EU patent that did not take into account EPO needs. At the same time, the ineffectiveness of EPO litigation could not be remedied without consent of the EU for reasons of competence. All this meant that, in other words, any plans developed for the EU level would have to also consider improvements for the EPO level. This, in essence, meant that somehow the two systems would have to be joined – at least for the matter of enforcement. Via EPLA therefore, the stalemate over the EU's patent plans had suddenly taken on an entirely new dimension: Any stalemate on the EU level would also translate to a stalemate on the – otherwise excellently functioning – EPO level. This created a new sense of urgency among stakeholders and fostered their readiness for compromise."

1146 See for an excellent historic overview of different attempts to come to a unitary patent in Europe the work of J. PILA, 'An historical perspective I: The unitary patent package' in J. PILA, C. WADLOW (eds). *The Unitary EU Patent System* (2015 Hart Publishing). See: pp. 9–32. Furthermore, also see T. JAEGER, 'What's in the Unitary Patent package?' *Max Planck Institute for Innovation and Competition Research Paper* No. 14–08 (2014). See: esp. at pp. 2–11. Also see the work of

we will in this dissertation continue with the most recent attempt. An attempt which *does* seem to have found the necessary traction to push the issue of fragmentation of rights and the lack of central enforcement forward.

This is the creation of a *European Patent with Unitary Effect*, and the *Unified Patent Court*, leading to not only a single unitary patent right, but also creating the desired system of central enforcement. As with previous attempts, negotiations have been notoriously tricky and arriving at the stage where the proposed system is standing now have not been an easy task. However, this time the will to come to a tangible result seems to prevail. After various political and legal hurdles were taken and partially overwon with respect to compatibility with EU Law of the proposed court, language issues and cost disputes, finally two Regulations have been adopted that form the legal heart of the Unitary patent.[1147] These are Regulation 1257/2012 – which sets up the Unitary Patent and entails the need for a Unitary Patent Court[1148] – and Regulation 1260/2012 – which is on translation arrangements. The Unified Patent Court Agreement itself was signed on February 19th 2013 in Brussels in the form of an intergovernmental treaty[1149] and forms the legal basis as well as the main framework for litigation, together with the implementing Rules of Procedure (ROP) of the UPC.[1150]

Whilst the envisaged system has been heavily criticised for having been built on shakily legal foundations[1151] and essentially can and should be seen as a political

A. ILARDI, *The New European Patent* (2015 Hart Publishing). See: pp. 6–37, on the attempts undertaken in the period 1960–2000 and the period thereafter, up to the introduction of the European Patent with Unitary Effect via the process of enhanced cooperation between Member States.

1147 T. JAEGER, 'What's in the Unitary Patent package?' *Max Planck Institute for Innovation and Competition Research Paper* No. 14–08 (2014). See: p. 6.

1148 See recital 25 of Regulation 1257/2012: "Establishing a Unified Patent Court to hear cases concerning the European patent with unitary effect is essential in order to ensure the proper functioning of that patent, consistency of case-law and hence legal certainty, and cost-effectiveness for patent proprietors. It is therefore of paramount importance that the participating Member States ratify the Agreement on a Unified Patent Court in accordance with their national constitutional and parliamentary procedures and take the necessary steps for that Court to become operational as soon as possible."

1149 Published in the *Official Journal of the EU*, June 20th 2013, Vol. 56, OJ C175.

1150 Unless otherwise specified, references made to the Rules of Procedure (ROP) will be to the 18th version of these Rules, drafted on October 19th 2015 and lastly revised on March 15th 2017.

1151 For instance see the article of Drexl, in which he goes into the conflict of the UPC system with primary EU Law, and the question of jurisdiction of the CJEU. He rightly states that political pressure to come to a concrete result in the establishment of the system has prevailed over legal compatibility. See: J. DREXL, 'The Unitary Patent System: on the unconstitutional misuse of conflict-of-law rules' *Max Planck Institute of Innovation and Competition Research Paper* No. 15–01

compromise between a large number of stakeholders, the resulting outcome of this all is that the envisaged system is now poised to start. From that moment, plaintiffs under the UPC have the possibility of obtaining an EU-wide injunction.[1152] But the sword also cuts in the other way, defendants making a counterclaim or those willing to strike down a unitary patent, can now easier invalidate that patent for the whole EU territory.[1153]

Whether the UPC, once it starts it operations, will become a success in general remains to be seen of course: much depends on the quality and the predictability of UPC case law, and the trust stakeholders eventually will have in the system. With respect to *preliminary injunctions* this is very much the same and it eventually depends on how the UPC handles the requests it receives for preliminary relief: is it seen as conservative or liberal in granting such a remedy?

However, that notwithstanding, it is submitted that it is likely that preliminary injunctions will be perceived as being attractive for plaintiffs; not only because of the larger territory that the remedy now serves, but also because the possible bifurcation of normal patent proceedings under the UPC can lead to a stay of infringement proceedings, pending a ruling by the Central Division on validity issues.[1154] This may positively influence the number of preliminary injunctions sought, as interim measures can still be requested in the period awaiting this outcome.[1155]

Institutional framework of the UPC and judges

The UPC litigation system will be characterised by a multi-layered and decentralised structure. It will consist of a Court of First Instance (CFI) and a Court of Appeal (CoA).[1156] The CFI is split into local or regional divisions – every Member State is entitled to set up a locally hosted division,[1157] although certain countries are also setting up a regional division jointly[1158] – and a more specialised Central Division, for which the cases are distributed between Paris, London and Munich, depending

(2015). Also see the criticism of Ullrich: Apart from fundamental legal problems of the system, Ullrich also believes that the unitary patent itself is asymmetrically designed, resulting into a 'power patent' that which fits well with certain business models and certain protectionist strategies, but does not cater for interests of other patentees. See: H. ULLRICH, 'Select from within the system: the European patent with unitary effect' *Max Planck Institute for Intellectual Property and Competition Law Research Paper* No. 12–11 (2012).

1152 Art. 34 UPC Agreement.

1153 On the latter, according to Art. 65 (2) UPC Agreement, the Court may only do so on the grounds referred to in Art. 138 (1) and Art. 139 (2) of the EPC.

1154 Bifurcation is regulated in Art. 33 of the UPC Agreement.

1155 A. COOKE, 'Rules that reflect different traditions' *Managing Intellectual Property* (March 2015). See: pp. 90–92.

1156 Art. 6 UPC Agreement.

1157 Art. 7 (1) and (3) UPC Agreement.

1158 Art. 7 (5) UPC Agreement.

on the technological field at hand.[1159] Thus the Central Division court with respect to pharmaceutical disputes will be located in London, that dealing with ICT proceedings likely at the Central Division Court in Paris. The Central Division in Munich will deal for instance with mechanical engineering. The CoA is located in Luxembourg and deals with all technology issues on appeal. This division between courts is also the case for preliminary proceedings.[1160]

Two further remarks regarding the structure of the UPC must be made at this particular point:

The national courts of Member States dealing with patents will continue to exist next to the UPC: these national courts will firstly deal with strictly national patents (i.e. issued by the German Patent Office instead of the EPO), as well as with European patents as they are issued nowadays: namely *without unitary effect* (that is until a transitional period of seven years has lapsed).[1161] These national courts are also still entitled to grant preliminary injunctions with respect to patents that fall under their competence.

Secondly, the judicial panels of the CFI are multinational of composition and will consist of *three* experienced judges drafted from a pool of judges from UPC contracting states.[1162] The number of three judges is also the case for preliminary injunction proceedings: this is a major difference with certain preliminary injunction practices in some jurisdictions at the moment: as for instance, in The Netherlands, there is only one judge at a *kort geding* case. Another difference with some jurisdictions at the moment, is that CFI cases in the Central Division, will, by default, have a *technically qualified* judge on board. This judge has the qualifications and experiences in the relevant technology field, and will work along with two legally qualified judges.[1163] For a local or regional division of the CFI, the addition of a technically qualified judge is not mandatorily required, but a judge with such a qualification may be added (leading to a total of four judges) at the request of the parties[1164] or when it is deemed as being appropriate by the sitting judicial panel itself, in order to add more (relevant) technical expertise to the panel.[1165] Appeals are in principle heard by five judges: three legal judges and two technical judges[1166] and the CoA may hear preliminary injunction appeals (on the basis of Rule 220 (1) (c) ROP).

1159 Art. 7 (2) UPC Agreement. The future of the London branch has become unclear due to the 'Brexit' and whether this will reach existence will be dependent on when and in what form the United Kingdom joins the UPC.

1160 Art. 32 (1) (c) UPC Agreement, jo. Art. 33 UPC Agreement, enabling the local and regional divisions of the Court of First Instance.

1161 Art. 1 jo. Art. 3. UPC Agreement.

1162 Art. 8 (1) UPC Agreement.

1163 Art. 8 (6) UPC Agreement.

1164 Art. 8 (5) UPC Agreement. This request is subject to approval by the President of the CFI.

1165 Ibidem.

1166 Art. 9 (1) UPC Agreement.

§8.3. Legislative basis for preliminary injunctions and the legal test

Firstly, at this point it should be mentioned that the EU Enforcement Directive is not merely just any source of law for the UPC,[1167] but it, being Union Law, also has primacy. According to the UPC Agreement, the UPC shall apply EU Law in its entirety and shall also respect its primacy.[1168]

Whilst the judicial discretion of the UPC in granting or denying *permanent* injunctions ex Art. 63 of the UPC Agreement after infringement has been found seems to be very limited,[1169] this seems to be quite the opposite for *preliminary injunctions*. As will be seen below, the UPC Agreement, which is to be read together with the applicable ROP,[1170] seem to give a *very wide discretion* to the courts making up the UPC system, to decide on the grant of the preliminary injunction and also prescribes a balancing of interests exercise to be taken by the court.

The above is not surprising considering that a wide judicial discretion and at least the possibility to balance interests are to be seen as hallmarks of preliminary injunction proceedings, as we have also seen earlier in this dissertation. Nevertheless, it is submitted that it is positive to see that these two characteristics have been firmly anchored in the wording of Art. 62 of the UPC Agreement. This is for instance a major difference with the corresponding provisions of Art. 50 TRIPS as well as Art. 10 of the EU Enforcement Directive, in which the requirement to balance interests of both parties is not spelled out for *non*-ex-parte injunctions. However, as we have also seen in the national chapters above, the possibility to balance hardships has been acknowledged in most national courts, so the UPC's approach can be viewed as a codification of existing practice. Whether this balancing exercise indeed will

---

1167 Art. 24 (1) (a) UPC Agreement jo. Rule 33 and 34 ROP.

1168 Art. 20 UPC Agreement.

1169 Some commentators argue that based on the exact wording of Art. 63 UPC Agreement, as well as the history of the UPC Agreement and finally the purpose (*telos*) of Art. 63 UPC Agreement, there is not much discretion for the UPC to refuse a permanent injunction when infringement has been found. The seemingly discretionary wording of 'may issue' in Art. 63 of the UPC Agreement is simply to be understood as merely giving the court the legal authority to issue a permanent injunction, and should not be interpreted differently. See: M. MARFÉ, A. REETZ, C. PECNARD, R. FRUSCALZO AND R. VAN DER VELDEN, 'The power of national courts and the Unified Patent Court to grant injunctions: a comparative study' *Journal of Intellectual Property Law & Practice*. 10, No. 3 (2015), pp. 180–190. See: pp. 187–188. However, arguing the contrary is the work of: R.M. HILTY, T. JAEGER, M. LAMPING, R. ROMANDINI AND H. ULLRICH, in 'Comments on the Preliminary set of provisions for the Rules of Procedure of the Unified Patent Court' *Max Planck Institute for Intellectual Property and Competition Law Research Paper* No. 13–16 (2013). See: p. 8.

1170 Preliminary Set of Provisions for the Rules of Procedure for the Unified Patent Court', 18th version. Lastly revised on March 15th 2017.

take place regularly in the actual practice of the UPC is something different too, as we have seen regarding national court practices.

In any case, the first two paragraphs of Art. 62 UPC Agreement state the following:

> "(1) The Court may, by way of order, grant injunctions against an alleged infringer or against an intermediary whose services are used by the alleged infringer, intended **to prevent any imminent infringement, to prohibit, on a provisional** basis and subject, where appropriate, to a recurring penalty payment, the continuation of the alleged infringement or to make such continuation subject to the lodging of guarantees intended to ensure the compensation of the right holder.
> (2) The Court shall have the **discretion to weigh up the interests** of the parties and in particular to **take into account the potential harm for either of the parties** resulting from the granting or the refusal of the injunction."[1171]

Provisional measures, such as a preliminary injunction, shall be dealt with in summary proceedings that consist of both a written procedure *and* an oral procedure.[1172] For a better understanding of Art. 62 UPC Agreement, this should be read and considered in conjunction with the Rule 211 ROP to the UPC. Rule 211 (1) reiterates the legal basis that the UPC is entitled to grant a preliminary injunction. More importantly are paragraphs (2) and (3) of Rule 211 ROP. These elaborate directly on Art. 62 UPC Agreement and are worded as follows:

> "2. In taking its decision the Court may require the applicant to provide reasonable **evidence to satisfy the Court with a sufficient degree of certainty** that the applicant is entitled to commence proceedings pursuant to Article 47, that the patent in question is **valid** and that his **right is being infringed**, or that such **infringement is imminent.**
> 3. In taking its decision the Court shall in the exercise of its discretion **weigh up the interests** of the parties and, in particular, take **into account the potential harm** for **either of the parties** resulting from the granting or the refusal of the injunction."[1173]

A few elements from these provisions are worth looking closer at:

The first thing to consider, and this is positive, is that *imminent infringement*, is explicitly mentioned in both the UPC Agreement as well as in the ROP. This means that from day one the UPC system goes live, it is undisputed that the UPC is able to grant preliminary injunctions in situations of future, but imminent infringement

---

1171 Art. 62 (1) and (2) UPC Agreement. Paragraph (3) of this Article is omitted here. Emphasis added.

1172 Rule 205 ROP and Art. 52 UPC Agreement.

1173 Rule 211 (2) and (3) of the 18th version of the 'Preliminary Set of Provisions for the Rules of Procedure for the Unified Patent Court'. Draft version of March 15th 2017. Emphasis added.

as is for instance the case with many episodes of generic entry in the realm of pharmaceuticals. This may seem logical from the perspective of the covered European countries that we have looked into in this dissertation where this is a common practice, but it is here pointed out that it is only relatively recently that French courts have allowed a preliminary injunction to be granted in the case of imminent infringement.[1174]

Secondly, however, as can be seen when looking at the current wording of Rule 211 (3) ROP, it that it is merely an abbreviated version of Art. 62 (2) UPC Agreement. This has resulted into some concern amongst respondents to a public consultation on the ROP that there was *too little guidance* for the judicial panels of the UPC on how to exercise provisional relief:

> "<This> respondent believes that this rule provides **too little guidance on how to exercise discretion to grant provisional relief.** It is concerned that different local and/or regional courts will **adopt divergent approaches**. To promote consistency therefore and to reduce forum shopping and to discourage market-distorting practices **this respondent recommends additional guidance** should be given as to when injunctions should be granted."[1175] [1176]

However, the provision of additional guidance is something that has been rejected by the Drafting Committee of the Rules of Procedure, pointing out that the ROP *cannot and should not* attempt to modify the standards set by Art. 62 UPC Agreement.[1177] [1178]

1174 P. DEBRE, 'France: Preliminary injunctions in case of an imminent infringement' (February 5th, 2010); available at EPLAW Patent Blog: http://www.eplawpatentblog.com/eplaw/2010/02/fr-preliminary-injunctions-in-case-of-an-imminent-infringement.html (last accessed on 24 April 2017).

1175 See the UPC, *Digest of Changes to the 16th version of the Rules of Procedure of the UPC*, which covers the amendments made after the public consultation on the 15th version of the Rules of Procedure, see p. 135. Emphasis added. The document is available at: http://www.unified-patent-court.org/images/documents/rop-digest.pdf (last accessed on 25 April 2017).

1176 Similar concerns were also raised at the *Oral Hearing on the Rules of Procedure of the UPC*, held in November 26th 2014 in Trier with respect to the 17th version of the Rules of Procedure (which for preliminary injunctions are mostly the same as the current 18th version). See p. 485 and p. 489 of the transcript. Available at: http://www.upc.documents.eu.com/PDFs/2014-11-26_Hearing_Trier_ROP_UPC_transcript.pdf (last accessed on 25 April 2017).

1177 UPC, *Digest of Changes to the 16th version of the Rules of Procedure of the UPC*. See: p. 135.

1178 The Drafting Committee of the Rules of Procedure did, on that occasion, agree to slightly change Rule 211 (3) to better reflect UPC Art. 62, by adding the words "in particular, take into account the potential harm for either of the parties resulting from the granting or the refusal of the injunction."

Thirdly: although a link to *urgency* was missing in earlier drafts this has been remedied somewhat in the present text. Its absence was something that was critically remarked on by some commentators, as they viewed it was a *precondition* for the grant of interim injunctions; according to Hilty et al, it are recital 22[1179] and Art. 3 of the EU Enforcement directive, in combination with jurisprudence, that together require 'urgency' as a precondition for the grant of interim injunctions.[1180] Their criticism on this earlier draft seems to be partly heard, because in the subsequent (16th) draft and onwards however, with the insertion of Rule 211 (4) ROP, urgency in a *temporal* sense has been added as a factor to be taken into account and UPC courts will look at delay:

> (4) The Court shall have regard to any unreasonable delay in seeking provisional measures.

This does not cover *urgency in the sense of necessity*. The addition of the term 'urgency', instead of merely adding 'delay', was considered to be included in Rule 211 ROP, but no change was proposed, as the Digest of Changes shows, because the Drafting Committee found that the term 'urgency' is not part of the EU Enforcement Directive nor of the UPC Agreement. However, it is not completely out of the picture of the UPC: note that the plaintiff, as specified in Rule 206 (2) (c), should in its *application* for a preliminary injunction, should still point out the *necessity* of a preliminary injunction in his *application* for such a measure.[1181] Urgency is

---

1179 Recital 22 of the EU Enforcement Directive: "It is also essential to provide for provisional measures for the immediate termination of infringements, without awaiting a decision on the substance of the case, while observing the rights of the defence, ensuring the proportionality of the provisional measures as appropriate to the characteristics of the case in question and providing the guarantees needed to cover the costs and the injury caused to the defendant by an unjustified request. *Such measures are particularly justified where any delay would cause irreparable harm to the holder of an intellectual property right.*" Emphasis added.

1180 R.M. HILTY, T. JAEGER, M. LAMPING, R. ROMANDINI AND H. ULLRICH, in 'Comments on the Preliminary set of provisions for the Rules of Procedure of the Unified Patent Court' *Max Planck Institute for Intellectual Property and Competition Law Research Paper* No. 13–16 (2013). See: p. 7. Note that these comments were on the 15th version of the Rules of Procedure.

1181 Rule 206 (2) (c) ROP, states that the applicant should specify "*the reasons why provisional measures are necessary* to prevent a threatened infringement, to forbid the continuation of an alleged infringement or to make such continuation subject to the lodging of guarantees;" Emphasis added. Also, *urgency* is mentioned explicitly in Rule 209 (2) (b) ROP as a factor that the court should take into account, in examining the *application* and subsequently deciding whether to summon the parties for an oral hearing or to request the defendant for (more) information that may challenge the plaintiff's application.

then subsequently mentioned explicitly in Rule 209 (2) (b) ROP as a factor that the court should take into account, in in *examining the application* and subsequently deciding whether to summon the parties for an oral hearing or to request the defendant for (more) information that may challenge the plaintiff's application. Urgency can maybe play an indirect role this way, even when it is not mentioned as such in Rule 211.

In any case, the UPC will bring unique issues to urgency and delay, as one commentator rightly submits.[1182] A question[1183] could for instance be how the Unified Patent Court judges will assess urgency in the case when an infringement is firstly tolerated in an unimportant market for the plaintiff, i.e. a smaller UPC country, but when the plaintiff requests a provisional measure when the infringer attempts to enter a more key market for the plaintiff.

Furthermore, it is also clear that both the UPC Agreement and the ROP lack a reference to the 'public interest' as such. Instead, the UPC Agreement and the ROP only speak about the court taking into account the interests of 'the parties' or 'either of the parties'. The absence of an explicit reference to the public interest is not a surprising omission, perhaps, when one looks at current European tests where there is neither an explicit statutory requirement, nor a rich tradition of public interest factors being routinely considered in practice. However, it is in so far an omission since it, as seen, is an explicit element that is considered with respect to preliminary and permanent injunctions in the United States. The enactment of the UPC would have been an opportunity to introduce such a test to Europe. This too has been signalled by some respondents of the public consultation on the ROP[1184] who have suggested explicitly adding the 'public interest' to the wording of the Rules, but the Drafting Committee has here too repeatedly stated that the ROP are based on the wording of the UPC Agreement. Again, it was held that Art. 62 UPC Agreement does not foresee in this. This is an understandable answer from the Drafting Committee, as it is clear that with

1182 R. FREELAND, 'The Unitary Patent and and Unified Patents Court-first steps to a decision' (2013) on *Pharmaphorum*. https://pharmaphorum.com/views-and-analysis/the_unitary_patent_and_unified_patents_court_-_first_steps_to_a_decision-2/ (last accessed on April 10th 2017). Also see H. CLINE, E. GOUGE, 'The Unified Patent Court's approach to interim injunctions will influence businesses' patent strategies in Europe, say experts' (2016). Available at: http://www.out-law.com/en/articles/2016/february/the-unified-patent-courts-approach-to-interim-injunctions-will-influence-businesses-patent-strategies-in-europe-say-experts/ (last accessed on April 10th 2017).

1183 Ibidem, the issues are raised in both the Freeland and Cline and Gouge articles above.

1184 UPC, *Digest of Changes to the 16th version of the Rules of Procedure of the UPC*. See: p. 137 and p. 139.

this issue (as with others as we have already seen) the Drafting Committee did not want to go beyond the given standard in the UPC Agreement. However, that said, it is submitted that this is not necessarily a satisfactory outcome since the enactment of the UPC would have been an unique opportunity to add such a provision, also because a granted preliminary injunction with respect to a Unitary Patent is – given the size of the market that this covers – even more powerful and has a larger impact.

Fourthly, and lastly, it is clear that Rule 211 (2) ROP makes an express reference to a *valid* patent. As one respondent commenting on the ROP has pointed out, patent validity is not something expressly mentioned in Art. 62 of the UPC Agreement nor in Art. 9 (3) of the EU Enforcement Directive. However, as the Drafting Committee mentions, validity was expressly added to the ROP for reasons of clarity, as it is not possible to infringe an invalid patent.[1185] Whilst this seems to require that the UPC takes the validity issue into account when considering the grant of a preliminary injunction,[1186] it is also evident that this gives the UPC a wide scope of interpretation of when validity is *sufficiently clear* for a preliminary injunction to be granted. But, on this also note Rule 209 (2) (a) ROP; this states that in examining the application and subsequently deciding whether to summon the parties for an oral hearing or to request the defendant for (more) information that may challenge the plaintiff's application, the court shall particularly take into account "whether the patent has been upheld in an opposition procedure before the European Patent Office or has been the subject of proceedings in *any other* court."[1187]

§8.4. The UPC and an adequate security against an erroneous decision

As is currently the case, the UPC foresees in the option to require a form of security from the plaintiff in order to provide adequate compensation in the case it turns out that the granted preliminary measure was erroneous. The importance of compensation is something that has been stressed before in this dissertation. According to Rule 211 (5) ROP,[1188] which is on 'adequate security' it is stipulated that:

> "The Court **may** order the applicant to provide **adequate security for appropriate compensation for any injury likely to be caused** to the defendant which the applicant may be liable to bear in the event that the Court revokes the order for provisional measures. The Court shall do so where interim measures are ordered without the defendant having been heard unless there are special circumstances not to do so.

1185 Idem, at p. 140.
1186 Idem, at p. 141.
1187 Emphasis added.
1188 In previous drafts of the Rules, this was Rule 211 (4) ROP.

> The Court shall decide **whether it is appropriate to order the security by deposit or bank guarantee.** The order shall be effective **only** after the security has been given to the defendant in accordance with the Court's decision."[1189]

What seems clear from the wording is that the UPC, for regular preliminary injunctions, has a discretion ('may') to decide on ordering security, whilst for an *ex parte* measure this is an obligation.[1190] This makes sense, as the risk of taking an erroneous decision is likely to be higher when the defendant has not been heard. A few other issues are clear as well: firstly, when the court decides that such security is necessary, this should be provided for *in advance*, thus prior to the preliminary injunction becoming effective as the effect of the preliminary injunction is conditional on the provision of the adequate security.[1191] Secondly, the term 'adequate' seems to indicate that the court should use this as a benchmark in setting the amount and that it has the discretion to determine this level. Thirdly, the words of the ROP prescribe a model where the plaintiff in principle should have access to the necessary funds in advance in order to provide the adequate security, either for a bank guarantee or a lodged deposit. This is different with England where the plaintiff provides a cross-undertaking, which is only impacting a plaintiff's liability in the case this is called upon.

Another issue that emerges here, is whether a wrongly enjoined addressee is also entitled to claiming damages when the preliminary injunction turns out to be erroneous. This seems to be the case, as Rule 213 (2) ROP foresees in 'adequate compensation' – again at the discretion of the UPC court – [1192] basing itself on both Art. 62 (5) in combination with Art. 60 (9) of the UPC Agreement, stating:

> "Where provisional measures are **revoked,** or where they lapse due to any act or omission by the applicant, or where it is subsequently found that there has been no infringement or threat of infringement of the patent, the Court **may** order the applicant, upon request of the defendant, to provide the defendant with **appropriate compensation** for any injury caused by those measures."

1189 Rule 211 (5) ROP.

1190 As the UPC, *Digest of Changes to the 17th version of the Rules of Procedure of the UPC*, explains, at Rule 211 ROP: "This change clarifies that, where the Court orders provisional measures without hearing the other party (inaudita), it shall as a general rule order adequate security for appropriate compensation for any injury likely to be caused to the party which has not been heard. However, such security need not be provided if there are special circumstances not to do so (if e.g. no damage can occur)."

1191 This principle was confirmed in UPC, *Digest of Changes to the 16th version of the Rules of Procedure of the UPC*, at Rule 211 (4) ROP.

1192 See the UPC, *Digest of Changes to the 16th version of the Rules of Procedure of the UPC*, confirming the discretionary nature of this.

The determination of these damages happens in a separate damages proceedings and is regulated by Rule 125 ROP and further. Such a proceeding has to be initiated within one year of an order, ex Rule 213 (2) ROP.[1193] In this, the applicant for compensation due to a wrongly granted preliminary injunction, *inter alia* has to indicate the redress relied upon, the facts and evidence it bases this redress on and provide an assessment of the amount of damages that he believes are due.[1194]

It seems logical that the UPC gets a central role in this as well. If this was not so, a defendant would have to follow numerous national procedures in order to obtain damages incurred in a particular Member State, thereby basing himself on general principles of tort. However, it is too early to say how well applicants will really be compensated in the case an erroneous decision is taken: for now, it is simply wait-and-see how the UPC will exactly handle compensation claims in this and how generous and flexible it will be in this matter.

§8.5. The transitional period

For the first seven years after the start of the UPC and possibly with an extension of another seven years, there will be a *dual* system with respect to patent enforcement in the EU Member States that have signed up to the UPC: the UPC litigation system will operate alongside the litigation system as it is currently exists in Europe.[1195] The UPC will, in this period, have competence to adjudicate on infringement and revocation actions concerning both traditional European patents as patents with Unitary effect.[1196] This should be different, at least that is the idea, when European patents have been opted-out of the UPC system by patentees or when these patents already have been brought into litigation proceedings before a national court first. Then, these patents remain subject to the jurisdiction of the national courts of the Contracting Parties to the UPC.

The above may have a bearing on both the *approach* of the UPC, as well as on *the behaviour* of litigants that may consider their strategic options. The way in which the UPC will deal with enforcement of patents, including that via preliminary injunctions, may have a *direct effect* on whether patentees are willing to remain in the UPC system or instead decide on opting-out of the system for as long as possible. Although some unclarity has been signalled on whether the UPC may still be entitled to provide a preliminary injunction even when a patent has been opted-out, commentators have argued – after providing a detailed analysis

---

1193 Rule 126 ROP.

1194 Rule 131 ROP.

1195 Art. 83 (1) jo. (5) UPC Agreement. For a good background article to opting-out, see: P. ENGLAND, 'In? Out? What's it all about? Patent opt-out and withdrawal in the UPC' *Journal of Intellectual Property Law and Practice* 9, No. 11 (2014), pp. 915–922.

1196 Art. 3 jo. Art. 32 UPC Agreement.

on the complex underlying issues – that this is not likely to be the case and the decision of the patentee to opt-out also works with respect to the competence that the UPC has to issue a preliminary injunction.[1197] An opted-out patent would thus mean that the ball is then entirely with the national courts, when it comes to providing interim relief.[1198] A pro-patentee stance of the UPC, with a relatively relaxed approach to granting interim relief, may thus form one reason for plaintiffs *not* to opt-out and would have the added-benefit for the UPC to keep the patent (and subsequent litigation that may flow from it) within the system.[1199] Nevertheless, the abovementioned unclarity should be resolved as soon as possible, as the exact status of Art. 83 UPC Agreement can touch upon every valid European patent at the time the UPC comes into force.

1197 Van Gemert and Pors concluded after their analysis that: "Our conclusion therefore is that the Unified Patent Court does not have jurisdiction to grant preliminary injunctions if under Article 83(3) UPCA it does not have jurisdiction to grant final injunctions." P. VAN GEMERT, W. PORS, 'The effect of an opt out under Article 83 of the Agreement on a Unified Patent Court on jurisdiction for decisions on the merits and preliminary injunctions' (2013). Available at: http://www.eplawpatentblog.com/2013/August/The%20effect%20of%20an%20opt%20%20out%20under%20article%2083%20UPC%20Agreement.pdf (last accessed on 24 April 2017).

1198 This also seems to be implied by the UPC Preparatory Committee: "It is the Preparatory Committee's view that if an application for a European patent, a European patent or a Supplementary Protection Certificate that has been issued for a product protected by a European Patent is opted out (or during the transitional period the case is brought before a national court), the Agreement no longer applies to the application for a European patent, the European patent or the Supplementary Protection Certificate concerned. As a consequence the competent national court would have to apply the applicable national law." UPC PREPARATORY COMMITTEE, 'Interpretative Note on the application of Art. 83 UPC Agreement' (January 29th 2014). Available at: https://www.unified-patent-court.org/news/interpretative-note-%E2%80%93-consequences-application-article-83-upca (last accessed on 24 April 2017).

1199 However, note the view of Pinckney, who also writes about the unclarity of Art. 83 UPC Agreement regarding provisional measures. He points out that: "it is arguable that an action for provisional measures is not a separate action from an infringement action and that, therefore, provisional measures may be applied for in national courts during the transitional period, even in respect of an "opted-in" European patent." R. PINCKNEY, 'Understanding the transitional provisions of the Agreement on the Unified Patent Court' *European Intellectual Property Review* 37, No. 5 (2015), pp. 268–277. See: pp. 274–275. Also see the article of Paul England, in which he mentions additional reasons to be taken into account when deciding on opting-out or not. P. ENGLAND, 'In? Out? What's it all about? Patent opt-out and withdrawal in the UPC' *Journal of Intellectual Property Law and Practice* 9, No. 11 (2014), pp. 915–922. See: pp. 920–922.

§8.6. Risk of differences between local courts and forum shopping

Article 33 (1) of the UPC Agreement states that a preliminary injunction action will be brought before the local division[1200] (a) where the actual or threatened infringement has occurred or may occur; or (b) the local division where the defendant – or in the case of multiple defendants one of the defendants – has its residence or its principal place of business. This seems to offer a certain degree of choice to the plaintiff. This can in turn potentially lead to the issue of *forum shopping*, which can be fuelled by differences amongst local divisions of the UPC, in the degree of granting preliminary injunctions.

With every decentralised system, there is an inherent risk that despite the attempt to foster consistency and uniformity from above, differences between lower courts may remain or emerge. In a legal system, this could be for instance due to cultural reasons, legal tradition, preferences or more deliberately by the court as a way to attract more cases, possibly leading to a negative form of competition amongst the courts. Whether or not this fear is justified with the UPC, remains to be seen and it is submitted that problems may probably not be that severe in actual practice as this risk appears on paper. However, the flexible wording in which certain provisions of the UPC Agreement and ROP are provided, including that of Art. 62 UPC and Rule 211 ROP on what constitutes validity, delay and balancing in this context, can and most likely will lead to some differences between the various courts that make up the UPC. It is thus a fair concern that a local division with a reputation of being particular pro-patentee and being relatively open to granting preliminary injunctions, could lead to forum shopping issues and attract more cases than other, more conservative, local divisions.

Of course, the UPC Court of Appeal can and most likely will, attempt to address the widest differences between courts with its judgments, thereby giving further guidance on how the provisions of the UPC Agreement should be interpreted, in a push to bring more desired uniformity.[1201] However, until it does so, there will

---

1200 Instead of the local division, this can also be the regional division in which that Member State participates in.

1201 But more in general, outside the immediate topic of preliminary injunctions, Meier-Beck argues that in the beginning of the UPC, non-uniform proceedings may also be beneficial. The UPC Agreement prescribes in Art. 8 (3) that a local division should have two national judges from that Contracting State; this way the UPC can benefit from nationally gained experiences first, in the early and critical years of its operation. Over time, different local procedures would be more aligned, including by the mixture of personnel and a mutual dialogue between the local divisons and the central division. See: P. MEIER-BECK, 'Quo vadis, iudicium unitarium?' *Journal of Intellectual Property Law & Practice* 9, No. 3 (2014), pp. 241–245.

likely be differences between local divisions, that plaintiffs will experience or can attempt to use to their advantage.

§8.7. Patent trolls and the UPC

In 2013, a large group of technology companies wrote an open-letter pointing out their concerns with the proposed UPC.[1202] Apart from concerns on the issue of bifurcation, these companies also mentioned the role of injunctions and especially feared 'patent trolls', sometimes also known as *Non-practicing entities* (NPEs). Where their concerns on bifurcation are not of direct relevance for the UPC in preliminary injunction proceedings, that of NPE's may become so.[1203]

As is well-known, NPE's attempt to extort exorbitant licensing fees from other businesses by litigating (often) unpractised and dubious (in the sense of weak or minor) patents. The companies that drafted the open-letter fear that by the emergence of the UPC, NPEs could copy their profitable business model from the US to the EU.[1204] This is not only a risk with respect to litigation in the context of permanent injunctions, but may also be so with *preliminary* injunctions. We have already seen in this dissertation that the grant of a preliminary injunction can reduce or eliminate the activities of a business and that therefore an enjoined party can be forced to stop operations or conclude a non-beneficial settlement.[1205] Just as much as with respect to permanent injunctions, courts should also be aware of this in the context of preliminary injunctions, especially if Europe, with the Unified Patent and the UPC, is seen as an interesting area by NPE's to expand their business to.

However, the Unified Patent Court Preparatory Committee, in this also relying on the work of Harhoff, does not believe that the key aspects that facilitate NPE activity will be present under the UPC.[1206] Aspects of the US patent litigation system that are essentially supportive of patent trolling are, according to Harhoff,[1207] the following:

1202 D. HAKIM, 'Tech giants fear spread of patent wars to Europe' *The New York Times* (September 25th 2013). Available at: http://www.nytimes.com/2013/09/26/technology/tech-giants-fear-spread-of-patent-wars-to-europe.html?_r=1 (last accessed on 24 April 2017). The open-letter of the technology companies is to be found in full at: http://graphics8.nytimes.com/packages/pdf/business/26trolls-letter.pdf (last accessed on 24 April 2017).

1203 For a good general article on this, see: P. CLARKSON, W. WEYMIENS, 'Striking the balance between patent assertion entities and SMEs' *IAM Media* (2014). Available at: http://www.iam-media.com/intelligence/Patents-in-Europe/2014/Europe-focus/Striking-the-balance-between-patent-assertion-entities-and-SMEs (last accessed on 24 April 2017).

1204 Ibidem.

1205 See for more on this page 82 of this dissertation.

1206 UPC, 'FAQ: Impact of the UPC'. Available at: https://www.unified-patent-court.org/faq/impact-upc-0companies (last accessed on April 20 2017).

1207 See, D. HARHOFF, *Economic Cost Benefit Analysis of a Unified and Integrated European Patent Litigation System* (2009 Final Report). See: p. 49.

- high costs of legal proceedings;
- certain cost allocation rules (when parties bear their own costs instead of the loser pays);
- contingent fees for lawyers, creating incentives for lawsuits;
- high damage awards and risk of treble damages in the case of 'wilful infringement';
- pro-patentee posture of (certain) US courts and juries;
- low examination quality by the patent granting body, creating uncertainty about the scope of protection of awarded patents;
- a broadly defined extension of patentable subject-matter to software and business methods.

Harhoff submits, and with this the present author agrees, that Europe is and will be indeed likely less vulnerable to NPEs, as the patent system, deviates from the US in a number of aspects.[1208] This both seems to be currently the case, as it also likely will be in the future under the UPC. Especially convincing arguments of Harhoff, are those that in Europe, both now, as under the UPC, (1) cost allocation favours the winning party,[1209] resulting that the losing party pays all litigation costs. This, unlike the US, should form a financial deterrent to parties that 'simply have a shot at litigation';[1210] (2) there are no treble damages / excessive damages in Europe. An additional convincing factor in this context, is (3) that of a higher patent quality in Europe. As Ohly mentions, in Europe there is the possibility for other parties to oppose a patent at the EPO,[1211] ex. Art. 99–100 EPC (this is also possible later with the Unitary patent). This was something that until relatively recently was not

Available at: http://ec.europa.eu/internal_market/indprop/docs/patent/studies/litigation_system_en.pdf (last accessed on 24 April 2017).

1208 Idem, at p. 50. In the same light as below, see the article of A. MAYERGOYZ, 'Lessons from Europe how to tame U.S. Patent Trolls' *Cornell International Law Journal* 42 (2009), pp. 241–270.

1209 Art. 69 UPC Agreement, covers the legal costs distribution.

1210 This is also pointed out by Helmers, Love and McDonagh: in their empirical paper, they come to the conclusion that there may be a limited patent troll problem in the UK, but that a loser-pays regime is one of the best ways, namely 'more than other reasons' of counteraction against NPE activity. See C. HELMERS, B. LOVE, L. MCDONAGH 'Is there a patent troll problem in the UK?' *Fordham Intellectual Property, Media, and Entertainment Law Journal* 24 (2009), pp. 509–552. See: pp. 544–545.

1211 A. OHLY, '"Patenttrolle" oder: Der patentrechtliche Unterlassungsanspruch unter Verhältnismäßigkeitsvorbehalt? Aktuelle Entwicklungen im US-Patentrecht und ihre Bedeutung für das deutsche und europäische Patentsystem' *GRUR* (2008), pp. 787–798. See: pp. 791–792. Also see on this subject: A. MAYERGOYZ, 'Lessons from Europe how to tame U.S. Patent Trolls' *Cornell International Law Journal* 42, (2009), pp. 241–270.

possible in the US at the USPTO.[1212] However, this 'second look' can result in less chances for the emergence of the type of patents that NPEs thrive on, since other parties can often oppose them. Also, as Ohly mentions, Europe is stricter when it comes to patent *publication* requirements: in the US there are more exceptions to this, leading to a greater potential for surprise attacks for and by patent trolls.[1213]

Whilst thus on a structural level it may be more difficult for patent trolls to exploit the European system than in the United States, this does not mean that such problems are non-existent in Europe. After all, as Ohly points out, in Europe there is also patent protection for 'minor inventions', especially in the realm of IT, leading to potential hold-up potential.[1214] From this point of view, it is good that currently preliminary injunction courts have wide discretion to decide on the grant of a preliminary injunction and that they are not obliged to do so after the infringement of a NPE's patent is found.[1215] Whilst this is nothing new in the context of preliminary injunctions, this is different compared to permanent injunctions in some countries, where the court formally does not have this discretion and should in principle enjoin when infringement has been found.[1216] However, at the same time it is observed that with the UPC there is no formal requirement in the UPC Agreement nor the ROP that an invention has to be practiced. This can still however be rendered to be an important factor in future UPC case law, to be taken along in the balance of convenience test. At the moment however, the answer to the question of how the UPC will exactly deal with NPEs, both in the context of permanent and preliminary injunctive relief, is still to be awaited.

1212 As a result of the *America Invents Act*, a 'Post Grant Review' has been introduced in the US at the end of 2012. This allows third parties to challenge patent claims of granted patents at the USPTO in a separate proceeding. This can be done until nine months after the patent has been granted or reissued. It is submitted here that this Post Grant Review is a positive contribution to enhance patent quality in the US – but only when this is a review mechanism that will be regularly used by parties in actual practice. See the website of the USPTO on Post Grant Review: https://www.uspto.gov/patents-application-process/appealing-patent-decisions/trials/post-grant-review (last accessed on April 15th 2017).

1213 A. OHLY, '"Patenttrolle" oder: Der patentrechtliche Unterlassungsanspruch unter Verhältnismäßigkeitsvorbehalt? Aktuelle Entwicklungen im US-Patentrecht und ihre Bedeutung für das deutsche und europäische Patentsystem' *GRUR* (2008), pp. 787–798. See: pp. 791–792.

1214 Ibidem.

1215 Also see: P. CLARKSON, W. WEYMIENS, 'Striking the balance between patent assertion entities and SMEs' *IAM Media* (2014). Available at: http://www.iam-media.com/intelligence/Patents-in-Europe/2014/Europe-focus/Striking-the-balance-be tween-patent-assertion-entities-and-SMEs (last accessed on 24 April 2017).

1216 A. OHLY, '"Patenttrolle" oder: Der patentrechtliche Unterlassungsanspruch unter Verhältnismäßigkeitsvorbehalt? Aktuelle Entwicklungen im US-Patentrecht und ihre Bedeutung für das deutsche und europäische Patentsystem' *GRUR* (2008), pp. 787–798. See: p. 792.

§8.8. Competition law and preliminary injunctions under the UPC

Certain scholars have argued that competition law should also be taken along into preliminary injunction proceedings.[1217] The authors Petersen, Riis and Schovsbo argue that from the outset, the scope of the UPC Agreement seems to provide for this[1218] and that if a defendant is not allowed to make any allegations amount to abuse of competition law, it will in practice be impossible to prevent a preliminary injunction even in cases where this would clearly amount *to an illegal abuse of a dominant position.*[1219] Despite this, they expect that the UPC will be rather reluctant to engage into any competition law analysis in (preliminary) injunction proceedings, mainly due to its very specialised patent-law nature and a doctrinal isolation of the UPC.[1220] The authors Petersen, Riis and Schovsbo therefore suggest that the UPC should "acknowledge the institutional biases of the court and be careful to also include other relevant values and interests than the proprietary values and interests of patent law" and, additionally, they argue that that "the procedural rules leave significant discretion for the UPC to do this accordingly."[1221] The present author however, agrees with their prediction that the UPC will be reluctant to engage in competition law analysis in proceedings and that such an exercise would be a rather large step from current practice. It is submitted by the present author that competition issues can indeed be taken along in the balance of convenience – i.e. these arguments can tip the balance against a preliminary injunction if this remedy would immediately put the only competitor out of business – but it are arguments with a more classic antitrust character, such as an abuse of a dominant position, that seem out of place with the swift nature of preliminary injunction proceedings and the foreseen temporary status of a preliminary injunction itself.[1222]

1217 C.S. PETERSEN, T. RIIS, J. SCHOVSBO, 'The Unified patent court (UPC) Compulsory licensing and competition law' *Nordiskt Immaterieelt Rättskydd (NIR)* (2014). Available at: https://papers.ssrn.com/sol3/papers.cfm?abstract_id=2489006 (last accessed on April 27 2017). See: pp. 14–15.

1218 Idem, at pp. 14–15.

1219 Idem, at p. 15.

1220 Idem, at pp. 16–17.

1221 Ibidem.

1222 However, on this, see the article of A. OHLY, '"Patenttrolle" oder: Der patentrechtliche Unterlassungsanspruch unter Verhältnismäßigkeitsvorbehalt? Aktuelle Entwicklungen im US-Patentrecht und ihre Bedeutung für das deutsche und europäische Patentsystem.' *GRUR* (2008), pp. 787–798. See: pp. 793–794. There, Ohly mentions the law on abuse of a dominant position – although his comments were not made explicitly in the UPC context nor in the context of *preliminary* injunctions – as a possible remedy to deal with extreme cases of patent troll abuse, thereby also possibly preventing an injunction: "Liegt ein Missbrauch einer marktbeherrschenden Stellung vor, so kann er nicht nur von den Kartellbehörden verfolgt werden und zu Schadensersatzansprüchen Anlass geben.

§8.9. Intermediate conclusion

At the moment of writing, but also likely in the first period after the start of the UPC's activities, much is and will be unclear of how the UPC will deal with preliminary injunctions in its actual practice. It is submitted that this is inevitable with any new court and new set of laws. However, it is also to a certain extent unsatisfactory, as it is evident that UPC judges have very little to rely on in terms of specific and substantive guidelines, helping to decide on the grant of what is a very powerful legal remedy with ramifications for the whole European market. More could have been done on this.

Nevertheless, this does not imply that those drafting the UPC Agreement and the Rules of Procedure should be blamed for this: these officials have essentially written a solid legal basis and have provided a general legal framework for dealing with preliminary injunctions which is very much based on the TRIPS and the Enforcement Directive, but also has a little more flesh to it. With respect to preliminary injunctions, no more could have realistically been asked for. Additionally, the current wording of the ROP, in comparison with previous drafts, has been improved, by for instance including references to balancing and delay. It is thus now up to judicial practice by the UPC, to develop the remedy further and to provide a stable corpus of case law and offer guidelines. This is something that will take time, making at least the immediate future uncertain for those seeking a preliminary injunction and for parties that are confronted with a possible enjoinment of their business.

§ 8.10. De Lege Ferenda – Recommended best Practices for the Unified Patent Court to Deal with Preliminary Injunctions

§8.10.1. Introduction

At this point, it is of course unknown in which direction the UPC will head when deciding on preliminary injunctions. Norrgård and Nyland believe that, when looking at the wording of the UPC Agreement and the ROP, as well as the TRIPS agreement and the Enforcement Directive, that the room to manoeuvre for the UPC Court is substantial and not a single model can be ruled out.[1223] Also, they state that "due to the vagueness of the provisions, it is likely that the judges of the UPC will

---

Einiges spricht dafür, dass er auch dem Unterlassungsanspruch einredeweise entgegengehalten werden kann."

1223 M.L. NORRGÅRD, A. NYLUND, 'The requirements for preliminary injunctions in the unified patent court' in R.M. BALLARDINI, M.L. NORRGÅRD, G.N. BRUUN, *Transitions in European Patent Law: Influences of the European Patent Package* (2015 Kluwer International Law Publishing), pp. 189–206. See: p. 203.

bring to the table their national traditions."[1224] But they also point out that some harmonisation, resulting in a common ground will be found over time, when the UPC Court of Appeal deals with an issue. Given these observations, with which the present author fully agrees as we have seen, it is interesting to think of what such an approach should look like for preliminary injunctions. The attempt of this chapter is then to, based on examples from national case law and prior (theoretical) observations made in this thesis, point out the typical problems the UPC court will face when dealing with preliminary injunctions as well as the strength and weaknesses of current approaches to deal with these problems. As far as possible, it will be attempted to prescribe 'best practices' with thereby trying to stay within the scope of Art. 62 UPC Agreement and the relevant Rules of Procedure. It thus amounts to a *de lege ferenda* approach.

The following issues will be addressed below:

- urgency and imminent infringement;
- likelihood of patent validity;
- likelihood of patent infringement and harm
- balancing of interests and the public interest
- bond and damages.

§8.10.2. Urgency (temporal and necessity)

It is emphasised that a preliminary injunction is only to be granted when there is urgency in both a *temporal* and a *necessity* sense. Although urgency is not explicitly mentioned in Art. 62 UPC Agreement, Rule 211 ROP now refers to unreasonable delay. 'Urgency' as such is mentioned in Rule 209 ROP as something that the court should look into when examining the application and in deciding whether to continue with oral proceedings. How should the UPC ideally deal with the urgency issue?

§8.10.2.1. Urgency (temporal)

How long can a plaintiff wait, before he is too late to bring a preliminary injunction action? There is not an obvious answer to this, as it depends on the facts of the case and what the preliminary injunction judge deems to be reasonable.

In any case, it is submitted that with Rule 211 (4) a *flexible* approach should be taken with what constitutes unreasonable delay, rather than to adhere to any strict temporal deadline. It is then thus key that the court should take into account the reasons for *delay*, as national courts tend to do so now – regardless of whether this is an explicitly required notion, or more indirectly as an assessment of 'irreparable harm'. It is also submitted that the UPC should acknowledge early in its case law that this should not entail that the plaintiff should take a litigation risk in order to

---

1224 Ibidem.

be 'on time'. This is something that, as we have seen, various national courts have acknowledged as well. This means in any case:

- That the plaintiff under the UPC should have a reasonable time to collect evidence of infringement, and if necessary obtain expert evidence in order to build a stronger case. This way, the quality of the legal debate is enhanced – with for instance more clarity on the technical subject matter – and this way the chance of taking an erroneous decision, which is something the preliminary injunction court should tend to avoid at all costs, is further minimised.
- To await pending proceedings on validity, i.e. at the EPO in either opposition or appeal proceedings or at another UPC court.

Additional reasons that could excuse delay are:

- When both parties are still in negotiations, an amicable solution should be preferred above starting litigation as soon as possible and thus without the plaintiff risking to forego the remedy of still obtaining a preliminary injunction. It has been observed that licensing negotiations, in which one party is supported by a granted preliminary injunction, bring along problems of their own.
- There should be no duty for a plaintiff to actively observe the market. However, the plaintiff should act swiftly when it obtains concrete signs of a violation of its patent rights, otherwise risking non-excusable delay.

§8.10.2.2. Urgency (necessity)

We have already seen that urgency in the sense of necessity is not taken along in Art. 62 UPC Agreement nor in Rule 211 ROP. This does not mean however that it is completely off the table; it is submitted that this can still be taken along through the backdoor in the balancing test, as happens now in Germany for instance. Furthermore, there is still Rule 209 ROP in which the plaintiff should indicate in its application *why the measure is urgent.* The latter is a positive obligation: urgency in the sense of necessity should be something that the plaintiff should always set out and something that the court should look into. This should happen in a (pro)active manner and not only when the defendant questions the recourse to a preliminary injunction.

§8.10.2.3. Imminent infringement

As such, imminent infringement is undisputedly covered by Art. 62 UPC Agreement. This clarity is welcome: in France for instance, until recently, courts had not issued preliminary injunctions for imminent infringement. Whilst in Germany and The Netherlands this has been possible, courts have been strict with granting preliminary injunctions for imminent infringement and the same applies to England. The contentious issue for the UPC is thus not *if*, but *when* infringement is really deemed to be imminent. Issues that national courts have encountered in this context, which the UPC will likely encounter as well, are:

- What constitute preparatory actions by the defendant-alleged infringer leading to the conclusion that infringement is imminent?
- What role does previous market behaviour of the defendant-alleged infringer play in determining likely imminent infringement?
- What does it mean when the defendant-alleged infringer is not willing to give an undertaking not to infringe?

All these are issues that depend much on the constellation of facts. At the moment, national courts have – at least with pharmaceuticals – over the board treated these more or less in the same manner and have in general been reluctant in assuming imminent infringement too easily. It is submitted that this is correct: the bar should indeed be set high and imminent infringement should only be assumed when this is *very likely* to take place on a (very) short notice. Doing otherwise could lead to an over enforcement of a patentee's rights.

In general, this should mean that preparatory actions, previous infringing behaviour and not willing to give an undertaking not to infringe or not launch a competing product, by themselves should not be sufficient to enjoin business. Whilst taken together they can maybe serve as serious indications that infringement is imminent, it is submitted that rather a clear and distinct moment should be chosen to mark the moment infringement is really due. An example is that of what now happens when generic pharmaceutical companies register their products in the *Lauer Taxe* or the *G-Standaard.* Such clarity would benefit all parties and also prevent unnecessary litigation. Furthermore, it should also not be seen as a sign of imminent infringement when preparatory actions take place well before the expiry of the patent. This does not go well together with the notion that the bar for imminent infringement should be set highly.

§8.10.3. Validity

Establishing the likelihood of a patent's validity is of utmost importance and it is argued that more clarity on this topic is something that the UPC should establish as soon as possible by providing clear principles on how it will approach this matter when deciding on a request for a preliminary injunction. Guidance on this matter gives legal certainty to both possible plaintiff-patentees as well as to the defendant- alleged infringers. It is assumed that the UPC's approach on this can also can severely influence the number of cases that the UPC will receive. When strict on this requirement, presumably less plaintiffs will simply 'take a shot' and opt for a preliminary injunction.

There are three main issues here:

- Should there be a presumption of patent validity; when is a patent deemed sufficiently secure to base a preliminary injunction on?
- How to deal with prior diverging decisions from inside the court system on patent validity?
- What is the extent of the validity analysis itself?

§8.10.3.1. A patent's likelihood of validity – the role of presumptions

In deciding upon granting a preliminary injunction, the court's initial attitude towards a patent's validity can make a considerable difference. Whilst, as seen, the courts in most countries do not strictly require a patent to have gone through earlier opposition or invalidity proceedings as a *de facto* condition to grant a preliminary injunction, this is different with respect to the German practice, especially that of the Düsseldorf courts, which can be considered much more strict on this. Whilst in the end this is a matter of policy as much as a matter of Law, it is clear that there are options for the UPC here to choose from: a string of rulings clearly setting out the requirements to when a patent is presumed to be *hinlänglich gesichert* will be more than welcome and can greatly influence the magnitude and type of applications that will be brought.

Art. 62 UPC Agreement is silent on the issue of patent validity, whilst Rule 211 ROP only refers to a *valid* patent. Rule 209 ROP however, provides that the court, on deciding whether to continue with the case, takes into account "whether the patent has been upheld in an opposition procedure before the European Patent Office or has been the subject of proceedings in *any other* court."[1225] Although it is still uncertain how Rule 209 ROP affects Rule 211 ROP, it is submitted that the spirit of this provision is considered to be partly in line with, but still falling short of, the approach that is recommended below.

It is submitted that the UPC, in this matter, should follow a similar strict approach as has been developed by the courts in Düsseldorf, Germany, and set out in *Harnkatheterset*. This would mean that the UPC should in principle presume that a patent is not sufficiently likely to be valid when it has not undergone and survived a 'second look' in either (1) opposition proceedings at the EPO, or at (2) earlier court proceedings on validity regarding the same patent: (a) before the national courts of a Contracting Member State prior to the start of the UPC, (b) or before the national courts of a Contracting Member State prior to when a patent has been opted-in to the UPC system, or (c) before another UPC judicial panel in which the patent's validity was an issue that was considered.

There are several reasons why an approach similar to *Harnkatheterset* would fit with the UPC as well:

- Rule 209 (2) (a) ROP points out that (the outcome of) validity proceedings in *any other* court should be taken along.
- A strict approach with respect to patent validity recognises the special and extraordinary nature of preliminary injunctions and the risks involved. This way the chance of taking an erroneous decision is minimised considerably.
- It takes into account that determining patent validity is a complex issue that is best dealt with in a venue with more technical expertise and more time at hand than a preliminary injunction court has for this.

1225 Rule 209 (2) (a) ROP. Emphasis added.

- When the UPC grants a preliminary injunction, it will have an effect in the whole area covered by the UPC, therefore a relatively high standard regarding patent validity is warranted as well.
- Doctrinally, such an approach also better connects to the spirit and aims of bifurcation, which is after all one of the hallmarks of the UPC when it comes to 'normal', non-preliminary, injunction proceedings.

This does not mean that such a system should be too rigid; just as in *Harnkatheterset* a plaintiff should *still* be able to obtain a preliminary injunction even if the patent has not yet been challenged in prior proceedings. The UPC should provide a clear list of 'exceptional circumstances' providing grounds when a preliminary injunction can then potentially be considered to be granted nevertheless. Such an analysis could, just as under the German Düsseldorf doctrine, take place under the balance of convenience test.

It is also submitted that for certain (classes or types of) patents, the UPC can adopt a *general policy* constituting a special exemption to the general requirement that a patent should have first gone through earlier opposition or invalidity proceedings. This may be for instance the case with pharmaceuticals. This because, as has been observed, (generic) infringement can lead to particularly serious consequences for the patentee and for the level of innovation within the industry. By somewhat lowering the bar for a patentee of these classes or types of patents to obtain interim relief, it is submitted that a fairer balance is struck because the particular nature of these patents is then taken into account, along with the particular commercial aspects surrounding them.

§8.10.3.2. An evident error on validity from within the court system

Should a preliminary injunction court under the UPC be restricted in *not* granting a preliminary injunction because of a previous negative decision on a patent's validity of another court within the UPC? No, it is submitted that in exceptional circumstances it should also then be possible for a preliminary injunction to be granted, just as various national courts can do now. Such a situation could occur when a request for a preliminary injunction is made, but when the patent where the preliminary injunction is requested for has been invalidated in an earlier ruling and this invalidity is now pending appeal at the CoA. If a preliminary injunction court of the UPC would be bound to this earlier assessment of invalidity and thus forced to deny a preliminary injunction, this would lead to the situation that the plaintiff-patentee opting for interim relief would be victim of bad justice twice when it turns out at the CoA that the previous ruling on invalidity was wrong; firstly by virtue of the wrongly invalidated patent and secondly by the denying of a preliminary injunction that the plaintiff otherwise may have been entitled to. In such situations, a preliminary injunction court of the UPC should always be able to make its own assessment on validity and not be bound by the earlier invalidity ruling. It is argued however, just as is acknowledged in current national practices,[1226] that the bar in such a situation to set aside a previous ruling on invalidity should be high and that this can only happen in the case *evident errors* have been made in the prior invalidity decision, and when the patentee has a significant chance of his patent being restored again at a later stage.

§8.10.3.3. The extent of the validity analysis itself

Despite the 'recommended practice' above, that in principle a patent should have gone through prior contradictory proceedings, this does not mean that the preliminary injunction court can *solely* rely on this earlier decision. The UPC, when dealing with a request for a preliminary injunction, should therefore always look at the issue of patent validity itself and be confident that validity will still hold at a further trial on the merits. This is also the case with patents that have survived earlier opposition or revocation proceedings or those that are exempted from this. Therefore, a preliminary injunction court of the UPC should have the freedom to anticipate on *all* aspects of the likelihood of a patent's validity and not solely be restricted to invalidity arguments as provided by the defendant, although for reasons of efficiency this should be the natural starting point of the actual analysis.

It is finally submitted that, as has been suggested above in this dissertation,[1227] that the UPC should be able to delay the proceedings somewhat and invite *amici curiae* to submit briefs when this would provide much added value. As argued, in the majority of patent cases, taking out a little extra time for this would not make a significant difference, whilst it could improve the information position of the court and the quality of decisionmaking considerably.

§8.10.4. Infringement and/or harm

Sooner or later, the UPC will have to decide whether it looks only at infringement or *also at harm*, as a precondition for the grant of a preliminary injunction. In other words, what value will a preliminary injunction court under the UPC attach to the concepts of infringement and harm? Is (irreparable) harm something that should be seen as an explicit prerequisite for a preliminary injunction and something that should be proven by the plaintiff and assessed by the court, as is the case in the United States? Or should the focus mostly be on an infringement analysis, which, if found, entails that harms follow by default? In the latter case, an alleged lack of

1226 See for instance the cases of *Olanzapin* (Germany), *Novartis v Hospira* (England), and *AstraZeneca AB v Sandoz B.V.* (The Netherlands), all mentioned in the respective national chapters *supra.*

1227 See the reasoning in the main text at footnote 1133 of this dissertation.

harm can then still be argued by the defendant in the balancing of hardships exercise. It is clear that in the current legal tradition, the Anglo-Saxon countries put emphasis on harm, whilst, German and Dutch courts put more emphasis instead on a detailed infringement analysis.

§8.10.4.1. Likelihood of infringement analysis

The above does not mean that an infringement analysis *as such* is to be considered as a point of discussion. In all observed jurisdictions, the preliminary injunction courts conduct an infringement analysis and courts have proven to be quite willing in taking on technical issues as well, regardless of the more concise nature of the proceedings. This does not only mean anticipating issues of claim construction but also whether these claims are infringed, both in a literal sense as with respect to equivalence. All courts in principle put the burden of proof on the plaintiff to prove that the patent is indeed likely being infringed and that therefore interim relief is warranted. It is recommended that these practices should continue under the UPC. Here too, it is submitted that as has been suggested above,[1228] that the UPC should be able to delay the proceedings somewhat and invite *amici curiae* to submit briefs when this would provide much added value on this topic.

§8.10.4.2. An explicit requirement to demonstrate irreparable harm?

It is, however, submitted that the UPC should not make 'irreparable harm' as a *de facto* and explicit requirement that should *per se* be satisfied by the plaintiff. As is clear from the wording of the UPC Agreement and the Rules of Procedure, it is not likely that the UPC will do so; both documents seem to indicate that an examination of harms can take place as part of the balancing of hardships instead. This would be sensible: an explicit *de facto* requirement of proving irreparable harm is worth little as a separate prong when it is (too) easily assumed to be fulfilled, whilst the opposite – when irreparable harm has to be explicitly demonstrated by the plaintiff – is far from ideal either. The practices from the England and especially the United States show that the court should then be prepared to undertake a detailed examination and possibly become bogged down in a complex debate (e.g. see the *causal nexus requirement*) on what and when harm is really 'irreparable'. It is very much the question whether it is desirable that this should take place in an adjudicative venue that attempts to deal with patent issues in a swift manner. Addressing the degree of (irreparable) harm in the context of balance of hardships is a more flexible way to incorporate this instead.

1228 See the reasoning in the main text at footnote 1133 of this dissertation.

§8.10.5. Balancing of hardships and the public interest

We have seen that the national courts that have been looked at in Chapter 7 all have the *possibility* to balance the hardships or interests of parties against each other, even though they do not always do so in practice. This way, the courts are enabled to look at mitigating factors i.e. with respect to (in)validity and (lack of) harms. It is submitted, that this is highly desirable for various reasons: 1) bearing in mind the strong effect a preliminary injunction can have on either of the parties; 2) to prevent an overly rigid judicial approach to preliminary injunctions; 3) to prevent harsh and unjust situations from occurring. Therefore, it is good that the UPC has explicitly taken balancing on-board, as is also clear from the wording of Rule 211 ROP.

As a general comment on this however, it is submitted that simply *providing* this possibility is not enough. It is advised that the UPC takes a proactive approach in this and indeed actively balances hardships or interest of the parties in practice, rather than letting this merely be a *possibility*.

What can then be taken along in this exercise?

Firstly, as stated above, if the UPC takes a strict approach with respect to the likelihood of ***patent validity***, holding the principle that a patent should have been through prior opposition or invalidity procedures in order for the grant of a preliminary injunction to be considered, a first issue that can and should be dealt with under this prong is that of *factors* that can provide mitigation when a patent has not (yet) received this 'second look' before. Equally, just as under the German Düsseldorf courts' doctrine with *Harnkatheterset*, a similar 'list' of special factors and circumstances can be taken along, as these factors may point into the direction of a patent's validity. It is submitted that relevant factors, favouring the grant of a preliminary injunction, can be:

- When a patent has been licensed by many licensees for years and is attacked at the end of its lifetime.
- When there is only a short period left until the expiry of the patent.
- To prevent abuse, in the case of *prima facie* weak arguments of the defendant-infringer regarding the patent's invalidity.

Secondly, with respect to balancing ***harms and interests***, both of the plaintiff and the defendant, these can and should be considered – again in an (pro)active manner – by a preliminary injunction court of the UPC. As we have already seen, this means that in any case the following should be taken into consideration:

- Whether parties are in direct competition with each other; direct competition would be a factor in favour of granting a preliminary injunction.
- The remaining duration of a patent and how long a trial on the merits would normally take to complete; if the former is short and the latter would take longer, this would be a factor in favour of granting a preliminary injunction.

- Whether an alternative to a preliminary injunction is possible; i.e. a speedy decision on the merits in the form of accelerated proceedings.
- If not looked into before, the court under this heading can also consider arguments of delay and urgency.

It is not recommended that the UPC adopts a 'clearing the way' policy as a *de facto* obligation for the defendant to undertake, as is for instance the case with generic pharmaceuticals under the English doctrine. It is submitted that it is important that generic companies are as little restricted as possible in launching without delay when they believe that they do not infringe the plaintiff's patent, without the burden of having to go through – possibly unnecessary – court proceedings well in advance, in order to be allowed to (prepare for a) launch. The latter process takes considerable time leading to a generic company missing out on a First Mover Advantage, which is one of the main incentives for generic entry.[1229] Instead, patent infringement and patent validity issues should be assessed by a preliminary injunction court of the UPC and should in principle initially be proven by the plaintiff, instead of shifting this burden to the defendant.

This brings us to the ***public interest***. In Europe, arguments of this nature seem to be rarely used or invoked explicitly. It has been equally demonstrated that in the case of the United States this is different: there the public interest is routinely examined and addressed. This is unsurprising, considering the explicit public interest prong that the preliminary injunction 'test' in this country entails. We have seen that arguments that are made here include the following:

- A reiteration of the role patents have in society.
- Healthcare arguments.
- Safety-related arguments.

It is clear that neither the wording of Art. 62 of the UPC Agreement nor the ROP foresee in an explicit public interest prong as is the case in the United States. However, it is submitted that the UPC should nevertheless pay extra attention to specifically health and safety arguments that are made and that the court should find manoeuvring space to do so in the balancing of interests prong.

That public interests are also clearly on the mind of the EU legislator, is shown by the EU *Trade Secret Directive*. Although this legislation is aimed at harmonising and strengthening a different form of intellectual property protection, the wording of the legislation shows that a *well-balanced approach* is preferred by the legislator, that this includes public interests and that the protection of intellectual property rights is not absolute. Especially the wording of recital 21 provides a clear sense of direction:

1229 In line with the recommendation that the European Commission has made on this. EUROPEAN COMMISSION, *Pharmaceutical Sector Inquiry Final Report* (2009). See: p. 461. Available at: http://ec.europa.eu/competition/sectors/pharmaceuticals/inquiry/staff_working_paper_part1.pdf (last accessed on 20 April 2017).

> "In line with the principle of proportionality, measures, procedures and remedies intended to protect trade secrets should be tailored **to meet the objective of a smooth-functioning internal market for research and innovation**, in particular by deterring the unlawful acquisition, use and disclosure of a trade secret. **Such tailoring of measures, procedures and remedies should not jeopardise or undermine fundamental rights and freedoms or the public interest, such as public safety, consumer protection, public health and environmental protection, and should be without prejudice to the mobility of workers.** In this respect, the measures, procedures and remedies provided for in this Directive are aimed at ensuring that competent judicial authorities take into account factors such as the value of a trade secret, the seriousness of the conduct resulting in the unlawful acquisition, use or disclosure of the trade secret and the impact of such conduct. **It should also be ensured that the competent judicial authorities have the discretion to weigh up the interests of the parties to the legal proceedings, as well as the interests of third parties including, where appropriate, consumers.**"[1230]

Public safety, consumer protection, public health and environmental protection are thus explicitly mentioned as being important public interest categories that should be considered by EU Member States and their judicial authorities when enforcing trade secrets. It is submitted that it seems arguable that the UPC could draw on this Directive in analogy. After all, one could argue that the Unitary Patent system also ultimately aims "for a smooth functioning internal market in research and innovation" and it would be somewhat illogical, from a legal and policy perspective, if these categories of public interest grounds would not be considered for other forms of intellectual property protection, which too can directly affect incentives for research and innovation in the EU.[1231]

To then, in that context, simply brush these kinds of public interest arguments aside as not being relevant or as marginal when a likely case of patent infringement has been demonstrated, would be too formalistic and would not do justice to the notion that a granted preliminary injunction can have effects beyond the immediate parties that are involved in the litigation. When a public interest argument is invoked by one of the parties such an argument should at least be considered and in any case should a negative decision on this be adequately motivated by the

1230 THE EUROPEAN PARLIAMENT AND THE COUNCIL OF THE EUROPEAN UNION, *Directive (EU) 2016/943 on the protection of undisclosed know-how and business information (trade secrets) against their unlawful acquisition, use and disclosure*, June 8th 2016. See: recital 21.

1231 Note that beyond the recital, an explicit reference to the 'public interest' is also made in Art. 11 (2) (g) of the Directive, in which it is stated that Member States shall ensure that the judicial authorities take into account the public interest, amongst others.

court. Here too, as with aspects of patent validity and patent infringement and in line with what has been suggested earlier in this dissertation,[1232] the UPC should be able to delay the proceedings somewhat and invite *amici curiae* to submit briefs on the public interest affected, when this would provide much added value and significantly contribute to the quality of the decisionmaking.

That such a public interest argument is at times aligned with the interests of the defendant – in order to ward off a preliminary injunction – and that he may not act out of altruistic reasons, is inevitable. This should then be balanced against the public interest the plaintiff has in favouring patent enforcement. Also, a closer look at public interest grounds that the defendant invokes at the same time does not mean that patent infringement should simply be tolerated; in such a case, an attempt can be made to accommodate both the public interest that the defendant has flagged and the interests of the patentee by for instance ***tailoring*** the injunction, i.e. by allowing a limited number of infringing devices on the market, in order to cater to a specific group of patient's needs, or to prevent a safety risk.

Similarly, another issue that the UPC should make a decision on as soon as possible is how to deal with ***Non-practicing entities (NPEs)***. Given the large market that will be affected when the plaintiff receives a preliminary injunction under the UPC in combination with the relatively low litigation costs to obtain this EU-wide injunction, it is advised that the UPC takes a cautious approach to dealing with NPEs, also to prevent Europe turning into fertile ground for NPE behaviour in the first place. There is no formal arrangement made on this in the UPC Agreement or ROP, however one way to mitigate abuse has already been mentioned: to take a critical look at a patent's likelihood of validity. There is every reason, especially with weaker or minor patents or in obvious cases of non-practice, that there is a requirement that a patent's validity should have undergone a 'second look' at an earlier occasion. Another possibility is to address the non-practicing nature of such a patentee directly, specifically under the balancing of hardships prong, by for instance pointing out that – save when special interests or circumstances are applicable – later monetary compensation for the plaintiff in the form of damages will be deemed to be sufficient, as there is no obvious irreparable harm to the plaintiff since the NPE itself does not produce products or technologies that directly make use of the patent.[1233] Therefore a preliminary injunction would then not be warranted.

1232 See the reasoning in the main text at footnote 1133 of this dissertation.

1233 On this, see P. CLARKSON, W. WEYMIENS, 'Striking the balance between patent assertion entities and SMEs' *IAM Media* (2014). Available at: http://www.iam-media.com/intelligence/Patents-in-Europe/2014/Europe-focus/Striking-the-balance-between-patent-assertion-entities-and-SMEs (last accessed on 24 April 2017).

Lastly, as is pointed out by some academics,[1234] the UPC Agreement and the ROP have not stipulated whether the court can decide to issue a preliminary injunction that becomes effective after a certain period of time has lapsed: a '***grace period***'. Such a mechanism is used by the courts in some jurisdictions, such as The Netherlands and Germany ('*Aufbrauchfrist*') as we have seen. Whilst this grace period effectively grants the patentee less than claimed for and permits a temporary infringement of the patent,[1235] this thereby allows the court a higher degree of flexibility to take into account wider public interest considerations. It is recommended therefore that the UPC indeed provides itself the opportunity to do so when it considers this to be necessary.

§8.10.6. Bond and damages

A key way to provide defendants compensation in the case that an erroneous preliminary injunction is taken is to require financial security in advance, such as a bond, a bank guarantee and a cross- undertaking in damages. These form an important part of the *internal balance* of a preliminary injunction: whilst the patentee receives the desired interim relief, the patentee this way is also made clear that the court's decision is a temporary ruling, subject to change, plus that the defendant is – to a certain extent- financially protected against an erroneous decision. Despite that a requirement to post this financial security raises the bar to obtain a preliminary injunction somewhat, it is nevertheless submitted that the UPC court should indeed require this from applicants. From this perspective, it is a wise decision that the Rules of Procedure, in Rule 211 (5) ROP, have foreseen in the *possibility* that the UPC court can request a plaintiff to post a bond in advance, that is before the preliminary injunction becomes effective. Although the wording of the ROP gives the court discretion in this, it is submitted that the UPC, by default, should always decide on setting a bond and only in exceptional cases decide not to request this from the plaintiff.

Equally, as is argued above, the UPC should be generous in granting *compensation* in the form of damages to a wrongfully-enjoined defendant, in order to properly deal with the fall-out of this erroneous decision. It can do so under Art. 125 ROP, Art. 62 (5) and Art. 60 (9) of the UPC Agreement. In practice this means, it is submitted, that the UPC should accommodate such claims for compensation by the defendant, both in terms of the *amount* of damages that is to be granted as in taking a liberal stance in accepting evidence on the *causal link* between the harm of the defendant on the one hand and the plaintiff enforcing the wrongfully-granted preliminary injunction on the other hand.

1234 M.L. NORRGÅRD, A. NYLUND, 'The requirements for preliminary injunctions in the unified patent court' in R.M. BALLARDINI, M.L. NORRGÅRD, G.N. BRUUN, *Transitions in European Patent Law: Influences of the European Patent Package* (2015 Kluwer International Law Publishing), pp. 189–206. See: pp. 193–194.

1235 Ibidem.

§8.10.7. Concluding proposal

Concluding, it is thus submitted that the UPC should follow key elements of mainly the Dutch and German Düsseldorf court's practices, but should also incorporate several elements found in other jurisdictions. The main characteristics of the UPC's preliminary injunction approach *de lege ferenda,* thereby bearing in mind the limits given in the UPC Agreement and the ROP, are thus:

- Urgency is always to be assessed and the UPC should do so with respect to delay and to lesser extent also with respect to necessity. Both should be seen as relative instead of absolute concepts with for instance the plaintiff not being forced to take an unnecessary litigation risk. A preliminary injunction for imminent infringement is possible, when this is indeed very likely to occur.
- The UPC should opt for strict requirements regarding the likelihood of patent validity: in principle a patent should have either undergone and survived prior EPO opposition proceedings or invalidity proceedings by another national or UPC court, before a preliminary injunction can be considered to be granted. However, exceptions to this approach are possible in the balancing of hardships phase.
- A preliminary injunction court of the UPC, when dealing with a request for a preliminary injunction, should not be bound to a previous (first instance) court's decision on the invalidity of a patent when clear errors in rendering this decision have been made. The preliminary injunction court can then still decide to issue a preliminary injunction if this is warranted, thereby anticipating that the wrongful invalidation will later be corrected on appeal.
- There should be no set limitations with respect to a patent's infringement and validity analysis by a preliminary injunction court of the UPC. Whilst for reasons of efficiency, a court should follow the arguments made by the parties in this, it is entitled to look into the issues as far is it deems necessary, in order to be sufficiently convinced that this will adequately anticipate the subsequent trial on the merits. A court is thus not restricted to looking at the arguments made by the parties alone. The UPC should also be able to delay the proceedings somewhat, and invite *amici curiae* to submit briefs when this would provide much added value to the decisionmaking.
- The balancing of hardships should not merely be seen as a *possibility,* but as something that a preliminary injunction court of the UPC should actively undertake as part of its decisionmaking process. There should be room for both looking at issues of *validity* and *harms.* Equally, the court should examine public interest arguments, especially related to public health and public safety, that are made in this context and here too should it be able to invite *amici curiae* to submit briefs. Granting a preliminary injunction with a 'grace period', resulting in some time before a preliminary injunction becomes effective should also be possible, just as the 'tailoring' of a preliminary injunction.

- No principle of 'clearing the way' should be adopted: the burden should be on the plaintiff to demonstrate both the likelihood of patent infringement and patent validity in order to obtain a preliminary injunction.
- The requiring of a bond before a granted preliminary injunction becomes effective should become the default approach of the UPC.
- The UPC should be generous in providing compensatory damages to a wrongfully-enjoined defendant.

Literature and Case Law

Cited legislation

- DE – Patent Code (Patentgesetz) of Germany
- DE – Civil Procedural Code (ZPO) of Germany
- DE – Civil Code (BGB) of Germany
- ECHR – European Convention on Human Rights
- EU – Treaty on the European Union
- EU – Treaty on the Functioning of the European Union
- EU – Charter of Fundamental Rights of the European Union
- EU – Directive 89/105/EEC (on the transparency of measures regulating the prices of medicinal products)
- EU – Regulation 44/2001 ('Brussels I')
- EU – Directive 2004/48/EC (Enforcement Directive)
- EU – Regulations 1257/12 and 1260/12 (on the European Patent with Unitary Effect)
- EU – Directive 2016/943 (Trade Secrets Directive)
- INT- European Patent Convention
- INT- Agreement on Trade-Related Aspects of Human Rights (TRIPS)
- INT – WIPO Arbitration Rules (2014)
- NL – Civil Code (Burgerlijk Wetboek) of The Netherlands
- NL – VRO proceeding rules of the Court of The Hague, The Netherlands
- NL – Civil Procedural Code (Wetboek van Burgerlijke Rechtsvordering) of the Netherlands
- NL – Patent Code (Rijksoctrooiwet) of The Netherlands
- UK – Rules on Civil Procedure (C.P.R.) of the United Kingdom
- UK – Practice Direction 25A on Interim Injunctions (UK)
- UK – Senior Courts Act (UK)
- UPC – Agreement on a Unified Patent Court
- UPC – Draft Rules of Procedure of the Unified Patent Court (15–18th versions)
- UPC – Digest of Changes to the Draft Rules of Procedure of the Unified Patent Court
- US – Title 35 of the United States Code (Patent code)
- US – 21 USC §355 (US Drug Price Competition and Patent Term Restoration Act)
- US – Federal Rules of Civil Procedure (US)
- US – The America Invents Act

List of cited cases

Given in a chronological order per jurisdiction

International and European Union cases

- CJEU, C-53/96, *Hermés International v FHT Marketing Choice BV*, June 16th 1998. ECLI:EU:C:1998:292.
- CJEU, C-391/95, *Van Uden v Deco Line*, November 17th 1998, ECLI:EU:C:1998:543.
- European Court of Human Rights, Grand Chamber, *Markass Car Hire.Ltd. v Cyprus*, No. 51591/99, Judgment of July 2nd 2002. ECLI:CE:ECHR:2002:0702JUD005159199
- CJEU, C-539/03, *Roche v Primus*, July 13th 2006, ECLI:EU:C:2006:458.
- CJEU, C-4/03, *GAT v LuK*, July 13th 2006, ECLI:EU:C:2006:457.
- CJEU, C-275/06, *Promusicae v Telefónica*, January 29th 2008. ECLI:EU:C:2008:54.
- European Court of Human Rights, Grand Chamber, *Micallef v Malta*, October 15th 2009, Application number 17056/06, ECLI:CE:ECHR:2009:1015JUD001705606.
- CJEU, C-324/09, *L'Oréal v eBay*, July 12th 2011, ECLI:EU:C:2011:474.
- CJEU, C-70/10, *Scarlet v SABAM*, November 24th 2011, ECLI:EU:C:2011:771.
- CJEU, C-616/10, *Solvay v Honeywell*, July 12th 2012, ECLI:EU:C:2012:445.
- CJEU, C-314/12 *UPC Telekabel Wien v Constantin Film Verleih*, March 27th 2014, ECLI:EU:C:2014:192.
- CJEU, C-146/13 & C-147/13, *Kingdom of Spain v European Parliament and Council* of the European Union, May 5th 2015, ECLI:EU:C:2015:298.

The Netherlands

- Hoge Raad, *Panhonlibco*, January 15th 1960, NJ 1960 84.
- Hoge Raad, *Ciba Geigy v Voorbraak*, November 16th 1984, NJ 1985, 547.
- Hoge Raad, *Vredo v Veenhuis*, June 4th 1993, NJ 1993/659.
- Hoge Raad, *Boehringer Mannheim v Kirin Amgen*, April 21st 1995.
- Hoge Raad, *Procter & Gamble v Kimberley-Clark*, December 15th 1995, Bijblad *Industriële Eigendom*, No. 12, 1996.
- Hoge Raad, *Tetra Laval Food Koppens v Meyn Machinefabrieken*, October 26th 2001, ECLI:NL:HR:2001:AB2774.
- Vzr. Rechtbank Den Haag, *Eli Lilly v Ratiopharm*, April 7th 2008, KG ZA 08–63.
- Vzr. Rechtbank Den Haag, *High Point SARL v Koninklijke KPN N.V. et al and Ericsson Telecommunicatie B.V.*, May 26th 2009, KG ZA 09–157.
- Vzr. Rechtbank Den Haag, *Novartis v Actavis*, July 8th 2009, KG ZA 09–611.
- Vzr. Rechtbank Den Haag, *Global Factories B.V. v ZIUZ*, December 3rd 2010, KG ZA10–1216.
- Hoge Raad, *Yukos v Rosneft*, January 7th 2011, ECLI:NL:HR:2011:BP0015.
- Vzr. Rechtbank Den Haag, *Apple v Samsung*, August 24th 2011, KG-ZA 11–730.

- Gerechtshof Den Haag, *Aventis, Inc. v. Apothecon*, March 16th 2010, IEF 86883.
- Vzr. Rechtbank Den Haag, *Merck Sharp & Dohme v Teva Pharma B.V.* March 27th 2012, KG ZA 12–138.
- Vzr. Rechtbank Den Haag, *SCA v MTS*, February 20th 2012, IEPT20120220
- Gerechtshof Den Haag, *Boston Scientific v OrbusNeich*, March 13th 2012, IEPT20120313.
- Vzr. Rechtbank Den Haag, *Rhodia Chimie v PPG Industries Chemicals B.V.*, April 25th 2012, KG ZA 12–244.
- Hoge Raad, *AGA v Occlutech*, May 25th 2012, ECLI:NL:HR:2012:BV3680.
- Vzr. Rechtbank Den Haag, *Bayer Pharma AG v Sandoz B.V.*, June 27th 2012, IEPT20120627.
- Vzr. Rechtbank Utrecht, *Boehringer Ingelheim v Teva c.s.*, August 15th 2012, KG ZA 12–319 / KG ZA 12–559
- Vzr. Rechtbank Den Haag, Provisioneel vonnis, *Sanofi v Pharmachemie/Teva*, September 3rd 2012, IEPT20120903.
- Vzr. Rechtbank Den Haag, vonnis in kort geding, *Sanofi v Pharmachemie/Teva*, September 14th 2012, KG ZA 12–905.
- Vzr. Rechbank Den Haag, *DeLaval Holding AB v Boumatic Robotics B.V*, December 7th 2012, KG-ZA 12–1165.
- Vzr. Rechtbank Den Haag, *The Wellcome Foundation & GSK v Mylan*, April 17th 2013, IEPT20130417.
- Vzr. Rechtbank Den Haag, *AstraZeneca AB vs Sandoz B.V.* August 15th 2013, KG ZA 13–854.
- Gerechtshof Den Haag, *Sanofi v Teva*, August 27th 2013, ECLI:NL:GHDHA:2013:3376.
- Vzr. Rechtbank Den Haag, *Unilever N.V. v. Procter & Gamble Nederland B.V. et al*, December 19th 2013, KG ZA 13–1038.
- Vzr. Rechtbank Den Haag, *Novartis v Alvogen & Focus Farma*, December 23rd 2013, KG ZA 13–1160.
- Vzr. Rechtbank Den Haag, *Sirvis B.V. and Serrix B.V. v. Medical Brands B.V. and Progressare B.V.*, February 13th 2014. KG ZA 13–1464.
- Vzr. Rechtbank Den Haag, *Novartis AG v Sun Pharmaceutical Industries (Europe) B.V.*, May 12th 2014, KG ZA 14–185.
- Gerechtshof Den Haag, *Novartis v Alvogen & Focus Farma*, November 18th 2014, ECLI: NL:GHDHA:2014:3611.
- Gerechtshof Den Haag, *Novartis AG v Sun Pharmaceutical Industries (Europe)*, January 27th 2015, KG ZA 14–185.
- Hoge Raad, *Medinol v Abbott*, April 4th 2015. ECLI:NL:HR:2014:816.
- Vzr. Rechtbank Den Haag, *Matador v Bick*, April 22nd 2015, KG ZA 14–754.
- Vzr. Rechtbank Den Haag, *Coloplast A/S v Medical4you B.V.*, August 14th 2015, KG ZA 15–9.

Germany

- OLG Düsseldorf, Mitt 1996, 87.
- OLG Düsseldorf, March 1st 2007, Az. 2 U 98/06.
- OLG Düsseldorf, May 29th 2008, Az. I-2 W 47/07.
- BGH, December 16th 2008, Az. X ZR 89/07.
- LG Mannheim, February 27th 2009, Az. 7 O 29/09.
- OLG Karlsruhe, July 8th 2009, Az. 6 U 61/09.
- LG Düsseldorf, March 30th 2010, Az. 4a O 13/10.
- OLG Düsseldorf, April 29th 2010, Az. I-2U 126.
- OLG Düsseldorf, September 30th 2010, Az. 2 U 47/10.
- OLG Düsseldorf, January 20th 2011, Az. I-2 U 55/10.
- LG Düsseldorf, August 25th 2011, Az. 4a O 195/10.
- OLG Düsseldorf, November 10th 2011, Az. 2 U 41/11.
- LG München, February 1st 2012, Az. 21 O 26022/11.
- LG Düsseldorf, April 12th 2012, Az. 4a O 16/12.
- OLG München, July 26th 2012, Az. 6 U 1260/12.
- LG Düsseldorf, August 15th 2012, Az. 4a 0 109/12.
- LG Düsseldorf, September 4th 2012, Az. 4a O 83/12.
- OLG Düsseldorf, September 20th 2012, Az. I-W U 44/12.
- LG Düsseldorf, October 19th 2012, Az. 4b O 135/12.
- LG Düsseldorf, November 15th 2012, Az. 4b O 139/12.
- OLG Düsseldorf, January 17th 2013, Az. I-2 U 87/12.
- OLG Düsseldorf, February 14th 2013, Az. 4b O 187/12.
- OLG Düsseldorf, 13 Sept 2013, Az. I-2 U 26/13.
- LG Düsseldorf, October 24th 2013, Az. 4C O 84/13.
- OLG Düsseldorf, November 7th 2013, Az. I-2 U 94/12.
- LG Düsseldorf, May 8th 2014, Az. 4a O 68/13.
- OLG Düsseldorf, December 18th 2014, Az. I-2 U 60/14.
- LG Mannheim, January 27th 2015, Az. 2 O 203/14.
- KG Berlin, 20 Febuary 2015, Az. 5 U 150/14.
- OLG Karlsruhe, September 23rd 2015, Az. 6 U 52/15.
- OLG Düsseldorf, January 21st 2016, Az. I-2 U 49/15.
- OLG Düsseldorf, February 19th 2016, Az. I 2 U 54/15.
- BGH, May 10th 2016, Az. X ZR 114/13.

England

- House of Lords, *American Cyanamid v Ethicon* (1975) AC 396.
- *Roussel-Uclaf v. G D Searle*, 1977, FSR 125 (Ch).
- EWCA, *Series 5 Software v Clarke ltd* (1996) 1 ALL ER 853.
- *Peaudouce SA v Kimberley-Clark Ltd And Others*, (1996) FSR 680.
- EWHC, *SmithKline Beecham PLC & GlaxoSmithKline (UK) Ltd v Apotex Europe Limited et al*, November 28th 2002, EWHC 2556 (pat).

- EWCA *SmithKline Beecham PLC & GlaxosmithKline (UK) Ltd v Apotex Europe Limited et al,* February 14th 2003, EWCA Civ 137.
- EWHC, *Novartis v Ivax,* October 16th 2006, EWHC 2506 (pat.).
- EWCA, *Novartis v Ivax,* October 18th 2007 EWCA Civ 971.
- EWCA, *SmithKline Beecham PLC v. Apotex Europe Ltd.* (2007) Ch. 71, 89.
- EWCA, *Les Laboratoires Servier & Anr v Apotex,* July 9th 2007, EWCA Civ 783.
- EWHC, *Leo Pharma A/S and Leo Laboratories Limited v Sandoz Limited,* March 17th 2008, EWHC 541 (Pat.).
- EWHC, *Novartis AG v Dexcel Pharma Limited,* June 10th 2008, EWHC 1266 (Pat.).
- EWHC, *Les Laboratoires Servier v Apotex,* October 9th 2008, EWHC 2347 (Ch).
- EWHC, *Cephalon & Ors v Orchid & Anor, trading as Mylan,* November 19th 2010, EWHC 2945 (pat.).
- EWHC, *Merck Sharp Dohme Corp and BMS v Teva Pharma BV* March 15th 2012, EWHC 627 (Pat.).
- EWHC, *Protomed Ltd v Medication Systems Ltd,* December 10th 2012, EWHC 3726 (Ch).
- EWCA, *Novartis AG v Hospira UK Ltd,* May 22nd 2013, EWCA Civ 583.
- EWHC, *BASF SE v Sipcam UK Ltd,* September 12th 2013, EWHC 2863 (Pat.).
- EWHC, *Actavis v Boehringer Ingelheim,* September 23rd 2013, EWHC 2927 (Pat).
- EWHC, *Astrazeneca v KRKA,* January 24 2014, EWHC 84 (Pat).
- EWHC, *Warner Lambert v Actavis, NHS, Teva and others,* March 2nd 2015, EWHC 485 (Pat.).
- EWCA, *Astrazeneca v KRKA,* March 21 2015, EWCA Civ 484.

The United States

- US Supreme Court, *Marbury v Madison,* February 24th 1803.
- Federal Circuit, *Smith International Inc. v Hughes Tool Co,* October 6th 1983, 718 F.2d 1573.
- Federal Circuit, *Hybritech Incorporated v. Abbott Laboratories,* June 16th 1988, 849 F.2d 1446.
- Federal Circuit, *High Tech Medical Instrumentation Inc. V. New Image Industries,* 1995, F.3d 1551, LEXIS 4290.
- Federal Circuit, *Polymer Techs. v. Bridwell and Westmark,* 1996, F.3d 970, LEXIS 33384.
- Federal Circuit, *Doctor's Associates Inc. v Distajo,* February 24th 1997, F.3d 126.
- Federal Circuit, *Amazon.com v Barnesandnoble,* February 14th 2001, 239 F.3d 1343, LEXIS 2163.
- US Supreme Court, *eBay Inc et al. v. MercExchange L.L.C.,* May 15th 2006, No. 05–130.
- United States District Court for the Southern District of New York, *Sanofi –Syntelabo v Apotex Inc,* August 31st 2006, 488 F. Sipp. 2d 317, LEXIS 65127.
- Federal Circuit *Sanofi-Synthelabo v Apotex Inc.,* December 8th 2006, 470 F.3d 1368.

- Federal Circuit, *Abbot Labs v Andrx Pharms,* January 5th 2007, 473 F.3d 1196.
- Federal Cicruit, *Abbott Laboratories v Sandoz,* October 21st 2008, 544 F.3d. 134, LEXIS 21880.
- US Supreme Court, *Winter, Secretary of the Navy et al v. Natural Resources Defence Council, Inc et al.*, November 12th 2008, No. 7–1239.
- Federal Circuit, *Titan Tire Corp v New Holland Inc,* June 3rd 2009, 566 F.3D 1372.
- Federal Circuit, *Qingdao Taifa Group v United States,* September 28th 2009, 581 F.3D 1375.
- Federal Circuit, *Automated Merchandising Systems Inc. v. Crane and Co.*, December 16th 2009, LEXIS 27667.
- Federal Circuit, *i4i Ltd. Partnership v. Microsoft Corp,* March 10th 2010, 598 F.3d 831.
- Federal Circuit, *Robert Bosch LLC v Pylon Manufacturing Corp,* October 13th 2011, F.3D 1142.
- Federal Circuit, *Celsis in Vitro v Cellzdirect,* January 9th 2012, 664 F.3d 922.
- Federal Circuit, *Apple Inc. v Samsung Electronics Co (Apple I),* May 14th 2012, 678 F.3d 1314, LEXIS 9720.
- Federal Circuit, *Apple Inc v. Samsung Electronics Co (Apple II),* October 11th 2012, 695 F.3d. 1370, LEXIS 21085.
- Federal Circuit, *Douglas Dynamics LLC v Buyers Products Company,* May 21st 2013, 717 F.3d 1336.
- United States District Court for the Middle District of North Carolina, *Heart Imaging Technologies, LLC v Merge Healthcare Inc,* August 14th 2013, LEXIS 114679.
- United States District Court for the Northern District of Illinois, Eastern Division, *BRK Brands, Inc and Gary J. Morris v Nest Labs Inc.*, March 19th 2014, LEXIS 41375.
- Federal Circuit, *Apple Inc. v Samsung Electronics (Apple III),* November 18th 2013, 735 F.3D 1352.
- United States District Court for the Northern District of California, *Open Text v Box,* April 9th 2014, 36 F.Supp.3d 885.
- Federal Circuit, *Trebro Manufacturing v Firefly Equipment et al,* April 9th 2014, No. 2013–1437.
- United States District Court of Delaware, *Edwards LifeSciences v CoreValve and Medtronic,* April 15th 2014, LEXIS 51778.
- United States District Court for the Northern District of New York, *PPC Broadband, Inc. v Corning Gilbert Inc.*, June 5th 2014, LEXIS 76462.
- United States District Court for the Northern District of California, *Asus Computers Intnl. et al. v. Exotablet Ltd.*, August 12th 2014, LEXIS 111843.
- United District Court for the District of New Jersey, *Power Survey, LLC v Premier Utility Services, LLC et al,* November 21st 2014, LEXIS 163288.
- Federal Circuit, *Celgard, LLC v. LG Chem America, Inc,* August 12th 2015, LEXIS 14079 (non precedental).

- United States District Court for the District of Minnesota, *Rudolph Technologies, Inc. v. Camtek, Ltd.*, August 26th 2015, LEXIS 113007.
- United States District Court for the Western District of Washington, *BitTitan Inc, v SkyKick Inc*, August 27th 2015, LEXIS 114082.
- Federal Circuit, *Apple Inc. v Samsung Electronics* (*Apple IV*), December 16th 2015, No. 2014–1802.

List of cited literature

AICHINGER, M., PETRITZ, W., REICH, E., *Interim measures and the applicability of Article 6* (2012).

Available: http://www.ejtn.eu/Documents/Themis%202012/Written%20paper%20 Lisbon/Written_paper_%20Austria_1_%20Interpretation_and_application_of_ar ticle_5_and_6_of_the_ECHR%20.pdf (last accessed on April 22nd 2017).

ALLEN, D.W., 'Transaction costs' in MÉNARD, C., (ed.), *Transaction costs and Property rights* (2004 Edward Elgar Publishing).

ALLEN, S.A., 'Justifying 'the public interest' in patent litigation' *Indiana Law Journal* 88, No. 3 (2013), pp. 1047–1088.

AYRES, I., KLEMPERER, P., 'Limiting patentees' market power without reducing innovation incentives: the perverse benefits of uncertainty and non-injunctive remedies' *Michigan Law Review* 97, No. 4 (1999), pp. 985–1033.

BARTH, G., ZIMMER, F.J., 'The Olanzapine patent dispute: German court grants a preliminary injunction on a patent invalidated by the first instance Federal Court' (2008) Available at: http://www.grunecker.de/files/olanzapine_article.pdf (last accessed on April 24th 2017).

BATEMAN, R., 'Novartis v Hospira – Interim injunction granted pending appeal when patent found invalid' *Lexology* (August 1 2013). Available at: http://www.lexology.com/library/detail.aspx?g=f3655785-7f52-49b3-a104-4072195242e4 (last accessed on April 24th 2017).

BAUMANN, J.J., BELVIS, G.P., 'Better things come to a patent owner who waits – the need to fully assess the strategic risks of seeking preliminary injunctive relief in patent cases' *Intellectual Property Litigation* 16, No. 4 (2005).

BERNEKE, W., SCHÜTTPELZ, E. *Die einstweilige Verfügung in Wettbewerbsachen* (2014 C.H. Beck).

BERNIERI, R.J.F.M.C., *Ex-post liability rules in modern patent law* (2010 Intersentia Publishing).

BERNIERI, R.C., 'Ex-post liability rules: a solution for the biomedical anti-commons' in FLANAGAN, A., MONTAGNANI, M.L., (eds.), *Intellectual Property Law: Economic and Social Justice Perspectives* (2010 Edward Elgar Publishing), pp. 93–111.

BLACK, S.H, 'A new look at preliminary injunctions: can principles from the past offer any guidelines to decisionmakers in the future?' *Alabama Law Review* 36, No. 1 (1984), pp. 1–49.

BLAIR, R.D., COTTER, T.F., 'Rethinking patent damages' *Texas Intellectual Property Law Journal* 10 (2001), pp. 1–94.

BOSTEDT, F.P., *Vorsorgliche und einstweilige Maßnahmen zum Schutz der Menschenrechte* (2009 Peter Lang Verlag).

BOYCE, J.R., HOLLIS, A., 'Innovation, imitation and preliminary injunctions in patents' (2002), pp. 1–35. Available at: http://citeseerx.ist.psu.edu/viewdoc/summary?doi=10.1.1.214.6747 (last accessed on April 21st 2017).

BÖHLER, R., 'Einstweilige Verfügungen in Patentsachen' *GRUR* (2011), pp. 965–977.

BOLDRIN, M., LEVINE, D.K., 'The case against patents' *The Journal of Economic Perspectives* 27, No. 1 (2013), pp. 3–22.

BREAN, D.H., 'Will the 'Nexus' requirement of Apple v. Samsung preclude the injunctive relief in the majority of patent cases? Echoes of the Entire Market Value Rule' *San Diego Law Review* 51 (2014), pp. 153–207.

BRITISH GENERIC MANUFACTURERS ASSOCIATION, *Response by the British Generic Manufacturers Association (BGMA) to the DG Competition Pharmaceutical Sector Inquiry Preliminary Report* (2004).

BROOKS, R.R.W., SCHWARTZ, W.F., 'Legal uncertainty, economic efficiency, and the preliminary injunction doctrine' *Stanford Law Review* 58 (2005), pp. 380–409.

BROOKS, R.W., SCHWARTZ, W.F., 'Uncertain breach of contract and efficient preliminary remedies', *American Law and Economics Association Annual Meeting Working Paper* No. 110 (2008). Available at http://law.bepress.com/cgi/viewcontent.cgi?article=2440&context=alea (last accessed on April 20th 2017).

BUSCHE, J., STOLL, P.T., *TRIPS* (2007 Carl Heymanns Verlag).

BÜHLING, J., chapter 'Germany' in HOYNG, W., EIJSVOGELS, F., (eds.), *Global Patent litigation* (2015 Kluwer Law Publishing).

CALABRESI, G., MELAMED, D., 'Property rules, liability rules and inalienability: one view of the cathedral' *Harvard Law Review* 85 (1972), pp. 1089–1128.

CALFEE, J.E., CRASWELL, R., 'Some effects of uncertainty on compliance with legal standards' *Virginia Law Review* 70, No. 5 (1984), pp. 965–1003.

CAMERON, L.J., 'Preliminary injunctions in pharmaceutical litigation: the economics of irreparable harm' *Discussion Paper The Brattle Group* (February 2011). Available at: http://www.brattle.com/system/publications/pdfs/000/004/959/original/Preliminary_Injunctions_in_Pharmaceutical_Litigation_Feb_2011.pdf?1384877054 (last accessed on 24 April 2017).

CHAN, N.P., 'Balancing judicial misvaluation and patent hold-up: some principles for considering injunctive relief after eBay' *UCLA* 59 (2011–2012), pp. 746–787.

CHIEN, C.V. 'Patent amicus briefs: what the court's friends can teach us about the patent system' *UC Irvine Law Review* 1, No. 2. (2011), pp. 395–433.

CLARKSON, P., WEYMIENS, W., 'Striking the balance between patent assertion entities and SMEs' *IAM Media* (2014). Available at: http://www.iam-media.com/intelligence/Patents-in-Europe/2014/Europe-focus/Striking-the-balance-between-patent-assertion-entities-and-SMEs (last accessed on April 24th 2017).

CLINE, H., GOUGE, E., 'The Unified Patent Court's approach to interim injunctions will influence businesses' patent strategies in Europe, say experts' (2016). Available at: http://www.out-law.com/en/articles/2016/february/the-unified-patent-courts-approach-to-interim-injunctions-will-influence-businesses-patent-strategies-in-europe-say-experts/ (last accessed on April 10th 2017).

COASE, R., 'The problem of social cost' *Journal of Law and Economics* 3 (1960), pp. 1–44.

CONRAD, D.B., 'Mining the patent thicket: the Supreme Court's rejection of the automatic injunction rule in eBay v MercExchange' *The Review of Litigation* 26, No. 1 (2007), pp. 119–154.

COOK, T., 'The likely role of the UPC in pharma patent litigation' *Life Sciences Intellectual Property Review* (2013).

COOKE, A., 'Rules that reflect different traditions' *Managing Intellectual Property* (March 2015), pp. 90–92.

CORNISH, W.R., DREXL, J., HILTY, R.M., KUR, A., 'Procedures and remedies for enforcing IPRs: The European Commission's proposed directive' *European Intellectual Property Review* 25, No. 10 (2003), pp. 447–449.

CORREA, C.M., *TRIPS, A Commentary on the TRIPS Agreement* (2007 Oxford University Press).

COTTER, T.F., *Comparative Patent Remedies: A Legal and Economic Analysis* (2013 Oxford University Press).

COTTER, T.F., GOLDEN, J.M., 'Empirical Studies relating to Patents – Remedies' *University of Minnesota Law School Legal Studies Research Paper Series* No. 15–31. (2015).

COURT OF THE HAGUE, *Reglement VRO in octrooizaken* (2010). Available at: https://www.rechtspraak.nl/SiteCollectionDocuments/Reglement-versneld-regime-in-octrooizaken-VRO-reglement.pdf (last accessed on April 17th 2017).

CREMERS, K., ERNICKE, M., GAESSLER, F., HARHOFF, D., ET AL, 'Patent litigation in Europe' *Zentrum für Europäische Wirtschaftsforschung, Discussion Paper* No. 13–072 (2013).

CREUTZFELDT, D., *Die Dringlichkeit der Einstweiligen Verfügung im gewerblichen Rechtsschutz und im Urheberrecht* (2010 Peter Lang).

CUMMING, G., FREUDENTHAL, M., JANAL, R., *Enforcement of Intellectual Property rights in Dutch, English and German civil procedure* (2008 Wolters Kluwer Publishing).

DAMMERS, W.F., *Examining ex parte in rei patenti* (L.L.M. thesis 2009). Available at the website of the University of Tilburg, The Netherlands at http://arno.uvt.nl/show.cgi?fid=99971 (last accessed 17 April 2017).

DARCH, M.C., 'The Presumption of Irreparable Harm in Patent Infringement Litigation: A Critique of Robert Bosch LLC v. Pylon Manufacturing Corp.' *Northwestern Journal of Technology and Intellectual Property* 11, No. 2 (2013), pp. 103–119.

J.P. DAVIS, 'Taking uncertainty seriously: revising injunction doctrine' *Rutgers Law Journal* 34, No. 2 (2003), pp. 362–462.

DEAN, R.J.C., 'Varying the plaintiff's burden: an efficient approach to interlocutory injunctions to preserve future monetary judgments' *The University of Toronto Law Journal* 49, No. 1 (1999), pp. 1–52.

DEBRE, P., 'France: Preliminary injunctions in case of an imminent infringement' *EPLAW Patent weblog* (2010). Available at: http://www.eplawpatentblog.com/eplaw/2010/02/fr-preliminary-injunctions-in-case-of-an-imminent-infringement.html (last accessed on April 24th 2017).

DENLOW, M., 'The Motion for a Preliminary Injunction: Time for a Uniform Federal Standard' *The Review of Litigation* 22, No. 3 (2003), pp. 495–539.

DESOGUS, C., *Competition and Innovation in the EU Regulation of Pharmaceuticals,* (2011 Intersentia Publishing).

DEUTSCH, A., 'Preliminary injunction proceedings in German intellectual property disputes' *Journal of Intellectual Property Law & Practice* 8, No. 2 (2013), pp. 136–145.

DISARRO, A., 'Freeze Frame: The Supreme Court's reaffirmation of the substantive principles of preliminary injunctions' *Gonzaga Law Review* 47, No. 1 (2011–2012), pp. 51–98.

DORR, R.C., DUFT, B.J., 'Patent preliminary injunctive relief' (1978) *Journal of the Patent Office Society.* 60, No. 10 (1978), pp. 597–635.

DRAHOS, P., *A Philosophy of Intellectual Property* (1996 Dartmouth Publishing).

DREXL, J., 'The Unitary Patent System: on the unconstitutional misuse of conflict-of-law rules' *Max Planck Institute of Innovation and Competition Research Paper* No. 15–01 (2015).

DUFFY, J.F., 'Rethinking the Prospect Theory of patents' *University of Chicago Law Review* 71, No. 2 (2004), pp. 439–510.

DYLST, P., VULTO, A., SIMOENS, S., 'Overcoming challenges in market access of generic medicines in the European Union' *Journal of Generic Medicines* 9, No. 1 (2012), pp. 21–28.

EBBINK, R., 'Provisional cross-border jurisdiction in patent cases according to the CJEU in Solvay' (2013). Available at: https://www.boek9.nl/files/2013B9/Richard_Ebbink_-_Provisional_Cross-border_Jurisdiction_in_Patent_Cases_according_to_the_CJEU_in_Solvay.pdf (last accessed on April 23rd 2017).

EHRENZELLER, S.K., *Der vorläufige Rechtsschutz im internationalen Verhältnis* (2005 Mohr Siebeck).

ENGLAND, P., 'In? Out? What's it all about? Patent opt-out and withdrawal in the UPC' *Journal of Intellectual Property Law and Practice* 9, No. 11 (2014), pp. 915–922.

EPSTEIN, R.A., 'A clear view of the cathedral: the dominance of property rules' *Yale Law Journal* 106 (1997), pp. 2091–2120.

EUROPEAN COMMISSION, *Proposal for a directive of the European Parliament and the Council on measures and procedures to ensure the enforcement of intellectual property rights* COM 2003 46 final (2003).

EUROPEAN COMMISSION, *Pharmaceutical Sector Inquiry Final Report* (2009) Available at: http://ec.europa.eu/competition/sectors/pharmaceuticals/inquiry/staff_working_paper_part1.pdf (last accessed on 20 April 2017).

EUROPEAN COURT OF HUMAN RIGHTS, RESEARCH DIVISION, *Guide on Article 6 – Right to a fair trial (civil limb)* (2013). Available at: http://www.echr.coe.int/Documents/Guide_Art_6_ENG.pdf (last accessed on 20 April 2017).

EUROPEAN GENERIC MEDICINES ASSOCIATION, *Patent-related barriers to market entry for generic medicines in the European Union* Report drafted by ROOX, K., PIKE, J., BROWN, A., BECKER. S., (May 2008).

EUROPEAN GENERIC MEDICINES ASSOCIATION, *Submission to the European Commission's consultation on civil enforcement of intellectual property rights: public consultation on the efficiency of proceedings and accessibility of measures* (2013). Available at: http://ec.europa.eu/internal_market/consultations/2012/intellectual-property-rights/contributions/registered-organisations/european-generic-medicines-association_en.pdf (last accessed on April 19th 2017).

EUROPEAN OBSERVATORY ON COUNTERFEITING AND PIRACY, *Injunctions in Intellectual Property Rights* (2009). Available at http://ec.europa.eu/internal_market/iprenforcement/docs/injunctions_en.pdf (last accessed on April 20th 2017).

FEDERAL TRADE COMMISSION, *Authorized Generic Drugs: Short Term Effects and Long Term Impact* (2011). Available at: http://www.ftc.gov/sites/default/files/documents/reports/authorized-generic-drugs-short-term-effects-and-long-term-impact-report-federal-trade-commission/authorized-generic-drugs-short-term-effects-and-long-term-impact-report-federal-trade-commission.pdf (last accessed on April 21st 2017).

FOSTER, J.J., 'The preliminary injunction – a 'new' and potent weapon in patent litigation' *Journal of the Patent and Trademark Office Society* (1986), pp. 281–291.

FREELAND, R., 'The Unitary Patent and and Unified Patents Court-first steps to a decision' (2013) *Pharmaphorum.* Available at: https://pharmaphorum.com/views-and-analysis/the_unitary_patent_and_unified_patents_court_-_first_steps_to_a_decision-2/ (last accessed on April 10th 2017).

GARLAND, P., LARUSSON, K., 'Data exclusivity, Bolar exemption and generic drugs in the EU' *European Intellectual Property Law Review* (2007), pp. 128–133.

GERVAIS, D., *The TRIPS Agreement: drafting history and analysis* (2003 Sweet and Maxwell).

GOLDEN, J.M., 'Injunctions as more (or less) than Off Switches: patent infringement injunctions' scope' *Texas Law Review* 90 (2012), pp. 1399–1472.

GORE, A., 'Interlocutory injunctions. A final judgment' *The Modern Law Review* 38, No. 6 (1975), pp. 672–679.

GRIFFITH TOWLE, C., ZARCO, R., 'Proving irreparable harm, have the standards changed?' *American Bar Association – 35th Annual Forum on Franchising* (2012) pp. 1–33. Available at: http://zarcolaw.com/wp-content/uploads/2014/11/Proving-Irreparable-Harm-Have-the-Standards-Changed-ABA-2012.pdf (last accessed on April 24th 2017).

GROSSKOPF, O., MEDINA, B., 'Remedies for Wrongfully-Issued Preliminary Injunctions: The Case for the Disgorgement of Profits' *Seattle University Law Review* 32 (2009), pp. 903–941.

GUPTA, K., KESAN, J.P., 'Studying the impact of *eBay* on injunctive relief in patent cases' *University of Illinois College of Law Legal Studies Research Paper* No. 17–03 (2015).

HAKIM, D., 'Tech giants fear spread of patent wars to Europe' *The New York Times* (September 25th 2013). Available at: http://www.nytimes.com/2013/09/26/technology/tech-giants-fear-spread-of-patent-wars-to-europe.html?_r=1 (last accessed on April 24th 2017).

HALL, B.H., HARHOFF, D., 'Recent research on the economics of patents' *National Bureau of Economic Research Working Paper Series* (2012). Available at: http://www.nber.org/papers/w17773.pdf (last accessed on April 17th 2017).

HAMMOND, R.G., 'Interlocutory injunctions: time for a new model?' *The University of Toronto Law Journal* 30, No. 3 (1980), pp. 240–282.

HARHOFF, D., *Economic Cost Benefit Analysis of a Unified and Integrated European Patent Litigation System* (2009). Available at: http://ec.europa.eu/internal_market/indprop/docs/patent/studies/litigation_system_en.pdf (last accessed on April 24th 2017).

HARHOFF, D., CREMERS, K., GAESSLER, F., HELMERS, 'Invalid but infringed? An analysis of Germany's bifurcated patent litigation system' *Zentrum für Europäische Wirtschaftsforschung, Discussion Paper* No. 14–072 (2014).

C. HEATH, 'Wrongful patent enforcement – Threats and post-infringement invalidity in comparative perspective' *IIC* No. 3 (2008), pp. 307–322.

A. HEINY, 'Formulating a theory for preliminary injunctions: American Hospital Supply Corp. v Hospital Products Ltd.' *Iowa Law Review* 72 (1987), pp. 1157–1170.

HEINZE, C., *Einstweiliger Rechtsschutz im europäischen Immaterialgüterrecht* (2007 Mohr Siebeck).

HELMERS, C., LOVE, B., MCDONAGH, L., 'Is there a patent troll problem in the UK?' *Fordham Intellectual Property, Media, and Entertainment Law Journal* 24 (2009), pp. 509–552.

HENKEL, J., ZISCHKA, H., 'Why most patents are invalid – extent, reasons and potential remedies of patent invalidity' (June 2015, working paper). Available at: https://www.tim.wi.tum.de/fileadmin/w00bcy/www/Research/Publications/Henkel/Henkel_Zischka_Patent_Validity.pdf (last accessed on April 25th 2017).

HETTINGER, E.C., 'Justifying Intellectual Property' *Philosophy and public affairs* 18, No. 1 (1989), pp. 31–52.

HILTY, R.M., 'The role of patent quality in Europe' *Max Planck Institute for Intellectual Property and Competition Law Research Paper* No. 11 (2011).

HILTY, R.M., JAEGER, T., LAMPING, M., ROMANDINI, R., ULLRICH, H., 'Comments on the Preliminary set of provisions for the Rules of Procedure of the Unified Patent Court' *Max Planck Institute for Intellectual Property and Competition Law Research Paper* No. 13–16 (2013).

HILTY, R.M., LAMPING, M. (project leaders), *Declaration on Patent Protection; Regulatory Sovereignty under TRIPS* (2014). Available at: https://www.mpg.de/8132986/Patent-Declaration.pdf (last accessed on April 25th 2017).

HILTY, R.M., 'The role of enforcement in delineating the scope of IP Rights' *Max Planck Institute for Innovation and Competition Research Paper* No. 15–03 (2015).

HOPPE-JÄNISCH, D., 'Das Zögern zu Gunsten Dritter' *GRUR* (2015), pp. 1075–1082.

HOYNG, W., EIJSVOGELS, F., 'The Netherlands' in HOYNG, W., EIJSVOGELS, F., (eds), *Global Patent litigation* (2014 Kluwer Law Publishing).

HUGENHOLTZ, P.B., 'Een overbodige richtlijn' *IER* No. 4 (2004), pp. 247–248. Available at: http://www.ivir.nl/publicaties/download/951 (last accessed on April 22nd 2017).

HUYDECOPER, J.L.R.A., VAN NISPEN, C.J.J.C. (eds), *Industriële Eigendom, deel 1, bescherming van technische innovatie* (2002 Kluwer Publishing).

HYLTON, K., 'Property rules and liability rules once again' *Boston University School of Law Working Paper, Law and Economics* No. 05–17 (2005). Available at https://papers.ssrn.com/sol3/papers.cfm?abstract_id=818944 (last accessed on 17 April 2017).

ILARDI, A., *The New European Patent* (2015 Hart Publishing).

INMAN, P., CARTER, A., 'When the biter gets bit: Cross undertaking in damages' *The IPKat weblog* (May 22nd 2015). Available at: http://ipkitten.blogspot.nl/2015/05/when-biter-gets-bit-cross-undertakings.html (last accessed on 24 April 2017).

JAEGER, T., 'What's in the unitary patent package?' *Max Planck Institute for Innovation and Competition Research Paper* (2014) No. 14–08.

JEITSCHKO, T.D., KIM, B.C., 'Signalling, learning and screening prior to trial: informational implications of preliminary injunctions' (2011) *EAG Discussion Paper.* Available at the website of the US Department of Justice: https://www.justice.gov/sites/default/files/atr/legacy/2011/02/23/267542.pdf (last accessed on 21 April 2017).

KAPLOW, L., SHAVELL, S., 'Property rules and liability rules: an economic analysis' *Harvard Law Review* 109, No. 4 (1996), pp. 713–790.

KELKENSBERG, L., BREMER, J., 'Inbreuk v nietigheid in grensoverschrijdende gevallen; is de Nederlandse octrooirechter bevoegd?' *Berichten Industriële Eigendom* (October 2014), pp. 206–213.

KITCH, E., 'The Nature and the Function of the Patent System' *Journal of Law and Economics* 20, No. 2 (1977), pp. 265–290.

KRAMER, X.E., *Het kort geding in internationaal perspectief* (2001 Kluwer Uitgeverij).

KRAMER, X.E., 'Civiele sancties in het internationale geval in Europees perspectief' in VAN HOEK, A., KLOMP, R., LOOS, M., (eds.), *Offerhauskring vijftig jaar* (2012 Boom Juridische Uitgevers), pp. 73–81.

KUR, A., 'The Enforcement Directive – Rough Start, Happy Landing?' *International Review of Intellectual Property and Competition Law (IIC)* (2004), pp. 821 – 830.

KUR, A., 'A farewell to cross-border injunctions? The ECJ Decisions GAT v. LuK and Roche Nederland v. Primus and Goldenberg' *International review of Intellectual Property and Competition Law (IIC)* 37, No. 7 (2006), pp. 844–855.

KUR, A., 'Enforcement of unitary intellectual property rights: international jurisdiction and applicable law' *Journal of Intellectual Property Law and Practice* 10, No. 6 (2015), pp. 468–480.

LANDES, W.M., POSNER, R.A., *The Economic Structure of Intellectual Property Law* (2003 Harvard University Press).

LANJOUW, J.O., LERNER, J., 'Tilting the table? The use of preliminary injunctions' *Journal of Law and Economics* 44, No. 2 (2001), pp. 573–603.

LARSON, K., 'Enforcement: Legal implications of the European and Unitary Patent Systems for Non-Practicing Entity Patent Enforcement in Europe' BALLARDINI, R.M., NORRGÅRD, M.L., BRUUN, G.N., *Transitions in European Patent Law: Influences of the European Patent Package* (2015 Kluwer International Law Publishing), pp. 147–165.

LAWSON, C., 'The interlocutory injunction dilemma in patent infringement and invalidity disputes' *Australian Intellectual Property Journal* 21, No. 2 (2010), pp. 73–99. Version accessed via: https://research-repository.griffith.edu.au/bitstream/handle/10072/35487/66020_1.pdf;jsessionid=E8F91C09631731896AA6D48887041040?sequence=1. (last accessed on 17 April 2017).

LAYCOCK, D., 'The death of the irreparable injury rule' *Harvard Law Review* 103, No. 3 (1990), pp. 687–771.

LEE, T.R., 'Preliminary injunctions and the status quo' *Washington and Lee Law Review* 58 (2001), pp. 109–166.

LEIPOLD, D., *Grundlagen des einstweiligen Rechtsschutzes im zivil-, verfassungs- und verwaltungsgerichtlichen Verfahren* (1971 CH Beck Verlag).

LEMLEY, M., VOLOKH, E., 'Freedom of speech and injunctions in Intellectual Property Cases' *Duke Law Journal* 48 (1998), pp. 147–242.

LEMLEY, M., 'Ex ante versus ex post justifications for intellectual property' *The University of Chicago Law Review* 71, No. 1 (2004), pp. 129–149.

LEMLEY, M., WEISER, P.J., 'Should property or liability rules govern information?' *Texas Law Review* 85, No. 4 (2007), pp. 783–841.

LEMLEY, M., SHAPIRO, C., 'Patent holdup and royalty stacking' *Texas Law Review* 85 (2008), pp. 1991–2049.

LEUBSDORF, J., 'The standard for preliminary injunctions' *Harvard Law Review* 91 No. 3 (1978), pp. 525–566.

LEUBSDORF, J., 'Remedies for uncertainty' *Boston University Law Review* 61 (1981), pp. 132–172.

LEUBSDORF, J., 'Preliminary injunctions, in defense of the merits' *Fordham Law Review* 76 (2007), pp. 33–47.

LEWIS, O.H., '"The wild card that is the public interest': putting a new face on the fourth preliminary injunction factor' *Texas Law Review* (1994), pp. 849–892.

LICHTMAN, D., 'Uncertainty and the standard for preliminary relief' *John M. Olin Law & Economics Working Paper* No. 166 (2002). Available at: http://papers.ssrn.com/sol3/papers.cfm?abstract_id=344640 (last accessed on 17 April 2017).

LLOBET, G., 'Patent litigation when innovation is cumulative' *International Journal of Industrial Organisation* 21 (2003), pp. 1135–1157.

LYNCH, K.J., 'The lock-in effect of preliminary injunctions' *Florida Law Review* 66 (2014), pp. 779–821.

MACHLUP, F., *An Economic Review of the Patent System – Study of the Subcommittee on patents, trademarks and copyrights of the Committee on the Judiciary of the United States Senate* (1958 US Government Printing Office).

MACQUEEN, H., WAELDE, C., LAURIE, G., BROWN, A., *Contemporary Intellectual Property: Law & Policy* (2011 Oxford University Press).

MARFÉ, M., REETZ, A., PECNARD, C., FRUSCALZO, R., VAN DER VELDEN, R., 'The power of national courts and the Unified Patent Court to grant injunctions: a comparative study' *Journal of Intellectual Property Law & Practice* 10, No. 3 (2015), pp. 180–190.

MAROTTA, P., 'The injunction bond in high technology litigation: the need for reform' *Santa Clara High Technology Law Journal* 4, No. 1 (1988), pp. 19–47.

MARTENS, D.W., SGANGA Jr., J.B., *Pre-litigation patent enforcement* (2013–2014 Thomson Reuters).

MAYERGOYZ, A., 'Lessons from Europe how to tame U.S. Patent Trolls' *Cornell International Law Journal* 42 (2009), pp. 241–270.

MCGOWAN, D., 'Irreparable harm' *Lewis and Clark Law Review* 14, No. 2 (2010), pp. 577–596.

MEI, G., 'Interlocutory injunctions in IP Infringement actions in England and Wales and in Ireland – *American Cyanamid* revisited' *International Review of Intellectual Property and Competition Law* 46, No. 2 (2015), pp. 175–202.

MEIER-BECK, P., 'Quo vadis, iudicium unitarium?' *Journal of Intellectual Property Law & Practice* 9, No. 3 (2014), pp. 241–245.

MEIER BECK, P., 'Bifurkation und Trennung; Überlegungen zum Übereinkommen über ein Einheitliches Patentgericht und zur Zukunft des Trennungsprinzips in Deutschland' *GRUR* (2015), pp. 929–936.

MEIJERS, E.M., VERMEULEN, J.TH. (ed.), *Het kort geding,* (1946 Second Edition, Tjeenk Willink Uitgeverij).

MERGES, R.P.,'Of property rules, Coase and Intellectual Property' *Columbia Law Review* 94, No. 8 (1994), pp. 2656–2673.

MILLARD, E.E., 'Injunctive relief in patent infringement cases: should courts apply a rebuttable presumption of irreparable harm after eBay Inc. v Mercexchange?' *St. Louis Law Journal* 52 (2008), pp. 985–1035.

MILLER, G.P., 'Preliminary judgments' *New York University Law and Economics Working Papers* No. 138 (2008).

MOORE, K.A. 'Are district judges equipped to resolve patent cases? *Harvard Journal of Law and Technology* 15, No. 1 (2001), pp. 1–39.

MOORE, K.A., HOLBROOK, T.R., MURPHY, J.F., *Patent litigation and strategy* (2013 West Academic Publishing).

MORGAN, G., CAREY, P., 'Missed opportunity' *Intellectual Property Magazine* No. July/August (2013), pp. 36–37.

MÜHLENDAHL, A., 'Enforcement of Intellectual Property Rights – Is injunctive relief mandatory?' *IIC* (2007), pp. 377–379.

MÜLLER, F., 'Analysis of 222 smartphone patent assertions: more than 90% go nowhere, rest lacks impact' *FOSS Patents weblog* (published October 1st 2014). Available at: http://www.fosspatents.com/2014/10/analysis-of-222-smartphone-patent.html (last accessed 16 April 2017).

MULLENIX, L.S., 'Burying (with Kindness) the felicific calculus of civil procedure' *Vanderbilt Law Review* (1987).

NARODICK, B., 'Winter v. National Resources Defense Council: going into the belly of the whale of preliminary injunctions and environmental law' *Boston University Journal of Science and Technology Law* 15 (2009), pp. 332–347.

NELSON, R.D., and MAZZOLENI, R., 'Economic theories about the costs and benefits of patents' *Intellectual Property Rights and Research Tools in Molecular Biology* (1997 National Academy Press), pp. 17–27. Available at: http://www.ncbi.nlm.nih.gov/books/NBK233537/pdf/Bookshelf_NBK233537.pdf (last accessed on April 17th 2017).

NORMAN, H., *Intellectual Property Law – Directions* (2014 Oxford University Press).

NORRGÅRD, M., *Interimistiskaförbud i immaterialrätten* (2002 Kauppakaari Förlag).

NORRGÅRD, M.L., NYLUND, A., 'The requirements for preliminary injunctions in the unified patent court' in R.M. BALLARDINI, M.L. NORRGÅRD, G.N. BRUUN, *Transitions in European Patent Law: Influences of the European Patent Package* (2015 Kluwer International Law Publishing), pp. 189–206.

OHLY, A.,'"Patenttrolle" oder: Der patentrechtliche Unterlassungsanspruch unter Verhältnismäßigkeitsvorbehalt? Aktuelle Entwicklungen im US-Patentrecht und ihre Bedeutung für das deutsche und europäische Patentsystem' *GRUR* (2008), pp. 787–798.

OHLY, A., 'Three principles of European IP enforcement law: Effectiveness, proportionality, dissuasiveness' in DREXL, J., HILTY, R.M., ET AL (eds). *Technology and Competition – Contributions in honour of Hanns Ullrich* (2009 Larcier), pp. 257–274.

OHLY, A., 'European Fundamental Rights and Intellectual Property' in OHLY, A., PILA, J., (eds.) *The Europeanization of Intellectual Property Law; Towards a European Legal Methodology* (2013 Oxford University Press), pp. 145–163.

OHLY, A., STREINZ, R., 'Can the UK stay in the UPC system after Brexit?' *GRUR Int.* (2017) pp. 1–11.

PANSCH, R., *Die einstweilige Verfügung zum Schutze des geistigen Eigentums im grenzüberschreitenden Verkehr* (2003 Carl Heymanns Verlag).

PETERSEN, C.S., *Immaterialrettigheder og foreløbige forbud* (2008 Jurist- og Økonomforbundets Forl.).

PETERSEN, C.S., RIIS, T., SCHOVSBO, J., 'The Unified patent court (UPC) Compulsory licensing and competition law' *Nordiskt Immaterieelt Rättskydd,* (2014). Available via: https://papers.ssrn.com/sol3/papers.cfm?abstract_id=2489006 (last accessed on April 27th 2017).

PHILLIPS, J., 'eBay's effect on copyright injunctions: when property rules give way to liability rules' *Berkley Technology Law Journal* 24, No. 1 (2009) pp. 405–435; Available at: http://scholarship.law.berkeley.edu/cgi/viewcontent.cgi?article=1780&context=btlj (last accessed on April 24th 2017).

PIGNATTI, F., BOONE, H., MOULON, I., 'Overview of the European Regulatory Approval System' *Journal of Ambulatory Care Management* 27, No. April-June (2004), pp. 89–97.

PILA, J., 'An historical perspective I: The unitary patent package' in PILA, J., WADLOW, C., (eds.). *The Unitary EU Patent System* (2015 Hart Publishing).

PINCKNEY, R., 'Understanding the transitional provisions of the Agreement on the Unified Patent Court' *European Intellectual Property Review* 37, No. 5 (2015), pp. 268–277.

POLINSKY, A.M., SHAVELL, S., 'Legal error, litigation and the incentive to obey the law' *Journal of Law and Economics and Organisation* (1989), pp. 99–108.

PORS, W., 'Holland: cross border patent litigation revival 'Solvay v Honeywell' (January 2013). Available at: http://www.twobirds.com/en/news/articles/2012/holland-crossborder-patent-litigation-revival--solvay-honeywell-0113 (last accessed on April 23rd 2017).

POSNER, R.A., *Economic Analysis of Law* (1973 Little, Brown and Co).

POWERS, J., 'A status quo bias: behavioural economics and the Federal Preliminary Standard' *Texas Law Review* 92 (2014), pp. 1027–1051.

RAACK, D.W., 'A history of injunctions in England before 1700' *Indiana Law Journal* 64, No. 4 (1986), pp. 539–592.

RACHLIN, M., 'Developments in injunctive relief in health care patent cases' *Intellectual Property Litigation Committee Articles* (October 16th 2014). Available at at: http://apps.americanbar.org/litigation/committees/intellectual/articles/fall2014-0914-recent-developmentss-in-injunctive-relief.html (last accessed on April 24th 2017).

RADEMACHER, C., *Die gerichtliche Durchsetzung von Patent-und Markenrechten in Deutschland, Japan und den USA* (2010 Nomos Verlagsgesellschaft).

RENNIE-SMITH, C., 'Patent Enforcement in the United Kingdom' in HEATH, C., (ed.) *Patent Enforcement Worldwide: Writings in honour of Dieter Stauder* (2015, Third Edition, Hart Publishing), pp. 81–110.

RESIS, R.H., *Preliminary relief in patent infringement disputes* (2011 American Bar Association Publishing).

ROMEU, F.R., 'An economic theory of the regulation of preliminary measures' *European Journal of Law and Economics* 30 (2010), pp. 267–300.

RUEB, A.S., GRAS, E., JONGBLOED, A.W., *Compendium van het Burgerlijk Procesrecht* (2015, 20th edition, Kluwer Publishing).

SAMUEL, G., *A short introduction to the Common Law* (2013 Edward Elgar).

SAMUELSON, P., BEBENEK, K., 'Why plaintiffs should have to prove irreparable harm in copyright preliminary injunction cases' *I/S: A Journal of Law and Policy* 6, No. 1 (2010), pp. 67–94.

SCHNEIDER, F., *Die Leistungsverfügung im Niederländischen, Deutschen und europäischen Zivilprozessrecht* (2013 Mohr Siebeck).

SCHWAB, S., 'Coase defends Coase: why lawyers listen and economists do not' *Michigan Law Review* 87, No. 6 (1989), pp. 1171–1198.

SCHWARTZ, H.F., 'Injunctive relief in patent infringement suits' *University of Pennsylvania Law Review* 112 (1964), pp. 1025–1048.

SCOTT KIEF, F., *Principles of Patent Law* (2008, Fourth edition).

SHAPIRO, C., GOLDEN, J.M., 'Injunctions as more (or less) than Off Switches: patent infringement injunctions' scope' *Texas Law Review* 90 (2012), pp. 1399–1472.

SHAPIRO, S.E., 'Preliminary injunction motions in patent litigation' *IDEA: The Journal of Law and Technology* (1992–1993), pp. 323–348.

SHEHADEH, R., STEWART, M., 'An economic approach to the "Balance of hardships" and "Public interest" tests for Preliminary Injunction Motions in Patent Infringement Cases' *Journal of the Patent and Trademark Office Society JPTOS* No. 5 (2001), pp. 341–358.

SPRY, I.C.F. *The principles of equitable remedies* (1990 Sweet & Maxwell).

STEIN, L.W., 'The Court and the Community: why non-party interests should count in preliminary injunction actions' *The Review of Litigation* 16 (1997), pp. 27–63.

STELZER, J., 'Münchener Verfahren – Patente – Deutlich verkürzter Prozess' *IHK Magazin "Wirtschaft"* (August 2011).

STERK, S.E., 'Property rights, liability rules and uncertainty about property rights' *Cardozo School of Law Working Paper* No. 205, (2007). Available at: http://papers.ssrn.com/sol3/papers.cfm?abstract_id=1016168 (last accessed April 17th 2017).

STOLL-DE BELL, K., DEMPSEY, N.L.,DEMPSEY, B.E., *Injunctive relief; Temporary Restraining Orders and Preliminary Injunctions* (2009 American Bar Association).

STRAUS, J., 'Reversal of the Burden of Proof, the Principle of "Fair and Equitable Procedures" and Preliminary Injunctions under TRIPS Agreement' *Journal of World Intellectual Property* 3, No. 6 (2000), pp. 807–823.

SURABRAMNIAN, S., 'Different rules for different owners – Does a Non-Competing patentee have a Right to Exclude? A study of post-eBay cases' *IIC* (2008), pp. 419–451.

SUBIOTTO, R., *Generic pharmaceuticals – Expert paper* (June 17th 2014). Available at the website of the Organisation for Economic Cooperation and Development (OECD): http://www.oecd.org/officialdocuments/publicdisplaydocumentpdf/?cote=DAF/COMP/WD(2014)75&docLanguage=En (last accessed on April 19th 2017).

TONKENS-GERKEMA, W., in VAN MIERLO, A.I.M., VAN NISPEN, C.J.J.C., POLAK, M.V., (eds) *Tekst & Commentaar Burgerlijke Rechtsvordering* (2008 Wolters Kluwer).

TRIDICO, A., JACOBSTEIN, J., WALL, L., 'Facilitating generic drug manufacturing worldwide: Bolar exemptions worldwide' *WIPO Magazine* No. 3 (2014). Available at: http://www.wipo.int/wipo_magazine/en/2014/03/article_0004.html (last accessed on April 14th 2017).

ULLRICH, H., 'Select from within the system: the European patent with unitary effect' *Max Planck Institute for Intellectual Property and Competition Law Research Paper* No. 12–11 (2012).

UPC PREPARATORY COMMITTEE, *Interpretative Note on the application of Art. 83 UPC Agreement,* (January 29th 2014). Available at: https://www.unified-patent-court.org/news/interpretative-note-%E2%80%93-consequences-application-article-83-upca (last accessed on April 24th 2017).

UPC PREPARATORY COMMITTEE, *Oral Hearing on the Rules of Procedure of the UPC, held in November 26th 2014 in Trier.* Available at: http://www.upc.documents.eu.com/PDFs/2014-11-26_Hearing_Trier_ROP_UPC_transcript.pdf (last accessed on April 25th 2017).

UNIFIED PATENT COURT, 'FAQ: Impact of the UPC'. Available at: https://www.unified-patent-court.org/faq/impact-upc-0companies (last accessed on April 20th 2017).

USPTO, 'Post Grant Review'. Available at: https://www.uspto.gov/patents-application-process/appealing-patent-decisions/trials/post-grant-review (last accessed on April 15th 2017).

VAN DEN BROEK, B., 'The Lundbeck Saga' in *Liber Amicorum Willem Hoyng* (2013 Uitgeverij_deLex).

VAN GEMERT, P., PORS, W., *The effect of an opt out under Article 83 of the Agreement on a Unified Patent Court on jurisdiction for decisions on the merits and preliminary injunctions* (August 28th 2013). Available at: http://www.eplawpatentblog.com/2013/August/The%20effect%20of%20an%20opt%20%20out%20under%20article%2083%20UPC%20Agreement.pdf (last accessed on April 24th 2017).

VAN NISPEN, C.J.J.C., *Rechterlijk verbod en bevel* (1978 Kluwer Uitgeverij). VAUGHN, L.B., 'A need for clarity: toward a new standard for preliminary injunctions' *The Oregon Law Review* 68 (1989), pp. 839–884.

VERSCHUUR, A., VAN DONGEN, P., 'Commentary on Art. 70 (1) ROW' in GIELEN, C.H., VISSER, D.J.G., (eds.), *Tekst & Commentaar Intellectuele Eigendom* (2013 Wolters Kluwer).

VOGEL, B.J., ST. HILL, S., 'To enjoin or not to enjoin: what's come of the test since eBay?' *Landslide* No. 1 (2013). Available at: http://www.americanbar.org/publications/landslide/2013-14/september-october-2013/to_enjoin_or_not_enjoin.html (last accessed on April 25th 2017)

VON FALCK, A., 'Einstweilige Verfügungen in Patent und Gebrauchsmustersachen' *Mitteilungen der deutschen Patentanwälte* (2002), pp. 429–438.

WEBER, M.P., *Die Umsetzung der Enforcement Richtlinie ins deutsche Recht* (2010 Peter Lang GmbH).

WEBSTER, B.E., WALMLEY, S., 'Unclean hands and preliminary injunctions: the effects of delay in bringing patent infringement cases' *Journal of the Patent and Trademark Office Society* (2002), pp. 291–309.

WERTS, I., MAAS, W., 'Wat te doen met proceskosten uit kort geding na een andersluidend bodemvonnis?' *IE Forum* (2015). Available at: http://www.ie-forum.nl/artikelen/wat-te-doen-met-de-proceskosten-uit-kort-geding-na-een-andersluidend-bodemvonnis (last accessed on April 23rd 2017).

WHITEHEAD, B., JACKSON, S., KEMPNER, R., 'Managing generic competition and patent strategies in the pharmaceutical industry' *Journal of Intellectual Property Law & Practice*. 3, No. 4 (2008), pp. 226–235.

WILLOUGHBY, R., chapter 'The United Kingdom' in HOYNG, W., EIJSVOGELS, F. (eds.), *Global Patent litigation* (2014 Kluwer Law Publishing).

WU, Y.T., 'How will Ebay v Mercexchange affect preliminary injunction?' *NTUT Journal of Intellectual Property Law and Management* 3, No. 1 (2014), pp. 34–55.

WYATT, L., 'Rebuttable presumption of public interest in protecting the public health – the necessity for denying injunctive relief in medically related patent infringement cases after eBay v Mercexchange' *Chicago-Kent Journal of Intellectual Property* 13 (2013), pp. 298–326.

ZUCKERMAN, A.A.S., 'Interlocutory remedies in quest of procedural fairness' *The Modern Law Review* 56 (1993), pp. 325–341.

ZUCKERMAN, A.A.S., 'Quality and Economy in Civil Procedure – The case for commuting correct judgments for timely judgments' *Oxford Journal of Legal Studies* 14, No. 3 (1994), pp. 353–387.

www.ingramcontent.com/pod-product-compliance
Ingram Content Group UK Ltd.
Pitfield, Milton Keynes, MK11 3LW, UK
UKHW021848100926
8556IPUK00020B/1116

9 783631 786987